1001 Ways

to Introduce Your Child to the Bible

KATHIE REIMER

BROADMAN
&HOLMAN
PUBLISHERS

Nashville, Tennessee

To my priceless family:
Jim, Mark, Lisa, Jenifer, Scotty, Nichole, Graham, and Micah.
Who couldn't undertake any challenge with a
cheering section of encouragers like you?
May the Lord bless you for the indescribably precious gift from God's own
hand that each one of you is to me, second only the the gift of all gifts –
Jesus Christ, our Lord and Savior.
By the way, I love everybody in this house!

Copyright © 2002 by Kathie Reimer

Published in 2002 by Broadman & Holman Publishers
Nashville, Tennessee

Scripture taken from the HOLY BIBLE, NEW INTERNATIONAL VERSION.
Copyright © 1973, 1978, 1984 by International Bible Society. Used by permission
of Zondervan Publishing House. All rights reserved.

Cover design and layout by Ed Maksimowicz.

A catalog record for this book is available from the Library of Congress.

ISBN 0-8054-3836-X
1 2 3 4 5   06 05 04 03 02

TABLE OF CONTENTS

What's the Book About?

Each chapter will begin with a key verse such as, "In the beginning God created the heavens and the earth" (Genesis 1:1), and a brief summary statement of the book's main message.

The study of each Bible book will then be introduced with a short narrative, presenting the big picture of what the child will encounter in that book, and setting the stage to introduce the people in that part of God's eternal drama of life.

Who are the People in the Book?

After the introduction to each Bible book, the major characters will be introduced to the child by the qualities they exhibited, the emotions they expressed, the relationships they had with God and with other people, and the experiences that affected them. They will be presented as the real people they were, at actual times and places in history, with strengths and weaknesses to which even a child can relate. The people of God's Word will become real friends, heroes, or villains to your child, and the written testimonies of their lives will begin to impact your child's life.

The Stories and Activities

First, by meeting the characters in God's Book about life, a child can then begin to understand that their intriguing and inspiring stories are an integral part of a bigger picture in the scheme of past, present, and future events. A perception can begin to form in a young child's mind that God's loving creation of the natural world, man's tragic fall and continual struggle with sin and personal missteps, God's single way of salvation and reconciliation through Jesus' death and resurrection, and His final and absolute victory through the return and everlasting reign of Jesus our Lord are events that fit together in a loving and redemptive Divine plan and purpose for us all.

What Can I Learn?

To help insure that a child will not simply picture the Bible as a book of interesting people and stories, this section of each chapter will present a child-friendly review of some of the lessons and principles that have been displayed in the lives of its people and their stories.

Scripture Verses

Key verses will also be included. You may want to help your child memorize them. Suggestions and activities designed to help your child memorize key verses are included.

Teaching Tips

Here are a few practical, how-to tips for Mom and Dad, Grandma and Grandpa, teachers, and everyone who loves a child, as you teach and apply God's Word to young hearts and lives. May the Lord bless, guide, and fill you with wisdom as you perform life's greatest privilege: presenting the Almighty God to the next generation of receptive hearts.

1. Begin each new book of the Bible by spending one day's learning session on each Bible person, helping your child become acquainted with him or her. A good way to begin is by reading the Bible narrative included in the chapter or telling it to your child in your own words. Be enthusiastic and animated as you describe these very real people, conveying to your child that they actually lived and experienced the same feelings and struggles that we do today. The goal in teaching our children is to enable the people in the Bible to come alive to them and help open their hearts to want to learn more about the Bible and the people in it.

You may choose to present the narratives describing the people of the Bible before, after, or during any of the activities that follow it. Find a time each day when the child is receptive to spending the highest quality time with you, and custom-fit the way you present God's Word to the way your child responds and learns best.

If a child can understand early in his life that Adam, Eve, Abraham, David, and the disciples were people with energy and emotion, too, he will begin to formulate the desired perception that God's Truth relates to him, and that God unconditionally loves the little unique person He made him/her to be.

Always remember that the wonderful stories and lessons of God's Word are much more alive, relevant, and timeless than the latest fad character, and your child will come to treasure them much more than a passing interest as the lessons penetrate her mind and heart. Remember, too, that instilling God's Word in a child's heart is not like any other teaching you will ever do. Each time you share Bible stories and truths, the Lord Himself, in the Person of the Holy Spirit, will be speaking through your willing words as you instruct and inspire your child, and, simultaneously, working in her impressionable heart as she listens and participates.

2. If you wish to continue with the same Bible person for several days or revisit a Bible character you've already met review the narrative by retelling it, or ask your child to tell you about the specific Bible friend. Then ask leading questions about the Bible person, such as for Adam and Eve: "Who was the first man God made? Who was Eve? Where did they live? Did they always do good things?"

3. Use as many activities as you wish related to the people you are learning about, as long as your child remains interested. Your goal is to make learning about the Bible and its people fun for him!

Follow the same format in presenting the stories and Bible lessons section of each chapter to your child. Tell or read the narrative/story and do one or more hands-on activities as often as time allows and her attention span dictates. It is a real plus to stop the Bible learning before she gets bored, leaving her eager for the next spiritual lesson.

4. If you wish, as each book of the Bible is completed, ask your child to draw the name of the book or you may print it for him, or design the name on your computer. He may then color it and tape it to the door or around the walls of his room in a Bible book chain or stick it on the shelves of a Bible "bookcase" outline on a door or wall. This bookcase can be made with masking tape and will help him understand and visualize that the Bible is made up of many fascinating books. In addition, he will be introduced to some of the new-sounding names of the Bible's books. Learning their general location with the whole Bible will be an advantage when he

begins to look up verses for himself!

5. You also may want to celebrate the conclusion of each book study with a treat or a small reward commemorating the priceless time you have spent together and the adventures you have enjoyed in learning about God and His Word. The celebration can be simply a big hug, a round of applause for your child's graduation to a new book of the Bible, a trip to the Treasure Box for a treat and trinket, lunch together at the mall, or a trip to the Christian bookstore for a new book or video.

Regardless of the specifics of how you teach, you will be on your way to training a little Bible scholar and helping to indelibly shape his life for time and eternity! What could possibly be more important or rewarding?

Here are a few items that will come in handy to have as you teach your children about the Bible:

1. Holman Bible Publisher's *Read to Me Bible for Kids NIrV.*

2. A flannel board or flannel/felt cloth.

3. An enlarged photo of the child to use as a paper doll or stick puppet

4. A Bible scrapbook/journal to glue pictures, write observations or comments, do written activities, or to keep a record of your journey through the Bible.

5. A prayer box with names or pictures of people.

6. A Kindness Sack with ideas for different kind deeds to pick and do each day.

7. A box of scarves, strips of cloth, sandals, etc., for Bible-time dress up

8. A Treasure Chest or Blessing Box with small inexpensive (or free) toys or treats to keep on hand as incentives, rewards for a job well done, "thanks for being you!" gifts, or to use in various games and activities described in the chapters that follow. They can be picked up for very little expense at neighborhood garage sales, in stores that sell birthday favors, discount stores, or Christian bookstores. Some items to consider are small Bibles, storybooks, glow-in-the-dark crosses, small pictures of Jesus, WWJD bracelets, gum, candy, or fruit snacks. Trade with another mother for an assortment of games, toy characters, and gadgets that clutter every child's closet. Remember, another child's trash will qualify as your child's treasure.

Genesis — God's Book of How the World Got Started

"In the beginning God created the heavens and the earth" (Genesis 1:1).

What's the Book About

God made an amazing world for people to live in. He started right away to show His love for them by helping them and leading them, just as He does for us!

In the Very Beginning

Genesis is a book about how the world got started. It tells how God was always here and how He made the beautiful world, with the sky, water, sun, moon, stars, plants, trees, and flowers. Then God added all kinds of fish, bugs, birds, and other animals to live in His amazing world.

All the time He was making things, God was getting the world ready for the very best thing He ever made – people. The first people God made were a man named Adam and a woman called Eve.

After we learn about Adam and Eve in the Bible book of Genesis, we will meet many more of God's people and hear about how He loves them and takes care of them, just like He does for us!

Let's Meet the People of Genesis

Adam and Eve were the very first people God made. They were very happy in God's beautiful garden, and God gave them everything they needed. But they disobeyed God, and they were very sorry and ashamed. God never stopped loving them and taking care of them.

Cain and Abel were Adam and Eve's first two children. Their story is very sad, because Abel was the very first person to die ever.

Noah was a man who loved and obeyed God. When a big flood came and destroyed everything, God kept Noah and his family safe inside a huge boat called an "ark." Noah loved God and worshiped Him.

Abraham was a man who trusted and followed God even when it was hard to do. Sarah was his wife. They were very old and had no children, until God gave them a special baby boy named **Isaac.**

7

Isaac also loved and obeyed God. **Rebekah** became Isaac's wife.

Abraham had a nephew named **Lot**, who made some very bad choices.

Jacob was Isaac's son, who wanted God to bless him, and **Esau** was Jacob's twin brother, who was very different from Jacob. Jacob's wife was **Rachel.**

Joseph, one of Jacob's many sons, had some adventures that seemed bad but turned out good because Joseph loved and served God. God was taking care of Joseph.

Here Are the Places of Genesis

The Beautiful Garden – "The Garden of Eden" was the first home God made for the first people, and it was absolutely perfect until Adam and Eve disobeyed God.

The Mountains of Ararat – were where Noah's big boat stopped when the huge flood was over and the waters that covered the whole earth dried up.

Babel – the place where some foolish people tried to build a giant tower to show how great they were. They even thought they were greater than God.

Caanan – Abraham, Sarah, and Lot traveled to this land and made it their home.

First There Was God and Nothing!

(A song with motions)

What will I need? Your voice, arms, and legs
Where is it in the Bible? Genesis 1
How long will it take? About 5 minutes
What age child? 1-8 years
Will it work in a group? Yes
Can it be played in the car? With limited motions.
Will it work in a school classroom? Yes, preschool–3rd grade

Sing this happy creation song from the book of Genesis to the tune of "Ten Little Indians."
First there was God and nothing, nothing.
(Cover eyes with hands)
First there was God and nothing, nothing.
First there was God and nothing, nothing.
All God's world was DARK!

Then God spoke, and He made light.
Then God spoke, and He made light.
(Make a flashing motion by quickly opening and closing hands over your eyes.)
Then God spoke, and He made light.
Now God's world was LIGHT!

God made sky, and God made water.
God made sky, and God made water.
(Point up to sky and then wiggle fingers as you bring your hands down.)
God made sky, and God made water.
God made the water WET!

Then God made the big, round world.
(Hold hands over your head like a ball.)
Then God made the big, round world.

Then God made the big, round world.
All God's world was ROUND!

God made grass and trees and flowers.
(Wave arms like a tree.)
God made grass and trees and flowers.
God made grass and trees and flowers.
Now God's world was GREEN!

Next, God made the pretty animals
(Crawl or hop like an animal.)
Next, God made the pretty animals.
Next, God made the pretty animals.
Living in GOD'S WORLD!

Last of all, God made the people.
(Point to self and others in the room.)
Last of all, God made the people.
Last of all, God made the people.
PEOPLE are the BEST!

God's Empty World and How He Filled It Up

(A hands-on storytelling activity)

What will I need? 1. A flannel-covered board or a flannel or felt cloth that can be draped over a large pillow or couch cushion. 2. Black, blue, and yellow felt cut-outs about 8-10 inches square; a brown felt cut-out either square or round; a yellow felt sun, moon, and stars; green fringed grass and trees, and colored flower shapes. 3. Magazine or book cut-outs of animals and a man and a woman (preferably from a Bible story of Adam and Eve), with a velcro strip or piece of felt attached to the backs to allow the pictures to stick to the flannel background.

(Parents: Keep these shapes and pictures to reuse.)

Where is it in the Bible? Genesis 1–2
How long will it take?   10-15 minutes
What age child? 1-6 years
Will it work in a group? Yes
Can it be played in the car? No
Will it work in a school classroom? Yes, preschool–3rd grade.

Tell a simple version of the creation story, asking your child to place the appropriate cut-out shapes or pictures on the flannel board as you mention what God made on the various days of creation. Your story may be something like this:

"Before God made His world, everything was DARK and BLACK. (Put up a black square on the flannel cloth.) God didn't want just darkness, so on the very first day, God made LIGHT. (Put up the yellow square.) He called the light, 'day,' and the darkness, 'night.' (Put black square beside the yellow one.) What do you like to do during the DAY? (Point to yellow shape.) What do we do at NIGHT? (Point to the black shape.) God was happy that He had made day and night, and He said that they were good.

Then on the second day, God made the SKY. (Put up the blue square and take the black and yellow ones down.) God was getting the sky ready for birds to have somewhere to fly.

On the third day, God made the world, with its DIRT and DRY LAND. (Put up the brown shape). Then He took water and made OCEANS, LAKES, and RIVERS. (Point to the blue shape.) God made PLANTS, TREES, and FLOWERS on His world to make it beautiful, and to be food for the animals and people that He would make very soon.

(Put up the green and flower shapes.) Everything God had made was good.

On the fourth day, God made more amazing things. He made the SUN (Put sun up), the MOON (Put moon up) and the STARS (Put stars up). God saw that His sun, moon, and stars were good, too. On the fifth day, God made all kinds of FISH to live in the oceans, lakes, and rivers He had made (Put up pictures of fish). He made BIRDS (Put up bird picture) to fly in his huge, beautiful sky, and everything was good, and God was pleased with what He had made.

On the sixth day of making His world and filling it up, God made all the ANIMALS. He made dogs, cats, lions, and tigers. (Name and put up whatever animal pictures you have.) He made them different colors, with different kinds of "outsides." Some had skin, like snakes or elephants, others had shells, like turtles and snails, and many of them had fur. Some had stripes, some had spots, and most of them had tails. They looked different from other kinds of animals; they sounded different; they acted different, but God made them all. The animals were all good because God made them.

Now God's world was all ready for the very best thing He would make, the thing He loves the very most – PEOPLE. So God made ADAM, the man, and EVE, the woman (Put up their pictures) so He could show them His love and care, and they could love God back. Then, God saw that everything He had made, especially the people, were VERY good! And, on the seventh day of creation, God rested and enjoyed His wonderful, beautiful world."

For babies and young children:

1. Tell the story of creation very simply, something like this: "God is good to us! He

made the day. (Put up yellow square.) He made the night. (Put up black square.) God gave us the world and the sun, the moon and the stars. (Put up these shapes.) God made the fish that swim and birds that fly. Then God made the first people. (Put up pictures of a man and woman. Name them Adam and Eve.) God is VERY good and loves all His children very much."

2. Cut out four or five large pictures of God's creations: animals, trees, flowers, or people. Mount pictures on pieces of cardboard, round the corners for babies, and cover with clear adhesive paper, like contact paper. Tell the creation story holding the Bible where your child can see it. Place the pictures on the open Bible and remove them one by one for the baby to see as you talk about each thing God made and how good He is to us!

3. Cut out large pictures of God's created world and glue them on the sides of a small, sturdy box, covering the whole box with clear adhesive paper. Let your baby or young child turn the box over and around as you describe each thing that God has made. Say, "Thank You, God, for being so good to us!"

Hang Up a World

(A messy art activity and a noisy game)

What will I need? A large round balloon, several sheets of newspaper and strips of paper, flour and water to mix together with a spoon to make a paste to use as glue.
Where is it in the Bible? Genesis 1–2
How long will it take? About 45 minutes to an hour to make the world and 15-30 minutes to play the game.

What age child? 2-10 years
Will it work in a group? Definitely!
Can it be played in the car? No, impossible to even imagine!
Will it work in a school classroom? Yes, preschool–4th grade

Spread the newspaper on the table or floor where you will be working. Expect a bit of mess, since you and your child will be making paper mache with newspaper strips, flour, and water glue! Inflate the round balloon and tie it tightly. Mix flour and water to form a paste about the consistency of gravy. (It may even be tasted during this project!) Dip newspaper strips in the mixture, allowing excess glue to drip back into the bowl, and drape them over the balloon, covering it completely several times. If you want to prolong the fun (a little unlikely for parents, but entirely possible for children!), allow the newspaper-covered balloon to dry for a day or two and repeat the process of covering it with a few more layers of newspaper. You are making a world to be used like a piñata for the second half of the fun!

When the balloon project is dry, paint it blue and brown (or use fast drying markers), for the oceans and land. Use this quality work time with your child to talk about the wonders of God's handiwork, and to discuss the amazing attributes of your child's favorite animals, and any other aspect of God's world that your child finds especially interesting. If he/she is old enough to understand, explain to him/her that a world so intricate could not have just happened without a very powerful and intelligent Creator. Give God honor even as you work together on this project.

When the piñata world is completed, cut a flap near the top and place a plastic bag of wrapped candy or other small treats inside the balloon. (Use the plastic bag if your child doesn't want to wait for the glue to dry). Tie a string to the balloon and hang it from a sturdy ceiling fixture, plant hook or beam, with a sheet spread underneath to protect the carpet, if inside.

Explain to your child that the Bible says that God hung the world on NOTHING when He created it, and how awesome He is to be able to do something so incredible. Remind your child that God can do ANYTHING!

At the start of the game, ask your child or group to sit on the floor near you as you read with enthusiasm the Bible account of creation from Genesis 1. If your child is too young to sit still for very long, paraphrase the passage in your own words. Then, let your child attempt to break the world with a bat or stick and enjoy its contents! Before each swing (or before each new child gets a turn), ask your child to name something God made from Genesis 1. End the activity by thanking God for the fun it is to learn about Him and His world.

Alternate activity: If you want to avoid the time and mess involved in the piñata project, inflate a balloon (a blue one, preferably) and explain that the balloon is the part of the world that is water and draw simple continental shapes with a brown or green felt-tip marker. Explain to your child that the Bible says the world is round (Isaiah 40:22), but that for a long time people thought it was flat. Talk about how mighty God is, how He made the world round like the balloon, put us on it and keeps us from falling off by creating gravity. Explain that although we cannot see gravity, it is real. It is God's way to "stick" us on the world and help make it a good place to live. Remind your child that God is right here with us, too, even though we can't see Him with our eyes right now.

God Made You, Kangaroo!
(A rhyming game and musical activity)

What will I need? A cassette or CD player and a favorite praise tape
Where is it in the Bible? Genesis 1; 2:19-20
How long will it take? 10-15 minutes
What age child? 2-9 years
Will it work in a group? Yes
Can it be played in the car? Only Activity 1
Will it work in a school classroom? Yes, preschool–4th grade

1. Begin this funny rhyme by clapping to establish the rhythm (not too fast or you'll have trouble fitting in some of the words!) or just chant it without clapping:
God made YOU, Kangaroo.
God made your SMILE, Crocodile.
God made the PLANTS, tiny ants.
God made the AIR, Panda Bear.
God made the SKY, birds that fly.
God made the TREES, Chickadees.
God made the GROUND, Basset Hound.
God made the SUN, Pelican.
God made the MOON, silly Baboon.
God made the LAKES, hissing snakes.
God made it ALL, Giraffe so tall.
God made ME, Honey Bee

2. Play this musical game with your child or a group of children. Instruct children to decide on an animal to pretend to be, but not to say its name. Ask them to act like that animal and make its sound as they move in a circle while the music plays. When the music

stops, the children must freeze in place. Let the children guess which animal the other children were imitating.

People, People
(A slightly noisy naming game)

What will I need? Two or more players, your imagination and voices
Where is it in the Bible? Genesis 1-2
How long will it take? 3-10 minutes
What age child? 2-9 years
Will it work in a group? Yes
Can it be played in the car? Yes
Will it work in a school classroom? Yes, preschool–4th grade

Mom or Dad will begin this game by naming a series of animals God made, interjecting the name Adam or Eve frequently in the list. Each time a person is named, the child must say, "People!" Say, "God made dogs, cats, trees, Adam, ('People!') horses, cows, Eve, ('People!') giraffes, ducks, Adam, ('People!') zebras, lions, Eve,('People!') Adam,('People') snakes."

Remind your child that Adam and Eve were the very first people God made and that they are everybody's great, great, great, great, great, grandparents! Take turns telling the Genesis story.

For babies and young children: Say this chant, "People, people! God made people! God made Adam. God made Eve. God made PEOPLE!" God made YOU!" (Tickle his tummy and give him a great big hug!)

A "Mud" Man
(A yummy art activity)

What will I need? 1. Chocolate cookie dough 2. Chocolate cookie crumbs 3. A piece of waxed paper, foil, or counter to roll out dough and make your "mud man"
Where is it in the Bible? Genesis 1:26-31 and Genesis 2:7, 15, 18-23
How long will it take? About 15-20 minutes to make and 10-15 minutes to bake
What age child? 1-10 years
Will it work in a group? Yes, make sure all the children have enough dough to make their own mud men.
Can it be played in the car? You and I are both smiling, aren't we?
Will it work in a school classroom? Yes, students love to cook and eat. Preschool–5th grade.

If you are not using packaged cookie dough, let your child help you make the dough (or you can use clay, if you don't want to eat your project!) as you tell the story of God's creation of Adam. If you wish, read the Genesis story and talk about how God had gotten everything just right for the man and woman, Adam and Eve, that He was soon going to make. Talk with your child about how much God wanted to make people to love and be with and take care of, and how He loves us just as much as He loved the very first people He made.

Elaborate as much as you wish on all the amazing things God makes people be able to do, to think, to feel, to love, to worship, etc., emphasizing how very good God is all the time and how thankful we should be that He made us and loves us so much. As you share with your child your own faith and trust in the Lord, help your child make a man out of mud, like God made Adam out of the "dirt" of the ground.

Instruct your child to roll his dough in chocolate "dust" (cookie crumbs or sweetened cocoa mix). Then ask him to roll a cylindrical body, add a head, arms, legs, facial features, etc., (or roll out the dough and cut out a boy shape with a cookie cutter) bake the mud man and let him cool. Say a simple prayer of thanks before enjoying your mud man and milk!

For very young children: Use a very simple narrative of the creation of Adam as you help him make a mud man, or as he watches you make one. Say, "God made a man. He called him, 'Adam.' We'll make a cookie man and call him 'Adam,' too. God made (your child's name). God LOVES (your child's name)! Thank you, God, for making (your child)."

God Made Me!
(A loving rhyme)

What will I need? Just you and your child
Where is it in the Bible? Genesis 1 and 2
How long will it take? One well-spent minute or less
What age child? Baby–5 years
Will it work in a group? Yes
Can it be played in the car? Yes, without the mirror or with a safe one he can hold
Will it work in a school classroom? Yes, preschool or kindergarten

Place your baby or young child in a position where he can look into a mirror that you hold before his face or prop against his crib wall (or walk around among a group of young children, carrying a mirror, pausing to let each child look into it). As he looks at his reflection, lovingly say this little rhyme several times, gently touching his tummy as you say,

"God made the flowers.
God made the trees.
God made the animals
And God made ME!"

How "Bad" Got Started in God's Good World
(A story and activity from Genesis 2, 3)

God made a man named Adam and a woman to be his wife named Eve. He put them in the beautiful Garden of Eden with plenty of food and water to eat and drink. Their job would be to take care of the garden and to enjoy it!

The garden was the most wonderful place anyone has ever lived. There was nothing in the garden to hurt Adam and Eve or cause trouble in any way, because there was nothing bad at all in God's perfect world. Even the animals were not afraid of Adam and Eve, and Adam and Eve were not afraid of any of the animals.

But in the middle of the garden grew two special trees. One was called the "Tree of Life" and the other was named the "Tree of the Knowledge of Good and Bad." God was so kind and loving that He let Adam and Eve eat fruit from ALL the trees except for the "Tree of the Knowledge of Good and Bad." God wanted to keep only good things in His wonderful world so that the people would never have to know what bad is like. So He told Adam never to eat the fruit from that one tree.

One day the devil (Satan) came to Eve in the garden. He looked like a special kind of snake (or serpent) so that Eve would not know who he was or what bad things he was trying to do. He began to talk to her and said, "Did God really say you couldn't eat ANY of the fruit in this garden?" "No," said Eve to the devil, "The only fruit we can't eat is on the one tree. God said if we eat it, we will die."

The devil was trying to trick Eve, and he said to her, "That's not true. You won't die! Why, if you just eat some, you'll become wise like God!" Eve looked at the fruit, and it looked very good to eat, because things that are bad (sin) sometimes look good to us. When we feel like doing something bad, that is called temptation, and it's the devil's way of trying to get us to do wrong.

Eve forgot that no one will ever be as wise as God; she foolishly did what the devil said and took a bite of the fruit. Not only did Eve do wrong, but she gave some of the fruit to Adam to eat, and he did!

Even while they were eating the fruit, they realized they had done something wrong. They were embarrassed and ashamed. They even tried to hide from God. But that's impossible. Sure enough, the Lord God was right there in the garden, and He called to Adam and asked him if he had eaten the fruit from the tree he had been warned not to eat!

Adam sadly said, "Yes," but then he tried to blame Eve and say it was her fault. Eve then tried to blame the snake! God knows all things, and He knew what had really happened. Because they had sinned and disobeyed God, God had to cover them with animal skin clothes. Because they disobeyed (sinned), Adam and Eve had to leave the beautiful garden home that God made for

them to enjoy. Later, they did die, just as God had warned them they would.

Oh, how they wished that they had obeyed God, because He always knows and wants the very best for us all. But God never stopped loving Adam and Eve and helping them, just as He does for us!

Activity: Take a few minutes to talk about the story with your child. Then act out modern-day scenarios in which your child might be tempted to do wrong and disobey God's Word. Some examples might be sneaking candy from the candy jar, saying something that isn't true, or not sharing your toys. In each of the situations, ask your child to first show the wrong way to act, and then the right way.

God Made Music!
(Making and using instruments)

What will I need? 1. Plastic eggs, rice, or dried beans, and glue or hot glue 2. A cardboard roll to decorate, dried peas or rice, and heavy tape
Where is it in the Bible? Genesis 4:19-20
How long will it take? 15-30 minutes
What age child? 1-11 years
Will it work in a group? Yes
Can it be played in the car? No
Will it work in a school classroom? Yes, a fun class project for preschool–6th grade

Ask your child where he thinks music came from. Show him in the Bible that God had the great idea for music. Talk about your favorite instruments that make music. Ask your child whether she likes slow or fast, happy or sad music better. Say a thank you prayer to God for His great idea of music!

You and your child may enjoy making some of these simple rhythm instruments and using them to keep time with Christian music in your own "homestyle" band.

Rain-sounding shakers – Fill colored plastic eggs half-full of rice or small dried beans and hot-glue them together for child-size shakers.

Rain-sounding sticks – Decorate the outside of a paper-towel or wrapping paper roll by painting it or gluing cut-out shapes from shiny wrapping paper, tissue paper, or construction paper. When the outside is dry, cover one end of the tube with heavy tape, making sure it is completely sealed, and pour a cupful of dried beans or uncooked rice into the tube. Seal the other end with tape and play the instrument by tilting the tube gently from end to end. The falling beans or rice will sound like rain!

Listen for the Treasure!
(An adventure in following directions)

What will I need? Small treats and treasures to hide.
Where is it in the Bible? Genesis 6:8, 13-22
How long will it take? 15-30 minutes
What age child? 2-9 years
Will it work in a group? Yes, fun!
Can it be played in the car? No
Will it work in a school classroom? Yes, great fun inside and outside the room. Keep it simple for preschoolers, but make the listening clues more complicated for older children.

Before you embark on your treasure hunt, hide a few small surprises in various places in the house or yard and a small "treasure chest"

box containing a few pieces of candy, a treat, a toy, a small new Bible, Bible storybook, or picture of Jesus.

Explain that you and he are going on a listening adventure. Explain to him that Noah listened to God. Share the story with your child and let the listening treasure hunt begin!

Tell your child that he must listen to you to find out where the treasure is hidden. He should find one thing at a time until he finds the treasure chest. Tell him the first clue, something like, "Go to a place where you can sit to read and look under something you find there." When your child finds that treasure, let him keep it and give him the clue to find the second one, etc., until the treasure box is found. If the treasure inside it is the Bible or picture of Jesus, talk about how those are the very best treasures of all! Thank him for being such a good listener, like Noah. Share with your child that listening to God is such an important way to make His heart and ours glad!

This Is the Way that I Obey!
(A song activity)

What will I need? Your voice and a friend to sing along with you
Where is it in the Bible? Genesis 6:22; 7:5
How long will it take? 3-5 minutes
What age child? Baby to 8 years
Will it work in a group? Yes
Can it be played in the car? Yes
Will it work in a school classroom? Yes, preschool–3rd grade

Sing this echo to the tune of "This Is the Day That the Lord Hath Made." You and your child should switch singing roles the second time through.

Tell your child the story of Noah's obedience to God and discuss how happy Noah must have been that he listened to God and obeyed Him.

Here's how the song goes:
"This is the day (echo: 'This is the day')
That I will obey. (echo)
Jesus is GLAD (echo)
When I do obey. (echo)
This is the day that I will obey.
 Jesus is GLAD when I do obey.
(all sing these two lines)
This is the day (echo)
That I WILL obey." (all together)

Two-by-Two
(An art project and a matching game)

What will I need? 1. Poster board, construction paper, or a large, brown grocery bag 2. A white paper like poster board
3. Something to draw or color with
Where is it in the Bible? Genesis 7:1-9
How long will it take? 45 minutes to an hour
What age child? 2-10 years
Will it work in a group? Yes, for individual projects or small group projects
Can it be played in the car? No
Will it work in a school classroom? Yes, pre-school–5th grade

Help your child cut out a big boat shape from poster board or paper. On the boat shape, cut eight or ten window-type flaps that can be folded open and closed. Glue the outside edges of the boat on another piece of light or white posterboard. Behind two different flaps, (not side-by-side) suggest that your child draw two matching animals, then

two more different animals, etc., until all the windows have a picture of an animal in them. Close all the flaps and number them.

Ask your child to choose a window number and open it. Tell him that he should try to find the other animal that looks just like the first one. Close the flaps of the pictures that don't match, and encourage your child to keep trying to find twin animals until all of them have been found.

Talk about the wonderful and amazing story of God protecting all kinds of animals along with Noah's family so that the world could start over again after the big flood, with many more animals and many more people.

Rainbow Celebration!
(An art activity and active game)

What will I need? 1. A paper plate, strips of different colored tissue paper, a spray bottle of water 2. A plate, fork, and a plastic knife, a banana, and dry powdered gelatin in more than one flavor and color
Where is it in the Bible? Genesis 9:1-17
How long will it take? 20-30 minutes
What age child? 2-11 years
Will it work in a group? Yes
Can it be played in the car? No
Will it work in a school classroom? Yes

Discuss how happy Noah and his family must have felt when the rain was over, the water was gone, and they could leave the boat! Read what the Bible says happened in Genesis 8:16-22 and do one or more of these rainbow activities to remind you of God's great promise.

Activity 1. On a small, white paper plate let

the child arrange strips or small squares of tissue paper. Then, with a shaker or a gentle spray bottle filled with water, she may pretend to "rain" on the "rainbow" paper. As she does, the colors from the tissue paper will appear on the plate, leaving behind a rainbow of color.

Activity 2. Give your child a banana, a small plate, and a child-friendly knife to slice the peeled banana into small rounds. Sprinkle several colors of dry gelatin on the banana slices, creating a pretty and delicious rainbow effect. Better plan to have several extra bananas for seconds.

One Hundred? That's a Lot!

(A counting game)

What will I need? One hundred things to count: buttons, jellybeans, pennies, dried beans, pasta, etc.
Where is it in Bible? Genesis 18:6-12
How long will it take? 15 minutes
What age child? 2-9 years
Will it work in a group? Yes, really well
Can it be played in the car? No
Will it work in a school classroom? Yes, good activities for preschool–5th grade.

Help your child understand that God did an amazing thing for Abraham and Sarah. When she was 90 and he was 100 years old, God gave them a baby boy! Share the wonderful story about God's promise to Abraham and how He always does what He says He will. To make Abraham and Sarah's ages seem more understandable, use one or more

of these 100 things activities:

1. Place 100 small items into a transparent container and let your child examine the amount of items inside. If you wish, let him pour the contents onto a paper towel and help him count them or just see how 100 looks spread out before him!
2. Take a 100-step walk and see where it takes you, looking back to see how far you came.

Be sure to explain again that "100" reminds you of our friend Abraham in God's great Bible and that having a baby when someone is that many years old is something only God can do.

Better Pack Your Bags!

(An active game)

What will I need? 1. Two suitcases or grocery sacks 2. Two shirts, pants, jackets, caps, pairs or gloves or shoes to put in the suitcases
Where is it in the Bible? Genesis 12-13
How long will it take? 10-15 minutes
What age child? 3-10 years
Will it work in a group? Yes, great fun as a relay.
Can it be played in the car? No.
Will it work in a school classroom? Yes, preschool–6th grades

Place two suitcases or grocery bags side by side at one end of a room or yard. Place the same number of similar items of clothing in each. All of the clothing may be oversized to make them go on easily.

Form two teams and at the "Go!" signal both players or the first player on each relay team must rush to their suitcases and put on the clothes, trying to be the first player completely dressed. If you are playing with a relay team, the first child to dress runs back to his team, takes off the clothes, hands them to the second runner who runs back to the bag or suitcase, puts on the clothes, and the cycle begins again.

Tell your child about Abraham's trip to a brand new home and describe all the many things he must have had to pack (see Genesis 13:1-6). If you have ever traveled with a family pet, imagine how difficult it must have been to take along herds of sheep and cows! Explain to your child that not only did Abraham and his family and all his animals and everything he owned have to be packed up to travel, but also he did not even know where they were going. But God knew where they should go, and Abraham trusted God!

Here's a traveling song you might want to sing in honor of Abraham.
(To the tune of "Camptown Races")
"God has sent me on a trip, Do da, do da.
Not by plane and not by ship. Oh, do da day!
Gonna walk all night, gonna walk all day.
Going to a brand new home. Oh, do da day!"

Divide It!
(A thinking and doing game)

What will I need? A cookie, a drink, dry cereal pieces, or fruit slices to share; a bag of items of two colors, sizes, shapes, or types.
Where is it in the Bible? Genesis 13
How long will it take? 15-30 minutes
What age child? 1-10 years
Will it work in a group? Yes, with partners "dividing" things
Can it be played in the car? Not very well
Will it work in a school classroom? Yes, in

pairs, maybe as a friendly contest to see how many partners can divide a bag of small items into two groups within a certain time limit.

Explain that when Abraham's family, his nephew Lot, and Lot's family got to the new land, they had to decide how to share or divide up the land. Tell the story and divide several things with your child. Use a cookie or cracker, a full glass of some drink poured into an empty glass, making them both half-full, equal numbers of cereal pieces, or fruit slices, etc.

If you wish, you may provide your child with a sack or shoebox containing items of two different colors, shapes, sizes, or types. Ask your child to divide the items into two groups and pretend that one group of items belongs to Abraham and the other to Lot, just like the land they divided between their families and animals.

If you are in a group, let the children think of some things to use to divide themselves into groups:
1. By hair color
2. By shoe type
3. By shirts style
4. By jeans or other pants

Finish the story by explaining that Abraham was kind to let Lot choose first, but Lot's choice was not so wise. The land he chose was near cities where people did not love and obey God. Finally, the Lord had to destroy those cities (Sodom and Gomorrah) because they were very bad.

The Big Test
(Genesis 22)

Share this beautiful story with your child in such a way that it will not frighten him, or cause the magnitude of God's command to Abraham to overshadow a wonderful message. God provides for what we need just when we need it, and whatever He asks of us, God will provide for us the necessary resources. God must be first in our lives because He is GOD, and He is good.

Isaac grew to be a young man. One day God told Isaac's father Abraham to take his son to a mountain called Moriah and offer him there to the Lord in worship. That seemed to Abraham like a very strange and hard thing to do, because people usually gave lambs or doves to God for their offerings, but Abraham trusted and obeyed God, because He knew God is good.

The next morning, Abraham prepared his donkey, chopped some wood to take along, and started walking with Isaac and two special helpers toward the place God had told him to go. When Abraham saw the place ahead of them, he told the helpers to stay with the donkey while he and Isaac went to worship God on the mountain.

Abraham made a pile of rocks called an altar, and put the pieces of wood on it. Isaac laid down on the wood to be an offering to God, just like the lambs that God's people usually gave to God when they worshiped Him.

At that moment, an angel of God called loudly to Abraham, "Abraham, Abraham! I know that you love God more than anyone else because you were going to give Him the son you love so much!" Just then, Abraham noticed a ram (sheep) that was nearby, with its horns caught in the bushes. Abraham put the ram on the wood instead of Isaac and offered it to God in worship. God promised to bless Abraham and to give his family many grandchildren and great-grandchildren to love. That was very good news to Abraham.

The "Don't-Look-Much-Alike" Twins

(Two funny art activities)

What will I need? A paper plate, a stick or ruler, crayons or markers, and strong tape.
Where is it in the Bible? Genesis 25:19-34 and 27:1-40
How long will it take? 15-30 minutes
What age child? 2-10 years
Will it work in a group? Yes
Can it be played in the car? Yes, but only the verbal activities
Will it work in a school classroom? Yes

Isaac and Rebekah got a wonderful surprise from God – twin boys. They named them Jacob and Esau.

Pretend to be "look-alike" twins (like looking at your reflection in a mirror) and take turns imitating the actions of the other person as you face each other. Then explain that Jacob and Esau did not look alike and were very different in the ways they acted, too. Describe the ways the twins boys were different:

Jacob:
1. had smooth skin
2. liked to stay around home
3. wanted God and Isaac, his father, to bless (do a good thing for) him

Esau:
1. had hairy skin
2. liked to go outside and hunt and do quiet things
3. didn't care much if God or Isaac did good things for him until it was too late

Tell the story of how Jacob played a dirty

trick on Esau and took away the special bless-ing that Esau, who was the oldest, was sup-posed to get from Isaac. Explain to your child that Esau did not care very much about important things until Jacob played a trick on him and took them away. Then Esau wished he could have the those things back!

Play this easy "What's Valuable?" game. Here's how: Make the following statements to your child and let her tell you what she thinks is more valuable in each one.

"I have a diamond ring and a torn-up old piece of paper. Which one shall I throw away and which one should I keep?"

"I have a broken toy car and a new shiny toy truck. Which one shall I keep?"

"I have a Bible and a candy wrapper. Which one shall I throw away?"

"I have new tennis shoes and old torn socks that won't fit me any more. Which ones shall I keep?"

Esau threw away something really valuable that he should have kept – the good things his father Isaac wanted to give to him and say to him. Later, Esau was very sorry. Esau choose a bowl of food that he ate, and then it was gone and he got hungry all over again! Unlike Esau, we understand that some things are very important: our family, our church, the Bible, and especially, Jesus!

Remind your child that Jacob had some very good things about him. He loved God, and he loved his family and wanted them to be kind to him. But Jacob also did some very bad things; he did not always tell the truth, and he tricked his father Isaac, who was very old and couldn't see.

Discuss with your child that all of us have to choose if we will be and do good and obey

God or if we will do bad. We should ask God to help us and He will.

Provide crayons or markers for your child and ask him to make a happy face on one side of a paper plate or paper and a sad face of the same person on the other side. Add hair or make your Jacob puppet as simple or elaborate as you wish. Explain that when Jacob did what God wanted him to, he was happy, but when he did not, his face and his heart were sad.

Make a picture of hairy Esau on a paper plate. To add hair use dry spaghetti or other pasta, yarn or string, Easter basket grass, or whatever you have handy that will work.

Very Many Sons
(A concentrating and guessing game)

What will I need? A dozen boiled eggs and waterproof markers or 12 different colored jelly beans

Where is it in the Bible? Genesis 29:30-35, 30:1-43

How long will it take? 15-30 minutes

What age child? 2-10 years

Will it work in a group? Yes

Can it be played in the car? Yes, if the driver doesn't try to play!

Will it work in a school classroom? Yes, preschool–5th grade

Tell your child that God was always faith-ful and kind to Jacob, even though Jacob did not always do the right things. Jacob learned that it is very important to love and obey God more than anything else, and God blessed Jacob very much. God gave Jacob a big fam-ily. He had 12 boys and some girls, too! You can find their names in Genesis 29:31-35 and

Genesis 30.

Play a "who's missing?" game with your child. Explain that even in families where there are many children, every child is very important to God. If you are using a dozen boiled eggs to represent the 12 sons of Jacob, mark each one differently using a waterproof marker. You may even choose the write their names on the eggs. Place the eggs in the carton with the symbols visible or use colored jellybeans for a real challenge for older children.

Pretend that the 12 eggs are Jacob's sons. Ask your child to hide his eyes, then take away one. Tell your child to open his eyes and see which egg is missing. Continue to identify missing eggs or jellybeans, and discuss how important every member of your family is to God and to each other!

Trouble and More Trouble!

(The story of Joseph from Genesis 37–41)

Joseph had some BIG problems! His brothers were jealous of him. They took away his beautiful coat and threw him in a deep, dark well. Then they told their father Jacob the terrible story that Joseph had died, but he was still very much alive. His brothers saw a group of people who were on their way to Egypt to buy and sell things, and Joseph's brothers sold him! Can you imagine that?

Joseph found himself in a strange land, far away from his whole family. He did not know anybody there! Still, God was right there all the time, so Joseph was never really alone.

But Joseph's troubles weren't over yet! Other bad things happened to him, but God made all the bad things work together in very good ways.

Remember that sometimes things happen to us that seem bad by themselves, but God changes those bad things into good things.

Talk about some of the things that happened to Joseph that seemed very bad, and God then changed them into something good! Here are some of the problems Joseph had in Egypt:

1. Joseph went to work for an important man named Potiphar, who liked Joseph very much. But Potiphar's wife told a lie about Joseph and got him put in jail!

2. While Joseph was in jail, he met the baker, the man who cooked for the king, and the butler, one of the king's special helpers. Both of them had dreams that bothered them. (Do you ever have bad dreams?) God told Joseph what the dreams meant, and Joseph told the baker and the butler. The butler's dream meant he would get out of jail soon and go back to his old job for the king. That was good news for the butler. Joseph asked the butler to please help him get out of jail, too, but when the butler went back to his old job at the king's house, he forgot all about Joseph! So Joseph stayed in jail! Now that seems like trouble, doesn't it?

3. Two long years later, Pharaoh, the king, had a dream that bothered him. Pharaoh's strange dream was all about fat cows and skinny cows, and he wanted to know what it meant (Genesis 41:1-36). Finally, the butler remembered Joseph in jail and told Pharaoh that Joseph knew how to tell what dreams meant. Joseph got out of jail at last. Remember, he had done nothing wrong to be put in jail.

4. After all the things that happened to Joseph that seemed so bad, God made him become one of the Pharaoh's special helpers.

He became a very important man in Egypt. He even got to wear the king's ring and beautiful clothes. Joseph was not angry about the problems he had. He just wanted to be able to do good and help people and, especially, to please God (Genesis 41:39-40, 46, 51-57).

Moving to Egypt

(A word game)

What will I need? Your voice and your good memory
Where is it in the Bible? Genesis 45-47
How long will it take? 15-20 minutes
Age age child? 3-11 years
Will it work in a group? Yes
Can it be played in the car? Yes
Will it work in a classroom? Yes, preschool–5th grade

Tell your child the ending to Joseph's great story about when he moved his whole family to their new home in Egypt, where there was plenty of food for them to eat. Play this familiar traveling game as a reminder that God moved Joseph's family from the home they lived in to a new home in a different place, because He knew that was the best thing for them to do. If you or someone your child knows has ever made a move to a new location, relate some of the good things that have come as a result of that move.

Then, play "I'm moving to Egypt and I'm taking along a _____(name anything you want)." If you want more challenge for older children, stipulate that all items they choose to take along must begin with a certain letter, like "E." The items might be silly things that could NEVER fit into a suitcase!

End the game by explaining that Joseph died in Egypt when he was an old man, and God had made his life good, just like He promised. Tell your child that even though Joseph went to heaven with God, his family kept growing and growing on earth and in the next book of the Bible, Exodus, we will see just how many people came to be in Joseph's family.

What Can I Learn from Genesis

1. God made us and loves us.

2. God kept His promises to the people in Genesis. God always keeps His promises to us, too.

3. The people in the book of Genesis sometimes did wrong things and made bad choices.

4. God always was with the people in the book of Genesis, and He was always helping them. We need God to help us, too.

5. God's people in Genesis were happy when they obeyed God and did what was right. Obeying God makes us happy, too.

Important Verses to Remember

Genesis 1:31 – "God saw all that he had made, and it was very good. And there was evening, and there was morning – the sixth day."

Genesis 2:7 – "The Lord God formed the man from the dust of the ground and breathed into his nostrils the breath of life, and the man became a living being."

Genesis 8:22 – "As long as the earth endures, seedtime and harvest, cold and heat, summer and winter, day and night will never cease."

Genesis 18:14a – "Is anything too hard for the Lord?"

Genesis 50:20 – "You intended to harm me, but God intended it for good to accomplish what is now being done, the saving of many lives."

A Devotional Thought for Parents and Teachers

Doesn't it seem strange that a little baby comes into life without an acquired knowledge of anything at all? He knows nothing from experience or observation about television, computers, tennis shoes, pizza, or candy bars. He has absolutely no personal knowledge of the Almighty God, his very Creator, nor will he meet Him, unless he is introduced. That's precisely where we fit in – to introduce to our own child the infinite Lord. From the very beginning of our child's life, we are privileged daily to present to him the only One who had no beginning at all, and who, like our child, will never end.

Exodus God's Book About His People
on a Long, Long Trip "I am the God of your fathers, the God of Abraham, the God of Isaac and the God of Jacob" (Exodus 3:6a).

What's the Book About

God's people lived in Egypt and worked very hard because of a king named Pharaoh, who did not love God. God saw their sadness and heard their prayers, and He led them out of their hard life in Egypt to a new life in a beautiful land called Canaan.

A Great Escape and a Long, Long Trip

As the book of Exodus begins, God's people have lived in Egypt since Joseph moved his family there 400 years before! Joseph's family has grown and grown, until there are more than two million people in Egypt who love God and worship Him. They are the Israelites or Jewish people, the very big family that God had promised to give to Abraham a long time before.

Egypt has a new king called Pharaoh, who does not love God and will not obey Him. Pharaoh is cruel to God's people, and they pray to the Lord to help them. In the exciting adventures of Exodus, God helps His people escape from this harsh king, and they begin a long trip through the hot desert to the promised land.

Let's Meet the People of Exodus

Moses was the leader of God's people, who sometimes made mistakes and got himself into trouble. Even when Moses acted badly and made wrong choices, God still loved him and used him to do great things.

Jochebed and **Amram** were Moses' parents, who loved him and hid him from Pharaoh when Pharaoh tried to kill all the Israelite boy babies.

Miriam was Moses' big sister, who helped protect her baby brother from danger when he was hidden in a basket on the river.

Pharaoh was the King of Egypt, who didn't love God and absolutely would not obey Him. Even after Pharaoh disobeyed, God gave him more chances to do what was right.

Pharaoh's daughter was the princess, who found baby Moses in a basket on the river and then adopted him to be her own son.

Aaron was Moses' brother and the High Priest (pastor) of God's people. Aaron often told the people what God and Moses wanted them to know, since Moses wasn't a very good speaker and Aaron was!

Joshua was a brave leader of God's people, who wasn't afraid to do what God asked of him.

Here Are the Places of Exodus

Egypt – the land where God's people worked hard as slaves

The Nile River – a long, important river in Egypt

Midian – a hot, sandy desert land where Moses lived for awhile and took care of sheep

Red Sea – a big sea that God's people crossed over

Sinai – a piece of land that points to the middle of the Red Sea

Mount Sinai – a mountain near where God's people camped, where God gave Moses His 10 special laws and other important rules to obey, because He loved His people.

STORIES AND ACTIVITIES FROM EXODUS

A Hard Time in Egypt

(Exodus 1–2:10)

Joseph brought his family to live in the land of Egypt, and they lived there for 400 long years! While they were in Egypt, more and more babies were born into Joseph's family until there were more than two million people who believed in God and loved Him.

The bad news was that Egypt got a new king called Pharaoh. Pharaoh did not love and obey God, and he was cruel to God's people and made them work very hard. This harsh king began to worry that there were too many people who loved God in his land. He thought of a terrible idea to stop their families from growing. Pharaoh commanded that all boy babies be killed!

At the same time, there was a father and mother named Amram and Jochebed who loved God. They wanted their boy baby to be safe from Pharaoh, so Jochebed made a tiny little basket and carefully put baby Moses in it. She put the little boat in the river, close to the plants along the edge of the water, and she asked Moses' big sister Miriam to watch what would happen to the baby.

Soon, one of the daughters of Pharaoh, a princess, came to the river to take a bath. She saw the little boat in the river and heard the tiny baby crying! As the princess looked at baby Moses in the basket, Miriam rushed up to her and asked, "Would you like for me to find a lady to take care of the baby and feed him for you?" When the princess said, "Yes," Miriam ran and got Jochebed, Moses' own mother, to take care of her OWN baby. This was the way God kept Moses safe.

Later, when Moses was a little older, Jochebed took Moses to Pharaoh's palace, where he lived until he became a man. Moses never forgot what God had done for him in loving him and keeping him safe, just like God does for us.

Moses and Aaron Meet the Mean King
(A royal wrestling match)

What will I need? Paper, crayons, glue, and scissors
Where is it in the Bible? Exodus 4:18–5:5
How long will it take? 5-10 minutes
What age child? 2-9 years
Will it work in a group? Yes
Can it be played in the car? Yes
Will it work in a school classroom? Yes, preschool–4th grade

Play a funny little "King Thumb" wrestling game like this: For each player, cut a small strip of paper (about 2" by 1") with points cut on one side to look like a crown. Tape the ends together to fit the thumb of each player, and slide the crown on each "King Thumb." Then instruct everyone to pick a partner and stand facing each other. Each player must use the same hand, close it into a fist, raise his thumb, and then open his fist a little to inter-lock with his partner's hand. Partners fingers should be joined together, with their thumbs upright. King Thumb wrestling is about to begin! At the signal, each player will try to push his partner's thumb down in a friendly competition! Remind the players that this is silly wrestling.

Explain that Moses and Aaron were sent by the Lord to talk to Pharaoh and that a real battle of the kings began. Tell the story from Exodus 4 and explain that Pharaoh could never win the struggle against God.

More and More Trouble
(A repeating rhyme)

What will you need? Your voice and a good memory
Where is it in the Bible? Exodus 9
How long will it take? Only about 5 minutes
What age child? Babies to 10 years
Will it work in a group? Yes
Can it be played in the car? Yes
Will it work in a school classroom? Yes, preschool–5th grade

Here's a repeating rhyme similar to "The House that Jack Built" that you may use teach your child a dramatic spiritual history lesson. If you wish, after each new additional plague is added in the rhyme, repeat the previous ones or just quote them in the order it is written:

"These are the PROBLEMS that Pharaoh caused:
This is the WATER they couldn't drink. (act like it tastes bad)
These are the FROGS, causing a stink. (hop up and down, holding nose)

These are the LICE that weren't very nice.
(act itchy)

These are the FLIES with the buggy eyes.
(make your eyes look big)

These are the COWS, all falling down.
(say moo and fall down)

These are BOILS that made them frown.
(hold stomach and look sick)

This is the HAIL with the fiery tail.
(look up, cover head to protect self)

These are the GRASSHOPPERS, jumping around. (jump around)

This is the DARKNESS that covered the town. (hold arms out in front like you can't see where you're going)

This is the NIGHT, so sad and DARK.
(bow head, rub eyes like crying)

This is Pharaoh with the HARD, HARD HEART. (shake finger at him and look angry)

These are the PROBLEMS that Pharaoh caused!

A Sad, Sad Night and a Great Escape

(An archeological dig)

What will I need? First project: 1. A lump of play dough, clay or homemade dough in which to wrap small treasures such as rocks, shells, jewels, buttons, wrapped candy, toys, coins, or other interesting objects 2. A plastic table knife or craft stick for digging.
Where is it in the Bible? Exodus 12:29-42
How long will it take? 5-20 minutes
What age child? 2-11 years
Will it work in a group? Yes
Can it be played in the car? Probably not
Will it work in a school classroom? Yes

Give your child a lump of dough in which you have already hidden treasures to be excavated. Explain that in many parts of the world scientists called archeologists have worked in places called digs to remove dirt and rock and see what may be buried underground from people and cities that were there years before.

Tell them that many interesting things have been found that tell us how they lived. A favorite place for archeologists has been the land of Egypt. Talk about the treasures that can be seen above the ground: pyramids, the Sphinx, and other ancient buildings. If possible, show pictures of these and explain that God's people, the Israelites, probably helped to build them when they were Pharaoh's slaves in Bible times. Remind your child that while they were slaves, the people of God were treated cruelly, but that they prayed to God, and He heard their cries and helped them get away from Pharaoh.

Tell them the story of the night God's people escaped from Egypt. As you do, let them listen and quietly dig in their dough to see what treasures are buried there. Open the Bible to Exodus 12:29-42 and tell the story in your own words.

From a Happy Song to a Bad-tasting Drink

(A simple science experiment)

What will I need? 1. A small can or bottle of juice or soda 2. A punch can opener 3. A straw 4. A small lump of play dough or clay
Where is it in the Bible? Exodus 15:22-29
How long will it take? 5-10 minutes
What age child? 2-10 years

Will it work in a group? Yes
Can it be played in the car? No
Will it work in a school classroom? Yes, preschool–5th grade

Try these experiments:
1. Help your child make a small hole in a can of juice. Ask him if he thinks he can drink the juice, and let him try. Then, make another hole in the can lid and ask him to attempt to drink the juice again. Explain that the second hole lets air get into the can to help push the juice out.
2. Open a bottle of juice or soda. Add more liquid until the bottle is full and place a straw in it. Before trying to take a drink, completely close the opening of the bottle around the straw with play dough or clay. Ask your child to see if this juice is drinkable or undrinkable. (He won't be able to drink it until the clay is removed.) When he learns he cannot get the juice to come through the straw with the clay around it, explain that, like in the can experiment, air must get into the bottle and help to push the juice up into the straw.

Use this practical illustration to tell the story from Exodus 15:22-29 as your child finishes the juice and, perhaps, enjoys a snack with it. See how God made the bad water drinkable and how He promised to help us take good care of our bodies, when we obey His helpful rules and do what is right.

God's "Perfect 10"
(The ten commandments)

What will I need? 1. Your voice and memory 2. Gloves made from felt or gardening gloves 3. A permanent marker, small pictures from paper or felt, a couple of coins

Where is it in the Bible? Exodus 20:1-17
How long will it take? 5 to 10 minutes
What age child? 3-11 years
Will it work in a group? Yes, and would make a good group learning project
Can it be played in the car? Yes.
Will it work in a school classroom? Yes, it is desperately needed!

Use one of these ways to learn the ten commandments:
1. Sing a song about the ten commandments. (Sing this to the tune of "Ten Little Indians.")

One, two, three commandments,
Four, five, six commandments
Seven, eight, nine commandments,
Ten good rules from God.
One, you shall have no gods before me.
Two, you shall not make any idols.
Three, you shall not use my name badly.
These are God's good rules.

Four, make God's day very special.
Five, obey your father and mother.
Six, you must not kill one another.
These are God's good rules.

Seven, keep promises in your marriage.
Eight, don't steal any thing around you.
Nine, don't lie, and
Ten, don't covet.
These are God's Ten Rules!

2. Make a pair of child-size gloves from felt. Trace around his hands, enlarge the outlines and glue, sew, or staple the edges together. If you prefer, you may buy a pair of child's gardening gloves to use.
On each glove finger, beginning with the baby finger on the left hand and going to the baby finger on the right, number them 1-10

near the base of each finger. Near the tip of each finger and thumb glue one of these visual reminders to help your child learn and recall the commandments.

1 - a crown shape made from shiny gold or silver foil paper (no other gods before Him. He's our King.)

2 - a circle with a diagonal line across it and the word, "no," inside

3 - a mouth or smile shape, cut from red felt or paper

4 - a simple outline of a church with a steeple, from paper or cloth

5 - a simple drawing of the faces of a smiling father and mother

6 - a round, sad face with eyes closed and mouth turned down in a frown

7 - a red heart shape

8 - a couple of shiny coins

9 - a round face, with an "O"shaped mouth, like someone talking

10 - a face, with eyes looking over to the side and frowning (seeing something he wants that belongs to someone else)

The People Are Bad, and Moses gets Mad!

Here's the story from Exodus 19–20; 32:

A little while after God's people crossed the Red Sea they came to a place called Sinai where there was a special mountain. Moses climbed up the side of Mt. Sinai to meet and talk with God.

God told Moses to help the people remember how good He had been to them and how very special they were to Him. God promised that His people would have a won-derful life if they would keep on loving and obeying Him. All the people said, "We will do everything God asks us to do!" But soon they forgot.

God told Moses that in two days the people would see a dark cloud come down over the mountain. God would meet with Moses again, and everyone would see God's mighty power. Just as God said, on the third morning there was thunder and lightning and a big cloud came down upon the mountain. The people heard a sound like a trumpet. There were fire and smoke near the top of the mountain. Not only did the people hear and see all that, but they even felt the ground under them shake in a big earthquake. Moses went up the mountain again into the cloud to talk with God.

The people knew that the things they had seen, heard, and felt meant that God was with them. They also understood they were not to try to climb the mountain while Moses was there talking to God.

Moses listened carefully to all the rules God gave him so he could tell the people. Moses stayed on the mountain a long time while God wrote down some very special rules, called the ten commandments, on two flat pieces of rock. God also told Moses exactly how to build a very special tent church, called the tabernacle.

When Moses didn't come back right away, the people got tired of waiting. They asked Aaron, Moses' brother, to make them a new god out of gold to take care of them and lead them across the desert. Aaron said "yes" to the people and used all their gold jewelry to make a golden calf to worship. When Moses learned what God's people were doing, he was very angry. As he came back down the mountain holding the tablets, he saw the calf and the dancing and threw the tablets down and they broke into pieces. Then he took the golden calf and melted it in the fire.

Even though God's people had done very bad things and had to be punished, the Lord gave Moses two new flat stones and wrote His ten good rules all over again. This time, Moses stayed on the mountain for forty days and nights, and when he came back down, his face was shining from being with God.

What I Can Learn from Exodus

1. When God's people cried to Him for help, He heard them and helped them. When we pray to God, He hears us and helps us, too.

2. God took His people out of their unhappy life in Egypt into a new, beautiful land because they followed Him. He will take us away from our sins, and one day move us into the happiest home of all – heaven.

3. God was kind enough to give the Israelite people, and us, His special rules to help us do the right things and be happy.

Important Verses to Remember

Exodus 3:14a – "God said to Moses, 'I AM WHO I AM...'"

Exodus 15:2 – "The Lord is my strength and my song; he has become my salvation. He is my God, and I will praise Him . . ."

Exodus 23:25a – "Worship the LORD your God . . ."

Exodus 29:46a – "They will know that I am the LORD their God . . ."

A Devotional Thought for Parents and Teachers

Exodus. Extraordinary is the best word that describes what we discover in this wonderful book. We see God's extraordinary love, provision, and protection for His children demonstrated through His is extraordinary power. God's children saw his love displayed in their escape from Egypt, at the Red Sea, through a burning bush, in the daily manna, under a cloud of protection, by a fire at night, and in so many other ways. It's is so humbling to think that God's extraordinary love and protection for His children has never changed. Just like the children of Israel we can take comfort in knowing that God is with us day and night. His is our great cloud of protection and love that will never, ever leave us.

Leviticus **God's Book About Worship**

"I will walk among you and be your God, and you will be my people. I am the Lord your God" (Leviticus 26:12-13a).

What's the Book of About

1. Loving God and worshiping Him
2. Thanking God for being so good by bringing our offerings to Him
3. Living healthy and happy like God wants us to
4. Learning what "holy" means

Special Days and Special Ways to Worship Our God

Leviticus is about the kind of days we all love – parties and holidays. It's about happy, celebration times when God's people worshiped Him and thanked Him for being so good.

Leviticus is also about quiet times of thinking about God and the important things He wants His people to know as they obey Him, stay healthy and live a happy and "holy" life. Best of all, Leviticus tells us some wonderful things about Jesus – long before He is even born.

Let's Meet the People of Leviticus

Moses was still the leader for God's people. Moses listened to what God wanted him to do and to tell the Israelite people, and then he and his brother, Aaron, told the people what God had said.

Aaron was the High Priest (or pastor) for God's people, and his two sons, **Eleazar** and **Ithamar**, helped him.

The Israelites were God's big "family" of people, who had left Egypt and were traveling to the wonderful new land God had waiting for them.

Here Are The Places of Leviticus

The wilderness - (desert land) near the bottom of Mt. Sinai. God's people are camped there during the whole book of Leviticus.

Find an Offering

(A scavenger hunt game)

What will I need? Your child and your house or yard
Where is it in the Bible? Leviticus 1–7
How long will it take? 5-20 minutes
What age child? 3-11
Will it work in a group? Yes
Can it be played in the car? Yes, by looking around for objects inside the car.
Will it work in a school classroom? Yes, preschool–6th grade

The book of Leviticus describes how God's people were to bring offerings to Him. The offerings were supposed to be the very best gifts the Israelites could bring to God, and He told them just what they should be. It was very important that the animals, the grain, or whatever else the people gave was absolutely perfect.

The important reason for that rule was because the offerings they sacrificed to God were like "pictures" of Jesus, the Lamb of God. Jesus did not have any sins and would one day give His perfect life for all the people in the world. After Jesus would die for all the sins of everybody, no one would have to bring animals to sacrifice to God anymore. They could have all their sins taken away, obey God, and show Him their love by giving their hearts and lives to Jesus.

Send your child on a hunt in the house or yard to find something they would give to God if they had no money and wanted to show Him their love. (Tell your child that God had made special offering rules for poor people because He loves all people just the same, rich and poor, and He wants everyone to be able to worship Him.) Ask your child to bring the item back to a designated location or take you to see it if it can't be moved and tell why he would give it to God.

Discuss the most valuable thing every person owns that he can give to God, his very own heart and life.

The Giving Game

(A relay game)

What will I need? Something to pass to another person
Where is it in the Bible? Leviticus 1-7
How long will it take? 5-15 minutes
What age child? 2-11 years
Will it work in a group? Yes, better in a group
Can it be played in the car? Yes, but for passengers only, by passing things back and forth
Will it work in a school classroom? Yes, preschool–6th grade

Leviticus 1-7 explains to the Israelite people what offerings they should bring to God and how they should give them. Play this Giving Game as an illustration of the fact that God made all of us to enjoy giving gifts, good things, and affection (hugs and kisses) to others and, especially, to God.

If only you and your child are playing The Giving Game, pass items back and forth several times. If you are in a group, form one relay team and pass objects down the line and back, or make two teams for a friendly race. Give something to somebody else in various ways:

1. First, hand an item to another player.

2. Give something to someone with your hands behind your backs.

3. Put on mittens or gloves or cover hands with plastic bags and pass coins, buttons, or some other small objects to someone that way.

4. Then, give something special to someone – pray with your child, asking God to help you both know about someone who needs help that you can give. Make tasty sack lunches with your child and hand them out; gather clothes or toys that you can give to those who need them; collect extra cans or boxes of food that you can give; give more than "things"–give a hug, a smile, and a kind word to everyone you meet. The desire and commitment to be a giver starts early in a child's life and will become a lifelong attitude and practice! Remind your child that when we give to others, we give to God.

Five Special Ways of Giving to God

God gave His people five special ways they could show their love for Him and give an offering. When people love someone, they like to give presents to them, and these offerings were the Israelite people's presents to God. We still give gifts to God–the songs we sing, the prayers we pray, the kind things we do for other people, the money we give to help other people learn about His love, the way we obey and do the things we should, the times we listen to Bible stories and verses about Him and, most of all, we can give Him OURSELVES!

Even when the Israelite people in the book of Leviticus gave their five offerings to God, He wanted most for them to give Him their hearts and lives and their LOVE—and that's still the very best offering that we can give Him, too.

The five special offerings God's people gave in Leviticus were:

1. The Burnt Offering to pay for all their sins. (Leviticus 1)
2. The Grain Offering to worship God and show Him their love. (Leviticus 2)
3. The Fellowship Offering to say "thank you" to God for being so good to them. (Leviticus 3)
4. The Sin Offering to pay for the wrongs they didn't mean to do and to show that they understood that sin is serious. (Leviticus 4)
5. The Guilt Offering to pay for sins they did that hurt God and other people. (Leviticus 5:14-19)

The Perfect Five

(A musical reminder)

What will I need? **Your imagination**
Where is it in the Bible? **Leviticus 1-7**
How long will it take? **10 minutes**
What age child? **2-10 years**
Will it work in a group? **Yes**
Can it be played in the car? **Yes**
Will it work in a school classroom? **Yes, pre-school–5th grade**

Tell your child that God gave the people of Israel five special ways to bring an offering to Him in order to worship, obey, and please Him. Talk about how kind God was to let His people know exactly what pleases Him, so that they wouldn't have to always guess and be worried that they might not get it right! Explain that we always want to please God and make His heart happy because He is so kind and good and "deserves" everything good we can do for Him and bring to Him to show our love.

Sing this musical reminder of the five offerings. The tune is "The Ants Go Marching One By One."
"God's people go marching one by one. Hoorah! Hoorah!
God's people go marching one by one. Hoorah! Hoorah!
God's people go marching one by one
Across the sand in the desert sun
And the Lord is with them day, by day, by day.
March, march, march, march (repeat)

God's people are camping two by two. Hoorah! Hoorah!
God's people are camping two by two. Hoorah! Hoorah!
God's people are camping two by two.
They look from their tents at the mountain-side view
And the Lord is with them day, by day, by day.
March, march, march, march (repeat)

God's people are listening three by three. Hoorah! Hoorah!
God's people are listening three by three. Hoorah! Hoorah!
God's people are listening three by three. Hoorah! Hoorah!
As God takes them on to victory!
And the Lord is with them day, by day, by day.
March, march, march, march (repeat)

God's people are giving four by four. Hoorah! Hoorah!
God's people are giving four by four. Hoorah! Hoorah!
God's people are giving four by four

As they bring God gifts, their sins are no more.
And the Lord is with them day, by day, by day.
March, march, march, march (repeat)

Their offerings number five by five. Hoorah! Hoorah!
Their offerings number five by five. Hoorah! Hoorah!
Their offerings number five by five
To worship our God Who is ALIVE!
And the Lord is with us day, by day, by day.
AMEN!

The Very Hot Offering (the Burnt Offering)

(A hot and cold cooking activity, and a science experiment)

What will I need? Activity 1. Slices of hot dogs or smoky links, pineapple, and cheese. Activity 2. 1 bowl full of (tolerably) hot water, 1 bowl of lukewarm water, 1 bowl of cold water, a kitchen timer or clock
Where is it in the Bible? Leviticus 1:6-17
How long will it take? 15-30 minutes
What age child? 3-11 years
Will it work in a group? Yes
Can it be played in the car? No
Will it work in a school classroom? Yes, pre-school (with careful supervision)–6th grade

Talk with your child about the burnt (cooked) offering that the Israelites gave to God. The people were supposed to bring a sheep, goat, or ox and if they were poor, doves or pigeons to give to God as a sacrifice, or offering (a little bit like the money we bring to church to give to God).

The animal had to be perfect. Aaron (or his sons), would cook it on a pile of rocks, like a campfire. The smell of the meat cooking and the smoke went up to God to show Him that His people loved Him and were sorry for their sins. The animal had to die for the people's sins because God's people needed to understand that sin is very serious and had to be "paid for" by the animal giving up his life. Then the sins of the people could be taken away, just like the smoke from the sacrifice disappeared into the air.

Ask your child if he knows why we don't cook animals today for a burnt offering to give to God (Hebrews 10:1-18) and how we get our sins taken away. Here are two activities you and your child may do together as you discuss the Very Hot Offering.

1. Hot Cooking - In a skillet or electric fry pan, brown several kinds of cubed foods that can be put on a toothpick and eaten as a shish-kabob. Enjoy the good cooking smells, and tell your child that the smell of the burnt offerings cooking on the altar in Bible days went up to God and was pleasing to Him.

2. Is Hot Hot? - Fill 3 bowls full of water, one with rather hot water, one with lukewarm water, and the other with cold. Instruct your child to put her left hand in the hot water and her right hand in the cold water and keep them there for three minutes. When the time is up, ask your child to take both hands out of the water and shake them off. Immediately put both hands into the room temperature water and ask her how the lukewarm water feels to her left hand. How does the water feel to the right hand?

(Both your child's hands adapted to the water they were in first, and now the messages the hands' sensory receptors are sending to the brain are confused. The right will sense the lukewarm water is hot, to the left hand the lukewarm water will seem cold .)

I Feel Bad for What I Did Guilt Offering
(A fun game)

What will I need? Your imagination, index cards with hypothetical good and bad situations on them, and a large picture of a happy face and a sad face
Where is it in the Bible? Leviticus 5:14-15 and 6:7, 7:1-10
How long will it take? 15-30 minutes
What age child? 3-11 years
Will it work in a group? Yes
Can it be played in the car? Yes
Will it work in a school classroom? Yes, preschool–6th grade, with age-appropriate situations

Write hypothetical good and bad situations on index cards. Add your own to these: "I took a toy that didn't belong to me, and I kept it." "I saw a lady drop some money from her purse, but I picked it up and kept it in my pocket." "My daddy said, 'Eat all your hamburger and French fries, but I put them back in the sack and threw them away when he wasn't looking.'" "I read a book to my little brother." "I put my 'tooth fairy' money in the offering at church."

Turn all the cards over and take turns choosing one to read or to read for your child. Decide if the situation is good or bad. You may then either place the card on a big happy face or a big sad face.

Talk about the fact that we all, even parents, do bad things sometimes and that God has given us a "voice" inside us called our conscience that helps us to know when we have done wrong and to feel badly about it. When we don't feel good about what we have said or done, we need to remember not to do that same thing again, and we should tell God and the people we have hurt or disappointed that we are sorry.

The Israelite people had an offering that they brought to God that was called the Guilt Offering, or the "I Feel Bad For What I Did and I Am Sorry" Offering. Explain that we don't need to bring an offering like they did because Jesus already died for our sins. What we need to do is to tell Him we are sorry and ask Him to forgive us, and He will.

Holy, Holy, Holy
(A quiet activity and discussion)

What will I need? 1. A rope, string, or piece of yarn 2. A sign that says "special place"
Where is it in the Bible? Leviticus 18–22
How long will it take? 15-30 minutes
What age child? 3-11 years
Will it work in a group? Yes
Can it be played in the car? Yes, with a little creativity
Will it work in a school classroom? Yes, pre-school–6th grade

Rope off an area of the house or yard and designate it as "a special place." Explain you are pretending that the air in there is special, the ground or carpet is special, and so are the rocks or bugs. Tell your child that no one is allowed to go into the special place for 15 minutes.

As you are waiting the 15 minutes talk about things in a museum that people are not allowed to touch and why not. Ask your child if there is anything in grandma's house, or a neighbor's, in your own home, at church, or school that he is not allowed to touch or play with and discuss the reasons why not.

Explain further that the Bible tells us in Leviticus about some very important things and people that should be treated in very careful ways because they belonged to God. Things that belong to God or tell us about Him are called holy, like the Holy Bible.

Discuss with your child the value of our Bible as God's special Word and the respectful way we should always handle and pay attention to it. Explain that in the Bible special, holy things were sometimes set aside and marked by pouring oil on them so everyone would know how important they were and that they were to be used to honor God.

Talk about other things that are very important to God like His special day for us to worship each week, the part of our money that belongs to Him, prayer, and you. God made people to belong to Him, but He lets everyone choose if they will become God's own special child. Have you decided yet that you will give your whole life to Jesus? How wonderful if you have or will.

What Can I learn from Leviticus

1. God wanted His people, the Israelites, to love Him, to worship Him, and to serve Him. He wants us to love and worship and serve Him, too!

2. God's people did wrong things and sinned against God. They needed to be sorry and ask to God to forgive them. When I do wrong things, I sin against God. I also need to tell Him that I'm sorry and ask Jesus to forgive me, and He will!

3. God's rules for being healthy and living well were for His people, and if I obey God's good rules in the Bible, they will help me to live and a happy and healthy good life!

4. The Israelite people celebrated God's goodness in different ways. God is so good everyday that He gives me many reasons to celebrate, too!

Important Verses to Remember

Leviticus 11: 44a – "I am the Lord your God; consecrate yourselves and be holy, because I am holy."

Leviticus 18:2 – "Speak to the Israelites and say to them: 'I am the Lord God'."

Leviticus 19:2b–4 – "Be holy because I, the Lord your God, am holy. Each of you must respect his mother and father, and you must observe my Sabbaths. I am the Lord you God. Do not turn to idols or make gods of cast metal for yourselves. I am the Lord your God."

Leviticus 19:18 – "Don't seek revenge or bear a grudge against one of your people, but love your neighbor as yourself. I am the Lord."

Leviticus 19:32 – "Rise in the presence of the aged, show respect for the elderly and revere your God. I am the Lord."

A Devotional Thought for Parents and Teachers

We live in an incredible time in the history of mankind. Our lives are full of modern conveniences, medical breakthroughs, and technological marvels that provide assistance with hundreds of tasks. We live daily lives of ease and luxury compared to the generations of people who have preceded us.

But with all the advantages of modern daily life, we face some critical risks. Near the top of our list of things to guard against is the danger of adapting to the climate and culture of our day so that we lose our precious distinctives as children of the Most High and Most Holy God.

As believers in the Almighty, all-loving God, we are reminded in Leviticus that He does have expectations of us but that all He requires of us in worship and conduct are the direct result of His love and concern for our well-being and because He is worthy of the very best that we are and do for Him in spiritual service. We are reminded through God's messages and interaction with the Israelite people that we are to be different morally, ethically, and spiritually from the unbelievers around us – even as our lives play out right in the middle of 21st century.

God is good and worthy of our praise and service. Sin is extremely serious and must be rejected and avoided at all personal costs through His ever-present power and help.

Numbers God's Book About a Big Mistake
and a Hard Lesson "... for they followed the Lord wholeheartedly" (Numbers 32:12b).

What's the Book About

God's people, the Israelites, are getting ready to go into the land God promised them. However, before they enter the promised land they make some BIG mistakes in not trusting God and not doing what He wants them to. God gives His people a second chance to obey Him and to try again to move into the promised land, called Canaan, that He has waiting for them.

A Very Big Campout

Numbers starts with the Israelites in a HUGE campout at the bottom of Mt. Sinai. There were tents everywhere covering miles and miles of desert sand! Can you even imagine two million people, all camping, cooking, and living together in tents?

How did there get to be so many of God's people? They all came from Joseph's family that moved to Egypt when they didn't have enough food in their homeland of Canaan. Remember in Exodus, God was good to Joseph's children and grandchildren. He gave them more babies that grew up to have babies of their own. Joseph's family lived in Egypt for more than 400 years.

God kept the promise that He made to Abraham that his family would one day outnumber the stars! It's that big family that is camping in the desert. God is taking them back to the home they had to leave when they ran out of food a long time before. But now Canaan has plenty of food, and God wants His people to be able to live again in such a wonderful home.

God's people have learned about obeying the Lord's good rules, and now they are going to do something that is a great big job – they are going to count everybody!

Counting the people was a very good idea so they would know how many men would make good soldiers when they had to fight God's enemies. The people also needed to be put into smaller family groups (tribes), instead of one giant crowd, for traveling and camping.

There were 12 tribes, and every tribe was named after the family of Joseph. The leader of every group carried a tall pole with a flag at the top of it. When all the people traveled across the desert, they stayed together in their groups, and everybody could see where they were supposed to be by looking at their tribe's flag. That was a very good way to make sure nobody got lost, especially the children!

Everything was going fine until the people forgot how good God is and began to grumble and complain about the heat, the water, the food, and especially their leaders, Moses and Aaron.

Let's Meet the People of Numbers

Moses was still the leader of God's people.

Aaron was Moses' brother and the "pastor" of God's people, and **Eleazar** was one of his sons, who became the next pastor after Aaron.

Miriam was Moses' big sister who watched over her baby brother Moses when he was in the basket on the river. In the book of Numbers she is grown up. Miriam loved to make up and sing songs of praise to God!

Joshua and **Caleb** were two brave men, who believed God and obeyed Him even when other people did not. These two men got to go into the beautiful land God promised, because they trusted God. We can always trust God, just like Joshua and Caleb did.

Balaam was a man who tried to act good on the outside, but inside his heart was really greedy and bad. God spoke to Balaam in a very unusual way, and Balaam learned that we should always listen to God and obey Him.

Here Are the Places of Numbers

Mount Sinai – the mountain where God gave Moses the ten commandments and where the people are counted at the beginning of the book of Numbers. While the Israelite people are camped here, they get ready to fight battles with enemy armies.

The promised land – Canaan, the beautiful land that God had promised to give to Abraham's huge family one day. It's the same land that Joseph and his family left 400 years before when they moved to Egypt. Now God's people are on their way back!

Kadesh-Barnea – this desert land was right next to Canaan. God's people spent quite a bit of their time in Kadesh-Barnea before they went into their new homeland. Miriam died there, and this is where Moses hit the rock when God told him to speak.

Moab's flat lands – (The Valley of Arabah) God's people camped on this flat land near the Jordan River and the town of Jericho just before they went to the promised land.

STORIES AND ACTIVITIES FROM NUMBERS

Grumble, Grumble, Gripe, Gripe!

(A role play)

What will I need? A bell or just a hand clap and you

Where is it in the Bible? Numbers 11:1,4; 12:1-16; 14:1-4, 16:3,41; 20:3; 21:5

How long will it take? 5-15 minutes

What age child? 3-11 years

Will it work in a group? Yes, really well

Can it be played in the car? Yes

Will it work in a school classroom? Yes,

preschool–6th grade

Explain that one of the things the Israelite people did that really made Moses and God unhappy was to grumble and complain. Read and talk about all the things they fussed about. They forgot God was taking care of them and would give them everything they needed. Even Moses' own sister Miriam became a grumbler. When they fussed to each other, nothing changed. But when they grumbled to Moses, Moses told God about the problem, and God was the One who could, and did, do something about it.

41

Play this game with your child, acting out two different ways of talking and behaving. Begin by pretending to be talking with a friend in a very happy, friendly manner.

Then signal to change into grumblers. Start frowning, folding your arms in front of you in a huff, turning your backs on each other, and giving each other dirty looks. Shake your fingers at each other and say, "Poor me, poor me, everything's so bad."

End the game by explaining that God's people were not happy when they were grumbling, but when they were working together and being thankful they were happy! Sing this song to the tune of "The More We Get Together the Happier We'll Be."

The more we work together, together, together
The more we work together
The happier we'll be.

For your job is my job
And your friend is my friend.
The more we work together,
The happier we'll be.

The more we grumble, grumble
We grumble, we grumble
The more we grumble, grumble
The sadder we'll be.

Our work will not get done
Our work will be no fun.
The more we grumble, grumble,
The sadder we'll be.

Great Big, Juicy Grapes!
(A fun and active game)

What will I need? You and your child
Where is it in the Bible? Numbers 13:17-33
How long will it take? 10-15 minutes
What age child? 3-11 years
Will it work in a group? Yes, best in a group
Can it be played in the car? No
Will it work in a school classroom? Yes, preschool–6th grade

Share with your child the exciting story of the spies, grapes, and grasshoppers. The report of the two positive and 10 negative spies and the resulting effects it had on the Israelites is a turning point in their history and a tremendous lesson for us all about the importance of trusting God no matter how things look to us at times.

"Bunch" up with your child in a "bunch-of-love-huddle." Huddle first with your backs together. Bunch up, connecting only one body part at a time, heads together, then feet, then shoulders, elbows, fingers, toes, hands, and even noses. Talk about the heavy bunch of grapes that the spies brought back to show Moses. Just think of all those delicious grapes God's people would have gotten to eat for 40 years, if they had just trusted and obeyed God. Ask Him to help you be a person who trusts God every day.

Don't Hit that Rock!
(A story about obeying God)

This interesting story from Numbers 20:7-13 is about God's telling Moses to speak to a rock. If Moses would do as God told him, then water would come out of the rock and the thirsty people and their animals could have water to drink in the hot, dry desert.

See if Moses obeyed God. Find out if the water came out as God said it would. See if God was pleased with what Moses did.

Moses was responsible to lead his people to follow every command of God because, not only does God deserve our total obedience, but also it would have been impossible to lead two million people without His direction in every matter. But Moses simply got mad. He'd had it with those grumbling people. He made it sound like he and Aaron were the ones who would be making the water come from the rock. His disobedience was serious as the penalty makes evident. We need to be careful in today's world not to treat our willful disobedience and sin, nor our child's, too lightly.

Help your child to understand that Moses was the leader of all the people of Israel, and it was very important for him to obey and trust God so that the people would follow his example and obey God, too.

Talk about how sad it was that Moses was not able to go into the new land because of the wrong thing he chose to do. Emphasize that God's ways are always best, and we should always obey Him.

If you want to play a game, roll a "rock" (a ball or wadded-up paper shaped with masking tape) back and forth to your child or in a circle of children, keeping your hands behind your backs at all times. You may use only your body, your feet, and head to roll the ball.

Snakes, Snakes, Everywhere!

(A digging and discovering game)

What will I need? 1. Fishing worms or gummy worms 2. A plastic tub, box, or roasting pan 3. Cornmeal, graham cracker crumbs, or Easter basket grass
Where is it in Bible? Numbers 21:4-9
How long will it take? As long as the activity remains fun
What age child? 2-10 years
Will it work in a group? Yes
Can it be played in a car? No
Will it work in a school classroom? Yes, it would be a fun "center" for younger children.

Discover snakes in one or more of these ways: dig for rubber fishing worm "snakes" or gummy worms in a plastic tub, a shallow box or a large roasting pan. 1. Cover the "snakes" with cornmeal. 2. Use gummy worms and graham cracker crumbs so your child can taste them, or use colored Easter basket grass. If you use Easter grass, you may choose to fill a pan with water and let your child "fish" for snakes in the swamp with tongs or a long-handled fork.

Tell your child the incredible and inspiring story of the serpent of brass. Explain the snake on the pole was a kind of example of what Jesus would one day do when He would be lifted up on the cross. Explain that just as looking at the brass snake would make people well and keep them from dying from their snake bites, trusting in Jesus and His death on the cross will take our sins away and let us live forever with Him one day.

Let's Try It Again!
(A walking game)

What will I need? You and your child and your imagination.
Where is it in the Bible? Numbers 22–36
How long long will it take? 5 to 15 minutes
What age child? 2-10 years
Will it work in a group? Yes
Can it be playing in the car? No
Will it work in a school classroom? Yes, preschool–4th grade

Stand side by side with your child and walk (or walk in place) like the following:
A soldier in the army
A tightrope walker
An older person with a cane
A person in a hurry
Someone sneaking around
A gymnast on a balance beam
Someone barefooted on hot sand or rocks
A person with a broken leg or only one leg
A ballerina

Explain to your child that the Israelites have been traveling around the desert getting no where for 40 years, and the older people have all died. Now, the younger people are ready to try going into the promised land one more time.

Ask your child if he has ever felt like that on a long trip. Has he ever said, "When will we ever get there?"

God Can Even Use a Donkey
(A "Don't look!" game)

What will I need? A pillow and paper "tails" backed with double-sided tape
Where is it in the Bible? Numbers 22-24
How long will it take? 15-20 minutes
What age child? 2-11 years
Will it work in a group? Yes
Can it be playing in the car? The story, but not the game
Will it work in a school classroom? Yes, preschool–6th grade

Play the game Pin the Tail on the Donkey or the "real people" version of the game. Tie a pillow your child's back so he becomes the tail-less donkey! Family members must close their eyes and try to put the paper tail on the donkey's back. Take turns being the donkey, and have fun seeing where the tails "end" up.

Tell this story of Balaam:

It is an intriguing story about God's power and sovereignty that began when King Balak of Moab, who is an enemy of God's people, got very worried at the size of God's army and the strength God had given them to defeat the armies of their enemies. Because King Balak did not believe in the true God, he asked a magician named Balaam to try to do a little "hocus-pocus magic" and make some bad luck come upon God's people so that they would not be able to win a battle against the Moabite armies.

Balaam knew about the true God, but he believed in other false gods, too, and worshiped them. He had no idea how powerful God was – nor did King Balak. So some messengers of the evil king brought money to

Balaam to pay him to go to where God's army was gathered and to do "bad magic" on God's people. That night God spoke to Balaam and told him not to do what the king wanted.

Balaam decided not to take King Balak's money and told him that he wouldn't curse the army of God's followers. When the king offered him a palace filled with gold and silver, and offered to give him great honors, greedy Balaam agreed to do what the king wanted. God allowed Balaam to saddle his donkey and start off to do his magic on His army. God was very unhappy with Balaam and placed an angel right in the middle of the road ahead of him, holding a sword in his hand to stop Balaam.

Donkeys were the cars of Balaam's day, and the magician was definitely about to have "car trouble!" His donkey saw the angel in the road, but Balaam couldn't yet see the angel. Then the donkey bolted off in fear into a nearby field.

When the angel changed locations, the donkey tried to squeeze past him with Balaam on her back and scraped his foot along the wall on the side of the road! Every time the donkey wouldn't go where Balaam wanted her to, he would beat her with his stick. Finally, the donkey lay down in the middle of the road and wouldn't budge at all! Balaam missed the important point that God was preventing him from going to do his evil, greedy deed.

God allowed the donkey to speak (a very easy thing for the One who created donkeys to do) and asked Balaam why he was treating the the donkey so mean when he had always served Balaam well. Just then, the Lord allowed Balaam to actually see the angel, and the angel spoke to him. God's messenger told Balaam to go where God's army was camped near the land of Moab, but to say only what God told him.

Since Balaam recognized God's power and authority, even though he was did not worship the one true God, he went with King Balak to offer a sacrifice on a mountain above where God's people were camping. The king thought that Balaam would then do his bad magic on the Israelites below. Instead, God told Balaam a BLESSING (a good prayer and message) to give to His people, and Balaam did.

God used a magician who didn't even serve Him and a donkey for His own purposes because He is God, and He will do what is right and good through whatever means He chooses.

The Big Fight!
Numbers 31

Explain to your child that even though God was going to give His people the land He had promised them, they ran into some enemies along the way. These people did not love nor worship the true God; they worshiped false gods called idols, who were not God at all! The enemy had armies of soldiers who had moved into the land promised to the Israelites.

Before the Israelites could settle down in their new home, they would have to fight the enemy people and get them out of the land. God promised His people that if they would obey Him and follow Him, He would help them win every fight, and God always keeps His word.

One of the enemy armies were the Midianites (the people from Midian). The Midianites were people who did not love God and absolutely refused to worship Him. They also were trying to get God's people to stop worshiping God and to serve their false god, Baal, and that's very serious. It was so serious that God's armies had to fight to stop them from trying to do this bad thing. If God's soldiers did not fight against the Midianites, God's people might have started doing the same evil things that the Midianites did, and that must not be allowed to happen. God loved His people so much that He had to protect them from evil and from danger! God helps to keep us safe from harm and evil, too, because He loves us so much.

What Can I Learn from Numbers

1. God did many wonderful things for His special people, the Israelites. When I think about all the great things God does for me, I remember how good He is, and I love Him more and more.

2. The Israelite people first learned from Moses how good God was and what He wanted them to do. Then it was their job to DO what God had said to them. In the same way, the first thing I learn is about God's goodness and what He wants me to do, and then I want to do what He asks me to because I love Him.

3. Moses did some wrong things when he was the leader of God's people, but God forgave him and kept on helping him to do what was right and good again. Even when I do wrong and make mistakes that hurt God's heart, He still loves me. I should tell Him I'm sorry and keep doing what is right again.

Some Important Verses to Remember

Numbers 6: 24-26 – "The Lord bless you and keep you; the Lord make his face to shine upon you and be gracious unto you; the Lord turn his face toward you and give you peace."

Numbers 15:41 – "I am the Lord your God, who brought you out of Egypt to be your God. I am the Lord your God."

Numbers 23:19 – "God is not a man, that he should lie, not a son of man, that he should change his mind. Does he speak and then not act? Does he promise and not fulfill?"

Numbers 23:21 – "The Lord their God is with them; the shout of the King is among them."

Do you have a child who has a tendency to have to learn everything the hard way? The warnings, the experiences, the consequences of the actions and errors of others seem to have no effect on him. Somehow he seems to think that the danger won't hurt; the mistake won't cause pain, and the thrill of the challenge will overshadow the risk.

So often with the children we love, we desperately wish they could see from our vantage point and learn from our experiences and mistakes. We don't want them to be hurt, disappointed, to get off track, or to make painful choices, but they plunge head-on and THEN they learn. How we want them to avoid pain and regrets.

Our heavenly Parent must feel that way so often about us, His unconditionally-loved children. His people in the book of Numbers with their lack of obedience, gratitude, and faith caused them pain and impeded their progress–and so does ours! Every new generation seems to need to reinvent the wheel when it comes to learning spiritual lessons, but God is patient and faithful and full of tender love for all His children, just as you are for yours!

Thank Him today for warning us and for loving and forgiving and loving again.

Deuteronomy The Book About How Good

God Is "Be strong and courageous . . . The Lord himself goes before you and will be with you; he will never leave you nor forsake you" (Deuteronomy 31:7a-8).

What's the Book About

1. Thinking about (remembering) all the good things God has done for all His people
2. Learning about God's good rules and obeying them
3. Loving God with all our heart, soul, mind, and strength

Moses Talks to God's People

After God helped His people escape from their hard life in Egypt, He began to take them to the beautiful land called Canaan that had been promised to them by God. The Israelite people had never lived there like their ancestors.

The trip across the desert to the new land was only supposed to take about 11 days, but God's people didn't do a very good job of always following and obeying Him. When the book of

Deuteronomy begins, the people have been walking around and camping in the desert for 40 years!

The adults have all lived and died, and they didn't even get to go into the new land because they did not obey and follow God. Their children have already grown up. When Moses talks to them the first time in the desert of Arabah where they are camping, the Israelite people are right beside the Jordan River where they can see Canaan. The problem is that a group of people that do not love God have moved into the land, and they must be driven out before God's people can move in. There have already been some fights with the enemy armies, and God has helped His people win every war, when they have obeyed Him. There will be more fights before all the enemy people will be gone, but God will help the Israelites move in to Canaan, just as He promised He would.

Deuteronomy all takes place in only a few weeks of time. As it begins, Moses is ready to give God's people three different "talks" to help them know how to live and behave when they get to their new home.

Let's Meet the People of Deuteronomy

Moses is still the leader of God's people, but he is growing very old, and it will soon be time for Moses to let Joshua become the new leader of God's people.

Joshua is Moses' helper who became the second leader of God's Israelite people. Joshua trusted God and was very careful to obey Him.

The **Israelite People** are still camped in the desert after 40 years, but they are almost ready to go in to their new homeland Canaan.

Here Are the Places of Deuteronomy

The Jordan River – The Jordan River flows right beside the promised land where God's people are getting ready to make their new home. When it is the right time for the Israelite people to walk across it, God will make sure that the water in the Jordan River opens up like it did in the Red Sea.

The Arabah Valley – This land is on the east side of the Jordan River, where the Israelite people are camping. While God's people are in the Arabah Valley, Moses talks to them about how God wants them to live in the new land. This is also the land where God buried Moses after he died.

Mt. Nebo – The mountain God let Moses climb at the end of his life to see the promised land. Moses could not go into the promised land because he disobeyed God and struck the rock to get water when God told him only to speak to the rock.

Three Special Talks

(A silly talking game)

What will I need? Three people
Where is it in the Bible? Deuteronomy 4:44–28:68
How long will it take? 5-15 minutes
What age child? 3-11 years
Will it work in a group? Yes
Can it be played in the car? Yes
Will it work in a school classroom? Yes, preschool–6th grade

Instruct the players that at the count of three you are all going to begin talking at once on three different subjects. Everyone must continue talking until you say the words, "Stop talking now," when all the talkers must become silent.

Before beginning to count, ask the players what they would like to talk about: the family pet, something they enjoy, a favorite video, etc,. When you and the other players know what their subjects will be, all of you should stand facing each other in a circle. Count to three, and each player must then begin to talk out loud about his subject while looking at each other. After you say, "Stop!" and all is momentarily quiet, count to three again. Do this "stop and go" conversation several times.

The last time, explain that Moses also spoke in threes. He had three special times of talking to God's people as they got ready to into the new land. Here's what Moses said:

The First Talk: Moses tells the people about all the amazing things God had already done for them and for their parents until that very day that Moses is talking to them. Moses wants the people to know how good and kind and powerful God is! And Moses knows how important it is for God's people to obey Him.

The Second Talk: Moses talked to the people about God's good rules, the ten commandments. He wanted the Israelite men and women and boys and girls to know how God wanted them to be and to act when they got into their new life in the new land. God is kind to tell us through His leaders so we don't have to guess what we should do.

The Third Talk: After Moses talked to the people about what they should do, he asks them to please obey the rules God gave them. Moses knew that the grownups and children needed to understand that God's rules are the very best. The Lord knows what is best for all His children.

A Brand New Leader

(A follow-the-new-leader game)

What will I need? A strip of masking tape at least 5 or 6 feet long. No heavy duty tape, please.

Where is it in the Bible? Deuteronomy 31-34

How long will it take? 5-10 minutes

What age child? 2-10 years

Will it work in a group? Yes

Can it be played in the car? No

Will it work in a school classroom? Yes, or on playground, for preschool–5th grade

Place a strip of masking tape on your floor or carpet for a balance beam or tightrope. Ask your child to follow you as you walk on the tape. Make the event as dramatic as you want it to be, with exclamation like "Be careful" and "Watch out below."

When you are almost to the end of the tape, shout, "change leaders!" At that command, both of you or all of you must make a careful about-face, and the child at the other end of the line will become the new leader. Reverse leaders as many times as you wish, changing the way you walk on the tape any time the leader chooses to do so. You may jump, hop, crawl, walk backwards, or whatever you think to do. If you are playing with a group, after each leader's turn, the leader should go to the middle of the line until everyone has gotten to lead at least once.

Read to your child from Deuteronomy 34:4-12, the beautiful ending to Moses' life of leadership and the beginning of the responsibilities of the new leader Joshua, who took his place. Read with as much expression as you can, but first set the scene for your child:

Moses has climbed up Mount Nebo from which he can see the city of Jericho and the land God promised His people. Explain that the Lord points out to Moses where all the tribes will be living in the new land, and Moses can see the beautiful blue water of the Mediterranean Sea and the Jordan River and the palm trees in the city of Jericho far below. But Moses will not get to go into the land. (Remember that Moses disobeyed God and hit the rock when he was told to speak to it instead.) God is giving him the next best thing – to be able to see how good it will be for His people to live there. Since Moses loves God's people, too, he is very happy for them.

What I Can Learn from Deuteronomy

1. Moses almost didn't do what God asked him to because he wasn't a very good speaker. But when Moses said, "Yes" to God, the Lord made him a great leader. Even if there are things I can't do very well, when I say "Yes" to God, He will make me able to do all that I need to.

2. Moses helped God's people remember God's good rules so they could obey them. It's good for me to learn and remember the things God tells me in the Bible to do so I can do them all my life.

3. God didn't want the Israelite people to obey Him just because they had to or because they were afraid to, but because they loved

God and wanted to please Him. God wants me to obey His Word because I love Him.

4. God's people could choose if they would obey Him and trust Him. So much good came to them when they followed God and so much trouble came when they did not. I can choose if I will love and trust God. He will make my life good when I do, and I will make His heart glad.

Important Verses to Remember

Deuteronomy 1:29b-30a – "Do not be terrified; do not be afraid of them. The Lord your God, who is going before you, will fight for you."

Deuteronomy 4:29b – "You will find Him if you look for him with all your heart and with all your soul."

Deuteronomy 4:40 – "Keep his decrees and commands, which I am giving you today, so that it may go well with you and your children after you and that you may live long in the land the Lord your God gives you for all time."

Deuteronomy 5:6-21 – The Ten Commandments
1. "I am the Lord your God, who brought you out of Egypt, out of the land of slavery. You shall have no other gods before me" (v. 6-7).
2. "You shall not make for yourself an idol in the form of anything in heaven above or on the earth beneath or in the waters below" (v. 8).
3. "You shall not misuse the name of the Lord your God, for the Lord will not hold anyone guiltless who misuses his name" (v. 11).
4. "Observe the Sabbath day by keeping it holy" (v. 12a).
5. "Honor your father and your mother" (v. 16a).
6. "You shall not murder" (v. 17).
7. "You shall not commit adultery" (v. 18).
8. "You shall not steal" (v. 19).
9. "You shall not give false testimony against your neighbor" (v. 20).
10. "You shall not covet your neighbor's wife. You shall not set your desire on your neighbor's house or land, his manservant or maidservant, his ox or donkey, or anything that belongs to your neighbor" (v. 21).

Deuteronomy 8:6 – "Observe the commands of the Lord your God, walking in his ways and revering him."

A Devotional Thought for Parents and Teachers

All of us have memories from our past, some pleasant, some painful, some regretted, some enjoyed again and again in our moments of nostalgia. Memories can be a tremendous motivational and instructional tool, especially as they relate to our personal walk with God.

We can review in our minds the goodness of God to us, the sting of our sins and our perception of divine disapproval or disappointment, the expressions of His grace, so desperately needed and freely extended again and again, the deep, dark spiritual valleys and high, exhilarating mountaintops, the ever-present personal God, in times of awareness and those when circumstances have caused us not to sense His presence at all.

But no matter the memories we personally treasure or regret, one thing is certain: they are our memories. Deuteronomy teaches us that every member of each new generation begins with a clean slate upon which must be written one's very own spiritual birth and journey. The memories and experiences of a generation of parents is not automatically incorporated into the lives of their children.

God reminded His people through the words of Moses that not only must adult believers choose to obey and serve the Lord, but they must take very seriously their responsibility to introduce their children to the faithful God Who has provided countless memories of His presence, His power, His provision, and His never-ending, unconditional love. To fail to share Him with our children would be our most tragic oversight. To see them grow into God-serving adults is our highest privilege and greatest of all accomplishments.

Joshua God's Book About a New Home for His People

" Have I not commanded you? Be strong and courageous. Do not be terrified; do not be discouraged, for the Lord your God will be with you wherever you go" (Joshua 1:9).

What's the Book About

1. Learning that we can trust God's ways more than our own
2. Understanding that God gives us new chances to do right after we make mistakes and do wrong
3. Learning what God wants us to do and then doing it
4. Deciding that we are always going to follow God and obey Him

A New Home for God's People

As the book of Joshua begins, God's people are still camping in tents, but this time their tents are set up along the side of the Jordan River. The people are finally ready to go into God's special new home that He promised to give them a long time before.

Before Moses died, God let him climb Mt. Nebo and see the promised land. Now the people have a new leader, Joshua. Joshua and his friend Caleb are the only two people left from their generation who will get to enter Canaan.

The people must have been very excited to be entering their new home. Joshua and God's people trust God to help them, and He will. But before they can settle down in Canaan and build their homes, they first have to cross the Jordan River, fight some enemies who have taken over God's land, watch what happens when people don't trust and obey God, and see the Lord do some amazing things for them!

Let's Meet the People of Joshua

Joshua was the new leader of the Israelites. Joshua loved God, trusted Him, and obeyed Him. While he was their leader, the Israelites followed his good example!

Rahab was a woman who lived in Jericho, the first big city God's people came to after they crossed the Jordan River. She did not know God, but she had heard about Him and decided to trust Him and to help His people. Rahab was the mother of Boaz and one of the great, great, and more greats, grandmothers of King David.

Achan was a very foolish man who thought he could steal and

53

hide it from God. Besides that, Achan didn't think God would care what he had done wrong. Achan's sin caused a lot of trouble for all of God's people. When we do wrong, it hurts other people, too. He was punished for his sins, just as we are, because God does care what we do, and He wants us to do what's right.

Here Are the Places of Joshua

The Jordan River – the water God moved apart to let His people walk across. The river was so full at that time of year that it was overflowing its banks. God chose that special time to show how powerful He was so the people would know they could trust and follow Him.

Gilga – where God's people camped after they crossed the Jordan River. There they built a monument out of 12 stones to help themselves and their children remember what God had done for them.

Jericho – the first big city that God's people had to capture to be able to move into their new land. It was a strong city with a huge wall all around it. Only God's mighty power could have made the wall fall down so that His people would be able to go into the city and live there. Even a big, strong city full of enemy people was no match for the strength and power of our God.

Ai – the next small town that God's people had to fight after Jericho. Ai should have been an easy battle to win, but the Israelites lost the first battle there. They lost because Achan had stolen something and lied about what he had done. God could not bless His people until everyone was following Him again.

Gibeon – the city where the people tricked Joshua and God's leaders into signing their names on a promise that they would not fight the Gibeonites or make them leave the land of Canaan. This was a problem because Joshua and the other leaders of the Israelites did not ask God what He wanted them to do, and that caused some trouble for God's people.

Valley of Aijalon – the place where God made the sun to shine longer that it ever had before, or ever after, so His people could win the fight with five enemy armies.

Be Brave, Be Strong and Obey

(Some things to do to show your muscles)

What will I need? A few of these items: balloons on the ends of a stick for pretend barbells, soup cans, heavy book, an old magazine, bubble wrap, or wadded-up newspaper or brown paper sack
Where is it in the Bible? Joshua 1:5-8
How long will it take? 10-15 minutes
What age child? 3-11 years
Will it work in a group? Yes, taking turns being strong.
Can it be played in the car? Not too well
Will it work in a school classroom? Yes, preschool–6th grade

Read Joshua 1:5,9. This is the important message that God gave to Joshua at the beginning of his leadership of Israel.

Help your child understand that those words are very important to us since the Bible was not just written for God's people who lived back in Bible days.

Talk about the courage and strength it takes to follow God even when others do not. Emphasize the importance of obeying God and doing what is right even in the little things, like never telling even a "little" lie, never taking anything that doesn't belong to us, etc.

Help your child to understand that if we are strong for God in little things, we will very likely be strong when big decisions and temptations come to us. Motivate your child to want to do right and be strong for God. Be sure to exemplify that very important behavior yourself as you live and play together every day. The strength and boldness displayed in you will be contagious to your child. After your chat, do some strong-person feats with much drama and effort. Pump iron with barbells made of a stick with and an inflated balloon attached to each end. Lift a huge boulder made from a pillow or a crumpled up paper sack. If you want to look the part of a strong person, stuff the shoulders of your shirt with wadded-up newspaper or paper towels for muscles and draw a phony handlebar mustache on your face with eyeliner pencil.

Remind your child that God is so good to us that we should want to love and serve Him with all our heart, all our mind, all our soul, and all our strength!

Two Spies, a Window, and a Red Rope

(Joshua 2)

The story of Rahab, the spies, and the red rope is an exciting one. Here's what happened in this true tale of adventure, intrigue, and rescue.

1. Joshua sent two spies to check out what Canaan was like and especially to see what the city of Jericho was like.

2. The spies got inside the wall of the city of Jericho and entered a house built into the city wall. It was the house of a woman named Rahab.

3. Rahab was not a good lady in the way she lived because she didn't know the true God and His good rules, but she had heard of

God's power. Her heart was open to learning about God and to helping His people.

4. Rahab hid the two spies on her roof when the king's soldiers came looking for them.

5. After the king of Jericho and his soldiers left Rahab's house, she begged the two spies to protect her and her family when the Israelites would later take over Jericho. She told the spies that she believed their God was the only true God of heaven.

6. The spies promised Rahab they would help her and her family when the Israelites moved into the land. Before they left Rahab's house, the spies told her that when God's people came back to Jericho, all her family must be safely inside her house and a red rope must be hanging from her window so the soldiers would know where she lived and could protect them.

7. The two spies escaped from Jericho by climbing down the red rope from a window in Rahab's house. They went to the mountains to hide for three days until the king and his men stopped looking for them.

8. When they were safe, the spies hurried back to Joshua and God's people and told them, "God will certainly give the land of Jericho to us, for the people inside the city are weak and afraid because they know our God is powerful!"

After you tell the story of Rahab write out the eight story segments on cards or paper. Then mix them up and let your child put them in the correct order.

You may also want to play a spying game with your child. Players begin the game by walking around the room or yard in different directions, not in a line or circle. While everybody is walking around, explain that you are all pretending to be spies. Tell everybody to have sneaky looks on their faces as they walk around and watch each other. Ask everyone to choose one person to spy on but not to let them know you are watching! Instruct players to sneak quick looks instead of staring at that person. Tell your spies to look at everyone, but to particularly notice what the one they are spying on is doing. After everyone has walked and spied for a while, let them take turns guessing who each other has been spying on.

God Did It Again

Share with your child this inspiring story from Joshua. Explain that the ark of the covenant was different from Noah's ark. It was a holy treasure of God's people, because it reminded them of God's presence and power.

The ark was a golden rectangular box with a lid. On the lid were two gold angels facing each other. Inside the ark were the ten commandments on the stone that God gave Moses; a container filled with manna, God's special bread that came down from heaven to feed the people in the desert, and Aaron's walking stick. Only the special family of pastors called Levites could carry the Ark of the Covenant.

When the Levites led God's people across the Jordan River, they stepped into the water. The river stopped flowing and stood up like two walls of water with a dry path in between them. The people walked safely across the river on the dry land.

Discuss how amazing and wonderful God's plan was for moving so many people across the flooding Jordan river. Talk about the problems they would have had if they had tried any other way to get across. Relate God's plan and provision for His people to the problems your family or child has today and how wonderfully God meets all our needs!

Twelve Very Special Rocks
(Questions and answers)

What will I need? A few large brown paper bags or construction paper or use large marshmallows, ice cubes, or rocks
Where is it in the Bible? Joshua 4
How long will it take? 15-20 minutes
What age child? 3-11 years
Will it work in a group? Yes
Can it be played in the car? Only the story and questions and answers
Will it work in a school classroom? Yes, preschool–6th grade

Help your child make 12 "rocks" from any of suggested materials. Ask her to see if she can pile the rocks on top of each other. Pretend to help her arrange the rocks, being as dramatic about the process as you wish! Then tell her you are going to explain what the pile of rocks are for. Sit near or around the rocks as you read from the Bible.

Talk about the 12 stones the people put in a pile to help them remember what God had done for them. Ask these questions and see if she can remember the answers. If needed, reread some verses.

1. How many stones were the leaders supposed to pick up?
2. Where would they get the stones?
3. Was there to be more than one pile of 12 stones?
4. Where would they put the second pile of stones?
5. Where was the ark of the covenant to stay while God's people were crossing the Jordan River?
6. What happened after the priests carried the ark out of the river?
7. How did the people feel about what God had done?

End your discussion by asking if she thinks it was a good idea for the people to pile the stones so that their children would see them and ask questions about them.

Share with your child what God has done for you and means to you. Share your personal testimony many times with your child as he grows up emphasizing your love for the Lord and the wonderful way He blesses you day after day, and year after year. Your personal spoken statement will impact your child forever.

The Walls Fall Down!
(A construction activity)

What will I need? Some of these: grocery bags stuffed with newspaper and taped shut across the top to form a block, or cardboard boxes of different sizes
Where is it in the Bible? Joshua 6
How long will it take? 15-20 minutes
What age child? 2-6 years
Will it work in a group? Yes
Can it be played in the car? No
Will it work in a school classroom? Yes, preschool–2nd grade

The exciting story of Joshua and the walls of Jericho falling down is an absolute favorite of children and adults alike. You will find it in most Bible storybooks or use the Bible account to present this awesome story of

God's plan and power.

Construct a wall out of the grocery bags or boxes.

Form a circle of children to march around the wall seven times, blowing trumpets and shouting and causing the wall to fall down and break apart. You may have to help some of the constructed walls fall down after the marchers have acted out their important role in this exciting, true action thriller!

A Sneaky Guy and a Gold Brick

(A sneaky game)

What will I need? A small block or box covered in gold paper or painted gold
Where is it in the Bible? Joshua 7
How long it will take? 10-15 minutes
What age child? 3-10 years
Will it work in a group? Yes
Can it be played in the car? No
Will it work in a school classroom? Yes, a good activity for preschool–5th grade

Tell your child the story of Achan.
Here are some elements you may want to present:
1. God told His people when they took over Jericho to destroy everything, but the things made of silver and gold, bronze, and iron. These things were to be used in the tabernacle to help them worship God
2. A man named Achan disobeyed God and kept a beautiful robe he found in Jericho, some silver worth $200, and a bar of gold worth about $500. Achan buried the things in the ground under his tent, and he thought no one, not even God would find out!
3. But God knew what Achan had done, and Achan's sin caused God's people to lose their fight against the little city Ai.
4. Joshua was upset about losing the battle, so he asked to God to help him understand what had gone wrong. God explained to Joshua that He couldn't bless the army because of Achan's bad deed.
5. Achan and his whole family were punished. We don't know if they had helped him steal or hide the things he took, but we know that in those times everybody in a family was hurt and had to share the punishment. When we do wrong today we also hurt the people who love us.

Explain that even though our ways of punishing crimes are different today, sin is still serious and still wrong.
6. If God had let Achan get away with doing wrong, it would have seemed like He didn't care if His people did good or bad, and He does.

After sharing the story of Achan, play a lighthearted game to help your child remember that it is important to obey God's Word.

Here's the game: You will need at least three players to sit in a circle on the floor, with an arms length distance between them. Choose another person to sit in the middle of the circle. The player inside the circle must cover his eyes with his hands while he counts from one to ten. The other participants will be passing the gold from player to player.

When the counter reaches the number nine, the person holding the gold will hide it somewhere on himself and try to act innocent. At the count of 10, the counter opens his eyes and has two guesses to find out who has the gold. If he guesses right, the two trade places. Otherwise, the game starts again until everyone has a turn inside the circle.

The Big Chase

Joshua 8

Explain that after Achan's sin and punishment, God's people fought the city of Ai again. This time they won, because they were obeying God.

God also told the people that this time they could keep any valuables they found. If only Achan had obeyed God and waited, God would have given him all the good things he needed.

God gave Joshua an inventive plan for winning the battle against Ai. Part of his army stayed hidden on one side of the city, while the other part pretended to be losing the fight and ran away. The army from Ai chased after the soldiers who were running away and left the city of Ai with no one to protect it. Then the hidden army went into the city and destroyed it with fire so their enemies couldn't move back in. The story of Ai is definitely about a big chase and a very smoky city.

God's Amazing Sun

(A cooking experiment)

What will I need? A basket, a piece of foil, a nail, and a potato
Where is it in the Bible? Joshua 10:1-15
How long will it take? Not really sure
What age child? 3-11 years
Will it work in a group? Yes
Can it be played in the car? No
Will it work in a school classroom? Yes, pre-school–6th grade

Share with your child some interesting facts about the sun by visiting the public library, your child's own book collection, or the internet. Here are a few facts:

1. God created the sun.
2. Without the light from the sun, all life on earth would come to an end.
3. Green plants need sunshine to make food, and you and all the animals on the earth need plants for food.
4. With no sun, we'd freeze to death! Even on cloudy days and cold days the sun is still shining!
5. Sunlight is made up of different colors, not just yellow or white. Sunshine contains the same beautiful colors you see in the rainbow!
6. Sunlight has hidden in it two kinds of rays, ultraviolet and infrared rays. The ultraviolet rays are the ones that give light and that make our skin turn darker or get tan when we are in the sunshine. Tanning is a protection that God put in our skin to keep some of the strong ultraviolet rays from getting through and hurting our body. The infrared rays are the ones that give us heat. God knew exactly how to give us both the light and the heat that we need to live! Don't forget to thank Him for the sun!

Tell the story about the one-of-a-kind day in history when the sun stood still so that God's people would have more time to win an important war. Even science verifies that about that time in history there was a longer-than-ever day recorded, but when the Bible tells us about it, that is enough to believe it!

If it's a sunny day, try cooking a potato in the infrared rays from the sun. This is very similar to the way microwave ovens cook food. Place a sheet of foil in a basket with the shiny side out. Make the foil as smooth as you can and tape it to stay in position.

Push a nail into the potato through the

bottom of the basket to keep it in place and aim the basket and potato toward the sun, changing their position occasionally during the day to absorb the most heat as the sun moves across the sky. The heat from the sun will warm the potato and finally cook it if the day is hot enough. If you want to cook outside during a cooler time of year, try melting something like butter, cheese, or chocolate.

Lots of Fights with the "ITES!"
(An active game)

What will I need? 1. Trash, dirt, or debris 2. Trash bags 3. Brooms, vacuums, mops, dust pans, or other cleaning supplies
Where is it in the Bible? Joshua 3:10; 11–12
How long will it take? 15-30 minutes
What age child? Involve the whole family
Will it work in a group? Yes
Can it be played in the car? No
Will it work in a school classroom? Yes, this is the kind of positive "war" that would benefit any classroom.

Tell your child that you want to talk about "ites!" When he asks what are they are, explain by reading Joshua 3:9-10.

Even though the promised land had already been given back to the Israelites by God, there were some enemies who had taken it over and were living there. All the funny-sounding names that ended with "ites" were enemy armies that God was promising to send out of the land that belonged to His people!

Show your child in Joshua 12 that God kept His promise. Pray and thank the Lord that He always keeps His promises to us, just

as He did for the people of Israel.

Find a clean-up project around your house or yard or car that could use the help of an army to conquer. Enlist your whole family in the army of the_____ (your last name and add "ites" to it). Your job is to tackle the clean-up project.

Divide the room, yard, or car into sections and your family into military teams. Give each member the appropriate cleaning weapons to fight the trash, dirt, or debris. Teams may then square off in the middle of the room, and at a signal, begin their battle. As each team finishes its assignment, members should come back to the middle of the room. The other team must then inspect their job to make sure it is satisfactory.

If you prefer to have a non-competitive war, enlist the whole family as one cooperative army of the best cleaners in all the war against trash! Set a clock or timer and see how long it takes your army to make their territory shine.

Peace at Last!
(Soothing smells)

What will I need? A good-smelling scent such as lavender or rosemary in a spray bottle or some other potpourri fragrance
Where is it in the Bible? Joshua 21:43-45; 23–24
How long will it take? 5-10 minutes
What age child? 2-11 years
Will it work in a group? Yes
Can it be played in the car? Yes
Will it work in a school classroom? Yes, a nice atmosphere for a classroom!

Talk with your child about the peaceful time that finally came for God's people after they moved into the land of Canaan. God had promised to give them a peaceful life, and every good thing the Lord had promised them came true!

Read Joshua 23:14-15 to see how important it was that the people kept obeying God so they could stay happy and peaceful. Pray that you will always stay true to God and serve Him, because He is so good and we love Him!

Make the room you are in seem peaceful by giving it a calming, pleasant atmosphere. Spray a potpourri fragrance like lavender or rosemary around the room (unless someone is allergic to them). There is some evidence that aromas such as those may actually have a calming effect on the brain, but if nothing else, they smell good! You can make your own scent by adding a few drops of lavender oil or dried rosemary to water in a spray bottle.

What Can I Learn from Joshua

1. Joshua was a good follower of God and a good leader of God's people, and they followed his example. Other friends notice if I love and obey God, and they may want to be like me. I have a chance everyday to be a good example to others.

2. God's people had some really hard things to do before they could be at home in their new land. God was always with them to help them when they needed Him and would let Him. God is always with me to help me, even when things seem hard for me to do and when they seem easy, too!

3. God knew the right way for the Israelite people to do the thing they needed to. When they followed Him, everything went well and when they didn't obey Him, things went wrong. When I let God lead my life, He will guide me in the very best way to go. I can trust Him because He knows best!

4. The Israelite people did not finish the job God gave them. They choose to do things the easy way instead. They soon found out that the easy way was not God's way, and it was really much harder than if they had just obeyed God. Sometimes I need to do things that seem hard even though I wish I could do something easy instead. Often the hard ways are the best ways, and God will always be there to make hard things easier.

5. Joshua asked God's people to never stop serving God so they could have the great life He promised them. Right now is a great time to decide to love and serve Jesus for the rest of your life.

Important Verses to Remember from Joshua

Joshua 1:7a – "Be strong and very courageous. Be careful to obey all the law my servant Moses gave you."

Joshua 3:5b – "Consecrate yourselves, for tomorrow the Lord will do amazing things among you."

Joshua 10:14 – "There has never been a day like it before or since, a day when the Lord listened to a man. Surely the Lord was fighting for Israel!"

Joshua 23:14b – "You know with all your heart and soul that not one of all of the good promises the Lord God gave you has failed."

A Devotional Thought for Parents and Teachers

Joshua was divinely placed in a position very similar to ours, He was appointed to be the leader and example of God's children. Joshua was an excellent role model for us to follow. This great man loved the Lord and obeyed Him even in the smallest details of life. As is true of successful leaders, Joshua could envision the positive outcome of his efforts. He could see God's people loving and serving Him, and living peacefully and happily in the place where the Lord had placed them.

Joshua modeled a trust in God for his followers, and he was able to challenge and motivate them to want to serve the Lord, too. Joshua's heart's desire was to equip and inspire the next generation to take up the mantle of leadership and to follow God wholeheartedly.

Isn't that why God placed us in the position we hold in the life of our child? Is anything we do more important? The same challenge that faced Joshua faces us today. We truly want to serve Him with our whole hearts and not to let the responsibilities of our homes, jobs, financial needs, and the temptations of the culture in which we live, crowd out the godly intentions of our hearts.

We must agree with Joshua and say we will serve the Lord.

Judges The Book About Twelve Heroes Who Saved

God's People "May they who love you be like the sun when it rises in its strength" (Judges 5:31b).

What's the Book About	The trouble God's people keep getting themselves into because they don't obey God—and the kindness God shows to them over and over and over again!

Joshua Dies and the People Disobey God	At the beginning of Judges, Joshua has died, and the people have started doing whatever they want instead of what God wants them to do. For more than 300 years, the Israelite people do the same things over and over again: 1. They disobey God. 2. Enemy armies take over their land. 3. They cry to God about their trouble. He sends a special leader, a "judge" to help them. 4. For a while, God's people worship Him and obey Him. 5. Then they forget and do the same wrong things all over again.

Let's Meet the People of Judges	**The Twelve Judges** of Israel were Othniel, Ehud, Shamgar, Deborah, Gideon, Tola, Jair, Jephthah, Ibzan, Elon, Abdon, and Samson. **Jephthah** was an army leader and a judge who served God but he made a foolish promise that was hard to keep. **Delilah** was the Philistine woman who tricked Samson into disobeying God and doing what she wanted him to do.

Here Are the Places of Judges	**Hazor** – was the place where King Jabin lived. He was the leader of God's enemies who treated God's people badly and who lost the fight against the armies of good Judge Deborah and God's leader, Barak. **Hill of Moreh** – was near where Gideon and God's army of only 300 soldiers won a battle with the huge armies of Midian by scaring them with broken pitchers, torches, and making a lot of noise until the Midianites gave up and ran away.

The Valley of Sorek – was where Samson fought thousands of the enemy Philistine soldiers with the incredible strength God gave him. It was also the place where Delilah lived, the woman who stole Samson's heart and cut his hair.

Eleven Brave Leaders and a Lady

(A silly affirmation activity)

What will I need? Just your voice and sense of humor
Where is it in the Bible? Judges 3-16
How long will it take? 5 minutes
What age child? 2-11 years
Will it work in a group? Yes
Can it be played in the car? Yes, fun to recite in the car!
Will it work in a school classroom? Yes, preschool–6th grade

Explain that for more than 300 years, every time God's people got into trouble by not obeying Him, the Lord would send a good judge or leader to help them have a good life again. Judges tells us the names of these twelve special leaders. To introduce your child to their names and to help her remember that the Judges were God's good helpers to His people, read this funny list of affirmations for the Judges:

"You're swell," Othniel
"You're my Bud," Ehud.
"You're up to par," Shamgar.
"Hooray for ya," Deborah.
"You're the one," Gideon.
"Hola,"("Hello" in Spanish) Tola
"Glad you're here," Jair

"Lovin' ya," Jephthah.
"You're the man," Ibzan.
"Keep on," Elon.
"Carry on!" Adbon
"You're # 1," Samson.
Ask your child who she thinks the lady judge was.

Read or tell the story of Judge Deborah from Judges 4-5. Here are some of the highlights:
1. God's people had sinned against Him once again. Their enemies, whose leader was a man named Sisera, were fighting the Israelites. Sisera's army had 900 iron chariots, which was pretty amazing and scary to God's people and to everyone else who lived nearby.
2. The Israelites finally prayed to God to help them fight against Sisera and King Jabin.
3. Even though God's people had disobeyed Him, God still heard their prayers and sent Deborah to help them.
4. Deborah was a judge, not a leader of the army, so she sent one of God's men, Barak, to lead 10,000 soldiers to fight the enemy.
5. Before Sisera's army could even come near Barak's army, God caused Sisera's men to be so mixed up and scared that they ran away without even fighting! Judge Deborah and Barak's army won the fight, because not even one of the bad guys was left when it was all over.
6. Sisera was not a very brave leader and ran

to hide in a cave, where he died at the hand of a woman named Jael.

Water, Water Everywhere
(Two water stories and activities)

What will I need? Water, squares of different kinds of fabric and one made of something similar to fake fur, and a measuring cup.
Where is it in the Bible? Judges 6:33–7:9
How long long will it take? Not sure. You'll be testing to see how long each fabric takes to dry.
What age child? 2-11 years
Will it work in a group? Yes
Can it be played in the car? No
Will it work in a school classroom? Yes, preschool–6th grade

Share with your child the story of Gideon and the sheepskin from Judges 6. Then do an experiment of your own with several different pieces of fabric and a piece of fake fur or something similar.

Ask your child to guess which kind of fabric will dry first after you get them all wet and hang them up to dry. After he has made his guess, check them once in a while.

As you watch to see the outcome of your experiment, ask your child if he can think of ways to help make the cloth dry faster. He may say to use a hair dryer, hang them over a heating vent, or set them in the sun.

God really does lead us and lets us know what we should do when we ask Him. Be sure to say thank you to Him.

While you are talking about water, ask your child what she would do if there were a river or stream nearby and she was very thirsty but had nothing with which to get water. Ask, "What if you needed to watch out for a tiger in the woods while you got a drink! How could you get a drink and watch for the tiger at the same time? (Explain to younger children that tigers don't live in the woods in our country.)

Tell your child that Gideon's army would face real danger, and God wanted Gideon to find out which men would make good, careful soldiers. Ask why God wanted Gideon to send thousands of soldiers home and leave Gideon with only 300 to fight the enemy. Why would Gideon be able to win the fight against the enemy armies that had many more soldiers. The next story in Judges 7:1-25 will give you the answers.

Do a simple "How much water will your hand hold?" experiment with the members of your family or group. Ask your child if she thinks her hand or yours will hold the most water? Find out by taking turns scooping water from the sink and immediately pouring each person's handful into a measuring cup. Compare the different amounts and let your child enjoy the fact that his guess was probably right.

Trumpets, Jars, Fire, and a Lot of Noise
(A noisy kind of painting)

What will I need? 1. Space outside or in the garage with newspapers on the floor 2. A large sheet of paper 3. A paper towel and scissors 4. Baking soda, white vinegar, measuring cups, and spoons 5. Baggies that zip close (This is important!)
Where is it in the Bible? Judges 7:7-25
How long will it take.? 20-30 minutes
What age child? 4-12 years

Will it work in a group? Yes
Can it be played in the car? Absolutely not!
The result would be very hard to explain to the officer in charge.
Will it work in a school classroom? Not inside the classroom, please! Preschool-7th grade

Enjoy with your child the story of Gideon's and God's victory over the Midianites. If possible, refer to a Bible story book for the details and a picture. Follow up the story with a bit of real-life excitement of your own with this exploding paint activity. Please resist the temptation to do this is someone else's garage. Spread out newspapers on the ground or in the garage where the experiment will take place.

Prepare zipped bags of exploding paint in four different colors. Here's how:

Cut a paper towel into four squares and put 2 tablespoons of baking soda into the middle of each square. Fold the sides of each square over the baking soda to form a little "package" with the soda inside. Place one package in each baggie.

Combine two teaspoons of paint or food coloring with one cup white vinegar and pour the colored vinegar into one of the plastic bags containing a paper towel. QUICKLY close the bag, place it on the big piece of paper and stand back! The baking soda and vinegar will combine, and the exploding paint will pop the bag open onto the paper. You don't want this to happen while you are left "holding the bag!"

Do this as many times as you like with different colors of paint. Messy, but thrilling, but still nothing compared to Gideon's thrill of victory over the Midianites.

Samson, the Strong
Samson, the Weak
(A making activity)

What will I need? A bunch of balloons or bubble wrap and a large sweatshirt and pants
Where is it in the Bible? Judges 14:5-6; 15:4-5; 16:4-30
How long will it take? 20-30 minutes
What age child? 3-11 years
Will it work in a a group? Yes, pretty funny in a group!
Can it be played in the car? No, too physical
Will it work in a school classroom? Yes, preschool–6th grade

Tell the story of Samson when he was strong. The reason God made him so strong was because of a special rule and a wonderful promise an angel made to Samson's parents.

Explain that God made Samson strong in a way that other people, even weight lifters and athletes are not. God planned to use Samson to save His people from the Philistines. The sad thing about Samson was that he did some very strong and amazing things with his body, but he wasn't very strong when it came to obeying God. Samson lost all of his strength for a while because he disobeyed God.

Samson became strong again at the very end of his life because he chose to obey God again. Encourage your child to decide right now that he will stay strong for God all his life and avoid the pain and sadness that Samson endured.

Make a strong guy or girl out of someone in your family by dressing them in an oversized jogging suit and stuffing as many small, inflated balloons into the suit as possible.

Now that looks strong, but being strong for God inside our hearts is what really counts, isn't it?

Discuss with your child the sad story of weak Samson from Judges 16:4-21. Explain that Delilah was a Philistine woman who did not love and serve God. She didn't love Samson, either. She made a terrible agreement with enemy leaders who promised to pay her a lot of money to find out the secret of Samson's strength. The Philistines wanted to make Samson weak so he would no longer be the strong leader of God's people.

Talk about how good and strong Samson started out when he was young, and then how Samson became so unhappy and weak when he stopped obeying God's Word. Help your child decide right now to follow God even when he is a teenager and an adult, because that early resolve will go a long way when temptations later come to him.

Explain that Judges ends with a big fight, not because God's people were having to fight more enemy armies, but because God's people were fighting against one of their own family. The whole saga is in Judges 19-20.

What Can I Learn from Judges

1. God's people in the book of Judges kept doing the same things over and over for many years: they obeyed God, then did not obey God and gave themselves lots of trouble. I can learn from the sins and foolishness of those people. It is so much better to just obey God all the time and have a great life!

2. When God's people were disobeying God and worshiping idols, there were always some special heroes who kept on serving God. The Lord used them in powerful ways to please Him and do His work. Sometimes I may have to be the only one who stays strong for God when other friends disobey Him. But, the Lord will use me, too, to do great things for Him!

Important Verses to Remember

Judges 3:4 – "They were left to test the Israelites to see whether they would obey the Lord's commands which he had given them through Moses."

Judges 5:3b – "I will sing to the Lord, I will sing; I will make music to the Lord, the God of Israel."

Judges 5:31b – "But may they who love you be like the sun when it rises in its strength."

Judges 16: 28a – "Then Samson prayed to the Lord, 'O Sovereign Lord, remember me. O God, please strengthen me just once more'."

One of our goals as parents and teachers is to instill in our children the character qualities that will enable them to stand strong for the Lord even when those around them are weak. Often our own human desire to fit in with our peers and to be a relevant part of our society causes us to shrink from going against the flow of public opinion, even though we have the liberty to do just that.

Throughout the book of Judges, God's people failed time and time again to be strong, instead blending in with the popular, evil influences of the unbelieving world around them. But in the middle of the crowd of compromising citizens there stood, head and shoulders above them all, those people God used for His Divine and redemptive purposes. They were the judges, and today those same types of people are called Christians.

God wisely included bad news in the Bible. If He hadn't, we would probably be overwhelmingly discouraged to see ideal people and a perfect society of the past that we, obviously, could never live up to. We might even have determined incorrectly that the Bible is simply not relevant anymore. He desires for us to learn from the negative as well as the positive examples of those who have lived before us.

Today as we learn from the Word of God and pass that knowledge on to our children, let's remember to pray that they will observe the dramatic tragedy that results from lives uncommitted to God and resolve to follow God's way for every day of their lives. God will make us as strong as we allow Him.

Ruth God's Book About Kindness and Love

"Where you go I will go, and where you stay I will stay. Your people will be my people and your God my God" (Ruth 1: 16b).

What's the Book About

Ruth is a beautiful love story. It tells about the love of a mother-in-law for God, Naomi's love for her daughter-in-law, and the love of a man for a woman. But most of all, the book of Ruth is about God's love and care for His children!

Ruth begins when things are bad for the Israelites. They are living in Canaan. There are enemies everywhere around them, and they don't have enough food to eat! Why are things so bad when God had promised that life would be so good in the new land?

The troubles came when God's people stopped obeying Him and started doing what they wanted to do. What they chose to do was foolish and wrong. Now their happy life had become unhappy.

Because life had become so hard in Canaan, Elimelech and Naomi took their two sons and moved to the land of Moab. They believed that there they could keep on serving God and have a good life.

After a while, Elimelech and Naomi's sons got married and lived happily until the father and the sons died. Naomi and her sons' wives, Ruth and Orpah, were left alone. Naomi decided to go back to her home in Bethlehem. Orpah stayed in Moab, but Ruth went to Bethlehem with Naomi. Some wonderful things happen there to Ruth.

Let's Meet the People of Ruth

Ruth was a girl from Moab who learned from her in-laws how to love and serve God. God took care of Ruth and sent Boaz to be her husband. She became the great-grandmother of King David. Later on Jesus would one day be in her family, too!

Naomi was the mother of Ruth's first husband, who died in the land of Moab. Naomi loved and obeyed God, and Ruth chose to go back to Bethlehem with Naomi.

Boaz was a kind man who owned a big grain field in Bethlehem. He made sure Ruth and Naomi had enough food to gather to eat. Later he married Ruth. They had a baby boy they named Obed.

Moab – the land where Naomi and Elimelech went with their two sons because their home in Canaan had become a bad place to live. Ruth was born and lived in Moab.

Bethlehem – the city in Canaan where Naomi and Ruth went to live after the men in their family died. Ruth met Boaz in Bethlehem and married him there. Later, Jesus was born in Bethlehem.

STORIES AND ACTIVITIES FROM RUTH

Naomi and Ruth Stick Together!

(A sticky situation)

What will I need? A bandanna or belt, three or more players
Where is it in the Bible? Ruth 1
How long will it take? 15-20 minutes
What age child? 3-11 years
Will it work in a group? Yes,
Can it be played in the car? Please don't!
Will it work in a school classroom? Yes, preschool–6th grade

Pretend to "glue" yourself to someone else in the family by using imaginary glue or by actually tying an arm or leg together with a bandanna or belt. Try different activities stuck together as a team. Try writing something, going outside to get the mail, watering the flowers, or making the bed.

Use the opportunity to tell or read the story of the loyalty of Ruth in sticking with her mother-in-law Naomi when Naomi needed her, even though it meant going to a new land and leaving Ruth's country behind. Use the moment to stress the importance of your family and church family and how people who love God and each other stick together.

A Big Bunch of Kindness and Barley

(A guessing experiment and a relay race)

What will I need? 1. A laundry basket and some pillows 2. Some bundles of twigs, grass, or uncooked spaghetti
Where is it in the Bible? Ruth 2
How long will it take? 10-15 minutes
What age child? 2-11 years
Will it work in a group? Yes
Can it be played in the car? As a discussion only
Will it work in a school classroom? Yes, preschool–6th grade

It's refreshing and motivating for all of us to hear inspiring stories of kindness and generosity. The story of Boaz and Ruth is definitely one of those stories! Share with your child this wonderful story of God's provision and protection and the love of a good man. Reinforce those important truths by trying a simple guessing experiment and playing a game together.

1. Guessing experiment: Ask your child to guess how many small pillows or other small items a laundry basket will hold. Give her time to look at the basket and the items that

will be going into it; then have her guess. Put the items in the basket (like Ruth may have put grain in hers) and count to see if your child was right in her estimate.

2. Gathering relay: Wrap eight or ten bundles of twigs or uncooked spaghetti and secure them with a rubber band or masking tape. Place half the bundles in a line across your yard or room at intervals several feet apart. Repeat with the remaining bundles, putting them in a parallel line about four or five feet away.

You and your child should each have a basket. Stand at the beginning of one a row of bundles. At the "go " signal, hurry down your line picking up the bunches of grain, much like Ruth may have done in Boaz's field. Instead of having a winner, express your enthusiasm at the end of the gathering by saying, "There! We got the job done!"

If you want to make the game more challenging, place 25 or more single bundles in the rows.

Match-Maker Naomi
Ruth 3

Try to think of some compound words that we use which may seem strange to us and don't appear to really mean what they say! Some examples: Dragonfly. Did you ever see a dragon fly? Butterfly. Did butter ever really fly? What is a matchmaker? Does a matchmaker make matches? Well, sort of.

Tell the story of Naomi's strange request. Explain that Naomi was asking Ruth to do something that Ruth did not understand, but she obeyed anyway. You may want to apply that principle to the parent-child or teacher-child relationship. A child doesn't always

understand why her parent makes a certain request, but she should obey, because parents that love God have her best interest in mind. The same is often true of what God places into our lives. We don't fully understand why, but we know He knows what's best for us.

There was nothing romantic nor immoral in Naomi's request and Ruth's action. It was a common practice for Israelite servants to lie at their master's feet and even share part of their covering at night. When Ruth did this, she showed Boaz that it was his responsibility (and the custom) to find a husband for her or to marry her himself. Boaz showed his kindness and integrity to Ruth, and before long, fell very much in love with her.

Here Comes Baby!
(A listening activity)

What will I need? A baby rattle or a plastic egg containing dried beans
Where is it in the Bible? Ruth 4:13-22
How long will it take? 5-10 minutes
What age child? 3-10 years
Will it work in a group? Yes
Can it be played in the car? Yes
Will it work in a school classroom? Yes, preschool–5th grade

The delightful story of Ruth and Boaz ends with the birth of a baby boy. The happy couple are blessed. Naomi, the grandmother, is blessed. All people throughout the ages of time are blessed because of the baby and his family tree. Baby Obed becomes the father of Jesse and the grandfather of King David, in whose family line our Savior, Jesus Christ, is born.

Now, do you think the story of Ruth and

Boaz is just an ordinary love story or a part of God's great plan? Ask your child if she thinks God has a plan for her life, too.

Play a baby rattle game with a real baby toy or a plastic egg filled with dried beans. Ask your child to hide his eyes or put on a blindfold and sit in the middle of the room. You, or a second player, shake the rattle in different locations in the room.

As the first player hears the rattle, he must keep his eyes closed, but point in the direction of the noise and say, "There's the baby." As you move from location to location, try to keep the rattle quiet until you reach the new spot. If you are in a group, use two rattles at a time. Take turns being the baby and the listener.

What Can I Learn from Ruth

1. Ruth was not just a poor girl who got lucky and married a rich man! God had a great plan for her life, even though she was just an ordinary young girl. God has a wonderful plan for my life, too, and I want to follow the adventure He leads me on!

2. Naomi and Ruth's story started with a lot of sadness in their lives. Things looked really bad, but Naomi kept on believing that God would take care of her and Ruth, and He did. I can and must always trust God, even when I am having a bad day. He will take care of me and make the sunshine days come again!

Important Verses to Remember

Ruth 1:16 – "But Ruth replied, 'Don't urge me to leave you or to turn back from you. Where you go I will go, and where you stay I will stay. Your people will be my people and your God my God'."

Ruth 2:12 – "May the Lord repay you for what your have done. May you be richly rewarded by the Lord, the God of Israel, under whose wings you have come to take refuge."

Ruth 4:17 – "The women living there said, 'Naomi has a son.' And they named him Obed. He was the father of Jesse, the father of David."

A Devotional Thought for Parents and Teachers

Mothers-in-law sometimes get a bad reputation. But if a mother-in-law can have the kind of godly influence on her son's unbelieving wife that Naomi did on Ruth, there's real hope and motivation for today's mothers-in-law.

God had a beautiful plan for Naomi, Ruth, Boaz, their son, and the children in generations to come. He has a wonderful plan for your life as a grandmother, a mother, a dad, or granddad. Time will reveal to you the way God will chose to work in the life of the your child and in the lives of your grandchildren, their children, and on and on until Jesus Himself comes back.

Make it a personal and continuing commitment to pray not only for the generations with whom you live and interact now, but for those who will come in the future and who will become recipients of your family heritage. Ask God to help you lay the foundation for a never-ending family chain of believers in the eternal family of our Lord and Savior, Jesus Christ. Nothing you do could possibly have more significance forever.

I Samuel God's Book About Some Happy Beginnings and Sad Endings

"Be sure to fear the Lord and serve him faithfully with all your heart; consider what great things he has done for you" (I Samuel 12:24).

What's the Book About

Samuel is about three important leaders in the life of God's people, the Israelites:
1. Their judge, Samuel
2. Their very first king, Saul
3. Their greatest king, David

Samuel Grows Up to be a Wise Leader

The book of I Samuel starts while the judges are still the leaders of God's people and, probably, while strong-man Samson is still alive. Eli, an old gentleman, is the High Priest, the good pastor, of God's people, like Aaron was when Moses was alive. Eli's life is almost over and God knows that His people will soon need a new High Priest.

Samuel is a little boy who grows up in the tabernacle. He becomes the Israelite's new High Priest after Eli is gone. In I Samuel, we meet Samuel's mother and father, Hannah and Elkanah; we also hear Hannah's special prayer!

First Samuel is also about God's people not being happy to just have priests and judges for their leaders. They want a king like all the neighboring countries have. The problem with wanting a king is that the people can very easily forget who their real King is – God.

God's people didn't understand that what they really needed was to obey God as their King, and He would help them with their problems. Samuel warned God's people that a human king would cause more troubles for them, and that's exactly what happened!

But since the Israelites cried so much for a king, the Lord gave them what they wanted, and Saul became their first king. Their next king was David. Having a king didn't fix their problems, though, and God's people had to keep on learning again and again that obeying God is what makes people great and strong.

Let's Meet the People of I Samuel

Eli was an old gentleman, the High Priest of Israel. Eli taught Samuel how to become the next High Priest so he could take over after Eli was gone. Eli was a good priest, but not a very good Dad; his two sons **Hophni** and **Phinehas** got into lots of trouble.

Hannah was the mother of Samuel. She prayed very hard that God would give her a baby boy, and He did! Hannah promised to give her son back to God, so Samuel lived in the tabernacle to learn how to be the next High Priest of God's people. Hannah kept her promise to God, and Samuel grew up to be a good leader for the Israelite people.

Saul became the very first king of God's people after they begged to have a king like their neighbor countries had. King Saul started out well as the king, but before very long he disobeyed God and became selfish and jealous.

Jonathan was the son of King Saul and David's very best friend. Jonathan loved David like a brother and was very good at helping and protecting him.

David was a shepherd boy who loved to write poems and songs and sing them to God while he took care of his father's sheep. God used David's music to help calm King Saul when he was upset. David was chosen by Saul to be his own bodyguard until Saul became jealous of David and tried to kill him. David was chosen to become the next, very important King of Israel and to be in the family of King Jesus.

Goliath was a mighty, giant soldier of the Philistines, the enemy of God's people. Goliath chose to fight against David, who was much smaller than he. Goliath and the Philistine army thought that such a giant-sized man would easily win the fight against young David, but God gave David the strength and power to win against the giant!

Shiloh – the city where the tabernacle was set up in Canaan. People traveled to Shiloh to worship God and offer their sacrifices and offerings to Him.

Mizpah – the place where Samuel called God's people together and asked them to pray to God to forgive their sins. While the Israelites were praying, the Philistines tried to attack them, but God kept His people safe. Saul was also chosen to be the first King of Israel at Mizpah, but he was crowned the king at **Gilgal.**

Elah Valley – the big stretch of land where Saul won many battles and where David killed the giant, Goliath.

The Wilderness – where David ran and hid from King Saul, who was trying to kill him. Sometimes David hid from Saul and the king's men in caves in the wilderness. Even when David had chances to kill King Saul, who was now his enemy, David refused to do so because he believed it would be wrong and David wanted to do right!

S T O R I E S   A N D   A C T I V I T I E S   F R O M   I   S A M U E L

God Gives Hannah a Present

(A musical game)

What will I need? 1. A picture of a baby that you can call baby Samuel, placed inside a shoebox 2. Several different kinds of paper to use as wrapping 3. Tape 4. A CD or cassette player and music

Where is it in the Bible? I Samuel 1:3-20

How long will it take? 15-30 minutes

What age child? 3-11 years

Will it work in a group? Yes, but it can be played with two people, taking turns

Can it be played in the car? No, just telling the story

Will it work in a school classroom? Yes, pre-school–6th grade, but for upper grades you may want to put a riddle giving clues about the baby in the box.

Before beginning the activity, secretly place a picture of a baby boy inside a small box and wrap it like a present in layer after layer of different kinds of paper, taping each layer separately so that they can be removed one at a time.

Sit down with your child near a CD or cassette player. You'll be turning the music on and off during the game. As the music begins, pass the mystery present from player to player, until the music stops. The person holding the present must then unwrap only the top layer of wrapping paper, exposing the next layer. Start the music again and resume passing the present. When the music stops again, the person holding the box must remove the next layer. Play until the last layer is removed, and the present is opened, revealing the baby or clues to the baby's identity.

Use this moment to share the story of Samuel and of his mother's intense prayer, and God's kind answer. Impress upon your child what an awesome gift from God he or she is! Pray with him, thanking the Lord for the specific attributes your child possesses and for the great plan God has for his/her life!

Samuel's Special Home
(A cut-out-a-mystery activity)

What will I need? A piece of paper and a pair of scissors
Where is it in the Bible? I Samuel 1:21–2:11
How long will it take? 10-15 minutes
What age child? 2-11 years
Will it work in a group? Yes
Can it be played in the car? Yes, if the one doing the cutting is a passenger.
Will it work in a school classroom? Yes, preschool–5th grade

Ask your child to watch as you cut out a mysterious clue to a Bible story. See if he can figure out what you are making. (Cut out the shape of a church by making a rectangular with a steeple and a cross on top of it.) Begin to slowly cut out the shape of a church, including a door that folds back and opens (asking often, "Do you know what it is yet?"). Save the steeple and the cross for the last.

When your child has identified your mystery object as a church, say, "Yes, it's a church, but it was also Samuel's house where he lived as a little boy. Discuss what your child might

like and not like about living inside your own church building. Ask him if he lived inside your church building, which room he would choose for his own bedroom and where the family would probably spend most of its time.

End the discussion by telling the story of Samuel's life. Talk about how hard it must have been for Hannah and Elkanah to live away from their little boy, but how they knew God had a special plan for Samuel's life and that made them happy and thankful.

Remind your child that God also has a very special plan for his life and that God is good to let you all live together at home.

Big Trouble for All the People
I Samuel 4–6

Talk about the ark of the covenant with your child and describe how it looked. It was a wooden rectangular box, covered inside and out with gold. It was made to be the special container for the ten commandments that God gave Moses. It also reminded the people of God's promises to them.

The ark of the covenant had a gold ring on each side for a gold-covered wooden pole to go through. This very special box could be carried wherever God's people traveled and lived. The ark had a lid of pure gold with gold angels facing each other at each end of the lid. Between the angels was the mercy seat where the High Priest would sprinkle the blood of an animal sacrifice every year to take away the sins of all the people.

This beautiful ark was the most special possession of the Israelite people, and it was kept in the tabernacle in a room called the

Holy of Holies. Only the High Priest was allowed to go once a year into that holy room.

So when the ark was stolen by the Philistines, it was a very serious problem. Here are some things that happened:

1. The Philistines were fighting and winning the battle against the Israelites.

2. The Israelite army foolishly thought all they had to do to win was to go get the ark from the tabernacle and carry it into battle with them. But that's not what the ark was to be used for. It had no special "magic" in it. Only God could help Israel win.

3. Because the Israelite army was not obeying God, they lost the fight and the ark of the covenant was captured by the enemy! Things looked very bad for God's people!

4. The Philistines put the ark in their temple with their false god Dagon, the rain god. They thought that if the ark brought good luck to the Israelites, it would do the same for them. But the next morning, their idol had fallen on its face in front of the ark of God. They set it back up, but the next day the head and the arms of their false idol were cut off and people in nearby villages began to get sick and to die. The Philistines decided the ark was bad luck. They tried to send it to other cities, but none of the other enemies of God's people wanted it.

5. Finally, the ark was sent back to the Israelite people, and they were glad to have it back.

We Want a King

(A king's cape decorating activity)

What will I need? 1. An old bathrobe or a piece of cloth that can be cut into a cape shape for a king or queen 2. Fake fur pieces, shiny buttons, fancy trim, sequins, fake jew-els, costume jewelry pieces 3. A glue gun or fabric glue

Where is it in the Bible? I Samuel 8:5b-22; 10:24-25

How long will it take? 30-45 minutes

What age child? 3-11 years

Will it work in a group? Yes

Can it be played in the car? Better not

Will it work in a school classroom? Yes, preschool–6th grade

Provide an old bathrobe or piece of cloth that can be cut into the shape of a cape then tied or fastened at the neck. Spread the robe or cape out where your child can glue royal-looking decorations onto it. As your child is busy decorating the robe, explain that the Israelite people already had the best King possible, God. They also had a good High Priest, Samuel, who helped the people know how to worship God. However, God's people kept saying, "We want a king! We want a king, just like our neighbors have!"

Samuel warned God's people that having a king would not be all good and that they would have problems. Read about some of the problems in I Samuel 8:10-19. Still, the stubborn people wanted a king, and they got one, but it certainly wasn't all good. They had to learn over and over again that the Lord is the real King and the One they must learn to trust to lead them!

The King Who Broke the Law

Ask your child to help you think of some things that break when you drop them (a cookie, cracker, egg, glass jar, flower vase, a pair of glasses). Mention that there is something else people can sometimes break, too – the law. Ask what happens to people when they break the law.

Think up some silly laws that you and your child must not break for a specified time limit. Some of these laws might be, don't use the word 'I' at all, don't laugh or smile, don't say a word, or don't scratch, no matter how much you itch.

If a law is broken, decide on a penalty like having to wash five cups even if they are not dirty. For younger children, make the penalty something like getting tickled or chased. Explain to your child that keeping the law is important. (Be sure to do it yourself, please.) Talk about what would happen if there were no laws for people. Use the discussion to lead into the story of the king who didn't obey the law of his own land.

Tell the story about the law that King Saul broke. Here are the main points of the story from I Samuel 13:1-14:

1. Saul had been King of Israel for one year.

2. Saul's son Jonathan led God's army to destroy the Philistine army's headquarters, but Saul took all the credit for the victory. He began to grow very proud of himself!

3. The Philistine army didn't give up easily; they came back to fight the army of Israel. The Philistines had 3,000 chariots, 6,000 men on horseback, and so many soldiers that they looked like sand on the seashore.

4. When the army of Israel saw all those soldiers, they got very scared and tried to hide in caves, bushes, rock piles, graveyards, and even in water pipes! They forgot how strong God is and that He was with them.

5. Samuel, the High Priest, was on his way to the battlefield to give a sacrifice to God before the fight began as a way of asking God to help them win the battle. Samuel was the only person who was supposed to offer sacrifices to God, and Saul had been told to wait for Samuel to come before they started fighting the battle.

6. King Saul got impatient. When he saw his army running away in fear, he went ahead and offered the sacrifice himself.

7. Saul took matters into his own hands and disobeyed God's important law. It was very serious, because King Saul had started doing things His way instead of God's. He thought that what he wanted to do was more important than what God told him to do, and that was a big mistake!

Read this account in I Samuel 15:1-23 about King Saul when there were animal sounds in the background. Acknowledge that the idea of cows mooing and sheep baaing seems a little funny at first, but it really was very serious. See how Saul again does what he wants instead of obeying God.

Brand New King David
(A cleaning and polishing activity)

What will I need? Some kind of silver polish, shoe or furniture polish, jewelry-cleaning solution, or car-washing supplies
Where is it in the Bible? I Samuel 16:1-13.
How long will it take? 20-30 minutes
What age child? 2-11 years
Will it work in a group? Yes, with clean-up teams
Can it be played in the car? No
Will it work in a school classroom? Yes, preschool–6th grade

Help your child make something look brand new by polishing or cleaning it. Whatever you clean together, make a point to make it look brand new. For example, if you wash and clean the car, spray some new car smell inside, if you have some.

Let your activity lead naturally into the story of the brand new king for God's people. David would be that kind. Ask your child if he would like it if someone poured oil on his head. Then tell the story of the anointing of shepherd boy David by Samuel. Explain that the oil was made by squeezing the juice out of olives, and sometimes a special perfume was added to it. The oil was poured from an animal horn on the head of the person who would become the next king – that was called anointing him.

When Samuel anointed David to become the next king, Saul was still king of Israel. Saul would be king for several more years. Saul had disobeyed God, so his son could not become king after him. His family could not be the king's family, even though that is what usually happened. But David was not from Saul's family.

Saul liked David at first and made him his own bodyguard, then his army commander. David played music and sang to Saul when the king was upset or unhappy. (I Samuel 16:14-23 and I Samuel 18: 4b-5) Later, King Saul became so jealous and angry toward David that he even tried to kill him.

A Giant of a Fight!
(Making a giant activity)

What will I need? 1. A roll of white or brown paper 2. Crayons or markers 3. Scissors and a piece of string, yarn, or strong tape
Where is it in the Bible? I Samuel 17
How long will it take? 20-45 minutes
What age child? 2-11 years

Will it work in a group? Yes, a good group project
Can it be played in the car? No
Will it work in a school classroom? Yes, preschool–6th grade and leave Goliath up for a while to enjoy in the classroom

Let your child tell you the story of David and the giant, Goliath. Emphasize that Goliath did not recognize that when he was fighting David he was also fighting God. He could not win against Almighty God!

David knew that God was with him. He was very confident that God would fight for him. People laughed at David and said bad things about him, even his own brother spoke against him, but David paid no attention to them. He went right on doing what he believed God wanted him to do, and David was the winner. Help your child to develop the personal strength of character that will enable him, too, to do what is right.

Have fun making a giant paper cut-out of Goliath. Unroll 9 feet of white paper, like shelf paper. Draw a simple outline of what Goliath might have looked like. If that's not too hard to do, trace around your child's head, shoulders, and arms (at his sides) at one end of the paper, then around his legs and feet at the other end of the paper. Add a long body in between.

Help your child color your giant Goliath then cut him out and hang him from the ceiling or something sturdy and high. If you would like, trace around your child. Color his paper likeness and let his paper cut-out be David. Tape David up near Goliath to show the difference in their sizes. Remember that David had giant faith in God and that's what counted.

Best Friends Forever

The wholesome friendship of the two young men, David and Jonathan, is a beautiful and inspiring glimpse into godly love and kindness. Through them, we are allowed to look at the way a friendship works when it is based on a relationship and commitment to God.

David and Jonathan had a friendship that was designed in heaven, and your child can enjoy those kinds of positive (but not necessarily perfect) relationships in his life, too. Pray that your child will develop wholesome friendships that will strengthen his walk with God.

Share the inspiring story of David and Jonathan and read I Samuel 23:15-18, their last time together. Talk with your child about how family and friends are loyal to each other, unless there is some immoral or unethical behavior that can not be condoned on one's part, and that should never be hidden from parents by their children.

What Can I Learn from I Samuel

1. God had a plan for Samuel's life even before he was born. God called to Samuel to begin serving the Lord when he was just a little boy! God knew all about me before I was ever born, too, and He has a great plan for my life. But I don't have to wait until I'm grown up to serve Him. I can start right now.

2. Some of God's people, like Eli and King Saul started out doing good for God but did not end up quite as well. I have my whole life ahead of me. I can chose right now, and every day of my life, that I will start good and end up good, too.

3. God was leading His people in the way they should go, but they decided that they wanted things to be done their way. They wanted a king like their neighbors had. I have learned that I need to be careful to follow God's good ways instead of my own and to be happy with what He gives me and the way He leads me.

Important Verses to Remember

I Samuel 1:27-28a – "I prayed for this child, and the Lord has granted me what I asked of him. So now I give him to the Lord. For his whole life he will be given over to the Lord."

I Samuel 2:2 – "There is no one holy like the Lord; there is no one beside you; there is no Rock like our God."

I Samuel 3:10 – "The Lord came and stood there, calling as at the other time, 'Samuel! Samuel!' then Samuel said, 'Speak, for your servant is listening.' "

I Samuel 12:24 – "But be sure to fear the Lord and serve him faithfully with all your heart; consider what great things he has done for you."

One of the universal challenges of parenting is being consistent in our expectations, discipline, and instructions to our child and in our reactions to him. Perhaps the greatest challenge of all involves consistency in our personal spiritual walk with the Lord as it is played out in full view of the observing eyes of our child!

It may be of some consolation (but no real excuse) that God has graciously shown us that even the great leaders of the Bible have suffered at the hands of their own human frailties. We can learn from their tragic mistakes, especially as those sins tremendously impacted the lives of their children. Resolve with God's ever-available strength, wisdom, and encouragement that we will live consistently to yield to Him as He gives us breath.

That may seem a little melodramatic, but there really is never a good time to let up in our spiritual resolve and commitment. In reality, how we live our lives will continue to impact our children as long as we and they live. What an awesome privilege to have that kind of influence on the life and potential of a child of God's!

May the Lord bless and strengthen you as you endeavor to live for Him from the beginning of right now until the ending of your earthly life.

II Samuel — God's Book About Good Times and Bad Times for David and God's People

"And David knew that the Lord had established him as king over Israel and had exalted his Kingdom for the sake of his people Israel" (II Samuel 5:12).

What's the Book About

The good things and the bad things that happened to David during his life as king of Israel and the great God that was (and is) always there in happy times and sad times are covered in the book of II Samuel.

The Story of a Shepherd Who Became a King

Second Samuel is an adventure that could be called, "David's Story." As we travel through the story of David's life, we find that the shepherd boy has grown up to be crowned King of Israel. He brings the ark of the covenant back home to the tabernacle where it belongs. David leads God's armies to finally finish the job of sending all the enemies of God's people out of the land of Canaan so the Israelites can live there in peace and happiness!

But, King David also made some bad choices and sinned so that he hurt himself, his family, and all of God's people. But David was sorry for his sins and asked God to forgive Him. God did just that. David was called "a man after God's own heart."

Let's Meet the People of II Samuel

David was the shepherd boy who became the King of Israel. He was a good king, but he also made some bad choices. God forgave David's sins and helped him.

Michal was the daughter of Saul that married David. Michal became mad at David one time when she saw him worshiping the Lord. God was not pleased with Michal for getting angry with David.

Mephibosheth was the crippled son of Jonathan and the grandson of King Saul. David was kind to Mephibosheth, just as he had promised Jonathan he would be.

Bathsheba was the wife of a soldier named Uriah. David sinned with Bathsheba and then had her husband put at the front of a battle so he would get killed. Bathsheba was the mother of Solomon, who became the next king after his father David.

Absalom was the son of David who wanted to be the king. Absalom secured an army and fought against David, but Absalom couldn't fight against God.

Here Are the Places of II Samuel

Hebron – the city where David was crowned the King of Judah and then king over all of God's people, Israel. (God's people were also in Judah.)

Jerusalem – the place where David fought one of his first battles and where he later brought the ark of the covenant to stay.

The Forest of Ephraim – where Absalom's army tried to fight King David's army so that Absalom could be the new king instead of David. Absalom's donkey ran under a tree in this forest. Absalom's hair got caught in the branches, and he died there.

STORIES AND ACTIVITIES FROM II SAMUEL

A Tongue-Twister Name
(A silly rhyme and a beautiful story)

What will I need? You, your child, and your sense of humor
Where is it in the Bible? II Samuel 9
How long will it take? 10-15 minutes
What age child? 3-11 years
Will it work in a group? Yes
Can it be played in the car? Yes
Will it work in a school classroom? Yes, preschool–6th grade

After reading the story, say this silly tongue-twister rhyme for your child:
Cain, Abel, Noah, Seth
Methuselah and Mephibosheth.

Jephthah, Jonathan
I'm out of breath!
But I can't forget the name, "Mephibosheth!"

Abraham, Benjamin,
Life and death.
David was kind to Mephibosheth.

Abigail, Abimelech
My good friend, Beth-
But I keep on thinking of Mephibosheth!

Who WAS Mephibosheth?
So glad you asked!

David Messes Up
(A messy art project)

What will I need? 1. A large sheet of paper and some newspapers to spread out 2. Several balloons 3. Several colors of liquid paints 4. Water 5. A needle or pin
Where is it in Bible? II Samuel 11
How long will it take? 15-20 minutes
What age child? 3-11 years
Will it work in a group? Yes

Can it be played in the car? No, please don't
Will it work in a school classroom? Yes, preschool–6th grade, outside please.

Familiarize yourself with the first 10 chapters of II Samuel and talk about the good news and good years that came after David became the King of Israel. Explain that now in chapters 11-24 the Bible shares with us some of the bad things that happened to King David that made him very sad and disappointed, especially in himself.

Ask your child why she thinks that God didn't just tell us about the good part of David's life in the Bible. The lessons that God's people learned from good and bad behavior and experiences are shared so that we can learn from them and not have to go through that same unhappiness ourselves! God is good to show us the bad!

These are a few of David's mistakes that you may or may not choose to share with your child:

1. He saw Bathsheba taking a bath and didn't turn around and look the other way. Instead, he sent for her and slept with her, even though she wasn't his wife.

2. He had Bathsheba's husband, Uriah, put right in the most dangerous part of the army where he would get killed. God was very unhappy with what David had done with Bathsheba and Uriah, her husband.

3. Bathsheba and David had a baby that became very sick and died. It was a sad day for David and Bathsheba, but later God gave them Solomon and other children.

4. David's children also did some of the same bad things David did. His sons Amnon and Absalom caused him a lot of trouble and sadness!

5. David's son Absalom tried to fight David and become the new King.

6. Absalom got killed, and David was very sad.

Since the subject of David's mess-ups is really very serious, do something a little more light-hearted with your child. Here's a messy painting idea to try:

Spread a big sheet of white or light paper on the ground outside. Squirt a different color of diluted tempera or watercolor paint into several balloons. Add some water to partially fill up the balloons and tie them tightly closed. Swish the water around a little to mix it with the paint in each balloon.

To do the actual balloon painting carefully stick a needle or pin into the balloons and point the leak toward the paper. Use the stream of paint as your brush making designs on the paper! God takes our real-life mess-ups and arranges them into a beautiful picture of His grace for others to see. Thank you, Lord.

What Can I Learn from II Samuel

1. David loved God and wanted to obey Him. He did a good job as the King for a long time, then David sinned against God and things began to go badly for him. God's ways are always best, and when I remember to obey Him, things will go better for me, too!

2. David told God that he was very sorry for the wrong things he had done in his life. Once he did this, he was able to praise God again! When I do wrong, I must tell God that I am sorry and ask Him to help me do better the next time! Then my heart will feel happy and peaceful again!

Important Verses to Remember

II Samuel 7:28 – "O Sovereign Lord, you are God! Your words are trustworthy, and you have promised these good things to you servant."

II Samuel 22: 2-3a – "The Lord is my rock, my fortress and my deliverer; my God is my rock, in whom I take refuge, my shield and the horn of my salvation."

II Samuel 22:4 – "I call on the Lord, who is worthy of praise, and I am saved from my enemies."

II Samuel 22:47 – "The Lord lives! Praise be to my Rock! Exalted be God, the Rock, my Savior!"

A Devotional Thought for Parents and Teachers

Good news/bad news, two steps forward and three steps back, we've all been there and can relate! But there are far more good times in the life of God's children than there are painful and difficult ones. Through them all, the Lord who loves us is here, just as He was with David.

How enlightening that even David had personal ups and down, high and lows. He failed God in ways that we pray we never will, and he reaped a harvest of repercussions that we cannot even imagine. But David truly repented and received God's forgiveness and restorative love. Through it all he held the incredible distinction of being a man after God's own heart. Why? Maybe it was because of his qualities of courage, patience, faithfulness, generosity, commitment, honesty, and candidness when confronted with his own sin. But it was primarily because our God is a God of unconditional love and grace. When we confess our sins, He sees only His own imputed righteousness revealed in us. Because of Jesus, we can all be people after God's own heart.

I Kings God's Book About Good and Bad Kings

and Wise and Foolish Choices
"So be strong, show yourself a man, and observe what the Lord your God requires: Walk in his ways, and keep his decrees and commands, his laws and requirements, as written in the Law of Moses, so that you may prosper in all you do and wherever you go" (I Kings 2:2b-3).

What's the Book About

The book of I Kings is about God's people and what happens when their leaders follow and don't follow God's ways.

Wise Kings, Foolish Kings, and a Family Feud

First Kings opens when King David's life is ending and his son Solomon is to be the new king of the Israelites.

King Solomon starts out well because he loves God and follows Him. He even leads the people to build a beautiful temple in Jerusalem. Solomon begins as a very wise and rich king, but then he makes some foolish choices and listens to people who do not love and worship God.

Before long, God's people have big problems because of their king's mistakes! The Israelites split into two feuding group instead of living in peace and fighting together against God's enemies. They even start worshiping idols instead of the one true God!

Right in the middle of the fighting, God sent a special prophet named Elijah to remind the people that they must turn back to God and obey Him again. God did amazing things through Elijah to show His awesome love and power and to teach the people that He is the only true God to love and to worship!

Let's Meet the People of I Kings

David is still the King of Israel as the book begins, but he dies shortly thereafter.

Solomon is David's son who became the new king of God's people.

Rehoboam was Solomon's son who became the king when Solomon died. He was not a good and wise king, and because of him, God's people split into two fighting groups. Two of the tribes kept Rehoboam as their king and lived in the Southern Kingdom of Judah.

Jeroboam was David's other son who became king of the ten tribes who lived in the Northern Kingdom of Israel. Like his brother, Jeroboam was not a good king either.

Elijah was a special preacher, a prophet, that the Lord sent to the land of Israel to help the people understand that they must worship and obey only the one true God.

Ahab and **Jezebel** were an evil king and queen who ruled the land of Israel when Elijah was God's prophet. Ahab and Jezebel would not listen to what God told them through Elijah, so things did not go well for them.

Here Are the Places of I Kings

Israel – the special home for God's people that He had given to them many years before. They lived there until Rehoboam became the king, and the land split into two kingdoms–the Northern Kingdom of Israel and the Southern Kingdom of Judah.

Jerusalem – the important city in the Southern Kingdom of Judah where Solomon built the beautiful temple for God's people to go to worship Him.

Dan and Bethel – two cities where King Jeroboam made a place for the people in the Northern Kingdom of Israel to go to worship two calf idols instead of the real God.

Mount Carmel – the mountain where Elijah had an important fire contest between the true God and the false gods, Baal and Asherah.

Solomon's Good Request

(A question and answer game)

What do I need? You, your child, and something to make a turban

Where is it in the Bible? I Kings 3:1-15 and I Kings 4:29-34

How long will it take? 10-15 minutes

What age child? 3-11 years

Will it work in a group? Yes

Can it be played in the car? Yes, a good car activity

Will it work in a school classroom? Yes, older preschool–6th grade

Ask your child to pretend to be the wisest child in all the world. Seat her in a special chair in front of you and wrap a cloth around her head like a turban. Ask her questions that need a wise answer, such as:

1. If you have a chance to eat a healthy dinner or just eat a whole bag of candy, what's the wise thing to do? Why?

2. If someone accidentally left a ladder leaning against the house, and you always wanted to see how the neighborhood looks from way up high, what would be the wise thing to do? Why?

3. If your soccer team is having an important practice, but you would rather go swimming, what is the wise thing to do? Why?

4. A sign says, "No trespassing," but there is a cute little dog standing there wagging his tail. What is the wise thing to do? Why?

5. A friend that you really like says, "Look! I found some cigarettes. Let's try one and see what it is like to smoke." What is the wise thing to do? Why?

Explain to your child that there was a king in the Bible who was very wise. His name was Solomon. Read what Solomon asked God to give him. Explain that Solomon wrote 3,000 wise sayings and over 1,000 songs.

Solomon Builds the Temple

I Kings 7

Begin a conversation with your child about the church you attend, what you enjoy about the worship service, what you have learned from the messages, how you enjoy seeing your friends at church, etc. Stop and thank God right now for your church (no matter how imperfect).

Continue your discussion by remembering what it was like for God's people to go church.

In Genesis, people worshiped God outside in front of altars where they cooked their animal sacrifices (offerings), and the smoke went to God to show their love for Him.

Then, when God's people were traveling in the desert they built a tent church right in the middle of their camp. People went there to meet God and to offer their sacrifices. King David wanted to build a permanent building, the temple, where all the people could come and worship God. Because David had fought so many wars and killed so many people, God did not let him be the one to build the temple. Solomon, King David's son, was chosen to lead the workers to build the temple in the city of Jerusalem.

Here are some interesting things to know

about the temple:

1. Solomon asked King Hiram of the land of Tyre to send special wood, cedar, and cypress, because they were the very best kinds for building. The cedar and cypress logs were sent on rafts down the water from Tyre to Israel, where they were carried on to Jerusalem.

2. Solomon was very kind to the workers who built the temple, and made sure they didn't have to be away from their homes for long periods of time. Solomon knew that a whole kingdom was strong when its families were strong.

3. Because Solomon and the people loved and respected God, they built the temple without the noise of a hammer or any other tool. That meant they had to do the noisy rock-cutting and other work miles away, then bring the wood and rocks to where the temple was quietly being built. They understood how awesome God is.

4. There were special bowls, cups, and furniture inside the temple, all used to worship God. Some of them would seem unusual to us today, but we have stained glass windows, crosses, pulpits, communion tables, songbooks, and other things in our churches that would seem strange to the people of Solomon's day, too.

The Queen Meets the King
(A treasure activity)

What will I need? A plastic tub containing treasures like beaded strips of Christmas tree garlands, colorful strips of plastic, shiny confetti, toy necklaces or garage sale jewelry, gold or silver painted rocks, shiny coins or wadded-up pieces of foil. Add a little clear dish detergent and a small amount of water to make the treasure slippery. Use tongs to search for your treasure.

Where is it in the Bible? I Kings 10

How long will it take.? As long as it is fun to play

What age child? 2-10 years

Will it work in a group? Yes, a small group at a time

Can it be played in the car? No

Will it work in a school classroom? Yes, preschool–4th grade

While your child is enjoying playing with the tub full of shiny treasures, tell him about the day when the Queen of Sheba came to Jerusalem to visit King Solomon. Read verses 1 and 2 to your child and ask why he thinks the Queen shared all her problems with the King. Find out how the Queen of Sheba felt about Solomon in verses 6-9.

Explain that the queen knew that Solomon was a wise and good king because of God's kindness to him and to Israel. Knowing God and loving Him was the most valuable treasure that King Solomon had, much more wonderful than all his jewels and spices and gold.

Rain, Rain, Come Today!
(A rain-making activity)

What will I need? 1. A large jar with a wide opening 2. A flashlight 3. Hot water 4. A metal tray of ice cubes or a small metal pan filled with ice

Where is it in the Bible? I Kings 17:1

How long will it take? Not sure, it's an experiment

What age child? 3-12 years

Will it work in a group? Yes, as an observation project

Can it be played in the car? No, sorry

Will it work in a school classroom? Yes, a science project for preschool–6th grade

Explain that Elijah was God's special prophet, a preacher, sent to Israel to remind the people that they must worship only the true God, not idols. Elijah went bravely into the palace of King Ahab and told him there would be no rain in the land for several years because his people were worshiping the false god Baal.

King Ahab was shocked by what Elijah said! Baal was supposed to bring plenty of rain to the land so their crops could grow well. But since Baal was not the true God, no rain fell at all. Even Baal's many priests couldn't get Baal to send any rain. For several years there was no rain, and all the rivers and brooks dried up, just like Elijah had said they would. Elijah knew what would happen, because God had told him what to expect.

Do a science experiment to see how clouds form and how rain falls from the clouds. Show how clouds are made in the sky by creating a little cloud in a jar. Put about one inch of hot water into a large jar and place a metal ice cube tray or a pan containing ice on top of it. Carefully carry the jar into a dark room or closet and shine a flashlight on it to look for the cloud. Keep watching to see if tiny raindrops begin to fall to the bottom of the jar from the cloud. King Ahab would have wished he could have made clouds and rain that easily!

Always Enough to Eat!
(A baking and eating activity)

What will I need? A cake mix that requires adding vegetable oil

Where is it in the Bible? I Kings 17:8-24

How long will it take? 30-45 minutes

What age child? 2-12 years

Will it work in a group? Yes, by allowing everyone to have a turn.

Can it be played in the car? No, you can understand why not.

Will it work in a school classroom? Yes, as a group project for preschool–6th grade

With your child as your assistant cook, mix and bake a cake that requires vegetable oil as an ingredient. After the cake has baked, enjoy eating a piece together as you tell the wonderful story of the kind lady and God's amazing miracle from I Kings 17:8-24. Be sure to thank God for giving you food and drink every single day!

Jumping Jehoshaphat!
(A jumping game)

What will I need? Your child and a jump rope

Where is it in the Bible? I Kings 22:41-50

How long will it take? 5-10 minutes

What age child? 3-11 years

Will it work in a group? Yes

Can it be played in the car? No, not a good place to jump rope.

Will it work in a school classroom? Yes, preschool–5th grade

King Jehoshaphat was a good king over God's people in the Southern Kingdom of Judah. Jehoshaphat led God's people to worship the true God for twenty-five years, but he made one mistake. Jehoshaphat did not tear down the altars and temples in the hills where some of the people went to worship idols. When he tried to destroy them, some of the people complained so much that Jehoshaphat wasn't able to get rid of the idols.

After talking about King Jehoshaphat have fun jumping rope to this jingle:

Jehoshaphat, Jehoshaphat! Was he fat or skinny?

Was he short? Was he tall? With lots of hair or not any?

Jehoshaphat, Jehoshaphat! One of Judah's good kings.
He served the Lord. He worshiped God. He did so many good things.

Jehoshaphat, Jehoshaphat! Let's jump and jump for joy.
For the good he did, and the God we serve, who loves each girl and boy.

What Can I Learn from I Kings

1. David was a good king, but not a great father. He didn't discipline his sons when they needed it. Because of this his sons lived bad lives and did some things that were wrong. When my Dad and Mom have to discipline me for something I have done wrong, I will try to remember that it is good for me to learn to do right.

2. Solomon's son Rehoboam listened to the wrong kind of friends who gave him bad advice. When he did what they said, he made a big mistake. I need to be careful when my friends tell me to do something I'm not sure is right. I need to check with somebody older and wiser who will help me know the best choices to make.

3. Solomon changed from being a very wise man to becoming a foolish man, who made lots of bad choices. It all started with just one small, bad choice that led to many other sins. I can learn to be careful to obey God even in the little ways.

Important Verses To Remember

I Kings 3:7, 9a – "Now, O Lord my God, you have made your servant king in place of my father David. But I am only a little child and do not know how to carry out my duties. So give your servant a discerning heart to govern your people and to distinguish between right and wrong."

I Kings 4:29 – "God gave Solomon wisdom and very great insight, and a breadth of understanding as measureless as the sand on the seashore."

I Kings 8:23 – "O Lord, God of Israel, there is no God like you in heaven above or on earth below–you who keep your covenant of love with your servants who continue wholeheartedly in your way."

I Kings 18:21, 39 – "Elijah went before the people and said, 'How long will you waver between two opinions? If the Lord is God, follow Him; but if Baal is God, follow Him. When all the people saw this, they fell prostrate and cried, 'The Lord–he is God! The Lord–he is God!' "

A Devotional Thought for Parents and Teachers

Much has changed since Solomon's day. There have been enormous scientific advances, tremendous progress in the fields of medicine, technology, transportation, psychology, military strategy, education, communication, and so much more. The world is a very different place since kings reigned over the people of God.

But two constants have remained, the goodness of God and His presence in the affairs of man, and the depravity of human nature. We want to think that we have advanced in every area, but the inescapable truth remains: the same forces that preyed on the people of Israel and ultimately brought about their moral and societal demise are the same influences that we are vulnerable to in the 21st century. How humbling!

We still experience jealousy, a desire for more and better things, and especially a love for money. Investment portfolios, the stock market, and positive financial profiles mean much to us. We desperately want to get ahead in life and are impressed with big names and influential people.

We, too, are careless with precious marriage promises. Infidelity is a way of life for many of our leaders and heroes. The pressures of time and the influences that surround us daily tend to weaken our devotion to God and keep us superficial in our commitment to Him. We don't like to admit it, but we, like Solomon, are at risk!

As influential adults in the life of a child, personally affecting more people than we will probably ever know until eternity, let's resolve by God's help and grace never to excuse the sins in our own lives that He points out to us, however small and justifiable they may seem. It's not the sins we don't recognize in our lives, but the ones we see clearly and excuse that most often lead us away from God. He loves us so much and wants only the very best for us and our children.

II Kings God's Book About Bad Kings, Good Kings, and God's Special Prophets

"The Lord warned Israel and Judah through all his prophets and seers 'Turn from your evil ways. Observe my commands and decrees . . . But they would not listen and were as stiff-necked as their fathers, who did not trust in the Lord their God" (II Kings 17:13, 14).

What's the Book About

The book of II Kings is about bad kings causing lots of trouble and God's leaders and prophets following God and doing so much good!

Good Things and Bad Things

At the beginning of II Kings, Elijah goes to be with God in a very amazing way. Elisha, Elijah's helper, becomes God's next special prophet. God does many miracles of love and kindness through Elisha, just as He did through the prophet Elijah before him.

Elisha reminds the people that the Lord is more loving and powerful than any idol, because false gods cannot feel or hear or help! Elisha's words to the people are that only the true God should ever be loved and worshiped.

Sadly, many of God's people still don't listen to Elisha. They keep on worshiping idols made of gold, wood, or stone. Until the people choose to turn back to God for His love and help, God will not do all the great and powerful things He wants to do for them.

Let's Meet the People of II Kings

Elijah was the prophet God sent to help the people come back to Him.

Elisha was Elijah's helper who became the next prophet to God's people in the Northern Kingdom of Israel.

The Shunammite Woman and her husband gave Elisha a room to stay in when he traveled through their town. Because she was kind to Elisha, he prayed that God would give her a child. The next year, she had a baby boy. When the boy later got sick and died, God helped Elisha bring him back to life.

Naaman was the army leader and hero in the land of Syria. He had a terrible disease called leprosy. A little servant girl who worked for Naaman's wife, told him about God's prophet Elisha. Elisha could heal Naaman, so God made Naaman well again!

Jericho – was the place where Elijah's life on earth came to an end as he went to be with God in a whirlwind. Then, Elisha became the next prophet to God's people in Israel.

Shunem – the town where Elisha brought a boy back to life and where he helped a woman get olive oil to sell for money that her family needed.

Gilgal – where Elisha took care of a group of young preachers by taking poison out of the stew they were about to eat. He made a little bit of food feed a lot of people. He even made the heavy head of an ax to float so it could be given back to its owner. He did it all by the mighty power of God. Gilgal is also the place where Naaman came to see Elisha and to ask the prophet to make him well from the disease of leprosy.

Dothan – the city where the King of Syria found Elisha and wanted to kill him. Elisha prayed that the Syrian soldiers would become blind so that he could capture them without getting hurt. God answered Elisha's prayer.

STORIES AND ACTIVITIES FROM II KINGS

A Bald-Headed Man

(A funny poem)

What will I need? Just you, your child, and the Bible
Where is it in the Bible? II Kings 2:23-24
How long will it take? 5-10 minutes
What age child? 3-11 years
Will it work in a group? Yes
Can it be played in the car? Yes
Will it work in a school classroom? Yes, preschool–5th grade

Read the dramatic story of the bald-headed man and the bears from II Kings 2:23-24 and add a little necessary explanation to this unusual story.

The men who were mocking and teasing Elisha about his bald head were not children, they were an immoral and evil mob who were from the center of idol worship in Israel.

When they mocked Elisha, they were really showing their great disrespect for God's power and the message Elisha spoke for Him. They were trying to keep him from telling them God's Truth, and that was very serious. Elisha didn't call for the bears to come and attack the men himself, God sent them as punishment for the evil in the hearts of the men and the way they behaved.

A very important message we can pass on to our children is that it is always important to show respect for the leaders, God sends to give His message of truth to us. Even when we don't agree with the leaders, we should pray for them instead of saying bad things about them. If they are doing something that doesn't please God, He is wise enough and strong enough to correct them and change their hearts.

When someone teaches us God's Word in truth, we need to respect him or her. There will be many times in our child's life that we will want him to listen and heed the messages God sends through a youth pastor or minister. We will be very thankful we taught our child to respect the leaders God provides to help us in our spiritual lives!

After telling the serious story from II Kings 2:23-24, lighten up things a bit with this silly mystery rhyme about hair. Ask your child to guess what you are describing in the rhyme.

Sometimes swirly, sometimes curly
Sometimes boyish, sometimes "girly"
Sometimes dark, sometimes light
Sometimes black, sometimes white.

Some wear braids, some wear twists
Some wear curls the size of fists.
Some wear it short, some wear it long
We have days when it looks all wrong!

Most everyone has some, some have more.
Some wear theirs clear down to the floor!
Some wear it flat, some wear it tall
Some have none of it at all!

What is it? Hair! What kind of person has none at all? Elijah must have been a man with little or no hair at all, but he was a man of God!

100 Hungry Men
(II Kings 4)

Read the beautiful example of how God provided food for the young prophets in Elisha's training school through a kind man named Baal Shalishah. Share with your child that since Elisha's day similar needs have been met in sometimes amazing ways for people who love and serve God.

If you have had a personal experience in which God has wonderfully met a need for you or your family or if you know of a testimony from someone else, be sure to share the story with your child. Explain that God did not only do wonderful and amazing things a long time ago to help His people, but He still does the same in our world today. Look for the many things God provides that are often overlooked or are considered to be coming from a more "natural" source, when they are really the evidence of God's gracious hand in your lives.

You may want to look for a book about the work of John Mueller, Mother Theresa, or a missionary who has experienced God's provision in their life. Help your child develop the habit of looking for opportunities to be a Baal Shalishah in someone else's life.

Make a giant cookie in a pizza pan or a foot-long subway sandwich and invite some friends, family or neighbors to enjoy eating it with you. Be sure they get to hear the story of Elisha and the 100 men, too.

The Little Girl Who Saved a Life

(A television interview)

What will I need? Something to pretend to use as a microphone and a box with a hole cut in the front to look like a television set. The box should also have the bottom removed so that your child can put her head into it and pretend to be on television.
Where is it in the Bible? II Kings 5:1-27
How long will it take? 10-15 minutes
What age child? 3-10 years
Will it work in a group? Yes, with some children as the audience and others being interviewed
Can it be played in the car? Yes, without the props
Will it work in a school classroom? Yes, preschool–5th grade

The story of Naaman and the little servant girl from Israel is a favorite of children! Enjoy reading parts of it directly from your Bible and telling part of it in your own words. If your child is familiar with the story, ask him to tell you the events that he knows as you fill in the narrative.

With the story fresh in your minds, conduct a television interview with your child pretending that she is the little servant girl. Ask questions for her to answer such as:
How did you become a servant? Whose servant were you (verse 2)?
Who was Captain Naaman? Was Captain Naaman an important man (verse 1)?
The Bible says that something was wrong with Naaman. What was it?
What did you tell Naaman's wife that probably made her very excited (verse 3)?

Continue asking questions that tell the story of Naaman being healed from leprosy. Remind your child that God often uses doctors, medicine, and the amazing way He made our bodies to help us get better when we are sick or hurt. We should always pray to Him to heal us, because He is the only one who can actually do that.

Taken Away

(A remembering activity)

What will I need? A tray with 8-10 small items such as a hair bow, a one inch screw, ink pen, a small toy, a rock, etc.
Where is it in the Bible? II Kings 17:37-40; II Kings 18, 24
How long will it take? 10-15 minutes
What age child? 5-12 years
Will it work in a group? Yes
Can it be played in the car? Not easily
Will it work in a school classroom? Yes, 1st–6th grade (Adjust the items on the tray to the age of your children.)

Show the items to your child. Ask him to take a good look and try to remember everything that is on the tray, because you are going to take away one thing, and he must guess what is missing. Ask him to close his eyes and turn his back while you remove one item from the tray. See if he can identify what you took away. Repeat the game several times, taking turns being the remover and the guesser.

The Bible tells us about something that was also taken away, God's own people. As they lived in the promised land and served and obeyed God, their lives were very good. God always knew what was best for His people and He wanted to bless them. But God's people did not always obey Him. God could not bless them when they were doing wrong and foolishly worshiping false gods. When the people started doing things their own way instead of God's good way, they grew more unhappy. God warned them over and over that they would have to be punished if they kept on disobeying Him, just like parents must do when their children will not obey them.

Finally, after God sent many prophets to warn the people of what would happen if they wouldn't obey God, He had to keep His word and punish them. God let an enemy army from Assyria march into the promised land and capture the people and take them away to a strange land where they would never be free again.

God's people in Judah stayed in their own land for a while longer, because they had more years of worshiping God with good kings than Israel did, but they also kept on disobeying God, too. Finally, (II Kings 24, 25:21b) they were also taken away from their homes in the promised land. They were captured three times by their enemies, the Babylonians, whose king was named Nebuchadnezzar. The leaders of God's people were taken away to the strange land of Babylon, where they lived for 70 years. If only they had just obeyed God, what a good life they would have had. Let's be sure to learn from the mistakes of God's people in the Bible so we won't have to learn from our own.

King Josiah and The Temple
II Kings 25

The people of God had been worshiping idols and had let the temple fall into bad shape, since it wasn't even being used. Because there had been so many evil kings leading the Israelites they had stopped serving the God, even the scrolls with God's Word and laws had been lost. Because God's Word was not being read to the people, they were not doing what was right.

When Hilkiah, the priest, found the Word of God in the Temple, he made sure King Josiah heard about the great discovery. When the king learned what was written in God's Word, he became extremely upset. The people were not doing what God wanted them to do. Once Josiah knew what God had said in His Word, he wanted the people to start right away to obey and serve God.

The king called for all the leaders and the people to come together to the temple. The whole book of God's law was read to them. After King Josiah and all the people heard what God told them in His Word, they made a promise to obey the Lord all time.

King Josiah and the people started right away to get rid of everything that had to do with worshiping idols. They began worshiping God just as God's people had done years before. King Josiah was a very good king, and the people were happy serving God. But after he died, another bad king came to the throne, and the people were sad.

Finally, God's people were taken away from their homes and their land by the Babylonians and couldn't come back for 70 years.

What Can I Learn from II Kings

1. Three young children in the book of II Kings were used in very special ways by God—the servant girl of Naaman's wife, 7-year-old King Joash, and 8-year-old King Josiah. If I give my life to God, He will use me—right now.

2. God can do anything. He shows us that is true in II Kings by doing some amazing things for the people through Elisha, the prophet/preacher. God can and will do everything that is best for me, no matter what it is, because He has all power, and He loves me.

3. When God's people kept on disobeying Him and paying no attention to what He told them, God had no choice but to keep His word and punish them, just as He had promised. I must obey my parents, my teachers, and especially, God—because I love them, they love me, and I don't want to be punished for doing wrong!

4. When King Josiah and God's people found God's lost Word hidden in the temple, they read it and right away started doing what God said! The Bible is very important to me. I want to learn what God says and then do it!

Important Verses To Remember

II Kings 6:17 – "And Elisha prayed, 'O Lord, open his eyes so he may see.' Then the Lord opened the servant's eyes, and he looked and saw the hills full of horses and chariots of fire all around Elisha."

II Kings 8:19 – "Nevertheless for the sake of his servant David, the Lord was not willing to destroy Judah. He had promised to maintain a lamp for David and his descendants forever."

II Kings 13:23a – "But the Lord was gracious to them and had compassion and showed concern for them because of his covenant with Abraham, Isaac and Jacob."

II Kings 17:36, 39 – "The Lord, who brought you up out of Egypt with mighty power and outstretched arm, is the one you must worship. To him you shall bow down and to him offer sacrifices. Worship the Lord your God; it is he who will deliver you from the hand of all your enemies."

We can relate to the real people and events of II Kings. We observe God doing amazing miracles through His prophets, Elijah and Elisha, in order to meet physical and spiritual needs of ordinary people. If we've truly been paying attention to what has happened in the events of our own lives, God has similarly met our own needs and wants, over and over again. Sometimes He has worked through ordinary means and circumstances, and sometimes He has temporarily set aside the natural for the supernatural–all for our benefit!

God dramatically opened the spiritual eyes of Gehazi, Elisha's servant (II Kings 6:16-17) and quelled all fear that had arisen in him at the sight of seemingly insurmountable events designed by the enemy to defeat the Lord's servants. Through Gehazi's incredible visual miracle, we are reminded that God's mighty unseen army also surrounds us at all times, with prior provision already made for every need and problem that we, too, may encounter.

Regardless of the surprise and devastating shock we may experience at the sudden and intense situations we find ourselves facing, the Lord who directs our lives and provides for our needs is never, ever caught off guard. He's totally prepared to reveal His presence and provision in His perfect time.

We must never be so foolish to assume that because God does not immediately call to our attention the unchecked attitudes and acts of sin in our own lives that He has chosen to overlook them and treat them lightly. God does notice the wrong we choose to do, and it does matter to Him. If we continue to regard lightly what He takes seriously, we, too, will feel the sting of His punishment in our lives. After all, we are His children and whom the Lord loves, He lovingly chastens.

We should desperately want to hear God's Word, read it, strive to understand what God is saying to us and desires of us, and then to set right out to do the Word in our daily lives. That kind of practical determination, coupled with the power of God, will transform the seemingly natural occurrences we experience into supernatural appointments and opportunities.

I Chronicles God's Book About the Way God

Led His People in the Past
"Give thanks to the Lord, call on his name; make known among the nations what he has done. Sing to him, sing praise to him; tell of all his wonderful acts" (I Chronicles 16:8-9).

What's the Book About

The book of I Chronicles is the historical record of how God led His people and took care of them from the time of Adam until the time of King David .

Making an Important List

The book of I Chronicles opens at the beginning of God's plan for the people He loves so much, starting with the name of the first man He made, Adam. The book reminds us that God took care of His people on a long trip from Egypt across the desert and gave them a wonderful new land, where they began to live. More and more of God's people were born and grew up there. I Chronicles gives us a long list of the names of the people of God who lived long ago and why they were important to the Lord and to us.

The rest of I Chronicles is about the story of David, the shepherd boy, who became the important King of Israel. We can read in I Chronicles, like we did in II Samuel, some good things about David and some news about God's people. We can learn again about the plans for the beautiful temple that David's son, Solomon, would build, where the people could worship God!

Let's Meet the People of I Chronicles

There is a whole long list of names of God's special people. You can read all of them in I Chronicles 1–9.

David is the shepherd boy who became the important King of Israel.

Solomon, was David's son, who became the new and very wise king of God's people after David died. Solomon was the one God chose to build the beautiful temple in the city of Jerusalem.

Here are the Places of I Chronicles

God's Promised Land – Israel was the special home for God's people that He gave to them and where they settled and lived.

Jerusalem – the important city where Solomon built the beautiful temple for God's people to go to worship Him.

The Name Game

(A naming game)

What do I need? A timer
Where is it in the Bible? I Chronicles 1–9
How long will it take? 10-15 minutes
What age child? 3-12 years
Will it work for a group? Yes
Can it be played in the car? Yes
Will it work in a school classroom? Yes, preschool–6th grade

Set a timer and see how many names of your child's friends he and you can name before the time runs out! If your child enjoys the game, set the timer again and try to beat the clock as you name as many fierce animals, sea creatures, colors, Bible people, etc. as you can. Instead of competing against each other, try to beat your own record as a team!

Help your child find I Chronicles 1–9 in his own Bible and explain it is where we find a long list of names of God's people. If you could read the list of names in those chapters fast enough to beat the timer, you would definitely win any naming contest. Tell your child that if the book of I Chronicles were long enough to include all the names of God's people who have lived since then and who love Him, your name and his name would be there, too!

The reason God put all those names in the Bible was to remind His people about the special family of believers they were a part of and that we are a part of, too.

One Extra-Special Man Named Jabez

(A prayer to share)

What do I need? You, your child, and a prayer time together
Where is it in the Bible? I Chronicles 4:9-10
How long will it take? 5-10 minutes
What age child? 3-12 years
Will it work in a group? Yes
Can it be played in the car? Yes, but the driver must not close her eyes!
Will it work in a school classroom? Yes, preschool–6th grade

Explain that in the long list of names there was one person that God told us more about than most of the other people. His name was Jabez. The Bible says that Jabez was important because he was one who prayed to God. That makes us feel special, too, because praying is something that both children and adults can do.

But the prayer Jabez prayed was important especially because of what was in Jabez's heart when he said the special words, "Bless me and enlarge my territory! Let your hand be with me, and keep me from harm."

Pray that wonderful prayer as a desire of your own heart for yourself and for your child. Help your child to understand that we need and want God:

1. To bless us. Ask what kinds of blessings or good things she wants that come from God.

2. To help us in our work. Talk about the wonderful fact that God is with us everywhere we are and is always ready to help us as we work and play.

3. To be with us in all we do. Remind your child that Jesus goes everywhere with us, hears every word we speak, and sees everything we do.

4. To keep us from evil and harm. Explain that it is good to ask God to keep us safe from anything that can hurt us, whether it is sinful actions, thoughts, and attitudes that hurt us or something that can hurt our body.

Pray with your child, using the prayer Jabez prayed as an example of some important things we need to talk with God about. At other prayer times, encourage your child to pray more spontaneous prayers so that he may grow in his personal, intimate communication and conversation with his loving Heavenly Father.

What Can I Learn from I Chronicles

The book of I Chronicles shows that God has taken care of His people for a long, long time and that there were many people who loved and served Him before I was even born! I know that God loves me and takes care of me, and I want people to know that I love Him, too.

Important Verses to Remember

I Chronicles 4: 9a-10 – "Jabez was more honorable than his brothers. Jabez cried out to the God of Israel, 'Oh, that you would bless me and enlarge my territory! Let your hand be with me, and keep me from harm so that I will be free from pain.' And God granted his request."

I Chronicles 15:16 – "David told the leaders of the Levites to appoint their brothers as singers to sing joyful songs, accompanied by musical instruments: lyres, harps and cymbals."

I Chronicles 16:10-11 – "Glory in his holy name; let the hearts of those who seek the Lord rejoice. Look to the Lord and his strength; seek His face always."

I Chronicles 16:23-25 – "Sing to the Lord, all the earth; proclaim his salvation day after day. Declare his glory among the nations, his marvelous deeds among all peoples. For great is the Lord and most worthy of praise; he is to be feared above all gods."

I Chronicles 16:34 – "Give thanks to the Lord, for he is good; his love endures forever."

A Devotional Thought for Parents and Teachers

We would be hard-pressed to find a more important message from the book of I Chronicles than the words of praise that David prayed in I Chronicles 29:10-13. Read and pray David's words to the mutual and eternal God you both love and serve and allow the words to be your personal and sincere expression of praise to the Lord, who is worthy of all our praise and honor.

II Chronicles God's Book About God's Beautiful Temple, Good Kings, and Bad Kings

"If my people, who are called by my name, will humble themselves and pray and seek my face and turn from their wicked ways, then will I hear from heaven and will forgive their sin and will heal their land" (II Chronicles 7:14).

What's the Book About

The book of II Chronicles is about King Solomon and the beautiful temple he built for God and about other kings, some who chose to follow God and others who did not.

A Trip Through Time to Meet 20 Kings

This special book starts by telling again the story of Solomon, the wise king. It tells us about the wonderful, beautiful temple that Solomon led God's people to build in Jerusalem and reminds us how important it is to worship God.

Second Chronicles takes us on a trip through time to meet 20 kings of the land of Judah. Most of them were so evil that we would run and hide from them, but five of them were good kings: Asa, Jehoshaphat, Uzziah, Hezekiah and Josiah. When good kings led God's people, they brought the people back to God by getting rid of the false idols and everything that did not please the real, living God. When the kings and the people loved and obeyed God, there was peace in their land. All was well with them. But when the bad kings led God's people away from God to serve the idols, they had lots of problems they couldn't fix.

God's people turned away from serving Him over and over again. Every time they were truly sorry for their sin, He would open His heart of great love to welcome them back and forgive everything they had done.

Solomon was King David's son, who became the wise and good king of Israel.

Rehoboam was Solomon's son, who was not nearly as good a king as his father. Rehoboam even caused the people of God to split into two waring groups instead of living as one family.

Jerusalem – the important city of Judah, where Solomon built the beautiful temple for people to come worship God.

STORIES AND ACTIVITIES FROM II CHRONICLES

Bible Match

(A musical trip)

What will I need? A bag of candy, some construction paper, and your favorite traveling music
Where is it in the Bible? II Chronicles
How long will it take? 5-10 minutes
What age child? 2-9 years
Will it work in a group? Yes
Can it be played in the car? Sure, pretend to travel while you travel.
Will it work in a school classroom? Yes, preschool–3rd

Play a candy matching game with your child. Provide a bag of candy that comes in various colors. Cut construction paper shapes out of corresponding colors. Spread the colored paper shapes out on the table, and ask your child to place the colored candy pieces on the papers that they match. Talk about things that match like twins, the two wheels on a bicycle, the four tires on a car, two ponytails in a girl's hair, two eyes, two hands, etc.

As your child divides up the candy by colors, talk about the way that I and II Chronicles match other books in the Bible. First Chronicles matches II Samuel, and II Chronicles matches I and II Kings. Tell your child that God planned the Bible that way so that I and II Chronicles can help us understand Samuel and Kings better. Ask why he thinks it is important to read the Bible and to understand what it says to us.

Talk sincerely with your child about your own love for God's Word and explain that God shows us what to believe and how to live our lives through the Bible. Discuss the two parts of the Bible: the Old Testament contains what happened before Jesus was born, and the New Testament relates what took place when Jesus came to earth and afterward. Talk about the 66 books of the Bible and the many different kinds of people God used to write His Word (shepherds, kings, preachers, farmers, doctors, fishermen, a tax collector, etc.).

Help your child understand what a treasure our Bible is. God has made sure that His Word has been protected so that we could have it today and learn all He wants us to know!

Tell your child that many children and adults in different parts of the world would give nearly everything they own to have a Bible. We should always treat God's Word with care and with thankful hearts.

What Can I Learn from II Chronicles

God's people had to learn the same hard lesson over and over: If we love and obey God, things go well for us, and we have peace in our hearts and in our land. Every time we stop following Him, we get ourselves in lots of trouble! I want to remember all my life that serving God is always the very best way to live!

Important Verses to Remember

II Chronicles 7:3b – "He is good; his love endures forever."

II Chronicles 7:14 – "If my people, who are called by my name, will humble themselves and pray and seek my face and turn from their wicked ways, then will I hear from heaven and will forgive their sin and will heal their land."

II Chronicles 16:9 – "For the eyes of the Lord range throughout the earth to strengthen those whose hearts are fully committed to him."

II Chronicles 30:9b – "For the Lord your God is gracious and compassionate. He will not turn his face from you if you return to him."

A Devotional Thought for Parents and Teachers

Every generation carries the awesome responsibility and privilege of passing on the Word of God to those within our sphere of influence. Those who have faithfully served the Lord in generations and centuries past serve as examples of faith. Their trust in God cannot compensate for any lack of commitment on our part. Nor can our personal faith be transmitted to our children without a conscious decision and an openness of heart on their part to receive God for themselves.

No matter the length of the list of one's godly genealogy, one break in that continuity of faith can plunge future generations into a downward tailspin of ungodliness and faithlessness. Tradition, customs, and ancestry alone is not enough. We must pass the Truth of God on to the next waiting generation and to the next. Our work is cut out for us as long as we live. Let's get on with it! There are some precious children and grandchildren counting on us!

Ezra — God's Book About His People Going Back Home and the Temple Being Rebuilt
"But now, for a brief moment, the Lord our God has been gracious" (Ezra 9:8a).

What's the Book About

The book of Ezra is about the first and second groups of God's people going back home to the promised land, rebuilding the temple, and learning how important it is to obey God's Word.

God Gives His People Good News about the Future

Ezra opens with God's temple completely ruined and God's people living in the land of Babylon, where they had not been free to go back home to their own land for almost 70 years. That was a long time! We can understand that it must have been a sad time for God's people.

Years before God's people were taken to live in Babylon, God told His prophet Jeremiah to tell the people that even though they would be taken away from their homes, God was still with them. He loved them, and one day they would go back home. That was great news! God also told the same awesome message to His prophet Isaiah. God told Isaiah that a king named Cyrus would help the people go back to their homes, and he did. Only God could have known the name of King Cyrus before he was born, and God told Isaiah to write about him.

God knows everything that will happen before it does. We can remember what happened in the past, but we don't know what will happen in the future. God knows everything, and when He tells us in His Word what will happen later, that's called "prophecy." What God says always comes true.

Just as God had said, King Cyrus of Persia fought against the Babylonians and Cyrus's army won. Then, King Cyrus announced that God's people could go back home. Zerubbabel led the first group of people back home to their homeland. Ezra, who believed what God had promised, led the second group of people back home later. It was a very exciting and happy time for the Israelites.

Let's Meet the People of Ezra

Cyrus was the King of Persia who won the war against Babylon. King Cyrus said that God's people were free to go back home, and they did!

Zerubbabel was a man who loved God and led the first group of God's people back to the promised land.

Haggai and **Zechariah** were two of God's prophets who helped the people stay strong while they rebuilt the temple, making it a beautiful place to worship God again.

Ezra was a teacher, preacher, and scribe (a writer) who led the second group of God's people back to their own homes.

Let's Visit the Places of Ezra

Babylon – The army of Babylon captured God's people here and kept them captive for 70 years.

Jerusalem – The temple and the city of Jerusalem were both destroyed by the Babylonians, but Zerubbabel and Ezra, God's leaders, helped rebuild the temple to worship God there again!

STORIES AND ACTIVITIES FROM EZRA

Let's Go Home
(A traveling home game)

What do I need? Paper, crayons, and a pencil
Where is it in the Bible? Ezra 1–2 and 7–8
How long will it take? 5-10 minutes
What age child? 3-11 years
Will it work for a group? Yes
Can it be played in the car? Yes, if you make the trip a looking adventure,
Will it work in a school classroom? Yes, preschool–5th grade

Take a picture of the outside of your house or ask your child to draw a picture of it. Then, help your child compose a story titled, "Our Home."

"My name is _____, and I live in a ____ (describe house) house on_____(address) in _____(city and state). In my family there are _____ (number of) people, my (siblings and parents) and _____ (number) pets. The kind of pets we have are _____, and their names are _____. I like my house because_____. I like the yard I have because_____. I like my neighbors. Their names are_____. Sometimes my neighbors and I like to_____. The very best things about my house and our neighborhood are _____.

The place we live is called our house, but it is the people in our family make it our home. Thank You, God, for my home.

Ask your child how he would feel if someone took your family away from their home for 70 years. Explain that God's people had that very thing happen to them. Ask how he would feel if he heard the great news that he could go home after being gone for a long time. Think about how things might have changed in 70 years.

Open your Bible to Ezra chapters 1, 2, 7, and 8 which tell how God's people went back home in two big groups. The first group went with a man named Zerubbabel, and the second group went home about 80 years later led by Ezra.

Take a minute to thank God for your home and family, because there are some people who don't have homes and families.

Now, Let's Get Busy

King Cyrus was now in charge of Babylon after his armies won the war with the Babylonians. Cyrus told the Israelite people they could go back home to the land God had given them. Cyrus even gave them back more than 5,000 gold and silver bowls and other valuable things that King Nebuchadnezzar had taken from the temple in Jerusalem when he destroyed it years before.

Soon, thousands of God's people and their horses, mules, camels, and donkeys traveled back home across dangerous territories to the promised land. God kept them safe all the way home.

One of the most important reasons the Israelite people were excited about going back home was so they could rebuild the temple. Many people gave their gold and silver to build it. One of the first things they did was to make an altar and worship God! The people were very thankful for God's kindness to them.

When the foundation of the temple was laid, the people had a big celebration, and some of the older gentlemen, who still remembered how Solomon's beautiful temple looked before it was destroyed, cried out loud with joy and thanksgiving!

Even though some enemies tried to stop the rebuilding of the temple, it was finally finished.

We're Very, Very Sorry
(An "I'm sorry" activity)

What will I need? You, your child, and his Bible
Where is it in the Bible? Ezra 9 –10
How long will it take? 10-15 minutes
What age child? 4-12 years
Will it work in a group? Yes
Can it be played in the car? Yes, a good car conversation
Will it work in a school classroom? Yes, older preschool–7th grade

Ask your child about the following situations. Who needs to be sorry to whom and why? Make up some of your own scenarios; here are a few for starters:
1. A child talks back to his mother.
2. A father embarrasses his son for a mistake he made, even though it was an accident.
3. A boy hits his friend.
4. A girl sticks her tongue our at another girl.
5. A child gets mad because his mother won't let him eat some cookies before dinner.
6. A mother forgets to keep her promise to her child.
7. A teacher doesn't bring the snack she told the class she would.
8. A boy comes running around the corner and bumps into a friend in the hall.
9. Somebody doesn't bother to pray for days and days.
10. A girl doesn't go to church because she wants to stay home and play instead.

If your child is old enough to complete an acrostic, here are some ideas to get you started.
I - insults
M - mean looks
S - selfishness

O - out of control, objecting
R - rudeness
R - rowdiness, ridicule
Y - yelling in class or church

Explain that when Ezra led the second group of God's people back to their homes, he was very sad to see that the people who were already there were not serving God as they should. Ezra prayed that God would help them to be sorry for their sins. Read Ezra 9:5-11 and explain the verses to your child. Then read Ezra 10:1 and see how the people reacted to Ezra's prayer!

Ezra held a special meeting of the leaders in front of the temple, and the Bible even tells us what the weather was like that day! Read Ezra 10:9 and 13 to see what the weatherman would have reported on that day!

How did the men act as they were meeting out in the open that day? Why did they act as they did?

What Can I Learn from Ezra

God promised His people that even though they had done wrong and had to leave their land and homes because of their sin, one day He would let them go back, and they did. I can count on God to always keep His promises to me, too.

Important Verses to Remember

Ezra 3:11 – "With praise and thanksgiving they sang to the Lord: 'He is good; his love to Israel endures forever'. "

Ezra 7:27a – "Praise be to the Lord, the God of our fathers . . . "

Ezra 8:22b – "The gracious hand of our God is on everyone who looks to him, but his great anger is against all who forsake him."

Ezra 9:15a – "O Lord, God of Israel, you are righteous!"

A Devotional Thought for Parents and Teachers

There are many encouraging messages in the book of Ezra:
1. God is always faithful to His people and keeps every promise He makes.
2. When God puts a passion in our hearts and minds to do a task for Him, He provides all the resources we will need, from start to finish, regardless of the opposition we may face.
3. Nothing good and great ever is accomplished for God and eternity without opposition, because God's enemy Satan is our enemy, too. Satan is relentless in his efforts, but he's on the losing team, and we will be victorious through Jesus Christ our Lord!
4. God's Word is an ageless, living sword that penetrates our thoughts, attitudes, and hearts. As we focus on what God says to us through the Bible, He will make us His new, clean, useful, and highly contagious servants, and our lives will be amazing.

Nehemiah God's Book About How the Walls Were Built and the People Returned to God "They realized that this work had been done with the help of our God" (Nehemiah 6:16b).

What's the Book About

The book of Nehemiah tells us about the third group of God's people who went back home. This is Nehemiah's own story about the things that happened as God's people rebuilt the walls of Jerusalem and what happened after they were finished.

A King Grants a Special Request

Nehemiah, an Israelite, is living in the palace of King Artaxerxes of Persia. Although two groups of God's people have already gone back to the promised land, some of the Israelites, like Nehemiah, are still living in the land where they were brought by their enemies years before. The people weren't free to leave for 70 years.

Because God's people had lived away from their homes for so long, many of them had been given jobs to do in the lands of Babylon, Assyria, and Persia. Nehemiah's job was to be the king's cup-bearer. A cup-bearer was one who made sure that the king's food and drink were safe to eat and drink, and Nehemiah did a good job.

Nehemiah had never been free to live in the promised land he called home, but he still loved the land, because it had been given to his people by God, and Nehemiah loved God. The city of Jerusalem, where the temple had been built by King Solomon and rebuilt by Zerubbabel, was in the promised land.

As Nehemiah's story begins, he has some guests who have come to visit him from Jerusalem. Nehemiah asks them a very important question and hears some very bad news.

Let's Meet the People of Nehemiah

Nehemiah took the third group of God's people back to Judah to live. He helped fix the broken walls and gates around the city of Jerusalem.

Ezra was the High Priest who read God's Word to the people and helped them start obeying God again.

Sanballat and **Tobiah** did not want anything good to happen to God's land or His people. The two men, and some of their mean friends, kept on teasing Nehemiah and the other workers, making their jobs harder as they worked to build the wall around Jerusalem. But God's people finished the wall, anyway!

<table>
<tr><td>Here are the Places of Nehemiah</td><td>Jerusalem – the important city where the temple had been rebuilt by Zerubbabel and God's people, and where Nehemiah went to live and rebuild the broken walls and burned gates.</td></tr>
</table>

STORIES AND ACTIVITIES FROM NEHEMIAH

Bad News for Nehemiah

Nehemiah was a man who loved God. He lived in a place called Shushan far away from his home in the promised land. Even though thousands of God's people had already gone back home, Nehemiah had not gotten to go with them.

Nehemiah lived inside the palace of King Artaxerxes in the kingdom of Persia. It was Nehemiah's job to be the king's cup-bearer. That meant that he had to make sure the king's food was safe for the king to eat and drink. The kings in those days had lots of enemies, and some of the enemies were so mean that they might even try to get rid of the king by putting poison in his food!

One day another Jewish man came to visit Nehemiah. The visitor's name was Hanani, and he had just come from the land of Judah, where many of God's people were now living again. Nehemiah asked his guest how things were going back home, but the news he heard was not good!

Hanani said that the wall, around the city of Jerusalem and the temple, was still torn down, and the gates were burned, too. That was terrible news to Nehemiah, because he knew how important the wall around a city was to the people. If there was no wall, the people were not safe from their enemies, and their temple could easily be torn down again! God's people were in danger, and Nehemiah was very upset about it!

The King Says "Yes!"
(A polite game)

What will I need? You and your child
Where is it in the Bible? Nehemiah 2:1-9
How long will it take? 5-15 minutes
What age child? 3-11 years
Will it work in a group? Yes
Can it be played in the car? No
Will it work in a school classroom? Yes, preschool–5th grade

As the story begins, Nehemiah has heard from Hanani that the wall around Jerusalem is broken down. Nehemiah is very disturbed to hear the sad news, and he wants to help rebuild the walls. Nehemiah prays and doesn't even eat for several days, because he is so upset about the walls of Jerusalem and the sins of God's people. He prays to God to help him ask the powerful king of Persia for a big favor. Nehemiah wants to take a third group of people back to their home in the promised land and let them build Jerusalem's wall again.

Four months later, Nehemiah gets his chance to ask the king the huge favor. Nehemiah was scared because the King might become very angry at his request to go home to Jerusalem, but he didn't let being afraid stop him. He prayed another quick prayer to God before he asked the permission of the king, and the king said, "Yes!" Nehemiah said "Thank you" to the king, but he thanked God most of all.

King Artaxerxes gave Nehemiah some letters to give to the leaders of the countries Nehemiah and God's people would pass through on their way back home, asking that the travelers might go through their lands safely. One of the letters was to Asaph, the man who took care of the king's forest. The king asked him to give Nehemiah wood to use in building the city walls, the gates, and even a house for Nehemiah. God hears us when we pray, and He gives us everything we need. Nehemiah traveled home and became a very good leader of God's people and, yes, they built the wall once more.

Ask your child if Nehemiah understood who really answered his prayers and helped him go home to Judah. Read again the last sentence of Nehemiah 2:8 for the answer. Read verse 10 to find out the names of the two men who were very angry at God's people. Remember their names, because they try hard to cause trouble for Nehemiah and the people more than once.

Play a game like "Mother, May I?" but call it "Your Majesty, May I?" as a reminder of Nehemiah's request to King Artaxerxes. Ask your child to pretend to be Nehemiah. You or another child pretend to be King Artaxerxes.

Go to opposite ends of the room or yard. Suggest different kinds of steps he should take to get to you, i.e. "Nehemiah, you may take three giant steps, one scissor step, one backwards step, three hops, etc., until he reaches the king. The players should then switch places.

Poor, Poor People
(A sharing and caring opportunity)

What will I need? Gift certificates for fast food, usable items to take to the Salvation Army or Goodwill, or some non-perishable food items
Where is it in the Bible? Nehemiah 5
How long will it take? Not long – but worth the time and effort!
What age child? 3-12 years
Will it work in a group? Yes
Can it be played in the car? Yes, your car will be the delivery "cheer-mobile."
Will it work in a school classroom? Yes, the planning and organizing part. Then you can go into action on a field trip or short excursion outside the classroom. Preschool–6th grade

Even while Nehemiah was busy building the wall around Jerusalem and fighting against enemies who wanted to stop the work, his mind was still on the people in the city who were very, very poor. The reason God's people were poor was because there were some very greedy and unkind leaders who were making the poor people pay big taxes and big amounts of money to buy land. When the good people couldn't pay the money they were charged, their land and homes were taken away. They even had to sell their own children to be slaves, and Nehemiah was very upset about that!

Nehemiah's heart was like God's when it came to poor people. In almost every book of the Bible, God shows us that He wants His people to take care of poor people, and that's what Nehemiah did! He told the rich, greedy leaders to stop charging the poor people so much money and warned them that God was upset with them, too! Nehemiah knew how important all people are to God, and they should be to us, too.

Decide with your child on a project that your family can do to help poor people:

1. Buy fast food gift certificates to hand out to homeless or jobless people.

2. Take good, usable items to Salvation Army, Goodwill, or other benevolence agencies, or buy some inexpensive new things to give directly to families in need.

3. Make it a habit every time you shop for groceries to add one or two non-perishable items to your cart to give to your church's food pantry, food drive, etc.

4. Sponsor a needy child or someone who wants to go on a mission trip.

If you create within your child a generous spirit of compassion toward other people and give her a practical outlet for expressing that concern at an early age, she will very likely continue that way of thinking and living for all her life. What a wonderful contribution to her personal fulfillment and to others who need her help!

What Can I Learn from Nehemiah	1. Nehemiah was a man who knew what he should do for God and did it. God tells me in His Word what I should do, and I will do it.
	2. Nehemiah knew that God was the One Who would help him build the broken walls of Jerusalem, and he remembered to PRAY to God as he did the work. I should remember to pray often to God about the things that matter to me, because He hears me and will help me.
Important Verses To Remember	Nehemiah 2:20a – "I answered them by saying, 'The God of heaven will give us success'."
	Nehemiah 4:20b – "Our God will fight for us!"
	Nehemiah 5:19a – "Remember me with favor, O my God."
	Nehemiah 9:5b-6 – "Blessed be your glorious name, and may it be exalted above all blessing and praise. You alone are the Lord. You made the heavens, even the highest heavens, and all their starry host, the earth and all that is on it, the seas and all that is in them. You give life to everything, and the multitudes of heaven worship you."

God is in the business of working through ordinary people to accomplish extraordinary things. Throughout the generations, God has worked in the lives of individuals whom He has gifted with specific temperaments, characteristics, experiences, and abilities that He wants people to use to get important jobs done. As we depend upon the Lord's power, and call upon His ever available resources like Nehemiah did, we, too, will be used in amazing ways.

Whatever else God equips and assigns us to do during our lifetime, can you really think of anything more wonderful than to be entrusted by God to raise His little children, the ones He has expressly placed in our lives and homes? What a challenge. What a privilege.

Esther God's Book About a Good Queen Who Saved Her People

"And who knows but that you have come to royal position for such a time as this?" (Esther 4:14b).

What's the Book About

The book of Esther is about a brave queen who saved God's people from an evil plan to destroy them.

God's Timing for a Beautiful and Brave Queen

God put Esther in the right place at just the right time. King Ahasuerus is the ruler of the huge kingdom called Persia. As the book begins, Esther and many others of God's people are still living in Persia, since they were taken there from their homes a long time before. King Ahasuerus, also called King Xerxes I, and his wife Queen Vashti live in the palace.

Queen Vashti has made her husband angry, because she wouldn't obey his orders, and she has been sent away from the king's palace forever. Now the king wants a new queen, and he decides to have a contest to chose one!

The story of Esther begins with a big party in the king's palace. Lots of important people in Persia are there to celebrate, and the party lasts six months! At the same time that the king's celebration is going on in the palace garden, Queen Vashti is giving a party for the women in another part of the palace. Soon afterward, the trouble starts!

Esther was the young Jewish woman who was chosen by King Ahasuerus to become the new queen of Persia and was used by God to save His people from a terrible plan to destroy them all!

Mordecai was Esther's older cousin. He even adopted Esther to be his daughter because her own parents had died. He worked in the palace and discovered an evil plan to destroy the King and another plan to get rid of all God's people! Mordecai helped Esther know what to do when things looked bad!

King Ahasuerus (King Xerxes I) was the king of the huge land of Persia after the first group of God's people had left to go back home. Many of God's people still lived in Persia, and King Ahasuerus was the king who ruled over them.

Haman was the Prime Minister of Persia. When Mordecai wouldn't bow down and worship Haman, Haman thought up a terrible way to get even and tricked the king to go along with his awful plan!

Here are the Places of Esther

Persia – the big kingdom where Ahasuerus was king and where Esther, Mordecai, and Haman lived.

STORIES AND ACTIVITIES FROM ESTHER

God's People are in Danger!

The story of Queen Esther and God's people is one of drama, suspense, and even romance, all the elements of a best-selling book or movie! Help your child enjoy the continuing story of the important events in Esther's life and begin to see God's plan working out through her. Sit down, open the Bible to Esther 3 and 4, and tell the story.

Esther has been chosen to be the new queen for King Ahasuerus (also known as Xerses) of Persia. Esther is a beautiful young Jewish girl who serves God. She has come to live in the palace at an important time for God's people.

Soon after Esther becomes the queen, her older cousin Mordecai becomes an important leader in the land, too. One day Mordecai hears about a bad plan by some enemies of King Ahasuerus to kill the king. Mordecai tells Esther, who warns King Ahasuerus, and his life is saved!!

Soon more bad news comes to Mordecai. Haman, the bad guy in the story, is the second most important leader in the land of Persia; he is the Prime Minister. Haman is very proud of himself, and wants everyone to bow down to him!

Mordecai refuses to bow down to Haman, because Mordecai worships and serves only the true God. This makes Haman furious, and he thinks up an evil plan to kill Mordecai and all God's people (the Jews). Haman tricks the king into agreeing to his evil idea that everyone must bow down to the king. King Ahasuerus sends a message throughout the land that all the Jewish people will be killed unless they bow down to this earthly king. Mordecai is upset and so are all the other Jewish people!

When Esther hears the terrible news about the danger to her people, she is very afraid for her people and for herself. Mordecai encourages Esther to go and talk to the king and try to change his mind about destroying God's people. Mordecai believes God has made Esther the Queen at that special time so she can save her people.

Esther, however, is afraid to go to the king to talk unless he calls for her. If anyone, even the queen, were to go into the king's court without his permission, she would be killed. She would be saved only if the king would hold up his golden scepter to her. Esther agreed to put herself in danger for her people, and she said she would go in and talk to the king. Before she went, she wanted all God's people to go without food and pray for her!

Esther Helps Her People
(A crowd of people on paper)

What will I need? A big sheet or roll of paper and a marker, crayon or pencil
Where is it in the Bible? Esther 5
How long will it take? 20-30 minutes

What age child? 3-12 years
Will it work in a group? Yes
Can it be played in the car? The story can.
Will it work in a school classroom? Yes, preschool–6th grade. Trace around every student to make a real crowd of people and let each student draw features, hair, and clothes on his or her own outline.

Continue telling the story of Esther to your child. Here are the main events:
1. Queen Esther went before the king even though she knew he might be angry toward her, and she could lose her life. King Ahasuerus raised his scepter toward her, which meant that he gave her permission to come and talk to him. He asked her what she would like to have from him and promised to give it to her. Esther was safe so far!
2. Esther asked the king and Haman to be her guests at a dinner party the next night. When they came, the king asked Esther again what she really wanted. He even promised to give her anything she asked. Esther only asked the two men to come to another banquet the next day.
3. That night, the king couldn't sleep and began to read some books in the palace. As King Ahasuerus read the books and papers, he found out that Mordecai had never been given any reward for saving the king's life from the enemies who had wanted to kill him.
4. The king asked Haman, "What should I do to reward a man who truly pleases me?" Evil Haman thought King Ahasuerus was talking about him, and he was delighted.
5. Haman suggested that the way to reward that kind of hero would be to parade the man through the streets on the king's own horse, wearing the king's crown and robe. What a big surprise Haman got when he realized that

Mordecai would be the one the king would honor and not him!

6. Guess who led Mordecai through the streets on the king's horse, wearing the king's robe, and crown. It was Haman! Haman was very upset by this.

Tell this story of Esther helping her people by making a giant picture of Queen Esther and some of the other Jewish people that lived in Persia. Spread out a large sheet or roll of paper on the floor. Ask your child to lie down several times on the paper and trace around only his head and shoulders each time, making the outlines of a crowd of people on the paper.

Look over the outlines and choose one to be Queen Esther. Draw faces, hair, clothes, and jewelry on the outlines. If you wish, draw a crown with jewels and a royal robe on Queen Esther and leave all the other faces blank.

Haman, the Horrible
(Mad, bad crackers to make and eat)

What will I need? Graham cracker squares, peanut butter, marshmallow cream, chocolate chips (optional), toasted English muffins, and red hot cinnamon candies
Where is it in the Bible? Esther 3, 5–7
How long will it take? 15-20 minutes
What age child? 3-12 years
Will it work in a group? Yes
Can it be played in a car? You could make the cracker faces at home and take them along for a snack.
Will it work in a school classroom? Yes, preschool–6th grade

Continue the story of Esther, the king, Mordecai, and Haman. Review what has happened in the story, if you wish, or just pick up with what happens next.

Haman has an awful plan to trick the king into killing all the Jews in the land including Queen Esther and Mordecai.

In the last part of the story, Haman is leading Mordecai through the streets of the land, because King Ahasuerus is honoring Mordecai for saving his life.

Now Haman is really angry! Haman wants to eliminate Mordecai so much that he has even built a high tower (a gallows) to hang Mordecai on for all the people to see. Haman is a horrible man.

After the parade in honor of Mordecai, the king and Haman come to Esther's second banquet at the palace. God has given Esther and Mordecai a plan to save His people, and Haman doesn't know what is about to happen.

At dinner, the king asked Esther what she would like him to do for her. This is what she says, "I would like you to save my life and the lives of my people, the Jews, from our wicked enemy, Haman." When King Ahasuerus understood that Haman had tricked him into a plan to kill the Jews, the king was very angry. He commanded that horrible Haman be hanged on the very same gallows that he had built for Mordecai.

After Haman died, King Ahasuerus gave Mordecai Haman's job as the Prime Minister of the land. An exciting new message was sent to the people throughout the land that all the Jews would be saved! God had saved His people through Esther and Mordecai.

Ask your child to help you think of some kinds of good news that you like to hear. Maybe you are going to have special company, you are going on vacation, it's a snow day from school, there's a church party tonight, etc. End with the good new that Jesus loves you!

After you tell the story of Haman to your child, make these mad, bad crackers together. Here's how:

Cover graham cracker squares or round cookies with peanut butter and marshmallow cream. Add chocolate chip eyes, nose, and frowning mouth on each mad, bad cracker, then gobble him up to get rid of him!

For red-hot mad guys, spread the peanut butter and marshmallow on a toasted English muffins and add chocolate chips or red hot candy faces.

| **What Can I Learn from Esther** | God chose just the right time and place for Esther to live in the king's palace as the queen. He put her there because He had a plan for her life. God made me and has a wonderful plan for my life, too. |

Important Verses to Remember

Esther 4:14b – "And who knows but that you have come to royal position for such a time as this?"

Esther 4:16b – "I will go to the king, even though it is against the law. And if I perish, I perish."

A Devotional Thought for Parents and Teachers

In Esther's day and culture, women were expected to stay in the background, to serve their families (which is still a blessed and noble calling!), and to remain out of the religious and political limelight. But Esther was an exception to the "politically correct" mindset of the day. She was an ordinary person that God used to be a key player in His plan for His people—because she was willing to follow Him against seemingly insurmountable odds.

She emerged at a time and in the place that God had divinely appointed to risk her own life and reputation in order to fulfill a "royal" assignment for the King of all Kings. Whatever our vocation and opportunity in life, God will use us to the degree that we are available and open to His leadership and Lordship. He wants to accomplish through us the divine purposes and plans that will impact others forever. May we always be willing to say, "Here I am, Lord—use me."

Job God's Book About Believing in God Even When Bad Things Happen "The Lord gave and the Lord has taken away; may the name of the Lord be praised" (Job 1:21b).

What's the Book About

The book of Job is about a man named Job who kept on trusting God even when bad things happened to him and how God made good come out of so much bad.

Job Has Great Faith, and Satan Loses

As the story of Job begins, things are going very well for Job and his family. He is a man who loves God and lives his life to please God. He has a big family, many servants, lots of animals, and all the money he will ever need.

Sometimes we think only good things should happen to people who serve God. Job probably thought everything would always stay good in his life, but the same world Job lived in is our world, too, and it's not perfect like heaven. Bad things can happen both to people who don't love God and to people who do love God.

Let's Meet the People of Job

Almighty God is all-wise and all-powerful. He was with Job when things were good and when they turned bad. Even though Job didn't understand why things happened as they did and even when Job couldn't feel or see God right there with him, Job still trusted God. God always knows what He is doing, and God is always good. God promises us that all things work for the good of those who love Him. God did that for Job – and God does that for us.

Satan, or the devil, was once an angel of God, but he chose to become proud and evil (I John 3:8). Since that time, he has been the enemy of God and our enemy, too. Satan wanted to hurt God by making Job stop trusting in Him, and he wanted to tempt Job so Job would hate God. In his attempt to bring Job down, the devil wanted to prove that Job loved God only because God had done so many good things for Job and his family. Satan thought that if bad things took the place of good things in Job's life, he would stop loving and serving God. He was wrong!

Satan didn't get what he wanted in Job's heart, and he won't get what he wants in ours either, if we stay close to God who is much greater than Satan.

119

Job was a good man who trusted and obeyed God in good times and in bad.

Job's wife and friends (Eliphaz the Temanite, Bildad the Shuhite, and Zophar the Naamathite) try their best to influence Job during his difficulties. His friends came to visit him and, at first, sat quietly and joined Job in his sadness. Before long, however, the men begin to talk and talk about what terrible things Job must have done wrong to have so many bad things happen to him! Even Job's wife told him he might as well just stop loving God and die!

Job's friends and his wife were mixed-up about how good God is and how loving and close He is to us when we are going through hard times.

Here are the Places of Job

The Land of Uz – The place where Job lived with his family.

STORIES AND ACTIVITIES FROM JOB

Happy Days, Sad Days

Retell the conversation between Satan and God and what happened to Job. (Help children understand that the pronunciation of Job rhymes with "robe.") Talk about how Satan's statement to God was a true picture of why some people trust God, even today. People who follow God only when everything is going well could be called "fair weather" believers. When trouble strikes, they stop following God, and that's exactly what Satan predicted would happen to Job if God stopped sending only good things to him! Aren't you glad Satan was wrong about Job?

Here are the bad things that the devil sent Job's way to try to make him stop trusting God:

1. Evil men came and stole Job's oxen and donkeys and killed his servants!
2. Job's enemies stole his camels and killed the servants who were taking care of them.
3. Job's house blew down in a mighty windstorm, and his children were killed.
4. Job got very sick and almost died.

Even after all these bad things happened to Job, the Bible says in Job 1:22, "In all this, Job did not sin by charging God with wrongdoing."

Spend some valuable time preparing your child for the inevitable fact that sometimes bad things happen to God's people. Explain that ever since the garden of Eden and the sin of Adam and Eve in the book of Genesis, our world has not been perfect. Now we have different kinds of bad in our world, instead of only the good that God wanted for us in His perfect plan for a perfect world.

Remind your child that everybody, those who love God and those who don't, have both good and bad things happen at times in their lives. Because of that, we all need more than ever to stay close to God, because He loves us and is always with us to help make us strong and to bring good out of the bad things that happen. Help your child understand that our God is stronger than Satan.

Thank the Lord for being with us on happy days and unhappy ones, too.

Job's Friends
(A game about friends)

What will I need? Ten or more pieces of paper or index cards and a pen or pencil
Where is it in the Bible? Job 3–37
How long will it take? 15-20 minutes
What age child? 3-12 (Adapt the situations on the cards to his age.)
Will it work in a group? Yes
Can it be played in the car? Yes
Will it work in a school classroom? Yes, preschool–6th grade

Make up a game called "Good Friend/Bad Friend" to help your child recognize at a young age that not all people we think are our friends give us good advice or present to us an example that we should follow. The ability to discern the acquaintances our child should emulate and those he should avoid is an invaluable resource for those years ahead (and even now!) when your child will need to be wise and strong in the face of "friend-pressure!"

Thumb through Job 3–37 as your child watches, and explain to him that all those chapters are a long, long talk that Job's friends had with Job about the trouble he was having. Job's friends may have meant well, but they gave him some bad advice. Job is wise not to agree with all they say and not to do everything they suggest! Even Job's wife doesn't tell him the right thing to do to make his troubles go away!

Then play the good friend/bad friend game with your child. On slips of paper or index cards, write hypothetical situations in which a friend gives your child some good or bad advice. Read them one by one or take turns reading one and then answering one. Ask your child if the message the friend is giving your child is good or bad.

Please explain that not all friends who tell us things we shouldn't listen to are bad people, but what they are trying to get us to believe or do may be bad. Even good people can give bad advice, but we need to be careful to choose friends who act and live in a way that is good for them and us–friends who help us to live for God.

Here are some kinds of situations to write on paper (include some that your child is facing or that you think that he will probably face at some time):
1. My friend says, "Let's take some money from your mother's purse and get candy at the gas mart down the street."
2. "Let's watch that scary movie that's on T.V. tonight, even though your Mom and Dad don't let you watch that kind of show at home."
3. "Look at this magazine I found. None of the people have any clothes on! Come here, I'll show it to you."
4. Your friend is saying bad words and thinks it sounds cool. "What's the matter?" he says to you. "Do you just talk baby talk?" You know he wants you to use the words he's

using, and you don't want him to think you're a baby.

5. "Why don't you just pretend to be sick today so you won't have to go to school."

6. "Will you go with me when our Sunday School class gives out food to the poor people?"

7. "I know it will be hard, but I think you should tell your teacher the truth."

8. "You mean you go to bed at eight o'clock every night? I think you're smart to obey your Mom and Dad and get all the rest you need."

9. "If you're not supposed to do that at your house, I don't think you should do it here at my house either, even though your parents aren't here to tell you, 'No'."

10. "Let's go to church instead of skipping out to go to the school party. After all, we're supposed to put God first, isn't that right?"

Awesome and Powerful God!

(A volcano-in-a-bottle! Watch out!)

What will I need? A small plastic water bottle full of warm water, red food coloring, a cup of vinegar, a heaping teaspoon of baking soda, and a kitchen funnel

Where is it in the Bible? Job 36–41

How long will it take? 15-30 minutes

What age child? 2-12 years

Will it work in a group? Yes

Can it be played in the car? The discussion can be–but not the volcano!

Will it work in the school classroom? Yes, preschool-6th grade

Chapters 36–41 in Job are full of amazing verses about the power and majesty of God.

Get excited together as you talk about what the verses tell us about our awesome God.

Job 36:26-29; 38:25-30; 34-38 – Clouds, evaporation, and rain

Job 36:29–37:5,14-24 – Thunder and lightning and heat

Job 37:6-13; 38:22 – Snow, frost and hail

Job 38:4-18 – The world and universe God created

Job 38:31-33 – The stars and constellations

Job 38:39-41; 39—The animal kingdom God made and takes care of

Job 40:15-24 – A large animal God made

Job 41:1-34 – Another huge creature of the sea and land ·

Talk with your child about other creations of God that show His mighty power, like the wind, the ocean waves, and volcanoes! Although anything you could make is a very small reminder of God's truly incredible power, it might be fun to erupt a volcano in a bottle as you talk about the Lord's greatness.

Tell your child that the Mauna Loa volcano in Hawaii is the world's biggest volcano. Discover more about it and other volcanoes from books, encyclopedias, and the Internet. Make your own volcano by setting a small plastic water bottle in your sink and filling it three-fourths full of warm water. Add a few drops of red food coloring and one cup of vinegar.

Here comes the exciting part. Hold a kitchen funnel just above the bottle top and quickly add a heaping teaspoon of baking soda. Eeeeeee-ruption! The mixture will immediately fizz and foam and overflow its "banks" in the bottle.

Explain to your child that God created all the chemicals and gases in our world and that vinegar and baking soda make the very same gas, carbon dioxide, that causes the hot liquid rocks underneath the earth's surface to erupt into active volcanoes! Amazing!

God's Happy Ending to Job's Sad Story

After Job had talked to his friends for a long time, and after God had spoken to Job about His own awesome goodness, His greatness and His power, Job understood that God's ways are best, even when we don't understand what He is doing or why. Job was sorry for the questions he had worried so much about, and he was able to see more clearly than ever before how great God is and how we can always trust His ways of doing things. Job told God how sorry he was for not trusting Him completely all the time. Then Job prayed for his friends also to understand God's goodness, which was the right thing to do!

An amazing thing then happened to Job— God gave him back everything he had lost and more! God blessed Job and his wife with children and all the same kinds of things he had owned before. In fact, God gave him twice as much as he had ever had before, and, as you would expect, there was a great celebration in Job's home. Even after all the trouble Job had, the Bible says that when he was an old, old man and his life was over, he had lived a long, good life. Only God can turn bad things into great good, like He did for Job—and He does for us!

What Can I Learn from Job

Even though Job was a man who loved God, he still had problems. But God was there with him all the time, when things were good and when things got bad. I may have some not-so-good days in my life, but God will never, ever leave me, and He will make good come out of bad, because He loves me, and I love Him.

Important Verses to Remember

Job 1:22 – "In all this, Job did not sin by charging God with wrongdoing."

Job 2:10b – " 'Shall we accept good from God, and not trouble?' In all this, Job did not sin in what he said."

Job 8:21 – "He will yet fill your mouth with laughter and your lips with shouts of joy."

Job 12:13 – "To God belong wisdom and power; counsel and understanding are his."

Job 19:25 – "I know that my Redeemer lives, and that in the end he will stand upon the earth."

Where do we even begin as we consider the practical application of the experiences of Job to our lives? All of us have had those times when it seems as though what's happening to us makes no shred of sense or seems to have no purpose. Often we feel those situations can't be fixed, and we've tried everything imaginable. God seems to be absolutely silent on the subject of our problems and pain. What can we learn from Job that will help us?

1. The problems weren't Job's fault. Although we often do bring trouble on our own heads, sometimes we really have done nothing we can think of to cause what is happening. Neither did Job. He was a good man who loved God, and you love God, too.

2. Job had lots of questions, and so do we. But Job didn't get all his questions answered. Eventually, after he recognized God's awesome greatness and presence, he didn't even mind not knowing the answers. He had to experience life one day at a time, without a clue as to why everything was crumbling around him. We also need to acknowledge that God is good and trust Him, without answers to all life's hard questions at least, not until heaven.

3. Job's situation appeared absolutely hopeless, but it never really was. Eventually that was obvious. When our faith and confidence in God is based upon rewards or prosperity, we're in bad shape when those things are removed from our lives, as sometimes they are. But when our faith is founded on the confidence that God's presence is ever with us and His divine purposes will come to pass through all circumstances we are never without hope or help.

4. After a break in hard times, we may not be restored by God in exactly the same way as Job was, but the message doesn't change. God is love, God is sovereign. Jesus said that anyone who gives up something for the Kingdom of God will be repaid, either in this life or in the life to come (Luke 18:29-30).

5. God sees our pain, and He is just. He will not only restore what we have given up, but he will give us more than we can even imagine throughout eternity in His wonderful presence. May God hold you right now in His loving, powerful arms, no matter where your personal journey has taken you this day. He is more than able to accomplish what concerns you today.

Psalms The Book of Songs and Prayers to Our Great God

"Let everything that has breath praise the Lord. Praise the Lord" (Psalm 150:6).

What's the Book About

The book of Psalms is about praising and worshiping God, because He is great and good. It's also about telling God we are sorry for our sins and knowing He will forgive us and help us.

God Is Worthy of Our Song of Praise

Psalms is a book of poems and songs, written by people who were telling God how they really felt. David and others who wrote the Psalms told God how much they loved Him and how awesome He is, but they also asked the Lord to help them when they were afraid or sad or in big trouble.

Some of the Psalms were written at times when God's people were full of great joy and happiness. They were celebrating God's goodness by singing and playing their musical instruments to Him, and God made sure their beautiful praise songs were written down for us to enjoy, too. Many of the praise songs we love to sing today are really Bible verses from Psalms.

Some of the verses from Psalms were written because God's people had done wrong and sinned against God, and they wanted to tell Him that they were sorry. They knew they could talk to God about anything, and He would love, help, and forgive them. God does the same for us today.

Let's Meet the People of Psalms

David was the King of Israel who wrote most of the Psalms. He wrote 73 in all.

Moses, Solomon, Asaph, Heman, Ethan and the sons of a man named **Korah** wrote the others.

The Psalms Books

Psalms can be put in to groups, like a set or collection of books that fit together, but are much more special than any ordinary set of books, because they are God's own Word. Here are some of the books of Psalms:

1. Psalms about God's Power and His Love (Psalms 1–41)
These Psalms are like the book of Genesis. They tell me that:

a. God made me, and He created all things.

b. I have sinned, like Adam and Eve did in the garden.

c. God loves me, forgives me, and saves me.

2. Psalms about God's Help with Our Problems (Psalms 42–72)
   These Psalms are like the book of Exodus. They tell me that:

a. God helped the Israelite people many, many times.

b. God helps me with my problems, too!

3. Psalms about God's Goodness and His Holiness (Psalms 73–89)
   These Psalms are like the book Leviticus. They tell me that:

a. God is more special and "holy" than anyone else.

b. That's why I should worship only Him.

4. Psalms about God's Greatness and His Kingdom
   (Psalms 90–106)
   These Psalms are like the book of Numbers. They tell me that:

a. God is our great King.

b. His Kingdom will last forever.

5. Psalms of Thanksgiving for God and His Word
   (Psalms 107–150)
   These Psalms are like the book of Deuteronomy. They are praise songs because:

a. God is kind and loving.

b. God's Word is wonderful and lasts forever.

I Am Strong
(Two science experiments)

What do I need? Your child, several friends or family members, and a chair
Where is it in the Bible? Psalms 1–41
How long will it take? 15-20 minutes
What age child? 3-12 years
Will it work in a group? Yes
Can it be played in the car? No, sorry
Will it work in a school classroom? Yes, preschool–6th grade

Ask your child who she thinks is the most powerful person in the whole world. God will probably be her correct answer. What are some things God has done to show us His power? (God created everything; He can change people's lives and forgive their sins; He raised Jesus from the dead; He parted the Red Sea; He heals people today; He makes people strong enough to stop taking drugs or treating other people badly; He puts families back together; etc.)

Ask her if she thinks the devil is powerful, too. (Yes, he is.) What are some things that make you think the devil is powerful? (He can persuade people to take drugs, hurt other people, steal from people, turn away from God who loves them, etc.) Is he as powerful as God? (No, Satan is not all powerful, only God is!) God is omnipotent.

Tell your child that since Satan does have some power, we must always trust God to help us be strong and do what's right.

Do one or more of these power experiments and enjoy some of the verses from the Psalms with your child whenever you get the chance. Think about reading a verse or two before you thank God for your food at meals, at bedtime, or before your child leaves in the morning for preschool or school.

Activity 1: Ask your child to see how much strong arm power he has. Instruct him to stand facing the wall with his feet slightly apart, to stretch his arms out full-length in front of him, and to place his palms against the wall, with his fingers pointing up.

Then, line up several people behind him, each one with his hands on the shoulders of the person in front of him or her. (To be fair the person right behind your child shouldn't be a whole lot larger and stronger than he is.) At your signal, everyone in line will try to push your child against the wall, and he will see if he has the power to withstand all his pushy friends!

He should be able to resist all their efforts because of the scientific principle that each person absorbs only the force of the pushing directly behind him. The force does not accumulate. The only person your child has to resist is the one right behind him. Remind him that we can also resist the power of the devil through the might and strength of our Lord Jesus Christ!

Activity 2: Yes, you can keep a good man (girl or boy) down! Tell your child that you believe she is so strong that she can keep a friend stuck in a chair with only one finger. Demonstrate by having the friend sit in a chair with her chin up, back against the chair, and head in an upright position. Instruct your child to put her index finger against her friend's forehead and press. Tell the friend to try to get up.

Her friend won't be able to get up because when we are sitting down, the place where gravity's pull is strongest is in the seat of the chair. In order to stand up, the center of gravity must shift to one's feet. To make that change, the head of the one sitting down must move forward and even a little pressure against her forehead makes that hard to do! Your child will be impressed with the strength in her own little finger!

Capture the moment to make the application that we must use what strength we have to do what's right. The power we have is like little finger strength compared to the power of the Lord and Creator of the universe, who wants to live in us and give us His own mighty power to live for Him!

How God Helps Us

(A yummy activity)

What do I need? To make ice cream you'll need two big cans or containers with lids, one larger than the other, like a 1 pound and a 3 pound coffee can; 1 cup of half and half or whipping cream, 2 tsp. vanilla, and 1 cup of sugar, table salt, or ice cream salt, crushed ice or ice cubes, a plastic bag or plastic wrap, and a rubber band

Where is it in the Bible? Psalms 42–72

How long will it take? 20-30 minutes

What age child? 3-12 years

Will it work in a group? Yes

Can it be done in the car? No

Will it work in a school classroom? Yes, preschool–6th grade

Open your Bible to Psalms 42–72. As you or your child thumb through the pages to become familiar with this part of the Bible,

explain that these are wonderful words about how God helps us. Ask your child to tell you some times when we need God's help. Include specific problems or challenges that may seem especially difficult to handle alone. Be sure your child knows that there is never a single moment when we don't need God. He provides the air we breathe, the time we have, our health, our energy, and our life!

Read verses of your choice or an entire Psalm if your child seems focused and interested.

Then, have fun with this activity. Roll Me Some Ice Cream, Please. Partner with your child to make ice cream by following these easy steps.

a. Stir ice cream ingredients together in a clean 1 pound coffee can with a lid. (See What do I need? above) Make sure the can is just about full. You may add more cream if needed.

b. Put the lid on the can, and be sure it fits securely. Cover the lid with a piece of plastic wrap or a plastic bag, and twist a rubber band around it tightly so it won't leak.

c. Inside the bottom of the larger container, put a layer of ice about two inches thick, and sprinkle some ice cream salt on top of it. Set the one pound can of ice cream mix inside the larger container on top of the ice. Add some ice to the spaces around the sides and top of the smaller container, layering salt and ice until the bigger can is almost full.

d. Here comes the fun! Sit on the floor facing your child some distance away and begin to help each other make ice cream by rolling the container back and forth

e. Keep on rolling for about 15 minutes, and then carefully peek inside the smaller can to check on the progress of your ice cream. Please be careful not to let any of the salty water leak inside the ice cream container. If the ice cream isn't quite frozen, roll a little longer. Then enjoy the finished product you helped each other to do!

Remember the point that many Psalms in this wonderful book tell us God helps us with every kind of problem we may face!

God's Goodness and His Holiness
Psalms 73–89

Talk with your child about things that are special to him—his Bible, church, family, a favorite toy or gift, a video he loves to watch, a special friend, and the Lord. Explain to your child that in Psalms God is called holy. That means that He is great and good and more important and wonderful than anyone or anything else. God's words that have been written in our Bible are so special that we call His Word the Holy Bible.

Explain that although we don't worship the Bible, we do treasure it, because it was written by people whom God gave the words to write down to tell His message. Many people have suffered and have even given their lives because they loved God and His special Word, the Bible. Let your child know that even today there are places in the world where people can't own a Bible, and they would give nearly everything they own if they could have just one small Bible like we have in our homes.

Take time to thank God for being so good and so holy. Read some of the verses about His goodness and holiness from Psalms 73–89. Then, give your child a small lump of play dough, clay, or silly putty and send him through your house or yard to make an impression of something special to him.

Explain that, although we have things and people that are special to us, none is nearly as precious or holy like our God. He is the most valuable and wonderful gift we will ever receive or have in our lives. The incredible thing is that this holy and awesome God has promised to come into our own hearts and lives when we ask Him!

If you would like to pray and invite Him into your life right now, just follow these steps:

1. Realize that you have sinned or disobeyed God, and you need Him to forgive you and be your own Savior. He chose to die for us and take our punishment so that our sins can be forgiven.

2. In a prayer, tell Jesus you are truly sorry for your sins and that have hurt Him. Ask Jesus to forgive (erase forever) your sins, and thank Him for dying for you.

3. Tell Jesus that He can be in charge of your life from now on. He can be your Lord and Master! He will!

Jesus will save you the very minute you pray that prayer and mean it! He will wipe away all your sins and begin to lead your life in the wonderful way He knows you should go. When your life on earth is over, you will go to heaven to be with Him forever, because He promised!

[NOTE TO PARENTS: For more information see Romans 3:23, 6:23, 5:8; 10: 13; John 3:16; 1:12. If you have never received Jesus Christ into your own life, this is a perfect day to do so. You can pray with your child, your family, or in a quiet moment alone with just you and God. You will forever be grateful you did.]

What Can I Learn from Psalms

God's people have loved Him and praised Him for His greatness, His kindness, and His love since He created the world and made the first man and woman! God's people still love Him, pray to Him in happy times and sad times, and sing their praises to Him—and so do I.

Important Verses To Remember

1. When I am feeling happy and thankful: Psalms 9, 16, 19, 27, 28, 118, 126, 136, 138
2. When I am afraid and I need God to protect me: Psalms 3, 4, 7, 16, 17, 18, 23, 27, 31, 46, 49, 56, 91, 118
3. When I am sad: Psalms 13, 23, 26, 34, 42, 43, 88, 143
4. When I am discouraged and want to quit: Psalms 29, 37, 43, 77, 145
5. When I need God to forgive me because I have done wrong: Psalms 32, 38, 40, 51, 69, 86, 103, 130
6. When I don't know what to do: Psalms 1, 5, 15, 19, 25, 32, 62
7. When I don't feel very important: Psalms 8, 15, 90, 138, 139
8. When I have problems and I don't know the answers: Psalms 4, 17, 34, 55, 86, 102, 142, 145

A Devotional Thought for Parents and Teachers

It's interesting to observe the parallel between the book of Psalms and the spiritual pathway we follow throughout life. The very first Psalm starts at the crossroads of two diverse options: the road to life and the pathway to death. It seems incredulous that anyone would truly choose death, but by attrition, procrastination, neglect, and unbelievable conscious choice, some do just that.

Once we truly begin traveling down the spiritual pathway, receiving our life from Jesus Christ, and growing in Him, we have deep within our being the intense need and desire to find in Him our strength, our comfort, our guidance, our encouragement. As He travels the road of life with us and provides for our every need, we come to understand more deeply and clearly that this was truly the right path to take. We want to express our gratitude to our eternal "traveling Companion" for leading us in the right direction and promising to be at our side, in our hearts, until the final steps of our journey into eternity and beyond.

Psalms express what is in our hearts and on our minds. We're not the first to have traveled this spiritual pathway, and we may not be the last. Little footprints mark the path right behind us as we glance back to make sure they are following us. David must not have lived so long ago, after all. He could be someone in our Bible study class, with all the 21st Century struggles, worries, defeats, and victories that are represented in all of us.

Because God has faithfully accompanied us on the journey, picking us up and dusting us off when we stumble and fall, we treasure the love and acceptance He extends us, in spite of all He knows about us. We want to thank Him.

Psalms is a practical, how-to book that give us pointers on expressing to the Lord the praise and gratitude we feel. God is worthy of all our adoration, and He enjoys hearing it from us in whatever form it takes.

Proverbs God's Book To Help Make Us Wise "For
the Lord gives wisdom, and from his mouth come knowledge and understanding" (Proverbs 2:6).

What's the Book About

The book of Proverbs tells us what it means to be wise. It also shows us how to be wise, fair, kind, careful, and pleasing to God in what we do and say.

God's Wise Words Help Us Know How to Live

Proverbs was written by God through the wisest man who ever lived, King Solomon. Solomon gives us many wise words, called proverbs, to help us know how we should think, act, and live. Proverbs tells us how we should think and act toward God, how God wants us to treat our family and other people, how we should use the money He gives us, and even how we should talk!

Solomon, and the other two men who wrote some of the last Proverbs, tells us that God actually hates some things, so we want to stay away from them. We learn in Proverbs that God wants us always to be honest and to tell the truth, that God is pleased when we do our work well, when we obey our fathers and mothers and that following His good ways will give us a happy and successful life! The book of Proverbs is very important, and it makes a lot of good sense, too!

Solomon wrote most of Proverbs while he was the King of Israel.

Agur and **Lemuel** may have helped to write some of the last proverbs in the book.

STORIES AND ACTIVITIES FROM PSALM

God Helps to Make Us Wise

Introduce Proverbs to your child by explaining that it is a book full of good ideas. It tells how we should live and what we should do in lots of different situations. Tell your child that these good ideas are called proverbs and that God gave King Solomon the wisdom to write them down so that we can live good and happy lives for Him.

Demonstrate what you mean about God's wise words by reading some of them from Proverbs 1 and 2. Explain to your child that wisdom comes from God.

Tell your child that we can know about a lot of good things, but wisdom, or being wise, means that we do good and right things, and that's much better. Help him understand that in his life he may meet many smart people, who know about lots of things, but the people who know God and His ways and do them are wise. We want to be God's wise people, and the book of Proverbs can help us!

Wise Words from Moms and Dads

(A song and an art project)

What will I need? White paper, markers, or crayons; a hole-puncher and yarn, thin rib-bon, or small metal rings

Where is it in the Bible? Selected verses from Proverbs

How long will it take? 5-30 minutes

What age child? 3-11 years

Will it work in a group? Yes

Can it be played in the car? The first activity would work in the car.

Will it work in a school classroom? Yes, preschool–5th grade

Tell your child that Proverbs has lots of important words for Moms and Dads to hear and do, but it also has some wise words for children to follow. Ask her to listen as you read and explain some of the important verses from the list below. Help her to understand that even though it is very important to listen to the words of parents and to obey, them it is much more important to listen to the wisdom of our Heavenly Father and to do what He tells us!

Wise words for children:

Proverbs 1:8

Proverbs 4:3-5

Proverbs 3:1-2

Proverbs 4:10-11

Proverbs 3:5-6

Proverbs 4:20-23

Proverbs 3:11-12

Proverbs 4:1-2

Then, do one or more of these activities to emphasize the importance of the position

God gave you as her Mom or Dad.

1. Ask your child to remember some of the important and wise things you have taught her such as, "Don't forget to brush your teeth." "Wear your coat when it's cold outside." "It's time for bed now." "Too much candy isn't good for you." "Be sure to listen to your teacher." "Jesus is with you everywhere you go, all the time." Talk about why these things are important.

2. Draw pictures of some things you have taught your child, putting each one on a separate sheet of paper. See if family members or friends can tell what is happening in the pictures. The pictures can be made into a keepsake book by punching holes along the edge and tying them together with ribbon, yarn, or metal rings. Name it your child's Book of Wisdom.

Wise Words about the Right and Wrong Kinds of Love

(Make windows of love)

What will I need? Colored acetate found at most craft stores (cellophane will work if you can't find acetate), scissors, and transparent tape

Where is it in the Bible? Proverbs 5–9

How long will it take? 15-30 minutes

What age child? 3-12 years

Will it work in a group? Yes

Can it be played in a car? No

Will it work in a school classroom? Yes, preschool–6th grade

Explain to your child that chapters 5–9 in Proverbs tell us about the right and wrong kinds of love, and the wrong kind is not really love at all. King Solomon knew what he was talking about, because during part of his life he followed God's ways faithfully, but some of the time he got careless and did things his own way. Later he was sorry that he hadn't followed God's plan all the time.

Use this time to guide the conversation in whatever direction you wish it to go and to whatever degree you feel is appropriate for your child's level of understanding. Even preschool years are a great time to begin instructing your child about godly relationships and conduct and to warn them that not everyone they meet will be trustworthy or good to associate with them.

Explain where real love comes from, and because of God's love, we can love Him back. Husbands and wives, parents and children, brothers and sisters, and friends can love each other with God's wonderful love.

Cover a window in your house with "love" in the form of transparent hearts. Cut heart shapes from red colored acetate, or use different colors of acetate and overlap them on the window to blend colors. Attach the hearts to your window with transparent tape, and watch how the room is filled with the colors of love when the sun shines through them.

Wise Words about the Right Way to Talk

Ask your child if it matters how a person talks. Why or why not? Explain to her that the Bible has some important things to say about how we talk to God and to each other, so there must be a right way to talk. Discuss some good ways we can use our speech and ways that we should not. Read some of the important verses in Proverbs that help us know how we should talk and then have fun getting your "tangs all tungled" up as you try these tongue twisters:

Honest Ollie often offers aid.

Lying leads to denying, sighing, and crying.

Stealing a meal still jails a male.

The bear's brass band beat the boar's bass bassoon.

Whispering walruses wait willingly for watermelon.

A big black bug bit a big black bear

Fuzzy Wuzzy was a bear; Fuzzy Wuzzy had no hair.

More verses about how we should talk:

Proverbs 10:14

Proverbs 15:1

Proverbs 25:15

Proverbs 17:27-28

Proverbs 12:15

Proverbs 25:18

Proverbs 12:18

Wise Words about Work

(An ant investigation)

What will I need? A clear jar of dirt and an anthill, a scoop, a screen for a lid or a lid with very tiny holes punched in it, a piece of black paper; bread, cracker, or cookie crumbs, and a moistened cotton ball

Where is it in the Bible? Proverbs 6:6, 10:4, 13-16; 22:13, 24, 26, 28:19-20

How long will it take? 30-45 minutes to make the anthill, but keep it for no more than a month since it's not the ants' real home

What age child? 4-12 years

Will it work in a group? Yes

Can it be played in the car? No

Will it work in a school classroom? Yes, preschool–6th grade

One of the most interesting verses from Proverbs is found in Proverbs 6:6, about ants. The reason Solomon talks about something so small as a tiny ant is because ants are such good workers. Proverbs describes a wise person as being someone who knows how to work!

Ask your child what lessons she thinks we can learn from this tiny member of God's kingdom. Then read more about ants and the hard work they do in Proverbs 6:6-11. Here are some interesting facts about ants:

1. Ants live together and work together in ant towns.

2. Ants have different jobs in their towns. Some keep the place clean and get rid of trash, others take care of ant eggs or take care of the baby ants, and others help to get food or to store it to eat later.

3. Ants talk to each other by sending out a smell that other ants can pick up with their antennae. They don't make a sound, but the other ants get the message!

After you have talked about God's amazing ants, read some verses from Proverbs about the kind of work wise people do. Make an ant farm in a jar, if you would like. Here's how:

Fill a clear glass jar about half full of dirt. Find a busy, bustling anthill and carefully scoop it up, along with some of the dirt around it and some nearby sticks and leaves, and put them into the jar. Cover it with a piece of net or screen or a lid with some very tiny holes that the ants can't crawl through.

Wrap black paper around the jar for a few days so the ants will think it's a good time to go underground. Wet a cotton ball occasionally and put it on the dirt for the ants' water supply and sprinkle bread, crackers, or cookie crumbs (add a few drops of honey now and then for a special treat) inside the jar every few days.

After a few days, remove the black paper and see if you can watch the ants working hard in their tunnels inside the jar. God says we can learn some wise lessons about work from His very tiny creatures, the ants.

Wise Words about Listening and Learning

Proverbs tells us that a wise person listens and learns. He doesn't think he already knows it all. After we learn something from God's Word, we are very wise to do what we have learned.

Foolish people can go to school for years and read many books and still not really learn much. If we are willing to be taught, we can learn a whole lot. A person who doesn't think he needs to listen and learn is not wise. He has another problem called pride. That kind of person thinks he knows a lot, when he really doesn't.

Listening to God's Word and learning to be wise has nothing to do with being smart or even going to school, although He certainly wants us to use our mind and to learn all we can.

Read a verse or two from Proverbs about listening and learning.

Ask your child to turn his back and to listen to some different sounds. See if he can tell you what they are: tearing a piece of paper, crumpling a piece of aluminum foil, a pop from a piece of bubble wrap, a spoon banging on a pan, your fingers snapping, a yawn, shaking keys, etc.

Explain to your child that even though there are sounds around us all the time, we get used to hearing some of them. Then we hardly even notice them. We can do the same thing with really important things we hear, like the things the people in our family say to us, the words our pastor tells us at church, or the directions our teacher gives us. We can listen but not really learn, and we want to do both important things.

Verses about learning and listening:
Proverbs 4:1-2
Proverbs 10:8
Proverbs 10:17
Proverbs 12:1
Proverbs 12:15
Proverbs 19:20

What Can I Learn from Proverbs

Proverbs offers an abundance of good and wise ideas about doing the right things. It tells me how to be a wise person. If I learn what God says, and then I do it, I will be wise!

Important Verses to Remember

Proverbs 3:5-6 – "Trust in the Lord with all your heart and lean not on your own understanding; in all your ways acknowledge him, and he will make your paths straight."

Proverbs 15:1 – "A gentle answer turns away wrath, but a harsh word stirs up anger."

Proverbs 16:3 – "Commit to the Lord whatever you do, and your plans will succeed."

Proverbs 17: 17a – "A friend loves at all times."

Proverbs 17:22 – "A cheerful heart is good medicine."

Proverbs 20:11a – "Even a child is known by his actions . . ."

A Devotional Thought for Parents and Teachers

As the book of Psalm motivates and assists us in expressing our praise and worship, the book of Proverbs helps us know how to live. Under the inspiration of the Holy Spirit Solomon puts so many practical gems of advice in capsule form to help guide us through the maze of a complicated everyday life. Proverbs is a "bottom-line" book. In our hectic world, that's exactly what we need. No fluff, no frills, just tell us what we need to do so we can get on with it.

Not only do we find out how God wants us to handle our money, our temper, our frustration with people who get under our skin, our personal work ethic, and the desire for success in our endeavors, but we also get some clear, no-nonsense advice on child-rearing and discipline. What parent doesn't need that!

One of the difficulties of conscientious parenting is sifting through the mounds of material available to us on child-rearing. How can any concerned parent determine the distinction between good and bad advice.

Solomon certainly wasn't a perfect parent. He must have made some major parenting mistakes with sons Jeroboam and Rehoboam. Solomon started out wise and ended up foolish. He made foolish decisions later in his life as he allowed success, fame, wealth, power, lust, and self-indulgence to lead his life astray. When the words of Proverbs speak to us about how to raise our children, they speak absolute truth and wisdom that we can depend on to work practically in the lives of the little ones we want to parent successfully and well.

Take time to sit down with the Lord and Solomon and see just what God wants you to do as a parent. As you read Proverbs, mark those who relate to your role as Mother or Dad. Ask the Holy Spirit to guide and equip you to do as He instructs. Your own Heavenly Parent is simultaneously parenting you as you lead your child. He wants only what's best for you both. You can absolutely trust the how-to instructions He shares from His heart of love!

You will see that the Lord pulls no punches. He is not concerned if He goes against the flow of contemporary thought and practice. He is God, and He is right.

Ecclesiastes God's Book About What
Matters and What Doesn't "Remember your Creator in the days of your youth" (Ecclesiastes 12:1a).

What's the book About

The book of Ecclesiastes helps us understand what is important–knowing and loving God–so that we don't have to waste a lot of time finding out for ourselves the hard way!

More Advice from Wise Solomon

Ecclesiastes would sound like some gloomy words from a very sad man if it didn't have such a happy ending. But the whole book is full of important things that help us know what's right and how to staying out of trouble. We'll be on the right course if we just follow the advice that Solomon gives us, and if we remember that the most important thing we will ever do is to know God and serve Him.

Let's Meet the People of Ecclesiastes

Solomon was the wise King of Israel, who wrote most of Proverbs and Song of Solomon when he was young. Then he wrote Ecclesiastes when, as an older man, he had made some bad mistakes and learned some important, hard lessons. We want to listen to what Solomon has to say and not make those same, sad mistakes ourselves.

STORIES AND ACTIVITIES FROM ECCLESIASTES

What Time Is It?

(A time experiment)

What will I need? 1. Two matching soup bowls and a ticking watch 2. A wooden dining room table or a wooden rail on a stairway and a ticking watch
Where is it in the Bible? Ecclesiastes 3
How long will it take? 10-15 minutes
What age child? 3-12 years

Will it work in a group? Yes
Can it be played in the car? Not too well
Will it work in a school classroom? Yes, preschool–6th grade

Read the verses and talk about what they mean. Solomon knew that during our lives we would probably experience all these things at different times, and he wanted us to understand that God has a plan for everything that happens to us.

Sometimes our lives will not be pleasant and happy, and some of the times will be hard to understand, but Solomon knew that without God the times we go through would make no sense at all. With God in our lives, He helps us all the time.

It is not important that we completely understand why there have to be times for war, for hating, and for anything that dishonors God, but we need to know that God's timing is important.

There are times when buildings need to be torn down, and new, better ones built; there are times when people are sad, times when war makes it necessary to kill, as sad as that is; and when we have to lose and be very sad. But in all times, we have hope and peace because our great God is in it!

Try one or both of these experiments with your child.

1. Time has an echo – Sit at a table and with a soup bowl on the table in front of you. Cup an identical bowl over your ear. Hold a ticking watch or clock about an inch above the bottom of the bowl on the table and move so that the bowl that is covering your ear is right above the bowl on the table. The watch will sound as if it is ticking right in your ear instead of inside the bowl on the table!

The reason for the strange ticking sound is that sound bounces off flat objects and can be caught in dish-shaped objects. What you are hearing is really the echo of the sound of the watch, not the actual ticking it makes.

2. Hearing time from a distance – You will need a long solid piece of wood like a dining room table or the rail on a stairway. Place a ticking watch or clock at one end, or ask someone to hold it there. Put one of your ears tightly against the other end; cover your other ear with your hand and listen. You will

be able to hear the watch ticking loud and clear, even if you are pretty far away, because sound waves travel through the wood right into your ear. Don't forget that time is a gift God gives us, and we want to always use it wisely for Him.

Two Can Be Better Than One

One of the wonderful gifts God gives us in life is the gift of friends, family, and companionship. He made us to have other people in our lives to make life more pleasant and friendly. God doesn't want us to spend our whole lives alone, just living for us and focusing on ourselves.

He wants us to be team players in His big family and to help, encourage, hug, comfort, and to enrich those around us. Solomon knew from experience that a team of two or three people can accomplish things that one person alone can't do nearly as well. Read Ecclesiastes 4:9-12 to your child and talk about what the verses mean.

Explain that many people think of God as our third partner, and when they read the last part of verse 12, they know He certainly is. He is the One who is with us in all that we do, everywhere we go, so we are never, ever alone.

Try one of these teamwork activities:

1. Play "wheelbarrow" with your child. One of you may be the "farmer" and the other one the "wheelbarrow" he is pushing to the garden. The wheelbarrow will get on the floor on his hands and knees, and the farmer will lift him up by his ankles (handles) and begin to push him slowly forward. (If your child is very young, with not a lot of arm and shoulder strength yet, keep the activity short, or

you be the wheelbarrow as he pushes.)

2. Find a sheet or tablecloth you no longer need and cut a hole in the middle of it, about the size of a jar lid. With your child catch the opposite edge of the sheet and lift and lower it to capture the air underneath like a parachute. Then, pretend that you are making ocean waves. Sit down and make small waves with the sheet. Place a ball or several balls on the sheet, and make a game of trying to keep it on the surface without letting it roll off the edge.

Please Don't Forget

The last chapter of Ecclesiastes is important, because it brings together everything that Solomon is saying to us. If Ecclesiastes 12 were not in our Bible, we might look back over Ecclesiastes and say, "Wow! What a gloomy outlook on life! Where's the hope?"

Hope is exactly what the book is about, because God makes an otherwise empty life full and and meaningful. Solomon wants to leave us encouraged, not discouraged, so he gives us the wonderful, happy verses in Ecclesiastes 11:7-8. Put these verses in your own words.

Solomon wants us to understand that knowing God and serving Him is the most important thing we will ever do in life, no matter how many other wonderful things also come our way. Chapter 12 tells us that if we try to live life without God, we will end up grumpy and hopeless, and who wants that! It also speaks to our children and teens about the great joy of being alive and serving God and that, in the very middle of those great and exciting years, they need to always remember God, their Maker and their Friend.

We must never forget God is the only One who can make us happy and satisfied and that one day will we meet Him face-to-face.

Here's a remembering game:

Tell your child, then let him tell you three things to remember and to do. Here are some examples: Stand up, stretch, touch a wall, clap three times, etc. After he has heard three instructions, ask him to do them.

Give other instructions to remember and do, adding one more thing to the list each time until you just can't remember a single thing more! Remind your child that there are definitely some things you should never forget. Read some of these Bible verses to discover what they are: Numbers 15:40, Deuteronomy 8:19, Psalm 77:11-12 and, of course, Ecclesiastes 12:1.

| What Can I Learn from Ecclesiastes | People try lots of different things to make them happy, but only God can do that for us! I will let God lead my life so that I can do well and be happy. |

People try lots of different things to make them happy, but only God can do that for us! I will let God lead my life so that I can do well and be happy.

Help your child understand that God never promises our lives will be perfect or that only good things will happen to us, but that He will take mixed-up messes and lovingly and carefully smooth them out for us. With God in our hearts and lives, our world will make much more sense and be much more beautiful and wonderful!

Ecclesiastes 3:1 – "There is a time for everything, and a season for every activity under heaven."

Ecclesiastes 3:11 – "He (God) has made everything beautiful in its time."

Ecclesiastes 5:10a – "Whoever loves money never has money enough."

Ecclesiastes 11:9a – "Be happy, young man, while you are young, and let your heart give you joy in the days of your youth."

Ecclesiastes 12:1a – "Remember your Creator in the days of your youth."

A Devotional Thought for Parents and Teachers

We don't have to be pessimists to understand that there is much hopelessness and emptiness in our world. We live in the greatest country in the world for freedom, prosperity, advantage, individuality, and opportunity. We truly experience the good life every day, by the world's standards. We are so blessed and so used to it that we now and then have to snap ourselves back to reality. Billions of people around the world can't even conceptualize a life with little pain or want.

In the very middle of peace and prosperity, the consciousness lies deep within us and quickly rushes to the surface when calamity comes. The reality is that we're frighteningly fragile and vulnerable and that all the pursuits we pour our time and energy into aren't really all that important, after all.

Education, talent and expertise, relationships, career, pleasurable activities, all have their value, but only in their proper place, all under the Lordship of Jesus Christ in our lives. Everything temporal must fade in its worth in the light of the priceless value of the eternal God.

Many good, well-intentioned folks just don't know how to find God amid the rubble of their lives, some of them in our neighborhoods and in our exercise class at the YMCA. We can be the heroes in their lives and hold up the light for them so they can find what they are truly searching for – God. We've found Him; we know where He is. Now, we must light the way for others.

Song of Solomon

God's Book About His Gift of Love Between a Husband and Wife "His banner over me is love" (Song of Solomon 2:4b).

What's the Book About

The book of Song of Solomon is about a man and his wife who love each other very much and their love as compared to Jesus' love for us.

A Very Beautiful Bride and the King Who Loves Her

Song of Solomon is the story of King Solomon and his beautiful wife who share a great love. Even though this book is the story of Solomon and his wife, God wants us to know that He is pleased with His plan for all husbands and wives and that He wants all marriages and families to be loving and happy!

God also wants us to know that Jesus loves His people, and we are even called His bride in the New Testament. Jesus loves us more than a husband loves his own beautiful wife, and He will do anything for us. He even gave up His own life on the cross because we needed our sins taken away. Thank you, Lord Jesus.

Let's Meet the People of Song of Solomon

King Solomon wrote about his own love story with the lady he loved so much that he took her to be his bride.

Solomon's bride was a young Jewish woman who loved Solomon dearly.

Here Are the Places of Song of Solomon

In a beautiful garden and in King Solomon's palace – These were the beautiful places where Solomon and his bride fell in love and got married. As the Song of Solomon begins, Solomon and the lovely lady are getting married.

A Beautiful Bride and a Handsome Groom

Tell your child that the Bible has a whole book about a wedding day and a marriage of two people who loved each other very much. It's called the "Song" of Solomon because it really is a love song. This would be a good time to show your child your wedding pictures and talk about why you love your spouse so much.

The bride in the Song of Solomon is a young Jewish girl and the groom is King Solomon. They are so much in love and so excited to be married to the person they love! That's the way it is with most brides and grooms. A wedding is usually a very happy occasion!

The Song of Solomon is also a picture of the love that Jesus has for His bride, and guess who that is? The Bible tells us in Ephesians 5:25 that Jesus is the groom, and the people who love Him and have given their lives to Him are His bride, or His church. He considers us very beautiful or handsome. He loves us even more than King Solomon loved his new wife.

Have fun with a silly wedding that most everybody will enjoy. If possible dress up the bride and groom using old clothes, construction paper, etc. Have a make-believe wedding with the lovely couple and be sure to get plenty of pictures for all to enjoy in the days ahead. If the bride and groom are the children in your family, save those keepsake pictures to show at their real wedding day in the years to come! They will be a treasure then.

A Lovely Lily and a Beautiful Rose

(Making some good-smelling potpourri)

What will I need? Some roses or other flowers, cloves, a little perfume or potpourri oil, and a small box that can be covered.
Where is it in the Bible? Song of Solomon 2:1
How long will it take? 20-30 minutes
What age child? 3-12 years
Will it work in a group? Yes
Can it be played in the car? Yes, but not making the potpourri
Will it work in a school classroom? Yes, preschool–6th grade

Ask you child this silly "knock-knock" joke:
Knock-knock.
Who's there?
Roseanne.
Roseanne who?
Roseanne the Lily of the Valley are two flowers mentioned in the Song of Solomon.

Read about those two kinds of flowers in Song of Solomon 2:1. These special flowers grew in the land of Israel where Solomon was king and where he and his new bride lived in the palace. There were probably some of these flowers growing in the beautiful gardens around the palace that Solomon and his wife could see when they looked out their window.

For Solomon's bride to be called by flower names was a way of saying that she was very lovely and special, and for that reason many people have called Jesus the "Lily of the

Valley" and the "Rose of Sharon." He's more wonderful than we can even imagine!

You can make your own good-smelling flower potpourri by collecting roses, wildflowers, cloves, cinnamon, or other fragrant flowers. Cut off the stems and place the flower petals with the spices in a covered box. Place the box in a dark corner of a closet or the garage and leave it there for about 10 days. Check to see if the flowers are dry, and if they are not, give them a few more days in the dark.

When the flowers are dry, sprinkle them with a few drops of your favorite perfume or potpourri oil. Keep your potpourri in a tightly-closed plastic bag when you are not using it, and add more perfume whenever you need it.

What Can I Learn from Song of Solomon

God made love and marriage and families, and His idea was a very good one. I'm thankful for the family God gave me and for the new family that I may have when I am older and get married. I'm especially glad to be in God's great family!

Important Verses to Remember

Song of Solomon 2:1 – "I am a rose of Sharon, a lily of the valleys."

Song of Solomon 2:11-12 – "See! the winter is past; the rains are over and gone. Flowers appear on the earth; the season of singing has come."

Song of Solomon 2:4 – "He has taken me to the banquet hall, and his banner over me is love."

A Devotional Thought for Parents and Teachers

God created within us the most basic need to give love and to receive love. In His wonderful plan for our emotional wholeness, He lovingly provides us with practical outward expressions of the intense, otherwise-unseen emotions we feel. When He places a feeling in our heart, He always provides a holy and acceptable vehicle through which to release it and express it in tangible, visible, meaningful, God-honoring ways.

Can you even imagine how things would be if there were no way to tell or show your husband or wife, child, parents, or long-time friend how deeply you treasure them? Wouldn't we just explode with all that love inside us? How sad life would be if we had no way of showing our loved ones our devotion to them and how equally tragic if we had no way of receiving the indescribable love they have for us in return?

Show your husband or wife, your child, your parent, a friend, or other loved-one just how much you adore them in some tangible way that they can feel and see today, and keep on showing and telling them!

If you're married, aren't you glad God put Song of Solomon in His holy Word so that we can know that there is no guilt, no sin, no ungodliness in the free and full expression of married love? God is good to us.

If you're not married, aren't you blessed, along with your married friends, to be the lovely, treasured bride of Jesus Christ and that he views you with a much more intense and focused love and affection than even the passionate bride and groom in Song of Solomon. Aren't you grateful that He has lovingly placed you into the eternal family of Christ. Let's all thank Him today for the gifts of love and affection.

Isaiah — God's Book About His People Coming Back to Him and Good News About Jesus

"But he was pierced for our transgressions, he was crushed for our iniquities; the punishment that brought us peace was upon him, and by his wounds we are healed" (Isaiah 53:5).

What's the Book About

The book of Isaiah tells us bad news about the problems God's people will have if they don't turn back to God. It also tell us the great news that one day Jesus the Savior would come!

Isaiah Tells the People About a Savior

Isaiah tells us the words prophet Isaiah spoke to God's people at a time when they were not following and obeying God. At first, the people liked Isaiah and wanted to hear what he was saying. When Isaiah told them the truth that they would be punished for their sins if they didn't come back to God, they got mad at him.

Isaiah's words came from God. God wanted the people to have a chance to do right and not have to be punished. God loved them far too much to let them keep on doing wrong. He does not want to have to punish people because of their sin.

Isaiah did not just tell the people bad news, he also told them the greatest news in all the world. Isaiah told them, and subsequently us, that Jesus would one day come to earth. Jesus would make a way for all people to be saved from their sins, so they could live for Him and go to heaven one day.

Isaiah has some incredible verses that tell us how Jesus would come, what He would be like, and what he would do for our sins. That is why Isaiah is called God's prophet, because a prophet tells what will happen in the future.

God told Isaiah to write about Jesus more than 700 years before He would be born. Only God could know that would happen and be absolutely right.

Let's Meet the People of Isaiah	**Isaiah** was God's special prophet who told the people the amazing message God had given to him.
	Uzziah, Jotham, Ahaz, Hezekiah, and **Manasseh** were the kings that lived during the time of Isaiah.
Here Are the Places of Isaiah	**Jerusalem** – the city where Isaiah did most of his speaking and writing.

STORIES AND ACTIVITIES FROM ISAIAH

God's Brave Preacher

Ask your child to use her imagination and act out some very brave things: pretending to walk across a swaying rope bridge over a raging river, riding a bucking bronco, jumping through a fiery hoop, or walking a tightrope. Use your imagination to think of others.

Explain that Isaiah was also a very brave person. He was brave because He did what God told him to do, even when the people didn't like what he was saying. Isaiah understood the greatness of God (Isaiah 6:1-8), and he wanted to do everything God asked him to do.

Begin helping your child gain strength while she is young to be willing to go against the crowd and follow the Lord's instructions for her life instead. Explain that sometimes doing what is right requires a person to be brave like Isaiah.

Encourage her by saying that God took care of Isaiah and made him strong. For 60 years he kept right on obeying God and telling others about Him. Isaiah cared about people and wanted them to know about God.

God's Amazing Color Change

(A remove-the-stain experiment)

What do I need? Liquid laundry bleach, red food coloring, measuring spoons, water, and two clear glasses about the same size.
Where is it in the Bible? Isaiah 1:18

How long will it take? 10-15 minutes
What age child? 3-12 years
Will it work in a group? Yes
Can it be played in the car? Not this one.
Will it work in a school classroom? Yes, preschool–6th grade

Pretend that you are the "Amazing Chango," and you are going to do a special trick to amaze your child. Because this activity contains bleach, take extra caution to protect children from coming in contact with it. To keep the suspense of the project going, do step two ahead of time.

1. Fill a clear glass full of water, and stir in three drops of red food coloring.

2. In the second glass, put one tablespoon of bleach and nothing else. It should appear to be empty.

3. Tell your child that you will now change the glass of red water to clear water.

4. Pour the red water into the glass containing bleach. Wait a few minutes, wave your wand over it, and, presto chango, the red will become clear water.

Read Isaiah 1:18 that tells about something red being changed to white. Explain that scarlet and crimson are both red colors that stain. If your child is old enough to understand the meaning of this beautiful verse, ask him to explain it to you. If he is not, help him to understand that our sins are dark like crimson, but Jesus takes them away and makes our hearts clean as snow, like the clear water in the glass.

Special Names for Jesus
(A very special art activity)

What will I need? A piece of art paper, a pencil, puffy paint or other thick paint like tempera, glitter, confetti, or tiny foil stars
Where is it in the Bible? Isaiah 9:6-7
How long will it take? 30-45 minutes
What age child? 3-12 years
Will it work in a group? Yes
Can it be played in the car? No, it involves paint.
Will it work in a school classroom? Yes, preschool–6th grade

Sit with your child and show him the wonderful words Isaiah wrote about Jesus in Isaiah 9:6. Read the verse with enthusiasm. Remind your child that Isaiah talked about Jesus coming to earth more than 700 years before He was born. Share how Jesus is all those things described in 9:6. We can talk to Jesus about any problem or need we have and He will help us. There is nothing Jesus cannot do.

Explain that Jesus came to bring peace between God and us. He did this because our sins separate us from God, from having peace in our hearts and peace with other people. This may be a good time to discuss with your child that sometimes war is necessary, because we have enemies who are not willing to live in peace. God's great plan from the beginning was perfect peace. When Adam and Eve sinned, peace with God was broken. Jesus came to repair or make a way for us to have peace by dying on the cross. That why He is called the Prince of Peace.

This would be a perfect time to share how Jesus is all those things to you. Your child will not forget the testimony of what Jesus Christ means in your own life. Your faith will be attractive and contagious to your child.

While you are sharing your love for Jesus, let your child do this simple but meaningful art project. Ask him which of the names for Jesus mentioned in Isaiah he likes the best. Then write it in big, fat letters across a piece of paper. Instruct him to fill in the letters with puffy paint or tempera paint; then before the paint dries, add glitter, foil confetti, or sequins on top of the painted letters. Help him display his new project in his room or on the refrigerator door for others to enjoy.

Our Enemy, the Devil
(A science experiment)

What will I need? An assortment of items like: a key, coin, spoon, nail, cotton ball, handkerchief, button, safety pin, etc.
Where is it in the Bible? Isaiah 14:12-15
How long will it take? 10-15 minutes
What age child? 5–12 years. Keep it simple for younger children.
Will it work in a group? Yes
Can it be played in the car? Yes, the discussion
Will it work in a school classroom? Yes

Using objects from the list above, do an experiment with your child to see which ones fall faster. Choose two different objects, hold them side by side, and drop them on the count of three. Let your child guess which one will hit the floor first; then drop the items at the same time.

After you have done a few experiments, explain that Isaiah tells us about one who fell from heaven to earth and even farther. Ask if she knows who that might be, and why he would have fallen out of heaven.

Read Isaiah 14:13-15 and explain that the one who fell from heaven was the devil. He was one of God's angels, made to serve God, but Satan became proud and decided (verse 13) he would take charge of all the angels. He even thought he could become like God.

Ask if Satan got his way? What happened to him? (He was made to fall out of heaven. He wasn't allowed to stay there, in that perfect place, because he didn't belong there.) The devil was sent by God down to hell, the place where he belongs.

If the subject of people going to hell is presented by the children themselves, you can help them understand that God doesn't want anyone to go there. He sent Jesus to die so we can give our hearts and lives to Him by asking Him to take away our sins. Then someday we will live with Him in heaven.

Mothers Don't Forget and Neither Does God

Read Isaiah 49:13-16. Explain God's people were feeling sad and lonely because their enemies had taken them away from their homes to Babylon, just like Isaiah said would happen. The people missed their homes, and they wondered if God had forgotten all about them.

Isaiah asked the people if they thought a mother could forget about her own child. Everybody must have thought, "Of course not!" Then, Isaiah said, "But even if a mother could forget her child and stop loving him, God would never stop loving His children." Isaiah reminded God's people that the Lord even knew their names and that God knew the sadness they felt over the walls of Jerusalem being torn down. Everything that matters to God's children matters to God.

Spend a few moments showing your child how deeply you love him. Take time to reminisce about your special memories of him. Here are some ideas: the first time you saw him, her first smile, his first step, the first time she got sick or hurt, his first birthday party and cake, her first friends in preschool, his first day of school, etc.

Jesus, Our Savior

How did the prophet Isaiah know so much about Jesus' coming to earth, and what would happen to Him here? God told him. God told Isaiah many things about Jesus that He wanted the people then and now to know: Here is a list of things God told Isaiah.

1. Jesus would be born into King David's royal family (Isaiah 9:6-7; 11:1-5).
2. Jesus, the Messiah, would be the foundation stone or cornerstone of His people's lives so they could be strong and successful (Isaiah 28:16).
3. When Jesus is in charge, the world will be joyful and happy, and there will be no more sadness and gloom (Isaiah 29:17-24; 36:8-10).
4. Jesus would be a servant who would show the whole world how good and kind God is (Isaiah 42:1-17).
5. Jesus would be the Savior, the One who could take away our sins forever (Isaiah 43:1-3).
6. Jesus would be the Light of the world (Isaiah 49:6).
7. Seven hundred years before Jesus was born, God told Isaiah that Jesus would be whipped, have his beard pulled out, and be spit in the face by His evil enemies (Isaiah 50:6-7).
8. Jesus would have to suffer and die as a sacrifice for our sins. Remember how God's people used to offer a perfect lamb to God as a sacrifice for their sins? That's why Jesus is called the Lamb of God (Isaiah 53:7).
9. Jesus, the Savior, would come alive again after He died (Isaiah 25:8).
10. God tells us to call on Jesus in prayer. He will forgive our sins (Isaiah 55:6-7).

If your child is old enough to understand, ask why he is thankful that Jesus died for our sins. You can explain that Jesus took the punishment for our sins because He loves us so much.

The discussion of sin with younger children can be approached by explaining that yelling or hitting when we're mad, telling lies, disobeying our parents, taking something that isn't ours – are all sins. We may think they aren't big things, but all sin is wrong. Every time we do wrong, we sin against God. It hurts His heart, which we don't want to do.

Explain Isaiah 53:5-9, then stop and thank God for coming as Jesus to suffer and die so we can have forgiveness and eternal life.

| **What Can I Learn from Isaiah** | I can learn that sin is disobeying God, which is very bad news. But Jesus came to earth to take away our sins, and that is very good news. |

| **Important Verses to Remember** | Isaiah 1:18 – " 'Come now, let us reason together,' says the Lord. 'Though your sins are like scarlet, they shall be as white as snow; though they be red as crimson, they shall be like wool'." |

Isaiah 6:3b – "Holy, holy, holy is the Lord Almighty; the whole earth is full of his glory."

Isaiah 9:6 – "For to us a child is born, to us a son is given, and the government will be on his shoulders. And he will be called Wonderful Counselor, Mighty God, Everlasting Father, Prince of Peace."

Isaiah 12:2 – "Surely God is my salvation; I will trust and not be afraid. The Lord, the Lord, is my strength and my song; he has become my salvation."

Isaiah 40:31 – "But those who hope in the Lord will renew their strength. They will soar on wings like eagles; they will run and not grow weary, they will walk and not be faint."

| **A Devotional Thought for Parents and Teachers** | There are so many directions that our thoughts could travel regarding Isaiah's words. We could focus on the call of God, judgment for the sins of individuals and nations whose hearts are unrepentant, the origin of evil, the coming of Jesus and with Him, hope, salvation, joy, and peace. Let's focus on Jesus. |

Spend some quiet moments reading these wonderful, amazing Scriptures about Jesus in Isaiah 9:2, 6-7; 11:1-9; 25:8; 29:17-24; 35:1-2; 36:8-10; 40:1-5; 42:1-17; 43:1-3; 49:1-7; 50:6-7; 52:13-15; and 53–55.

Try to imagine the miraculous accuracy of those prophetic predictions regarding the birth, life, and death of Jesus–how amazing, how moving, how motivating.

Isaiah was just the human scribe; he held the pen and repeated the words that were told him. God knew exactly what would happen to Jesus. He told this life-changing information to Isaiah, so he could tell us.

Jeremiah
God's Book About an Important Message Jeremiah Gave God's People

"'For I know the plans I have for you,' declares the Lord, 'plans to prosper you and not to harm you, plans to give you hope and a future'" (Jeremiah 29:11).

What's the Book About

The book of Jeremiah is prophet Jeremiah's sad message to God's people that their great city of Jerusalem will be torn down, and the people will be taken away by their enemies. He tells them this will happen because of their sins against God. But Jeremiah is also a happy message about God's love that never changes.

God Has Plans for His People to Prosper

Jeremiah's job as God's prophet is to tell the people what will happen, because they have stopped following God. It seems God's people have a hard time remembering to obey Him so that things will go better for them. The people don't like what Jeremiah is saying to them, even though it's what they need to hear. Instead of listening and obeying God, so they won't be punished for their sins, the people get mad at Jeremiah.

In this book we will read about all the bad things that happen to Jeremiah that he doesn't deserve. It tells how this brave preacher keeps on preaching and serving God. Jeremiah is tough about staying strong and true for God, but very tender in his heart, because he loves God, God's people, and the land God gave them. Jeremiah wants God's people to obey and serve God, Who loves them. Jeremiah cries because his heart is so broken, so he is called "the weeping prophet." If Jeremiah's heart is that sad over the sins of the people, can you imagine how God's heart was breaking? That's why God did something about the problem–He sent Jesus.

Let's Meet the People of Jeremiah

Jeremiah was a great preacher and wrote the book of Jeremiah. He told God's people to turn from their sinful ways. He experienced difficulties because of his message.

Josiah, Jehoahaz, Jehoiakim, Jehoiachin and **Zedekiah** were the last five kings of Judah before King Nebuchadnezzar of Babylon came into the land, tore down Jerusalem, and took God's people away from their homes. These men were all kings while Jeremiah was preaching and writing the book of Jeremiah.

Judah – the Southern Kingdom was the land where God's people were living before they were taken from their homes into Babylon for 70 years. People of the Northern Kingdom, called Israel, had already been taken away by the Assyrians. Jeremiah was preaching and writing to God's people in Judah and to the other countries that were their neighbors.

STORIES AND ACTIVITIES FROM JEREMIAH

God Knew Me Before I Was Born
Jeremiah 1:4-5

Talk to your child about how amazing it is that God already knew him, knew his name, loved him, could see him, and had a wonderful plan for his life before he was born. Show him special baby pictures of his that you treasure. Have an intimate sharing time with your child, as you affirm to him how precious he is to you and to God. In the warm atmosphere of love and affection, open your Bible and read the beautiful words that God spoke to Jeremiah.

No matter the circumstances and timing of your own birth or your child's, God had a plan for you, knew you, made you, loved you, and protected you. What an awesome God we have. What an incredible creation you are.

Jeremiah's in a Jam
Jeremiah 38:6-13

Jeremiah's important message to God's people was that they must turn back to God and away from their sins, or they would be punished. He even told them that the city of Jerusalem would be torn down by enemies. Then they would be captured and taken from their own homes. Jeremiah loved the people and their homeland. He wanted God's people to keep from sinning and sin's punishment. He wanted to tell God's people good news, but there wasn't any good news to tell.

God sent Jeremiah to tell the people to please turn back to God and obey Him. For 40 years, Jeremiah preached God's message to His people. The people had lots of time and chances to hear what God had to say, but they didn't want to listen. In fact, they got mad at Jeremiah for bringing them bad news, even though it was the truth. They made his life pretty miserable. Here are some of the things that happened to Jeremiah as he tried to serve God and help the people:

1. He was very poor and didn't have the things he needed.

2. He was thrown into jail (Jeremiah 37) and into a deep, muddy well (Jeremiah 38).

3. He was taken away to Egypt, when he didn't want to go (Jeremiah 43).

4. Jeremiah's neighbors turned against him (Jeremiah 11:19-21) and so did his own family (Jeremiah 12:6).

5. The other false preachers in the land who didn't know the true God hated Jeremiah (Jeremiah 20:1-2), and his friends stopped liking him (Jeremiah 20:10).

6. As if that weren't bad enough, the people he was preaching to wouldn't listen (Jeremiah 26:8).

7. Even the kings wouldn't listen to Jeremiah (Jeremiah 36:23).

Jeremiah was alone, with not a single friend, but God was with him, and that was enough.

Talk about all the trouble Jeremiah had while he was doing the right thing, obeying God, and trying to help God's people. Ask your child if Jeremiah deserved all those troubles.

Many people think that good things should happen to good people and bad things should happen to bad people. But that's not always what happens. Jesus was good, in fact he was perfect, yet He still had enemies and trouble. It wasn't fair at all. Some very bad and sad things happened to Jesus. He was killed on a cross, when He had done absolutely nothing wrong, but he did it because He loved us.

Sometimes people who don't know and love God cause trouble for those who follow and obey God, just as they did for Jeremiah. One of the bad things that happened to Jeremiah was that he was thrown into a deep rock-lined hole in the ground, a kind of well that was used to catch rain water. It was sure to have been dark, damp, and muddy. King Zedekiah was a weak leader who kept changing his mind about Jeremiah. The king told some men that they could put Jeremiah in the well and leave him there, where he would probably die of cold or hunger.

But, after a while, King Zedekiah sent thirty men to pull Jeremiah out of the well. God was taking care of Jeremiah and making sure he was kept safe. They lowered a rescue rope and some old clothes to pad the rope under his arms and lifted Jeremiah out. Read the story of the rescue from Jeremiah 38:7-13.

A Broken Pot that Got Fixed
(A clay dough project)

What will I need? 1 cup cornstarch, 1 cup flour, 1 cup water, a few drops of food coloring (optional), a mixing bowl, and a spoon
Where it is in the Bible? Jeremiah 18:1-6
How long will it take? 25-30 minutes
What age child? 2-12 years
Will it work in a group? Yes
Can it be played in the car? No
Will it work in a school classroom? Yes, preschool–6th grade

Mix the cornstarch, flour, water, and coloring to make cornstarch clay. Add flour as needed until the mixture is no longer sticky. Ask your child to shape it into some kind of pot. Make it a simple one by using a ball of clay that she can push her hand into to make a hole.

You might choose to make a decorated pot with nature prints. Place your hand inside the pot to stabilize it and gently press the object you are using–small leaves, sticks or pebbles–against the outside to make an impression in the clay.

Let the clay dry. To hurry up the process, place the clay pot outside in the sun, if the weather is warm, or on a pan in a barely warm oven. When the pot is thoroughly dry, your child may wish to decorate it with paint.

As you watch her paint, tell her the beautiful story the Lord told Jeremiah. In the story, the clay is like the people. The potter, the one who makes something out of the clay, is like God.

Even though the potter is shaping the clay to be beautiful and perfect, something happens to the clay pot. It has something wrong with it, and the potter can't use it. That's what happens to all of us. We all have done something wrong; we've sinned, and that keeps us from being beautiful and useful like our Maker. So, what does the potter do with the imperfect pot? Throw it away because it's no good? No!

The potter in the story starts to work again on the same marred pot. He shapes it and carefully molds it into a beautiful pot again, just like he wants it to be. That's what Jesus does with us, too. He made us to be good and beautiful and pleasing to Him. But then we sinned and became marred and broken, and the potter couldn't use us like that. Not only could Jesus not use us, but He cared too much about us to just let us stay marred and broken. He lovingly calls to us so that we will let Him shape us into what we're supposed to be.

Only Jesus can make our lives and hearts brand new. Be sure to thank Him.

The Book That Couldn't Be Burned
(A hide and find game)

What will I need? Two players and a small Bible

Where is it in the Bible? Jeremiah 36:5-7; 36:16-25, 32

How long will it take? 10-15 minutes

What age child? 3-11 years

Will it work in a group? Yes, one player can go out of the room as the group hides the Bible, then he can come back in and try to find it.

Can it be played in the car? No

Will it work in a school classroom? Yes, preschool–5th grade

The fact that the Bible has never been able to be destroyed is proof that it really is God's Word. God has protected it down through the ages. Many evil people have tried to get rid of God's Word by tearing it, burning it, burying it, or hiding it. Some people have tried to destroy it by saying that it is not all true or that it cannot be trusted for us to believe. People may choose not to believe and obey God's Word, but they will never be able to destroy it. It is still true.

Tell the story of Baruch, the secretary who wrote down the words God had given to Jeremiah. Read Jeremiah 36:5-7 and explain that Jeremiah was hoping very much that the king and all the people would listen to God's words, then turn away from their evil lives before it was too late.

Next, read 36:16-25 to see if the the king listened to and obeyed God's Word like Jeremiah and God hoped he would. See what happened (verse 32) after the king foolishly cut up and then burned up God's Word. Can the words of God ever be destroyed? No, they will stand forever. We can count on that!

Play a simple hide and find game with your child using a small Bible or New Testament. Take turns being the one to hide your eyes as the other players hide the Bible somewhere in the room or the house. If needed, you may give two clues about where the Bible is hidden. Or the player who hid the Bible may clap slowly if the one looking for the Bible is far away from it and clap faster as he gets closer to where it is hidden.

What Can I Learn from Jeremiah

The book of Jeremiah tells me that God's people finally had to be punished because they would not obey God, but God never stopped loving them. He promised there would be happier times in the future for His people. God kept His promise. Sometimes I do wrong and have to be punished because of it, but I can always know that God will never stop loving me.

Important Verses to Remember

Jeremiah 10:6 – "No one is like you, O Lord; you are great, and your name is mighty in power."

Jeremiah 17:7 – "Blessed is the man who trusts in the Lord, whose confidence is in him."

Jeremiah 17:10 – "I the Lord search the heart and examine the mind, to reward a man according to his conduct, according to what his deeds deserve."

Jeremiah 31:3b – "I have loved you with an everlasting love; I have drawn you with lovingkindness."

Jeremiah 33:15-16b—"In those days and at that time I will make a righteous Branch sprout from David's line; he will do what is just and right in the land. . . .This is the name by which it will be called: The Lord Our Righteousness."

A Devotional Thought for Parents and Teachers

Don't you find that there are times as a parent when you know more than you want to know. Your little children are so blissfully comfortable in their naive world of security and serenity, and you want that to be. You feel it's in your parental job description to provide a domestic environment that is stable, predictable, safe, and reliable as possible. She's only a child. He loves the simple world.

But you know more than you want to know about things in the very real world in which your children live. She may not know about stitches, break-ups, friends who talk behind your back, kidnappers, car accidents, betrayal, heartache, and terrorism, but you do. You know more than you want to know, and you pray for him and do your best to protect him. Then you wait for the inevitable conversations when you must communicate those things that you know to your children. It makes your heart sad. You want your babies to grow up in a world of ease and peace, but you know that will not happen.

With the feelings you share, you and Jeremiah are definitely kin. He, too, knew much more than he wanted to know, and it broke his heart. He just couldn't get over the fact that he knew God's people were headed for trouble, and it was their own fault. To make matters worse, it was avoidable. Even more painful than simply knowing, Jeremiah knew he must be the one to deliver the message to the people, and they were not going to like what he had to say.

Jeremiah knew the city of Jerusalem, which represented the golden age of comfort, security, and prosperity, would become a heap of ashen ruins. Jeremiah knew much more than he wanted to know, and he cried about it.

Jeremiah knew something else that most people did not fully comprehend. Jeremiah knew about grace. He knew that a Messiah would come and die to provide the peace and security that can truly reside within hearts, in spite of the lack of either in the world around us. As God talks to Jeremiah about what to tell His people, He selects the worst of the worst, the tribe of Ephraim, to mention as the object of His unwavering adoration, in spite of their wicked behavior and idolatrous hearts. God wants the people to know that nothing has changed in His heart toward them. It's perpetually overflowing with undying love, and they are not at all loveable.

All of us have been wayward children to some degree, but the degree is not what counts. Wayward is wayward; sin is sin, and God's grace is indescribable and free to all. The New Testament reminds us that if we are guilty of one sin, we're guilty of all of them. We need grace, and we need to know that God lavishly extends it to all who reach out to Him. This knowledge should give us meaning, purpose, and joy, even though we sometimes know more than we wish we knew. God's grace is sufficient, not only for forgiveness and restoration, but also to equip us to handle difficult situations of life.

Lamentations
God's Book About
Jeremiah's Sad News That Came True

"Because of the Lord's great love we are not consumed, for his compassions never fail. They are new every morning; great is your faithfulness. . . .The Lord is good to those whose hope is in him, to the one who seeks him" (Lamentations 3:22,23,25).

What's the Book About

The book of Lamentations is about the sadness that comes to God's people when they won't obey Him. . . . and the sadness that is in God's heart because His people are hurting.

Sad Memories for a Beautiful City

Lamentations is like a sad song, that's what "lamentations" means. Jeremiah and God's people are sad because their beautiful city, Jerusalem, has been torn down and burned. They have been taken away to the enemy land of Babylon to live for what will be a long time.

God is also sad, because He loves His people. God knew that if only they had loved Him and obeyed Him, all this terrible trouble they are having would never have happened.

But even in the middle of all this sadness, there's a bright light of hope and joy shining–God's kindness and faithfulness to His people never ends, and He is with them everywhere they go. He tells His very sad people that if they will turn back to Him and wait for Him to make things better, He will.

Let's Meet the People of Lamentations

Jeremiah was the prophet who wrote Lamentations. He wrote it like a poem that would be sung at a funeral. Jeremiah couldn't write a happy, cheerful book, because he was so sad for God's people who were having lots of trouble.

The people of Jerusalem were the people Jeremiah loved and wrote about.

A Sad, Sad Song

Lamentations 1–5

Open your Bible to Lamentations, and explain that although most books in the Bible are joyful and happy, this book is really a sad song. The reason it's so sad is because God's people have disobeyed Him and would not be sorry for their sins. Now the city they love, Jerusalem, has been ruined by their enemies, the Babylonians. The people have been taken away from their homes to live in the enemies' land.

Never Ending Love

(A search)

What will I need? You, your child, a Bible, and a place to search

Where is it in the Bible? Lamentations 3:21-26

How long will it take? 10-15 minutes

What age child? 3-12 years (Help younger children understand-never ending)

Will it work in a group? Yes

Can it be played in the car? Not too well

Will it work in a school classroom? Yes, preschool–6th grade

Recruit your child to go with you on a scavenger hunt through the house or garage for things that seem to have no beginning or end. Look for things such as rings, bracelets, tubes, cylinders, balls, wheels, etc. As you bring your assortment of never-ending things together, talk about things you can't see that have no end, especially God and His love for us.

Ask your child to help you find, or find by himself, Lamentations 3:21-26. Read the verses together. Mention that these verses are like beautiful, shining lights in the middle of a dark, sad story about God's people. They remind us that God's kindness, love, and goodness to us are new and fresh every single day. God's love is with us all the time. Be sure to thank Him for loving us.

What Can I Learn from Lamentations	God never stopped loving His people, and God loves me all the time, too!
Important Verses to Remember	Lamentations 3:21-23 – "Yet this I call to mind and therefore I have hope: Because of the Lord's great love we are not consumed, for his compassions never fail. They are new every morning; great is your faithfulness."
	Lamentations 3:25-26 – "The Lord is good to those whose hope is in him, to the one who seeks him; it is good to wait quietly for the salvation of the Lord."

Lamentations 3:40 – "Let us examine our ways and test them, and let us return to the Lord."

Lamentations 5:19 – "You, O Lord, reign forever; your throne endures from generation to generation."

A Devotional Thought for Parents and Teachers

We've all experienced sadness in our lives–sadness associated with loss, pain, separation, failure, betrayal, disappointment. Sadness is such an integral part of human existence, from Jeremiah's day and before to ours. Most of the time, we wish that wasn't the case. We can realistically acknowledge that times of sadness truly enhance our moments of gladness, but most of the time, we'd prefer the happy days.

We also share the same assurance with our brother Jeremiah that God always loves us. His love shines brightly upon us when we're sad or bad or mad or glad. Some absolutes never change, and His unending, unconditional love is the best of all life's certainties.

Ezekiel God's Book About the Great Things He Does for the People Who Love Him
"I will give you a new heart and put a new spirit in you; I will remove from you your heart of stone and give you a heart of flesh" (Ezekiel 36:26).

What's the Book About

Ezekiel is about the brave prophet Ezekiel and the unusual things he did to explain God's important message to His people.

God Gives His Prophet a Special Word

As the book begins, Ezekiel has lived for five years in the land of Babylon, where he was taken away with 10,000 of God's people. God comes to Ezekiel in a special dream and calls him to be His prophet. God wants Ezekiel to tell the people some important words about His power and His love, and Ezekiel says, "Yes!"

God's people are away from the land of Israel. Their enemies in Babylon won't let them go back home, so the Israelite people are discouraged. They are forgetting that God is still with them, that He still loves them, and that they must not forget to keep on loving and serving Him.

All the words that God speaks to His people through Ezekiel are not the happy words that they want to hear, but God's words are always important. Ezekiel is not afraid to say and do what God asks. The Prophet Ezekiel does some unusual things to help the people understand what God is telling them–God calls him the "watchman on the wall," a guard whose job it is to be sure the people are safe and protected. Ezekiel knows that if the people will serve God and obey Him, they are sure to be okay. If they do not, trouble will come! This is what Ezekiel has been sent to tell them.

Let's Meet the People of Ezekiel

Ezekiel was the brave preacher God chose to give His words to the Israelite people who had been taken away to Babylon. Some of God's messages came to Ezekiel in dreams, and he explained them to the people. At other times, Ezekiel acted out God's words in unusual ways to help God's people understand what He was saying to them.

Nebuchadnezzar was the King of Babylon when Ezekiel was preaching God's words to the Israelite people who lived there. Some of the dreams and messages that God gave Ezekiel were about King Nebuchadnezzar and what would happen to him.

Here Are the Places of Ezekiel

Jerusalem – the important city in the land of Judah where many of God's people still lived when Ezekiel was preaching.

Babylon – was where the enemies of God's people had taken them to live.

Egypt – the land from which God's people escaped long before when Moses was their leader. The Egyptian people did not serve the true God and worshiped many false gods. Some of God's words were also given to Ezekiel about Egypt.

Whee! Wheels!

(A spinning experiment)

What will I need? A large button with two holes and a piece of thin, strong string (dental floss or fishing line) 8-10 inches long
Where is it in the Bible? Ezekiel 1:15-21
How long will it take? 15-20 minutes
What age child? 3-12 years
Will it work in a group? Yes
Can it be played in the car? Yes, if you make the wheel deal at home.
Will it work in a school classroom? Yes, preschool–4th grade

Open your Bible to Ezekiel 1 and explain to your child that God Himself came to talk to Ezekiel in a very amazing and exciting dream. When Ezekiel realized it was actually God who was right there with him, he fell down on his face before God in worship and listened to everything He had to say.

A part of Ezekiel's special dream was about wheels! These were not just ordinary wheels, however. There were four wheels in sets of two, and one of them was inside the other wheel, so that the wheels could go in any of the four directions very easily. One wheel in each set faced North and South, and the other one faced East and West.

It seems like a smart arrangement, but why were the wheels made that way? What did they mean in Ezekiel's special dream from God? The wheels that could go any direction and travel everywhere showed Ezekiel that God is everywhere, and He is able to see all things. That was great news because it meant God never leaves us.

Make a spinning wheel to remind your child of Ezekiel's important dream. Thread the string through the two holes on a button to make a large loop. The button will be your wheel. Tie the ends of the string together and slide the button to the middle of the string.

Hold one end of the string loop in each hand and begin to twirl the button around and around in one direction until the thread is very twisted. Pull your hands apart to straighten the string and see what happens. Then, let the string relax just a little and see what happens. Keep straightening and relaxing the string, slowly and then quickly, to see what happens to the spinning wheel. See how long you can keep the button spinning.

The reason the button spins is that the twirling motion stores energy in the twisted string. When you straighten the string, the energy travels into the button and makes it spin. The spinning motion of the button passes the energy back to the string and then back and forth between the button and the string.

Each time the energy is transferred, a little bit of it is lost. Unless you keep adding more energy by pushing and pulling the string, the spinning wheel will slow down and eventually stop. A similar thing happens when a child twirls a swing around and around and lets it unwind in the opposite direction.

A Beautiful, Shining Man

Provide art materials for your child to make a picture of Jesus. Ask him to do his very best, but don't criticize his efforts if they are less than perfect. We can honor Jesus as we work with our hands to make a picture of Him!

When the drawing is completed to your child's satisfaction, ask him to carefully cover Jesus' robe or clothes with glue. Then sprinkle it with white, iridescent, or gold glitter. A good way to sprinkle glitter is to place the picture inside a box, where the extra glitter can be shaken off and returned to the bottle when you are finished with it.

The shiny look will remind you of the way Ezekiel saw God in his dream. Explain that a shining light often glows around the Lord when He is described in the Bible, because He is so pure and holy. If your child prefers to leave his drawing as it originally was, that is okay too.

Talk about how awesome and amazing Jesus is and that when the prophet Ezekiel saw Him in a dream, Ezekiel bowed all the way down to the ground on his face to worship Him! When we kneel down before God, we are showing Him that we understand how great He is and that He deserves all our praise and our attention.

I Should Eat a Book?

(A scroll that you can eat)

What will I need? A recipe for crepes or very thin pancakes
Where is it in the Bible? Ezekiel 2: 9; 3:1-3
How long will it take? 20-30 minutes
What age child? 2-12 years
Will it work for a group? Yes
Can it be played in the car? No
Will it work in a school classroom? Yes, preschool–5th grade

Tell your child that you are going to read a verse from the book of Ezekiel about a special dream, and you would like for her to listen carefully to learn the strange thing that God asks Ezekiel to do!

Read Ezekiel 3:3. Ask what a scroll is (a rolled up book of the Bible) and what God asked Ezekiel to do with the scroll. Then, ask if Ezekiel ate the scroll in his dream and if it tasted good.

Explain that just as food gives strength, energy, and health to the body, we read, listen to, and learn about God's Word because it makes us strong and wise. Then, we tell other people about God and His wonderful Word, like Ezekiel did.

Go to the kitchen and whip up some tasty crepe "scrolls" with your child. Use a recipe for crepes, or add a little extra milk to a pancake mix to make the batter thinner and the pancakes flatter. After you cook the thin pancakes, let them cool. Fill them with a spoonful of pudding, whipped cream, or ice cream. Roll them up like a scroll, securing them with a toothpick that can be removed before eating them together.

Sprinkle your scrolls with a little powdered sugar, if you wish.

Happy, Dancing Bones

(A create-a-person activity)

What will I need? Marshmallows, some small and large ones; toothpicks or pieces of drinking straws
Where is it in the Bible? Ezekiel 37:1-14
How long will it take? 15-30 minutes
What age child? 4-11 years
Will it work in a group? Yes
Can it be played in the car? No
Will it work in a school classroom? Yes, preschool–6th grade

Give your child some toothpicks and some large and small white marshmallows. Ask her to make a "bone-man" or "bone-lady" out of them by joining the marshmallows together with the toothpicks. She may enjoy eating some of the marshmallows while she is making her person.

As she creates the person, explain that one of Ezekiel's dreams from God was about bones! (Don't make it sound scary.) Ezekiel saw a valley full of old, dusty bones, and God asked Ezekiel if he thought the bones could ever live again. Ezekiel didn't know the answer to God's question, so he said to God, "You're the only One who knows if they can live, or not."

Then, God had Ezekiel tell the bones that He would make them become people again.

The bones rejoined, and skin and muscle covered them. But they were not breathing yet, so they were not really alive. God commanded the winds to blow from all four directions to make the bones come alive, and it happened! Ezekiel was amazed when he saw the huge crowd of people standing where there had been only dusty bones a little while before. Wouldn't you be amazed, too? God can do anything, since He's the One who made everything.

God explained to Ezekiel that his dream meant that even though God's people were in Babylon away from their land and homes, God still had a great plan for them in the years ahead. God's people would live and go back home to their own land again, just as God had promised them.

What Can I Learn from Ezekiel

Ezekiel preached to God's people about choosing to do right and to obey God so that He could be kind to them. I want to always choose to do what God wants me to even if other people around me make wrong choices.

Important Verses to Remember from Ezekiel

Ezekiel 11:19-20 – "I will give them an undivided heart and put a new spirit in them; I will remove from them their heart of stone and give them a heart of flesh. Then they will follow my decrees and be careful to keep my laws. They will be my people, and I will be their God."

Ezekiel 34:31 – "You my sheep, the sheep of my pasture, are people, and I am your God, declares the Sovereign Lord."

Ezekiel 37:27 – "My dwelling place will be with them; I will be their God, and they will be my people."

A Devotional Thought for Parents and Teachers

In our contemporary world, success is often evaluated by consumer demand, by user-friendly products, and by politically correct marketing. Ezekiel would have had a hard time getting his message across. The same, however, was true in his day. He presents to us an exemplary picture of what a servant of God is like, when society doesn't approve of the message or the packaging of the product.

Ezekiel didn't measure his success on positive feedback and the accolades of his contemporaries, he simply obeyed God and rested in the satisfaction that pleasing God was absolutely all that mattered. Ezekiel obviously understood that his own popularity and any degree of appreciation or acceptance on the part of the people for the message he delivered were irrelevant. It was not about him; it was about God. Success equaled obedience – period.

We, too, will be measured by our own faithfulness. We truly want Him to be able to work through us to impact those around us, but we also want Him to consistently work in us and on us.

It's easy for us to forget that God has an intense, intimate, personal interest in every single one of us. He knows us by name; He knows our strengths and our idiosyncrasies. He knows our secret passions, good and bad. He knows our fears and inadequacies. He loves us like an only child, and He doesn't evaluate our worth in the light of our achievements, our portfolios, or our accomplishments. We're just infinitely valuable to Him because He loves us.

Daniel God's Book About the God Who Is in Charge of Everything "Praise be to the name of God for ever and ever; wisdom and power are His" (Daniel 2:20).

What's the Book About

The book of Daniel is about four young men who loved God and obeyed Him and about our God, who is more powerful and awesome than anyone or anything!

A Lion's Den and a Fiery Furnace

Daniel begins when King Nebuchadnezzar of Babylon fought against the armies of God's people and won. Nebuchadnezzar decided to take some special Jewish boys back to Babylon with him to work in his palace. It didn't seem to bother Nebuchadnezzar to capture the young men and to move them away from their friends and families and the land they loved. He moved them to a strange land where the people did not love their God. Four of the young Jewish boys who were kidnapped by King Nebuchadnezzar were Daniel, Shadrach, Meshach, and Abednego.

Nebuchadnezzar thought he would be able to change the hearts of the boys and make them turn away from God, but he didn't know that these four were never going to stop loving and serving God.

Some very exciting and dangerous adventures happen to the four boys in Babylon, but God is always with them, and the Lord shows His mighty power to the people in Daniel's day and to us in some very amazing ways.

Let's Meet the People of Daniel

Daniel was a young Jewish boy who was taken away from his home to Babylon. Even there, Daniel kept on serving God.

Nebuchadnezzar was the king of the Babylonians, the enemies of God's people in Israel. Nebuchadnezzar learned some hard lessons about God, but he never really gave his whole heart to the true God. Nebuchadnezzar wanted to be his own god.

Shadrach, Meshach, and **Abednego** were the three young Jewish teenagers who were taken away to Babylon with Daniel by the enemy king Nebuchadnezzar. They kept right on believing in God and obeying Him even though they were far away from their families and homes in a strange land.

Belshazzar was one of the kings of Babylon after King Nebuchadnezzar died. He did not serve God, and he was sent a very surprising message from God in a very amazing way

Here Are the Places of Daniel

King Nebuchadnezzar's palace – the place where Daniel and his three friends lived and worked after they were captured and taken away to Babylon.

The fiery furnace – the very hot place where King Nebuchadnezzar had Shadrach, Meshach, and Abednego thrown when they would not bow down and worship the huge golden statue he had made. God was right there in the fire with them, and He kept them perfectly safe!

Belshazzer's banquet hall – the place where King Belshazzer had a big party, and God got his attention by writing a message on the wall.

The lion's den – the pit where Daniel was sent when he refused to obey the king's order to stop praying to God. Daniel knew that he must not ever stop obeying and serving God. God kept Daniel safe when he spent all night with the hungry lions. He sent an angel to shut the mouths of the lions; they didn't even scratch Daniel.

A Very Scary King and Four Brave Boys

Open your Bible to Daniel 1:1-21 and retell the story of King Nebuchadnezzar and the four Jewish boys whom he took from their homes and families to live and work in his palace.

Daniel was born during the time when good King Josiah was leading God's people to serve and worship the Lord. Daniel probably heard the prophet Jeremiah speak, and he learned as a little boy to love and obey God.

One sad day an enemy king named Nebuchadnezzar, the ruler in Babylon, attacked God's people, and the Babylonians won the fight. The enemy completely destroyed the temple in Jerusalem. King Nebuchadnezzar took some of the special gold cups from the temple that were used to worship God and gave them to his false god. (Remember these cups, they will show up again in another story about Daniel.)

As if that weren't enough, King Nebuchadnezzar ordered one of his men in Babylon to choose some of the strongest and wisest young men from God's people to take away to live and work in the palace of the king of Babylon.

Daniel and his three friends, Shadrach, Meshach, and Abednego, were chosen to be taken to Babylon. They loved God. They knew He was with them and would never leave them, no matter where they went. When they got to the king's palace, King Nebuchadnezzar even changed their names to try to make them Babylonians, but he couldn't change the love they had in their hearts for God.

Nebuchadnezzar also ordered Daniel, Shadrach, Meshach, and Abednego to eat the food and wine that the king ate and drank. That kind of food was against God's rules for His people. The four boys knew that obeying God was more important, so they made up their minds not to eat the king's food. They asked for permission to eat vegetables and drink only water instead.

The king's servant was worried about allowing the boys to eat different food than the king had commanded. He was afraid they would become weak and pale and sick, and then he would get in trouble with the king. However, the servant agreed to let the four boys try their vegetables and water for 10 days to see how they got along. At the end of the ten days, the boys were stronger and healthier than any of the other young men in the palace who had been eating the king's food. From then on, all the young men in the palace were ordered to eat only vegetables and drink only water.

The Lord blessed the four boys and helped them learn quickly. God gave Daniel a special gift of being able to tell what dreams meant. All four of them became helpers to King Nebuchadnezzar, and he asked them to tell him what to do when he had problems and questions. Because God was with Daniel, Shadrach, Meshach, and Abednego things went well for them, just as it will with us when we love God!

Encourage your child to stand strong for God's way when the time comes in real life that he must choose between doing what pleases God and doing what someone else thinks he should.

Way Too Hot for Comfort
(A silly musical instrument)

What will I need? A long piece of fishing line or large rubber bands looped together
Where is it in the Bible? Daniel 3
How long will it take? 10-15 minutes
What age child? 4-10 years
Will it work in a group? Yes
Can it be played in the car? No, but it would be a great story to tell as you go
Will it work in a school classroom? Yes, preschool–4th grade

The story of Shadrach, Meshach, and Abednego and the fiery furnace is one of the most exciting stories in the Old Testament. It is filled with divine truths that can influence our lives and the lives of our children.

The story of these believing young men also reminds us that God is with us and in us during any problems we face. These four had plenty of opportunities not to be committed to God. Peer pressure (they were probably young teenagers at this time) might have made them shun being different in that crowd, especially when they knew what the cost would be.

As you tell the terrific story, make it as dramatic as it truly was and help your child to understand that the flaming fiery furnace wasn't just a small fire. It was a huge, industrial-strength furnace that was used to melt metal and bend iron. Ordinarily, no one could have survived its blazing heat.

The flames dancing above the top of the furnace could be seen by the people and served as a deterrent to anyone who choose to disobey the King, except Shadrach, Meshach, and Abednego. Even the soldiers who went up to the furnace door were killed by the extreme heat.

The concept of such a furnace might boggle our minds if we hadn't witnessed the inferno resulting from the World Trade Center attack that melted solid steel beams in what was supposed to be an invincible structure.

Read as much of the actual narrative from the Bible as your child can understand and be sure to read to him Daniel 3:25. Ask your child who he thinks the fourth person was in the fire with the three young men.

After you read and discuss this story, read Daniel 3:15 and have fun naming the instruments that were played. See which ones are still being used today.

If you play or your child plays an instrument, how do you use the talent God has given to you? Make a point of playing and enjoying music that lifts your spirit and pleases the Lord. Developing that kind of musical taste in a young child will create in him a love for it all his life.

Make a silly instrument by stringing fishing line, dental floss, or rubber bands looped together between the legs of two kitchen chairs. Think of a funny name for your homemade instrument.

The Incredible Writing Hand
(An unusual letter)

What will I need? A small piece of paper; a pencil or pen, and a balloon
Where is it in the Bible? Daniel 5
How long will it take? 15-30 minutes
What age child? 3-12 years
Will it work in a group? Yes, the balloons would be a great group project!
Can it be played in the car? You could tell

the story on the way to the balloon store.
Will it work in a school classroom? Yes

Daniel 5 describes an unusual way a message was sent when King Belshazzer was having a big party for a thousand of his friends one night. King Nebuchadnezzar had died a few years before.

Belshazzer did not love God or serve Him. While the party was going on, the king remembered the gold and silver cups Nebuchadnezzar had taken from the temple when he destroyed it. (Remember those cups that had been used by God's people to worship Him?) King Belshazzer was drunk from all the wine he had been drinking at the party. He ordered the cups be brought to him and filled with more wine so he and his friends could use them to praise their false gods. God was displeased. It is not a happy ending to this story.

After learning about God's unusual way of writing a message to Belshazzer, write your own secret message to someone. Think of a general message you would like to send to someone you don't know. Write it on a small piece of paper. Be sure to tell a little something about yourself in the letter. At the end of your message, ask the person who gets it to let you know by e-mail, phone, or letter, or don't include any contact information at all in your letter if it makes you uncomfortable.

Roll up the message and slip it into a balloon. Go to a store that sells balloons and ask them to fill the balloon with helium. Go back home and let the balloon go. Keep watching it until it is completely out of sight. Someday you may hear from the person who found your balloon. It would be interesting to see how far away your message got.

Daniel's Furry Four-Footed Friends
(Fun with lions)

What will I need? Inexpensive furry slippers, a white or light-colored felt piece, a glue gun or fabric glue; a couple of clothes pins
Where is it in the Bible? Daniel 6
How long will it take? As long as your child is having fun
What age child? 2-12 years
Will it work in a group? Yes
Can it be played in the car? No
Will it work in a school classroom? Yes, preschool–5th grade

The awesome story of Daniel and the lions' den is a favorite of all of us and sure to be a favorite of your child, too! It is a wonderful lesson about prayer and God's faithfulness.

Try these lion ideas with your child:
1. Buy a pair of cheap fuzzy slippers, then add claws by cutting out felt triangles and gluing them on the slippers. They will transform your sweet child into a roaring lion and he may even want to prowl a little to some kind of jungle music.
2. Role-play the dramatic story of Daniel and the lions with your child, or draw a paper doll Daniel. Cut him out and glue him on a Popsicle stick, ruler, or paint stirrer. Then make a puppet for King Nebuchadnezzar.

To make the lions, draw pictures of several lions without legs. Cut them out, or cut some lion pictures from a magazine, trimming off the legs. Clip two clothespins to the lions where the legs should be so they can stand up. If you wish, glue on yarn for the manes of the lions and reinforce your drawings by attaching them to sturdy construction paper

What Can I Learn from Daniel

Daniel and his three friends all loved God and kept on obeying Him and doing what was right even when other people were doing wrong. God will help me be strong and do right, even when it's hard, and the people around me are doing wrong.

Important Verses to Remember

Daniel 1:8 – "But Daniel resolved not to defile himself with the royal food and wine, and he asked the chief official for permission not to defile himself this way."

Daniel 3:17-18 –"If we are thrown into the blazing furnace, the God we serve is able to save us from it, and he will rescue us from your hand, O king. But even if he does not, we want you to know, O king, that we will not serve your gods or worship the image of gold you have set up'. "

Daniel 4:3 – "How great are his signs, how mighty his wonders! His kingdom is an eternal kingdom; His dominion endures from generation to generation."

Daniel 6:22 – "My God sent his angel, and he shut the mouths of the lions. They have not hurt me, because I was found innocent in his sight. Nor have I ever done any wrong before you, O king."

Daniel 7:14 – "He was given authority, glory and sovereign power; all peoples, nations and men of every language worshiped him. His dominion is an everlasting dominion that will not pass away, and His kingdom is one that will never be destroyed."

A Devotional Thought for Parents and Teachers

The key players in the book of Daniel are Daniel, Shadrach, Meshach, and Abednego and King Nebuchadnezzar. The contrast between the two categories of people they represent is of eternal consequence. It marks the distinction between those who will spend eternity in heaven and those who live forever in hell, apart from the loving God Who desperately has tried to reach and touch them with no avail.

We wince when we hear it expressed so bluntly. Isn't there a nicer, more friendly way to talk about eternity? It's so startling, so final. Shouldn't we just shun the subject all together, since it makes people so uncomfortable? No, we can't, because God didn't.

Nebuchadnezzar was loved by God, in spite of his preoccupation with idol worship and his refusal to give his own heart and life to the sovereign Lord. Nebuchadnezzar came so close.

God gave Him dramatic opportunities to surrender, but Nebuchadnezzar just couldn't give up the throne of his own life where he reigned supreme.

There came a point in Nebuchadnezzar's life when he, like it will be for all of us, stood face to face before the sovereign King of all Kings and finally, he bowed in mandated submission, but to no avail. The opportunity to bow in chosen contrition had come and gone, again and again and again and then passed by forever.

The third person in the drama of Daniel and life is God Himself. He was in control in Babylon, in spite of the idolatry and evil forces at work. He has been at work in history, controlling events and destinies behind the stage where humanity plays out world events. At this precarious and uncertain time in our own shaken world, God alone knows what the outcome of circumstances will be, and He is eternally in control of it all. We can trust Him with the destiny of the world.

We can control our own lives—our personal, everlasting destiny. Jesus has already done His part. He has taken our punishment for sin in His own body on the cross, and He stands holding out to each of us the priceless gift of eternal life, saying, "Please, take it."

How can we possibly refuse the offering of His unspeakable gift of incalculable worth, when it's so available right now? To do nothing about where we will spend eternal time is to insure that we will not spend it in heaven with God.

If you are not sure you have ever truly settled the question of eternal life, won't you please pray right now, wherever you find yourself, and simply say, "Dear Lord Jesus, Thank you for dying for me and offering to me your free gift of forgiveness and eternal life. I know I have sinned and need your forgiveness. I ask you to forgive my sins and to become my Lord. I will give you my life to direct and use for your honor. I receive Your gift of eternal life and look forward to living with You forever one day. Thank You for saving and forgiving me. In Jesus' name I pray, Amen."

If you have prayed and have given your heart and life to Jesus in exchange for His eternal life, will you please tell someone who will rejoice with you in this decision. May the Lord bless you.

Hosea God's Book About the Love He Has for His People, Even When They Sin "Come, let us return to the Lord" (Hosea 6:1a).

What's the Book About

The book of Hosea is two love stories in one about Hosea and his wife Gomer and, especially, about God's love for His people.

God's Love Story for His People

Hosea is a love story, but it isn't like the love stories where two people live happily ever after. God even tells Hosea ahead of time that when he marries Gomer, she will not be a very good wife. That was not good news for Hosea, but he knew that God had a plan for his life with Gomer, and he married her and obeyed God.

Hosea and Gomer had several children, all with special names for special reasons and, just as God had said she would do, Gomer left Hosea to be with other men. What Gomer did to Hosea is called adultery. She was not a faithful wife like she should have been, and that made God and Hosea sad.

But the story doesn't end there. Because Gomer has sinned against God and Hosea, her life doesn't go well. In fact, things seem to get worse and worse for her while she is away from her family. Finally, she becomes a slave, serving other people just to have food to eat to stay alive!

When things were at their very worst for Gomer, God told Hosea to go find her and bring her back to be his wife and to love her, even after all she had done. Hosea obeyed God, and he found his sinful wife. He even paid money to buy her back from the person who owned her.

Even though the story of Hosea and Gomer really happened, it is also a picture of God's people Israel, who are called His bride. God loved His people much more than Hosea loved Gomer, even though Israel also left the true God for other false gods like Gomer left her husband Hosea.

God went to His sinful people and brought them back home to Himself, just like Hosea did for Gomer.

Hosea's story is also a beautiful picture of what Jesus did for us. We are like Gomer, because all of us have also sinned and done what we shouldn't have. But Jesus still loved us all the time. He came to us and bought us back, and redeemed us from the devil.

Jesus took us to be His forever and ever! If we believe in Him we will live happily ever after in His family with Him!

Let's Meet the People of Hosea

Hosea was God's special prophet, who told God's messages to the people.

Gomer and their children were Hosea's wife and family. They had lots of trouble because of the things Gomer did. But Hosea kept on loving his wife, just as God keeps on loving His people.

Here Are the Places of Hosea

Israel – the land where Hosea lived and told his story.

STORIES AND ACTIVITIES FROM HOSEA

Hosea's Disappearing Wife

(A scientific trick)

What do I need? Two clear glasses about the same size, warm and cold tap water; a spoonful of honey, salt, sugar, sand, pepper, cooking oil, coffee, a tea bag, and a spoon
Where is it in the Bible? Hosea 1–11
How long will it take? 10-15 minutes
What age child? 3-12 years
Will it work in a group? Yes
Can it be played in the car? No, sorry
Will it work in a school classroom? Yes, preschool–6th grade

Do this scientific disappearing trick for your child to observe and enjoy. Begin with a clear glass of warm tap water. Explain that many different substances dissolve or disappear when they are mixed with water. Do a test to see which of these will disappear when they are added to a glass of warm tap water:

Sand, salt, sugar, honey, tea in a bag, coffee, and cooking oil.

The tea, coffee, salt, and honey will probably dissolve with some stirring. Some will leave their color behind in the water, but the cooking oil and sand will not, no matter how much you stir.

Then try experimenting with warm and cold water to see which works best to make substances disappear. Fill identical glasses with very warm tap water and the other with cold. Add a little salt to each glass and stir. The salt should dissolve and disappear into the warm water first.

Tell your child this science experiment reminds you of someone who kept disappearing from the prophet Hosea's house, his wife Gomer! Explain that God had asked Hosea to marry Gomer so they could be an example to the children of Israel of what God's love was like.

Just as Gomer kept disappearing and running away from Hosea and her family, God's people were running away from following Him! Hosea tells the people that, just as Gomer's life did not go well when she left her husband, Israel would be punished and have lots of unnecessary problems if she didn't come back to serving God.

But, just as Hosea pays to rescue Gomer from the sad life she got herself into, God also will forgive His people when they are truly sorry. He will bring them back home to Him. Jesus redeemed us and paid for our sins by His own death on the cross, so we can be a part of the family He loves so much.

What Can I Learn from Hosea	See *What Can I Learn from Hosea, Joel, Amos, and Obadiah* at the end of Obadiah.
Important Verses to Remember from Hosea	Hosea 6:3 – "Let us acknowledge the Lord; let us press on to acknowledge him. As surely as the sun rises, he will appear; he will come to us like the winter rains, like the spring rains that water the earth." Hosea 14:9b – "The ways of the Lord are right; the righteous walk in them, but the rebellious stumble in them."
A Devotional Thought for Parents and Teachers	See *A Devotional Thought from Hosea, Joel, Amos, and Obadiah* at the end of Obadiah.

Joel God's Book About a Very Important Day

"And afterward, I will pour out my Spirit on all people" (Joel 2:28b).

What's the Book About

The book of Joel is about two kinds of important days, the sad day when God's people will have to be punished for their many sins, and the happy day when God will pour out His love on the people who love Him!

The People Get a Warning About Danger Ahead

Joel is about an important day that God calls, "the day of the Lord" (Joel 1:15). On that day, God will have to punish sin, because He is good and cannot allow evil to go on and on hurting people and destroying their lives.

God, through His prophet Joel, is calling His people to turn to Him and leave their awful sins behind. He promises that when they come to God and are sorry for their sins, He will open His great arms of love and welcome them in!

However, God loves His people far too much not to warn them that they are in danger if they keep on disobeying God and continue following false idols that help them. Joel tells those people that the day of the Lord will not be a happy time for them. It will be a day of judgment or punishment for their sins. Judgment is very sad and hurtful, and Joel says that our loving God is full of kindness, and anxious not to punish you!

If God were not full of love and kindness, He could just surprise the people and send the punishment for their sins without letting them know what was about to happen. But God wanted them to know the sad truth so they could change their hearts and their ways and not have to be punished at all!

Joel tells us the good news that the day of the Lord is not just a time of hurting and sadness for the people who don't love and serve God. It will be a great day of joy for those who have come to God to have their sins taken away and now love and obey Him. Joel tells us that everyone who calls upon the name of the Lord will be saved.

Let's Meet the People of Joel	**Joel** wrote the book. He was God's prophet to tell the people what God wanted them to know about the important "day of the Lord."

The people of Judah were God's people who had gotten careless about living for Him. They had turned their hearts away from God, who loved them, to selfishness, sin, and false gods. How foolish! God's message through Joel was not just to the people of Judah, it was to all people at all times everywhere! It's a message to us, too. |
| **Here Are the Places of Joel** | **Judah** – the Southern Kingdom was the land where many of God's people were living when Joel spoke and wrote God's words to them.

Zion – God's holy hill, a beautiful place where God dwells. |

STORIES AND ACTIVITIES FROM JOEL

Too Many Grasshoppers

(A bug check-up)

What will I need? A clear jar with a tiny holes punched in the lid and a grasshopper or cricket, grass, twigs, and a little water
Where is it in the Bible? Joel 1–2:27
How long will it take? 30-45 minutes
What age child? 3-12 years
Will it work in a group? Yes
Can it be played in the car? No
Will it work in a school classroom? Yes, preschool–6th grade

Try this activity that may bug your friends! If the time of year is good for finding grasshoppers or crickets, catch one and put it in a jar. If not, find a book with good pictures about insects at the library or bookstore. Add some grass and twigs and sprinkle in some water or add a damp cotton ball and, of course, a lid that has small holes poked in it.

Use a magnifying glass to examine your grasshopper up close. Decide if he is an insect. Insects have 6 legs in 3 pairs, 3 separate body parts, 1 set of antennae, and a hard shell-like skin on their body. Imagine what the world looks like from a grasshopper's-eye view. After you have checked him out thoroughly, let the grasshopper go back to his world.

You may want to do more bug watching and try the insect test on other kinds of bugs to see what you can learn about them before you let them go back home.

The book of Joel also describes bugs, but these are not insects the people were happy about. They were called locusts, and they came in huge groups that looked like big, black clouds. They would eat up all the plants and gardens throughout the land. Because of the locusts, there would be no food to eat when the people needed it.

Joel told God's people that even though a cloud of locusts coming to their land was bad, being punished for their sins would be even worse, if they didn't tell God they were sorry and begin serving God again. But Joel also makes it very clear to the people that God loves them very much and doesn't want to have to punish them. He wants them to return to Him and let Him be kind and loving to them. God is patiently waiting for them to do just that. Read Joel 2:12-13 to hear the kind words God speaks to His people.

What Can I Learn from Joel

See *What Can I Learn from Hosea, Joel, Amos, and Obadiah* at the end of Obadiah.

Important Verses to Remember from Joel

Joel 2:13b – "Return to the Lord your God, for he is gracious and compassionate, slow to anger and abounding in love, and He relents from sending calamity."

Joel 2:27 – "Then you will know that I am in Israel, that I am the Lord your God, and that there is no other; never again will my people be shamed."

Joel 2:32a – "And everyone who calls on the name of the Lord will be saved."

A Devotional Thought for Parents and Teachers

See *A Devotional Thought from Hosea, Joel, Amos, and Obadiah* at the end of Obadiah.

Amos God's Book About a Shepherd Who Was God's Spokesman
"Let justice roll on like a river, righteousness like a never-failing stream" (Amos 5:24).

What's the Book About

The book of Amos is about some bad things that were going on with God's people in the lands of Judah and Israel and about the people living nearby that were treating God's people badly. Amos tells all of the people God's words about what will happen to them if they don't straighten up and do what is right!

A Shepherd Obeys God to Deliver a Message

Amos' job is to watch over the sheep on the hills of Judah. He also takes care of sycamore trees. On ordinary days, Amos takes his flock of animals into the hills and sits near them all day long, making sure that his sheep are safe from wild animals and that they don't decide to wander away. Nothing exciting usually happens to Amos or his sheep.

One day something out of the the very ordinary happens. God comes to Amos in a dream and tells him that the real sheep, who have wandered away from Him, are His very own people in Israel and in the land of Judah, too.

God shares with Amos the bad news about what will happen to the people if they don't stop worshiping idols and pretending to be good when they are really selfish and proud, and if they don't stop mistreating the poor people. God can't just pretend that those bad things aren't really going on, because He sees and knows everything. Our holy God is good, and He must stop the evil ways of people and punish them if they don't change. He asks Amos to tell those important words to His people.

The message Amos has to deliver is not one the people want to hear. Even the priest Amaziah tries to make Amos stop talking. But Amos, like the other brave prophets in the Bible, keeps right on obeying God and speaking the words God has given him. Amos doesn't just tell bad news about sad things. He gives the people hope, because God is good.

Let's Meet the People of Amos

Amos was the prophet who wrote the book of Amos. He wrote it to tell the people that their sin must be punished, but that God wants to forgive sin and help His people do what is right.

The people of Israel were the people Amos mainly wrote about in this Bible book and delivered God's message to, but it is also to God's people everywhere!

STORIES AND ACTIVITIES FROM AMOS

An Amazing Stream of Water

(A science lesson)

What will I need? A pan, 1/4 cup heavy cream, vinegar, a stove, and a stream of water
Where is it in the Bible? Amos 5:24
How long will it take? 20-30 minutes
What age child? 3-12 years
Will it work in a group? Yes
Can it be played in the car? No
Will it work in a school classroom? Yes, preschool–6th grade

Read Amos 5:24 and explain the people of Israel had been doing a lot of bad things, and it didn't seem to bother them at all. God wants them to start living for Him. He also wants them to start doing so many good things for the people who need their help that they will be like a mighty flowing river of goodness, spreading throughout the land.

God's people had gotten selfish with the many good things that God had given them, and they had forgotten to share with the poor people who needed their help. Instead, the people who had plenty to share just kept it all to themselves, like a water faucet with the stream of water turned off! God wanted His people to let the goodness in their hearts flow out to others.

Do an experiment with a stream of water in your sink to show how hard the hearts of God's people had become. Here's how:

Warm some heavy cream in a pan, just to the simmering point. When it is simmering, slowly stir a few teaspoons of vinegar into the cream. The acid in the vinegar will react to the chemicals in the milk and, it will become rubbery, then hard like plastic.

Keep stirring the mixture until it becomes rubbery. Let it cool and rinse it under a stream of running water in the sink. What you have made is your own plastic.

That's what happened to the hearts of God's people. They became cool and then hard toward God and toward other people, when they should have been a stream of goodness and kindness. Let's decide right now that we will be that kind of good stream.

What Can I Learn from Amos	See *What Can I Learn from Hosea, Joel, Amos, and Obadiah* at the end of Obadiah.
Important Verses to Remember	Amos 5:14a – "Seek good, not evil, that you may live." Amos 5:24 – "But let justice roll on like a river, righteousness like a never-failing stream!"
A Devotional Thought for Parents and Teachers	See *A Devotional Thought from Hosea, Joel, Amos, and Obadiah* at the end of Obadiah.

Obadiah God's Book About Some People in the Mountains Who Face Big Trouble! "The day of the Lord is near for all nations" (Obadiah 14).

What's the Book About	The book of Obadiah is about some enemies, the Edomites, who live near God's people and keep causing them trouble. It's also about the great and loving God, who watches over His people and protects them from those who want to hurt them or destroy them like a good father protects his children.
A Very Short Message with a Powerful Punch	Obadiah is the shortest book in the whole Old Testament. It has only one little chapter, but it has a powerful message to tell us. Obadiah shows us that God does a very good job of watching over His people. He doesn't want anyone treating them badly. The Edomite people were big neighborhood bullies who kept bothering God's people. The book of Obadiah helps us to understand that God must sometimes punish His people for the wrong they do. Like a good father God never stops loving us and watching out for us, but He corrects us when we need it. Even God punishes His people from His heart of love, and for the very same reason that He protects them. God wants things to be well with His precious people!

Let's Meet the People of Obadiah

Obadiah was the preacher who wrote and spoke God's words to the Edomite people, who were treating His people very badly.

The Edomites were the people who lived in the mountains near Israel and Judah, but they kept attacking the Jewish people, stealing from them, and treating them badly. God was especially unhappy with the Edomite people, because they should have been the friends of God's people. They were even in the same family with the Jewish people, since Esau was their great, great, and more greats grandfather. Esau's father was Isaac, whom the Jewish people had as an ancestor, too. Obadiah was written to warn the Edomites that they were in serious trouble if they didn't start loving and serving God and leaving God's people alone!

Here Are the Places of Obadiah

Edom – the land in the mountains where the people who bullied God's people lived. God had a lot to say to them in Obadiah.

Jerusalem – the big, important city in the land of Judah, where God's people lived.

STORIES AND ACTIVITIES FROM OBADIAH

Get Down from That Tower!

(A building project)

What will I need? Blocks or boxes, cylinders or cardboard tubes, a toy action figure, small doll or toy animal
Where is it in the Bible? Obadiah 3-4
How long will it take? 5-10 minutes
What age child? 3-11 years
Will it work in a group? Yes, in small groups or as one large group
Can it be played in the car? Just the discussion
Will it work in a school classroom? Yes, preschool–5th grade

Read verses 3-4 in Obadiah and explain that the Edomites were neighbors of God's people, who lived in the mountains and among high cliffs. They were very proud of themselves, much too proud of themselves, because they thought they were more important than anyone else around them. They lived in a city that had been carved out of a high rock cliff, and the Edomites thought that no other people could ever be as smart or strong or as safe as they were.

Because the Edomite people were so very proud of themselves, they thought they could do whatever they wanted, even if it hurt or bothered other people. They would come down from their mountain homes into the land where God's people lived, and they would fight them, capture them, help their enemies do bad things to them, and steal whatever they wanted from them. Then they would hurry back to hide in their mountain houses and caves. The Edomites were behaving badly, and God was not happy with them.

That's where Obadiah fit into God's plan. He delivered God's message to the Edomites. He told them they would never be able to hide from God's punishment for their bad deeds. Obadiah said God could see them and find them anywhere. God made sure everyone understood that He loved His people and would see that all was well with them.

God's people today are those who have trusted Jesus as their Savior and have given their lives to Him. As we read in Obadiah, we can get a little look at what it means to be God's child.

The Bible says being too proud often causes a person, or whole land full of people, to fall, like falling off the top of a high tower. The right kind of proud means we understand we can do many wonderful things because God is with us, helping and leading us. We don't put all our trust in ourselves. We want to trust God.

Make as high a tower as you can with blocks or boxes. Place a small action figure or doll or a small toy animal on top and see how long he can stay there without the tower falling down. Remember to be thankful for all that God helps us to do. Let other people be proud of you, like you are of them!

What Can I Learn from Hosea, Joel, Amos, and Obadiah

God punishes sin when His people keep on doing wrong. He must show them that they can't keep on disobeying Him. But He also watches over His people and takes good care of them, because He loves them. I'm God's child, and He loves me, too. I want to do what He knows is best for me. Share with your child the wonderful truth that God wants only what is the very best for us, and He knows what that is.

Important Verse to Remember

Obadiah 3a – "The pride of your heart has deceived you."

A Devotional Thought from Hosea, Joel, Amos, and Obadiah For Parents and Teachers

The voices of God's courageous prophets seem to ring out in one message: God hates sin and must punish it, but He loves you and wants to be kind to you. Again and again He warns His people what's going to happen if they don't make some real and serious changes. As a parent, perhaps you feel that on some of those days all you do is stay on your child's uncooperative back and constantly warn him of his impending doom.

As the infinitely loving Father that God is, can't you almost hear Him saying to His children, "But I don't WANT to punish you, please just please do as I ask, so things can go better for you, and we can just enjoy being together? Why do you make life so hard on yourself when I want it to be so good for you?"

We relate as adults in the life of a child to what God must have felt toward His people in their disobedience. We also respond to the outrage God expressed with those who made life difficult for those same disobedient people He loved so much. God wanted no one to be mean and unkind to His children, and neither do we. Something powerful wells up deep inside us when those we love so much are misunderstood, maligned, or mistreated. We often do something about it! So did God.

He understands just what we feel toward the children He has given us, what we desire from them, and for them. We seem to find ourselves incredibly on the same page with the eternal, omnipotent Lord of the universe, because we're both parents–and we desperately want only the very best for our children.

Jonah God's Book About the Adventures of a Man Who Learned to Obey God
"I knew that you are a gracious and compassionate God, slow to anger and abounding in love, a God who relents from sending calamity" (Jonah 4:2b).

What's the Book About

The book of Jonah is about the adventures of the prophet Jonah who decided not to obey God and found out the hard way that it's important to do what God wants us to!

God's Prophet Takes a Wrong Turn on His Journey

The book of Jonah begins as God speaks to Jonah and tells him to go to the big city of Nineveh. The people in Nineveh do not love God and are not obeying Him. God is warning them that they are in big trouble if they don't change their bad ways. But Jonah does not like the people of Nineveh. He knows that if they are sorry for their sins and turn to the true God, He will forgive their sins and be kind to them. Jonah doesn't want that to happen. So Jonah sails away on a boat in the opposite direction, trying to get away from Nineveh and from God.

On the trip away from Nineveh, Jonah finds himself in serious trouble. As usual, things never go right for long when people turn away from God. Jonah is caught in a terrible storm, gets thrown overboard, and gets swallowed by a great big fish. Finally, Jonah understands that God means business and intends for Jonah to go to Nineveh and preach to the people there. Finally Jonah goes.

<table>
<tr><td>Let's Meet the People of Jonah</td><td>Jonah was the prophet God chose to go to Nineveh to tell His message to the people in Nineveh. But Jonah didn't like the people there and chose to disobey God. God had other plans, and Jonah learned the hard way that obeying God and following Him is always best!</td></tr>
</table>

Jonah was the prophet God chose to go to Nineveh to tell His message to the people in Nineveh. But Jonah didn't like the people there and chose to disobey God. God had other plans, and Jonah learned the hard way that obeying God and following Him is always best!

The boat's captain and other sailors that were on the boat Jonah took to try to sail away from God.

Here Are the Places of Jonah

Joppa – the city on the Mediterranean Sea where Jonah got on a boat to travel away from Nineveh, the city where God had told him to go and preach.

Nineveh – the city in Assyria where the enemies of God's people lived. God wanted the people in Nineveh to listen to His words, to become sorry for their sins, and to begin to serve Him. God sent Jonah to take His message to them, but Jonah didn't want to go! God was not pleased with the way Jonah was thinking and acting!

STORIES AND ACTIVITIES FROM JONAH

Jonah Runs Away from God

Most of us have heard the story of Jonah and the whale, a special, big fish that God sent to save Jonah's life in the stormy sea, but here is what happened:

God told Jonah to go to Nineveh and tell the people to turn from their evil actions and begin to follow the one true God. Jonah knew that if the people did as God said, He would erase all their sins and be kind to them. The people in Nineveh were Jonah's enemies. Jonah wanted them to be punished. He didn't want God to be kind to them.

Jonah was afraid to go to Nineveh, so he got on board a ship going to the city of Tarshish in the other direction. Jonah climbed down into a dark place inside the boat and tried to hide there from God.

While the boat was sailing along, a huge storm blew up. Even the brave sailors that were used to storms became afraid. The captain and the crew prayed to their false gods for help, but, of course, that did no good. They threw boxes and barrels overboard to try to keep the ship from sinking. All the time,

Jonah was sound asleep inside the ship. The captain found Jonah there and angrily told him to get up and pray to his God for help!

When the captain and sailors learned that Jonah was disobeying God, they decided to throw him overboard in an attempt to stop the storm. Even Jonah told them to throw him into the sea, because he knew he was the reason for the terrible, scary storm. The sailors even prayed to Jonah's God. When they threw Jonah into the water, the storm instantly stopped. The sailors were so amazed at the power of the true God that they worshiped Him and promised to begin to serve Him.

Meanwhile, God arranged for a huge, special fish to swallow Jonah to save him from drowning. Jonah remained inside the fish for three days and three nights. While he was in the fish, he prayed to God and asked for His help. Jonah was sorry for not obeying God, and he told Him so. Jonah promised to worship and serve God and to keep his promises to the Him for the rest of his life. Then, God ordered the fish to spit Jonah out onto the beach and it did.

Jonah went to Nineveh and preached. The people listened and turned to God right away. Just as Jonah knew He would, God forgave all their terrible sins. That made Jonah mad. He was so angry he didn't even want to live anymore. Jonah was acting foolishly.

While Jonah was angry about God's kindness, he went out by himself and sat under the shade of a tree to stay cool. When the hot sun made the leaves of the tree dry up, the Lord caused a vine to grow up quickly and shade Jonah with its big, broad leaves. God was kind to Jonah even when he was cranky and angry at God.

But the hot summer sun and a blistering wind dried up the vine and made Jonah even more miserable. He wanted to die more than ever. God said to Jonah, "You are feeling sorry for yourself just because the vine died. Why shouldn't I feel sorry for a city like Nineveh, full of thousands of people who need to know my love and care?"

A Three Part Fish
(A big art activity)

What will I need? A roll of white paper, scissors, crayons, markers, or watercolor paint
Where is it in the Bible? Jonah 1–2
How long will it take? 30-45 minutes
What age child? 3-12 years
Will it work in a group? Yes
Can it be played in the car? The story only
Will it work in a school classroom? Yes, preschool–6th grade

Tell your child the story of Jonah and the big fish. Cut sheets of paper large enough for you, your child, and a friend or another family member to wear like a shirt. The strips should be about five feet long each. Fold each paper in half, and cut a half-circle at the folded edge to make a hole for your head to go through.

Lay your folded papers side by side on the table or floor with the top edges at the same height. Draw the picture of one big fish across all three (or just two) papers, as if you were drawing on one wide sheet of paper. Make fins and gills and whatever designs you want your special fish to have, trying to match each section as much as possible.

When the drawings are finished, put the paper shirts on and stand next to each other in the correct order, trying to line up the sections to make one big fish. Stand in front of a mirror so your child can see the finished product. Then trade positions to see what a big change it makes in the way the fish looks.

Heat Wave

(A simple science experiment)

What will I need? A circle cut from poster board or lightweight cardboard, a pencil and a ruler, scissors, a thumbtack, and a wooden stick

Where is it in the Bible? Jonah 4

How long will it take? 15-30 minutes

What age child? 3-12 years

Will it work in a group? Yes

Can it be played in the car? No

Will it work in a school classroom? Yes, preschool–6th grade

Cut out a circle from poster board or lightweight cardboard and decorate it if you wish. Use a pencil and a ruler to divide the circle into six sections, and write a number on the top right corner of each section. Cut on each line toward the center of the circle, but stop cutting about one inch before you reach the center. Gently roll the numbered corners of each section toward the center and push a thumbtack through all of them and then into a wooden stick. Can you tell that you've made a pinwheel?

Hold the pinwheel above a heat source such as a lamp, a lighted bulb, or a heater, but not an air blowing heater, and watch what happens to the pinwheel.

When air is heated, the invisible molecules begin to move and set up currents which make the pinwheel start to spin. The moving of the air is called convection.

What Can I Learn from Jonah	See *What Can I Learn from Jonah, Micah, Nahum, Habakkuk, and Zephaniah* at the end of Zephaniah.
Important Verses to Remember from Jonah	Jonah 2:2a – "He (Jonah) said: 'In my distress I called to the Lord, and he answered me'."
	Jonah 2:9 – "But I, with a song of thanksgiving, will sacrifice to you. What I have vowed I will make good. Salvation comes from the Lord."
A Devotional Thought for Parents and Teachers	See *A Devotional Thought from Jonah, Micah, Nahum, Habakkuk, and Zephaniah* at the end of Zephaniah.

Micah God's Book About Who God Loves and What

God Hates "He has showed you, O man, what is good. And what does the Lord require of you? To act justly and to love mercy and to walk humbly with your God" (Micah 6:8).

What's the Book About

The book of Micah is a kind of picture of God and the people He loves and the sin He hates. The prophet Micah tells us that God hates sin and must punish it, but that He loves all people, even though we are the ones who do the sinning. God loves people so much that He sent His own Son Jesus to take the punishment on Himself that all of us deserve, because we have all done wrong.

Micah tells us about Jesus, and he even names the very place where Jesus will be born in Bethlehem. How could Micah know that fact 700 years before it would even happen? God told Him. Then Micah wrote down God's words for us to read.

God Gives His People a Glimpse of the Future

Micah begins at a time in the land of Judah when God's people think that things are going really well. There is plenty of food for everybody, and they have almost everything they need, but they are forgetting that God is the One who gives all good things to His people. God expects His people to live and act in the right way.

God's people are being selfish and doing many other bad deeds. They are also being unkind to the poor people in the land. They are pretending to serve and love God, but their actions do not show it. The Lord is not happy about that.

Micah warns the people that God can't let their bad behavior go on and on, even though He has given the people many, many chances to be sorry and to change the way they are acting. Micah tells them that one day before too long they will be punished for their sins. Since the people won't obey God's words, the punishment comes just as God said it would!

But, right in the middle of all Micah's bad news, comes the best news anyone has ever heard–that God forgives and erases sin and that He is sending His Son to take the punishment we deserve. As we talk about the book of Micah, we can see that sin is serious, but that God's great love is greater than all our sins.

God doesn't just say, "I love you," He does something to prove it. He promises to send Jesus to be "love in action," and then He keeps His promise–700 years later.

185

Micah was the prophet who told God's words to the people who lived in the lands of Judah and Israel.

The people who lived in Israel, Judah, and Samaria were the ones God spoke to through Micah, but God speaks to us in Micah's book, too!

Jerusalem – the important city in the Southern Kingdom of Judah.

Samaria – the important city in the Northern Kingdom of Israel. God's people lived in both places in Micah's day, and his words from God were for all God's people everywhere.

STORIES AND ACTIVITIES FROM MICAH

Things to Love, Things to Hate

(A game to play blindfolded)

What will I need? Construction paper, a marker or crayon, tape, small squares of paper, and a handkerchief or bandanna
Where is it in the Bible? Micah 3
How long will it take? 15-30 minutes
What age child? 3-12 years
Will it work in a group? Yes, by taking turns
Can it be played in the car? No
Will it work in a school classroom? Yes, pre-school–6th grade

Show your child the first three chapters of Micah. Explain that Micah tells God's people that they are doing things that make God unhappy. The people are pretending to love God and to do what He says, but they are really not doing what God wants.

Ask, can God just say to His people, "I know what you are doing, but that's okay. You can act as bad as you want. I don't mind." Ask your child what kind of parent would say to his child, "I know it's wrong to steal or to hurt other people, but you can just do whatever you want, and I won't try to stop you."

Explain that a mother and father who love their child will do everything they can to protect him from doing wrong and hurtful things. God also protects His people because He loves them. When He knew that His people in Israel and Judah were doing things that were hurting others and themselves, too, He had to warn them to stop. Finally, God had no choice but to punish His people when they wouldn't listen and obey Him. It was for their own good!

Play a "Fill the Heart With Love" game. Cut a large heart shape from construction paper or poster board and tape it to a door. On another large sheet of paper make a big "X" that covers most of the paper and tape it up beside the heart. The heart will represent things we should love and the "X," the things we should hate.

On small squares of paper, write the statements listed below, plus make up some of your own. If they relate to something we should love, draw a heart shape at the end of the statement. If the sentence concerns something we should hate, write an "X" after it.

Read one card at a time and ask if the message is something we should love or hate. Explain that God's Word tells us not to hate people, but to hate things that are wrong, evil, and hurtful. After your child has identified each statement, ask him to take a good look at where the heart and the "X" signs are on the door. Blindfold him, hand him the card with the tape attached, and ask him to try to stick it on the right spot.

When the game is over, pray with your child and ask the Lord to help you both to love and hate the right things. Ask God to fill your hearts with the things He loves!

Here are some "love and hate" statements:
1. taking money from a poor person just so you can have more for yourself
2. being gentle and patient with an older person who can't get around very easily
3. telling a lie
4. making another person get in trouble when he has done nothing wrong
5. stealing something and keeping it when it doesn't belong to you
6. being kind to a child who doesn't know about Jesus and doesn't get to go to church
7. telling the truth
8. singing praise songs to Jesus
9. helping someone who needs you
10. obeying God
11. being mean to someone
12. doing good things because you love God

Some of the things that we should hate are the very same things that God's people were doing wrong in Micah's day. God loved His people even then, but He hated their sins.

A Promise, a City, and a Special Baby
(A rhyming game)

What will you need? Your child and a Bible
Where is it in the Bible? Micah 4:3–4; 5:2, 5a
How long will it take? 10-15 minutes
What age child? 3-11 years
Will it work in a group? Yes
Can it be played in the car? Yes, if the driver keeps her hands on the wheel!
Will it work in a school classroom? Yes, preschool–5th grade

In Micah there is a wonderful mystery about a baby who will be born in a tiny city and grow up to be the King of Kings. Explain that He will be called the Prince of Peace. Read with expression Micah 4:3-4. Then, read Micah 5:5a.

Tell your child that those verses mean that one day when Jesus comes back to earth there will be real peace, no more fighting and war. There will be no more need for people to make guns and other weapons to fight their enemies, because there won't be any more war, ever. That was great news for the people in Micah's day, because they had been fighting wars for a long time. It's great news for us, too, because wars still go on today. When Jesus comes back, He will bring peace forever!

Play "We're Going on a Baby Hunt" to solve the mystery of who the special baby is and where the baby will be born. After the game, read Micah 5:2 and explain that many of the leaders in Micah's day were much too proud of all their money and power. They were sure that God's special baby would be born in the city of Jerusalem. However, the leaders weren't really serving God at all. Jerusalem was going to be torn down as punishment for their sins. God's special baby, Jesus, would be born in the tiny town of Bethlehem.

Jesus chose to become a human baby, who was really God at the same time, so that we can understand a little better who He is and what He is like. Also, we can know how to become His own children in a very personal relationship with Jesus, the Eternal God.

But now, let's go on a baby hunt:
Oh, we're going on a baby hunt, a baby hunt, a baby hunt. (Pretend you are rocking a baby.)
Oh, we're going on a baby hunt to find God's special baby. (Shrug your shoulders and gesture with your hands as if to say, "I don't know where He is.")

We're traveling to Jerusalem, Jerusalem, Jerusalem. (Slap hands on your legs to make the sound of a donkey trotting.)
We're traveling to Jerusalem to find God's special baby. (Shrug shoulders and gesture.)

We're swimming across the Red Sea, the Red Sea, the Red Sea. (Pretend to be swimming.)

We're swimming across the Red Sea to find God's special baby. (Shrug shoulders and gesture)

We're hiking across the desert, the desert, the desert. (Pretend to be hot and tired.)
We're hiking across the desert to find God's special baby. (Shrug shoulders and gesture)

We're climbing up Mt. Sinai, Mt. Sinai, Mt. Sinai. (Act like you are climbing the mountain.)
We're climbing up Mt. Sinai to find God's special baby. (Shrug shoulders)

We're sitting on a hillside, a hillside, a hillside. (Sit with arms folded in front of you.)
We're sitting on a hillside to find God's special baby. (Shrug shoulders)

We see a bright light in the sky, in the sky, in the sky. (Look up, squint, and shade eyes.)
We see a bright light in the sky and hear the voice of angels. (Cup hand around ear as if listening)

You hurry down to Bethlehem, to Bethlehem, to Bethlehem. (Slap hands on your legs fast to make the sound of running.)
You hurry down to Bethlehem; you find God's special baby. (Kneel down, bow your head, and fold your hands as if worshiping the baby.)

What Can I Learn from Micah

See *What Can I Learn from Jonah, Micah, Nahum, Habakkuk, and Zephaniah* at the end of Zephaniah.

Important Verses to Remember

Micah 4:3b-4 – "They will beat their swords into plowshares and their spears into pruning hooks. Nation will not take up sword against nation, nor will they train for war anymore. Every man will sit under his own vine and under his own fig tree, and no one will make them afraid, for the Lord Almighty has spoken."

Micah 5:2 – "But you, Bethlehem Ephrathah, though you are small among the clans of Judah, out of you will come for me one who will be ruler over Israel, whose origins are from of old, from ancient times."

Micah 5:4b-5 – "And they will live securely, for then his greatness will reach to the ends of the earth. And he will be their peace."

Micah 7:7 – "But as for me, I watch in hope for the Lord, I wait for God my Savior; my God will hear me."

Micah 7:8b – "Though I have fallen, I will rise. Though I sit in darkness, the Lord will be my light."

A Devotional Thought for Parents and Teachers

See *A Devotional Thought from Jonah, Micah, Nahum, Habakkuk, and Zephaniah* at the end of Zephaniah.

Nahum God's Book About a City That Kept on

Sinning "The Lord is good, a refuge in times of trouble. He cares for those who trust in him" (Nahum 1:7).

What's the Book About

The book of Nahum is about the kingdom of Assyria and their important city, Nineveh, but it's mostly about what happens when people keep on doing wrong and are not sorry about it!

Nineveh Sees the Lord's Anger

Nahum is the story of the land of Assyria and, especially, about their most important city, Nineveh. The Assyrian people were the enemies of God's people and were treating them unkindly. God loved His people and was displeased about the bad things they were doing. After all, He was their Heavenly Father, and the people of Judah were His children.

God told Nahum to tell the people of Nineveh that He would have to punish their bad behavior if they didn't change their ways. But they would not listen or obey God.

In fifty years, just as Nahum had prophesied, the city of Nineveh was completely torn down. God considers sin to be serious. The people of Nineveh found that out the hard way.

Let's Meet the People of Nahum

Nahum was God's prophet who told the people in the city of Nineveh what would happen if they did not start obeying God and treating His people right.

The people of Nineveh were proud of how powerful and important they were. They didn't think they needed to love or serve God. They found out they were wrong about that.

God's people in Judah were heartened to know that God was in charge of taking care of them and that the Lord would not let the Assyrians keep on treating them badly. God would help the people He loved, and He would not allow their enemies to keep on doing wrong.

Here are the Places of Nahum

Nineveh – the big city of Assyria where the people did not love God or obey Him. The people of Nineveh treated God's people badly which displeased God greatly.

The Bear and the Peacock

(An active game)

What will I need? Several feathers made from construction paper
Where is it in the Bible? Nahum 1–3
How long will it take? 15-20 minutes
What age child? 3-11 years
Will it work in a group? Yes
Can it be played in the car? No
Will it work in a school classroom? Yes, preschool–5th grade

Ask these questions, "Do you think it is good to be proud of someone? Is it okay for Moms and Dads to be proud of their child, like I am of you? Can you think of a time it is ever bad to be too proud?"

The people of Assyria, were too proud of themselves. They thought they were so great and powerful that they didn't need God for anything! They thought they did not need to pay any attention to God at all or to do what He said. The people in Nineveh were proud and foolish.

Read Nahum 1:2-3a to your child. Explain that God is the only One who has the right to punish those who mistreat His children. We must not try to take matters into our own hands and hurt people back who hurt us. God takes good care of His children because he loves us so much. To be an enemy of God or of His people is to be on the wrong side. Ask your child if she knows what bird is sometimes said to be proud. The answer is a peacock. Play "The Bear and the Peacock" to demonstrate the patience God has with people who are proud and sinful and to illustrate that in His own time God takes action against those who refuse to obey and serve Him.

Cut several large feather shapes from construction paper, and tuck them into the back of your child's belt or waistband. He will pretend to be a proud peacock. You pretend to be a bear, sleeping on the floor or the couch while the peacock dances around, teasing you, and trying to interrupt your long winter's sleep. Remind the peacock that whatever he does, he cannot touch you. Pretend to remain oblivious to the gestures, noises, and tricks of the peacock as he tries to get you to wake up.

Every once in a while, stretch a little, roll over, yawn sleepily, and open one eye to let the peacock know you know what's going on, but don't do anything for sometime. Then jump up suddenly and try to snatch one of the peacock's feathers. Chase him around a bit if space permits. When you have grabbed a feather from the proud peacock, the two of you may change roles, and your child will become the sleeping bear who's after you.

Help your child understand that God is patient with those who do wrong, but when it is His time to act, He acts.

What Can I Learn from Nahum	See *What Can I Learn from Jonah, Micah, Nahum, Habakkuk, and Zephaniah* at the end of Zephaniah.
Important Verses to Remember from Nahum	Nahum 1:3 – "The Lord is slow to anger and great in power; the Lord will not leave the guilty unpunished."
	Nahum 1:7 – "The Lord is good, a refuge in times of trouble. He cares for those who trust in Him."
	Nahum 1:15a – "Look, there on the mountains, the feet of one who brings good news, who proclaims peace!"
A Devotional Thought for Parents and Teachers	See *A Devotional Thought from Jonah, Micah, Nahum, Habakkuk, and Zephaniah* at the end of Zephaniah.

Habakkuk God's Book About God's Answers to a Man's Questions

"The Sovereign Lord is my strength; he makes my feet like the feet of a deer; He enables me to go on the heights" (Habakkuk 3:19a).

What's the Book About	The book of Habakkuk explores the questions the prophet Habakkuk asked God, the answers He gave, and the joy Habakkuk felt when he understood how loving and powerful God is and that God always knows and does best.
Habakkuk Complains, and the Lord Answers	Habakkuk had an inquiring mind. That expression means he had lots of important questions that bothered him and that he wanted to ask of someone who would have the right answers. He would need to ask God. Habakkuk was wise to bring his questions and worries to God and not to be afraid to ask the Lord to help him understand the things that didn't make sense to him.
	Habakkuk wondered why it seemed God wasn't doing anything to correct the bad things that God's people in the land of Judah were doing. He didn't understand why the bad guys sometimes seemed to get along so well while the good guys had trouble. It just

didn't seem right to Habakkuk that people could get away with doing wrong again and again and not get punished for it.

God very patiently answered Habakkuk's questions and let him know that everything God does is good and right, even if it seems like God moves slower than we want. The Lord tells us not be in a big hurry, as God works out all His good and fair plans in our lives and in the lives of the people who do evil all the time. God tells Habakkuk that bad will not win over good forever, because God is in control and can be trusted to do what is right. After Habakkuk heard God's answers, his questions disappeared. Habakkuk praised God for Who He is and what He does!

Let's Meet the People of Habakkuk

Habakkuk was the prophet who asked God important questions about good and evil and then wrote down God's answers for us to read in the book of Habakkuk.

God's people in Judah were not obeying God like they should have, and Habakkuk didn't understand why God was letting them get away with such bad behavior. God let Habakkuk know that He saw how His people were acting and that He would do something about it in His own time.

The Babylonians were the enemies of God's people who seemed to get along well, even though they did many bad and sinful things. Habakkuk didn't understand why God did not punish the Babylonians. God told Habakkuk that they would be punished for their disobedience and sin at the right time.

Here Are the Places of Habakkuk

Judah – in the Southern Kingdom where God's people lived when Habakkuk asked his questions of God.

The Answer Man

(A question and answer game)

What need I need? You and your child and a Bible

Where is it in the Bible? Habakkuk 1–2

How long will it take? 10-15 minutes

What age child? 3-12 years

Will it work in a group? Yes

Can it be played in the car? Yes

Will it work in a school school classroom? Yes, preschool–6th grade

Open your Bible and explain that Habakkuk was a prophet who wrote the words God spoke to him. A prophet spoke God's words, like our pastors and preachers do today, but God also told him about important things that would happen in the days and years to come.

Habakkuk was a man who kept asking why. "Why is there bad in the world?" "Why do bad people have good things happen to them and good people have bad things happen to them?" "Will the people who do bad things ever get punished for their sins?"

Habakkuk loved God and knew that God had the answers to his questions. He asked God to help him understand the things that didn't seem to make sense. God did just that. He listened to Habakkuk's questions in chapter 1 and patiently gave him the answers in chapter 2. Then, Habakkuk felt so much better as he came to understand that God has everything under control. He learned that God will do the right thing at just the right time.

Play "The Answer Man" game. Pretend that your child is on a television game show, trying to answer the questions you ask her. Make the activity as simple or elaborate as you wish. You may drape a sheet behind her and tape a big question mark on it for a backdrop, or you may want to cut a hole in the side of a big box and ask her to put the box over her head. Then she could speak through the opening.

Here are some questions you may want to ask, or you can make up your own according to your child's age and interests. The last two questions are ones that Habakkuk asked, too.

1. Why do cats have little soft pads of skin on the bottoms of their feet?
2. Why do dogs wag their tails and cats purr?
3. What things have a nice smell?
4. Would a balloon break if it fell from a table to the floor? Would an egg? A light bulb? A marble? A ball?
5. Why doesn't grass grow on sandy beaches at the edge of the ocean?
6. Why do deer have antlers on their heads?
7. What can a person's brain do?
8. Why did God give us fingernails?
9. How does electricity travel from the light switch on the wall to the light bulb?
10. Why are there bad things in the world?
11. Will God ever stop evil from going on and on?

| **What Can I Learn from Habakkuk** | See *What Can I Learn from Jonah, Micah, Nahum, Habakkuk, and Zephaniah* at the end of Zephaniah. |

| **Important Verses to Remember** | Habakkuk 2:20 – "The Lord is in his holy temple; let all the earth be silent before him."

Habakkuk 3:19 – "The Sovereign Lord is my strength; he makes my feet like the feet of a deer, he enables me to go on the heights." |

| **A Devotional Thought for Parents and Teachers** | See *A Devotional Thought from Jonah, Micah, Nahum, Habakkuk, and Zephaniah* at the end of Zephaniah. |

Zephaniah God's Book About Trouble and Hope

"The Lord your God is with you, he is mighty to save. He will take great delight in you, he will quiet you with His love, he will rejoice over you with singing" (Zephaniah 3:17).

| **What's the Book About** | The book of Zephaniah is about the trouble that will come to God's people if they don't start obeying Him and doing what is right. It is also about the hope that God gives to those who love and serve Him. |

| **An Uncertain Future for Jerusalem** | In Zephaniah, God's people in Judah are not obeying Him. The people have plenty of money, and are so comfortable that they have forgotten all about God. They are worshiping false gods like Baal and Molech. God couldn't let His people keep on acting like that. The Lord told Zephaniah to warn His children that they were in danger of being punished if they don't stop what they are doing, and say they are sorry for their sins.

Even though God scolds His people harshly, He still loves them. He also gives them wonderful hope in the words He spoke through Zephaniah. God even tells His people about the Savior, Jesus, who will come and to be the King of His people forever. The same God who will have to punish His people will be the very One who will save them from their sins. |

Let's Meet the People of Zephaniah	Zephaniah was the prophet who spoke and wrote God's words about punishment and love.
	God's people in Judah had gotten very careless about obeying God.
Here Are the Places of Zephaniah	Judah – a city in the Southern Kingdom where some of God's people lived. God's people who had lived in the Northern Kingdom of Israel had already been taken away from their homes by the Assyrians.

STORIES AND ACTIVITIES FROM ZEPHANIAH

Opposites
(A hard and easy game)

What will I need? A box covered with paper and a crayon
Where is it in the Bible? Zephaniah 1–3
How long will it take? 15-25 minutes
What age child? 3-10 years
Will it work in a group? Yes
Can it be played in the car? No
Will it work in a school classroom? Yes, preschool–4th grade

Cover a box with paper. Write the words "trouble" on three sides, and "hope" on the other three sides. Then toss the box and see which word it lands on. If it lands on hope, ask your child to do one of the hope activities from the list below. Be sure to include activities appropriate for your child's age. If the box lands on trouble, he must try to do one of the trouble activities. Remember, there is no penalty for not performing the activity well. The object is to contrast the difference in trouble and hope, and to emphasize that God wants to give us the best life possible.

Real trouble comes when we try to do things on our own without God's help.

When God's people disobey Him and go their own way, there is trouble for them, but when they love and serve God there is hope.

Hope activities:
1. Get a hug from someone in the room.
2. Get your favorite treat.
3. Ask someone in the room what they like about you.
4. Go somewhere fun today or tomorrow.
5. Watch a favorite video after the game.
6. Get to invite a friend over to play.
7. Get to play with your favorite toy.
8. Play a favorite game with your family.
9. Listen to one of your favorite songs.
10. Get high five's from everyone.

Trouble activities:
1. Try to stand on your head.
2. Try to do a cartwheel.
3. Try to name everyone in your family in less than 7 seconds.
4. Try to do the backwards crab walk across the room.

5. Try to explain how the engine of a car works.

6. Try to say the Pledge of Allegiance backwards.

7. Try to wiggle your ears.

8. Try to touch your nose with your tongue.

What Can I Learn from Jonah, Micah, Nahum, Habakkuk, and Zephaniah

God sees everyone all the time. He knows if they are doing what is right, or if they are doing wrong. When people keep disobeying God, He must do something to stop them and to help them understand they need to obey and serve Him. When people are sorry for doing wrong, God is anxious to forgive their sins and help them have a good and happy life. God loves me, and because He loves me, I love Him, too. I want Him to see me doing what is right

An Important Verse to Remember

Zephaniah 3:17 – "The Lord your God is with you, he is mighty to save. He will take great delight in you, he will quiet you with his love, he will rejoice over you with singing."

A Devotional Thought for Parents and Teachers from Jonah, Micah, Nahum, Habakkak, and Zephaniah

God is good all the time, but an integral part of His goodness is His holiness and perfect justice. Over and over in the books of prophecy it is brought to our attention that God sees and knows what is going on all the time. He is not an absentee landlord, keeping His hands off His creation once He brings them into being. He is never oblivious to the wrong that reigns around us, no matter how much the evidence may seem to point to the contrary.

He understands that His people are constantly exposed to the sinful behavior of those who don't honor Him. He also knows His children constantly struggle with encounters with the devil.

We identify with the "why" man, Habakkuk. Haven't we all wondered why the ungodly seem to prosper. We wonder why God allows terrorism to succeed, and to continue at the incalculable price of thousands of lives.

But we do not usually direct our why's to the One with the answers, as Habakkuk did with his questions. Somehow we don't feel it's proper to express our doubts, fears, and questions to God. We act as if we don't want God to be aware of how we really feel. We don't want to insult or upset Him, and we seem to think that if we don't tell Him, He won't find out.

Our children are not like us. They don't try to hide their fear, and mask their questions. They just blurt it out, "Why didn't God stop that from happening? Why do bad guys get away with the things they do? Why don't they ever get caught and punished?"

In the books of prophecy we hear the answer over and over, God sees, God knows, and God will act in His perfect time, and in His sovereign manner. His ways and purposes far exceed our capacity to understand. We can always trust Him in every one of life's situations, good and bad.

We should boldly ask Him "why." We should also be sure to also ask why He is so good to us? Why He love us so? I'm not sure why, but thank You, with all my heart.

Haggai God's Book About Putting Him First and about Finishing the Work We Start for Him

"Be strong, all you people of the land declares the Lord, and work. For I am with you, declares the Lord Almighty" (Haggai 2:4b).

What's the Book About

The book of Haggai is about the prophet Haggai who is reminding God's people to put God first. He tells the people to get busy finishing the job of rebuilding the destroyed temple in Jerusalem.

God's People Learn to Listen and Obey

Haggai motivates God's people to finish repairing the temple that the Babylonians had destroyed years before. The people had started the job, but had gotten tired and discouraged, and had quit trying.

The Lord was not happy with the people, who were more interested in making their own houses nice and comfortable than in rebuilding God's house. For the people to care more about their own homes than a place to worship meant that God was not very important to them. They were putting themselves first, before God.

God's people listened to Haggai, got busy, and finished rebuilding the temple.

Let's Meet the People of Haggai

Haggai was God's special servant, one of His prophets, who delivered the message that God's people needed to put Him first and finish the temple.

The people living in Jerusalem were the ones Haggai told to get busy rebuilding the temple so people could go there to worship God again.

Zerubbabel, the Governor of Judah, and **Joshua,** the High Priest, both helped the people rebuild the temple.

Here Are the Places of Haggai

Jerusalem – the important city where the temple was being rebuilt after it was destroyed. God's people needed the temple so they could all come together and worship God.

S T O R I E S A N D A C T I V I T I E S F R O M H A G G A I

We've Got to Keep Working

(An edible construction activity)

What will I need? Graham crackers; peanut butter, cheese spread, or frosting; paper plates to make your project on, and a knife
Where is it in the Bible? Haggai 1-2
How long will it take? 20-30 minutes
What age child? 3-12 years
Will it work in a group? Yes, individually or in small groups
Can it be played in the car? No
Will it work in a school classroom? Yes, Preschool–6th grade

God's people, the Jews, have come back home after living as slaves in Babylon for seventy years. King Cyrus told the people they could go back to the land God had given them years before in Abraham and Moses' day. Then they could rebuild the temple which had been destroyed.

God's people moved back home to Judah. Once home, they unpacked their bags, unloaded their tools, and started to work on the temple. They wanted to build a beautiful place where they could go to worship the Lord.

Before long they got tired of doing the work. Their enemies started causing problems for them as they tried to work. They forgot how important the job of rebuilding God's temple really was, and right in the middle of the project they quit working. The temple lay unfinished.

God spoke to His people through Haggai. He told them He wanted His temple finished. He would take care of them, giving them everything they needed to do the job. God would make sure their enemies didn't hinder their work. God needed their willing hands to do whatever it took to get the job done.

The people listened to Haggai. As soon as they built the foundation for the temple, God started blessing them. He didn't wait for the whole job to get finished before He started blessing them, because God wants to bless His people.

Pretend to be the Jewish people in Haggai's day. Begin to build a temple on a plate using crackers for the walls and peanut butter, frosting, or cheese spread for the mortar to hold them together.

While you are building your temple, act out these events:

1. You get tired of the hard work. (Say, "whew" and wipe your forehead. Rest for a minute, then get back to work.)

2. Your enemies come to fight. (Box the air as if you are fighting) and tease you (put your thumbs in your ears, wiggle your fingers and say, "nah, nah, nah, nah, nah." Sigh and look discouraged.)

3. You need a vacation. (Say, "I'm going to my house to rest. God's temple can just wait. My house is pretty, but this place is a mess." Quit building and leave the table.)

4. But, Haggai says, "We must get back to work. Come on, you can do it. God will give you the strength you need. God's temple is important, so we've got to finish building it for Him." The people did. (Start building your cracker temple with new energy. Then, enjoy eating your project together.)

What Can I Learn from Haggai

See *What Can I Learn from Haggai, Zechariah, and Malachi* at the end of Malachi.

Important Verses to Remember from Haggai

Haggai 1:2-4 – "'This is what the Lord Almighty says: 'These people say, 'The time has not yet come for the Lord's house to be built.' Then the word of the Lord came through the prophet Haggai: 'Is it a time for you yourselves to be living in your paneled houses, while this house remains a ruin?'"

Haggai 1:13 – "Then Haggai, the Lord's messenger, gave this message of the Lord to the people: 'I am with you,' declares the Lord."

Haggai 2:4b – "Be strong, all you people of the land, declares the Lord, and work. For I am with you, declares the Lord Almighty."

A Devotional Thought for Parents and Teachers

See *A Devotional Thought from Haggai, Zechariah, and Malachi* at the end of Malachi.

Zechariah   God's Book About the Coming King

"Rejoice greatly, O Daughter of Zion! Shout, Daughter of Jerusalem! See, your king comes to you, righteous and having salvation, gentle and riding on a donkey, on a colt, the foal of a donkey" (Zechariah 9:9).

What's the Book About

The book of Zechariah is about God's people finishing rebuilding the temple in Jerusalem. It is mostly about the wonderful King and Messiah, Jesus Christ.

Dreams about Trees, Horns, Scrolls, Baskets, a Chariot, and a Crown.

Zechariah is about eight special dreams that God gave to the prophet Zechariah, so he can tell God's people what they mean. The dreams are all about God's people rebuilding the temple, staying away from sin, and loving God with all their hearts.

The great news of Zechariah's message is that Jesus is coming to earth as a baby. He will be the King of Kings.

Let's Meet the People of Zechariah

Zechariah was the prophet who preached God's words to the people in Judah and Israel.

Zerubbabel and **Joshua** were leaders who helped Zechariah give God's message to His people.

Here Are the Places of Zechariah

Jerusalem – the important city in Judah where Zechariah gave God's wonderful message to His people.

A Lot of Dreams

(A grab bag of strange things)

What will I need? A bag or pillowcase with these items in it:

1. toy horse or a picture of a horse or of a tree
2. number "4" cut out of construction paper
3. ruler
4. dirty shirt
5. candle
6. rolled-up piece of paper
7. basket

Where is it in the Bible? Zechariah 1–6

How long will it take? 15-30 minutes

What age child? 3-12 years

Will it work in a group? Yes

Can it be played in the car? No

Will it work in a school classroom? Yes, preschool–6th grade

Let your child see how many chapters are in Zechariah. Mention it is much longer than most of the other Bible books around it. Show him how long the books of Habakkuk, Zephaniah, and Haggai are in contrast. Zechariah is also a very important book because it tells us many things about the coming of Jesus Christ, His life, and His death for our sins.

Most of the things God told Zechariah to tell the people wouldn't take place for another 500 years. God knows everything that will happen. He is God, and He made time.

Put the items below in a bag. Let your child reach in and take out one item at a time. Each item is a reminder of the special dreams God gave to Zechariah. Share this simple explanation of what they mean:

1. The horse or a drawing or picture of a tree (Zechariah 1:7-17). Zechariah saw an angel on a red horse. The horse was standing among the trees beside a river. Other horses and riders were behind the angel. The angel was looking around at all the people living in different lands, and noticed that everything was going well for them. God's people didn't think it was fair for Him to let the people who were acting so badly live so well. But God was giving everyone a chance to change, before He had to punish their sins.

2. The number "4" (Zechariah 1:18-21). In Zechariah's dream he saw four animal horns which represented the four enemies of God's people – Egypt, Assyria, Babylon, and Medo-Persia. He also saw four blacksmiths who pounded and shaped pieces of metal. The metal represented the other countries God used to fight the enemies of His people. God was saying the people who disobeyed Him would be punished for their sins.

3. A ruler (Zechariah 2:1-13). In another dream a man was measuring the city of Jerusalem. It meant that one day the city would be full of happy people again.

4. A dirty cloth (Zechariah 3:1-10). God was showing Zechariah that He washes away our sins and makes our hearts clean.

5. A candle (Zechariah 4:1-14). This dream was about the Spirit of God who lives in our hearts when we believe in Him. Just as a candle can't shine by itself, we need God to shine His light through us.

6. A rolled-up piece of paper (Zechariah 5:1-4). The scroll Zechariah dreamed about was God's Word which tells us how He wants us to live.

7. A basket (Zechariah 5:5-10). Zechariah saw a woman inside a basket The woman did bad things, and represented sin. She was sent back to Babylon, because God wants our sins to be taken far away from us. Jesus is the only One who can take our sins away.

8. Another horse (Zechariah 6:1-8). Again, Zechariah dreamed about horses. He saw four horses, pulling chariots in four different directions. They were looking for people who were treating God's people badly. Those unkind people were in big trouble and would be punished for the bad things they were doing.

God's Very Special Day

Celebrate a special day "just because." You may want to honor your entire family or you may wish to honor individual people. Just make it a special day.

Read Zechariah 14:9. Explain there would be a very special day when Jesus would come to earth as a baby. There will be another special day when He comes again. It will be a wonderful day for everyone who believes and loves Jesus.

If your child expresses some fear about the return of Jesus, comfort and reassure him that seeing Jesus will not be scary for those who know Jesus as their Savior. It will be more exciting than anything that has ever happened to us. Ask him how he would feel to see somebody he loves, and hasn't seen in a long time coming to see him. That's how we'll feel when Jesus comes back to earth.

What Can I Learn from Zechariah	See *What Can I Learn from Haggai, Zechariah, and Malachi* at the end of Malachi.
Important Verses to Remember	Zechariah 4:6b – " 'Not by might nor by power, but by my Spirit,' says the Lord Almighty." Zechariah 8:13b – "So will I save you, and you will be a blessing. Do not be afraid, but let your hands be strong." Zechariah 9:9 – "Rejoice greatly, O Daughter of Zion! Shout, Daughter of Jerusalem! See, your king comes to you, righteous and having salvation, gentle and riding on a donkey, on a colt, the foal of a donkey." Zechariah 14:9 – "The Lord will be King over the whole earth. On that day there will be one Lord, and his name the only name."
A Devotional Thought for Parents and Teachers	See *A Devotional Thought from Haggai, Zechariah, and Malachi* at the end of Malachi.

Malachi God's Book About Sin and the Promise of a Savior

" 'My name will be great among the nations, from the rising to the setting of the sun. In every place incense and pure offerings will be brought to my name, because My name will be great among the nations,' says the Lord Almighty" (Malachi 1:11).

What's the Book About

The book of Malachi is about God's love for everyone

God Is Loving, Patient, and Just

Malachi is the last book in the Old Testament. The temple in Jerusalem had been rebuilt nearly 100 years before Malachi starts to preach about God. God's people have a wonderful place to go to worship Him, but once again they have forgotten they must obey God. God has been faithful to them, but they are not being faithful to him.

Some of God's people have stayed true and strong for Him. Malachi tells those who have been faithful that God knows who they are, and He will reward them. He even calls the faithful people His jewels.

Let's Meet the People of Malachi

Malachi was God's prophet who delivered God's message that even though we sin God will forgive us. He will send the One Who will erase our sins forever–Jesus.

The Priests and God's people were the ones God scolded through Malachi, because they didn't really love God. They pretend to worship and serve Him. They had forgotten all the lessons they had learned when they had been made to work as slaves in Babylon. Now, God's people had started disobeying Him again.

Here Are the Places of Malachi

Jerusalem – the city where the temple was located. It is where Malachi preached to the people.

God's Beautiful Jewels
(Making jewels in your kitchen)

What need will I need? Several different colors of small packages of gelatin, a bowl, measuring cup, and spoon. Several flat containers in which to pour the gelatin.

Where is it in the Bible? Malachi 3:16-17

How long will it take? 30-45 minutes

What age child? 3-12 years

Will it work in a group? Yes

Can it be played in the car? Only the discussion

Will it work in a school classroom? Yes, pre-school–6th grade

Read Malachi 3:16-17. Ask your child to listen for a word that describes something very beautiful and valuable (jewels). Hold your child close and tell her that God thinks of her as His valuable jewel.

In Malachi's day many of God's people weren't loving Him as they should. There were some people who kept right on serving God. He called those people His jewels. God promises to take care of those who love and obey Him. He knows each of them by name. Talk about how God knows your child's name and everything else about her.

To illustrate the truth that God treasures those who love Him, make several different colors of gelatin with your child. Pour each one into separate flat containers to gel. When they are set, let your child help you slice the gelatin into cubes. Then put the different colored cubes into a clear dish so the colors can be easily seen. Top your jewels with whipped cream, and enjoy the treasure together.

What Can I Learn from Haggai, Zechariah, and Malachi	God's people in the days of Haggai, Zechariah, and Malachi were pretending to love Him. In their hearts He was not really important to them. That's why they didn't care about finishing the job of rebuilding the temple or following His rules.
Important Verses to Remember from Malachi	Malachi 1:2 – " 'I have loved you,' says the Lord." Malachi 3:6a – "I the Lord do not change." Malachi 3:8 – " 'Will a man rob God? Yet you rob Me.' But you ask, 'How do we rob You? In tithes and offerings'. "

A Devotional Thought for Parents and Teachers from Haggai, Zechariah, and Malachi

These prophets must have been reading our mail. The names and times have changed, but the facts, unfortunately, remain true today. Human nature is alive and well, and is nothing to brag about.

The "to do" lists of the people in Jerusalem must have been quite different from ours, but, nonetheless, they revealed the priorities of God's people. What are our priorities—be at work early, stay late again, be there, do that, work on that project. Oh, if there is any time left, work at the temple project, give food to the beggar by the gate, pray and thank God for all His goodness.

It was about priorities then, and it is still about our priorities. Values then, values now. We say that God is first in our lives, but what do all our "to do" lists say about that?

Matthew God's Book About Jesus, Our Lord and King

"She will give birth to a son, and you are to give him the name Jesus, because he will save his people from their sins. All this took place to fulfill what the Lord had said through the prophet: 'The virgin will be with child and will give birth to a son, and they will call him Immanuel'—which means, 'God with us'" (Matthew 1:21-23).

What's the Book About

The book of Matthew is about the special way Jesus was born, the amazing life He lived, and the way He died and came alive again to show us that Jesus is the Son of God, the One God promised the people He would send. Matthew makes sure we understand that Jesus is the King and Lord over everything.

A Long-Expected Promise is Fulfilled

Matthew begins as God's people are waiting for His Son, our Savior and Messiah, to come to earth. More than 400 years have gone by since any of God's prophets have given His words to the people. Now it is time for all God's amazing promises to be fulfilled.

The Old Testament prophets had promised that God's Son would come from King David's royal family. He would be the King of Kings forever (Isaiah 11:1-5).

Let's Meet the People of Matthew

Jesus is God's Son. He is the Savior of the world that the prophets of the Old Testament promised would come.

Mary was Jesus' mother. She was a virgin when she gave birth to Jesus.

Joseph was her husband and the father of her other sons and daughters.

John the Baptist was the cousin of Jesus and the person that was promised in the Old Testament who would announce to everybody when God's Son was soon to appear. John the Baptist also baptized Jesus.

Jesus' twelve disciples were the men that Jesus chose to be His helpers on earth. He taught them many important and amazing things.

The Pharisees were the religious leaders who gave Jesus a hard time and finally put Him on a cross to die.

Caiaphas, the High Priest and **Pilate**, the Roman Governor were Jewish leaders who had Jesus put on the cross to die. But even these leaders and their powerful soldiers weren't strong enough to make Him stay there. Jesus willingly chose to die for our sins, and He did.

Mary Magdalene was one of the women who came to Jesus' grave after He was buried. There she discovered Jesus was alive.

Here Are the Places of Matthew

Bethlehem – the small town where Jesus was born, as foretold by the prophets.

Jerusalem – the important city of Israel where the temple of God was located.

Capernaum – the big city where many people lived who did not know God. That's why Jesus moved there to preach and to show them who God really is.

Galilee – the land near the Sea of Galilee. Capernaum and Nazareth were located there.

Judea – the land near the Dead Sea where Jesus' friends, Mary, Martha, and Lazarus lived in Bethany, and where the city of Jerusalem was located. Jesus spent the last week before He died in Judea.

Then Came Jesus

Talk with your child about your family history. Try to name as many ancestors and family members as you can Talk about the individuals on your list, what they were like, what you think they might have been like if you never met them, what they did, and their love and service for God, if they were believers.

If you wish, you may draw or copy an outline of a tree on a piece of paper and ask your child to fill in the top part with the names or pictures of your family members.

Open your Bible to Matthew 1 and show your child the list of the names in Jesus' family. Explain that it was very important in Jesus' day to know about your family. It was really important for Jesus because God's Son had to come from King David's family line, which He did.

Jesus didn't have a human father like everyone else, Joseph was his stepfather and Mary's husband. God was Jesus' father. Because Jesus was born from Mary, He was a human like we are; but, because He was born of God, He was also divine.

One of the most beautiful truths of Jesus' genealogy is that some of the people in His own lineage were godly heroes; some were just ordinary people; some had questionable reputations; and others were just evil. God can use all kinds of people to accomplish His great purposes. But how much more wonderful to be a person God can use because we truly want Him to. Help your child to be that kind of person, as you reflect that attitude in your own life.

Joseph's Amazing Dream

Talk about the important story of the angel who came to Joseph in a dream and told him him that Jesus, the Savior, would be born to Mary. Joseph was troubled that Mary would have a baby, because he was not yet married to her and he was not the baby's father. As Joseph tried to figure out what was happening and why, God sent an angel to explain His wonderful plan to Joseph. Read about it in Matthew 1:20-23.

God explained to Joseph that the baby should be named Jesus, which means Savior, because He would be God's own promised Son. He would be the One who would save His people from their sins. After the angel spoke to Joseph, he understood that God was the baby's father and that this very special baby was like no other baby who had or would ever be born.

Joseph took Mary to be his wife. When the baby was born, they named Him Jesus, just as the angel had said. The precious baby Jesus grew up to die on the cross to save us from our sins.

The How-to-Be Attitudes

A very important part of Matthew's book is the words Jesus says to us in Matthew 5:1-12. We sometimes call them the Beatitudes. We could call them the how-to-be attitudes. Each of the verses tells us how to be happy or blessed. Jesus tells us to have joy in our hearts even when things are going on around us that aren't much fun. He said be happy :

– by not being too proud of ourselves (v. 5)

– by being sad about some things, especially, our sins (v. 4)

– by knowing that we still have lots of things we can learn because we don't know it all (v. 6)

– by wanting to do the good, right things that please God (v. 3)

– by being kind and loving to other people, even when they don't deserve it (v. 7)

– by keeping our hearts pure (v. 8)

– by trying to keep peace with other people and not cause trouble or argue (v. 9)

Jesus said that we can be happy even when other people are being very unkind to us and treating us unfairly (v. 10-12). That's amazing. He said there is a special prize in heaven for the people who are treated badly on earth, because they choose to follow and obey Jesus. We want to love Jesus all the time, even when it's hard.

To help you and your child remember the Beatitudes, here are some bee facts:

1. Bees are God's busy worker insects. They can carry up to half their body weight in nectar and they sometimes fly 6-8 miles to find a tasty field of flowers. Besides that, bees' bodies are really too heavy for their little wings to be able to carry them and make them fly, but God makes sure that they can.

2. Bees must gather up enough honey to last them through the cold winter, when the flowers aren't blooming, and food is hard to find. To make just one pound of honey, bees must fly about 50-100 miles. That's a lot of traveling.

3. As bees collect nectar, they also get pollen on their wings, which helps to fertilize other plants so they can grow and give us fruit and vegetables. Just as bees are very important in God's great plan for plants, we are important in God's great plan about how His people should be.

Twelve Very Special Helpers
(A funny drama)

What will I need? Your child, his imagination, and a sense of humor

Where is it in the Bible? Matthew 10:1-41

How long will it take? 5-10 minutes

What age child? 2–12 years

Will it work in a group? Yes

Can it be played in the car? Yes

Will it work in a school classroom? Yes, preschool–6th grade

Jesus chose 12 very special helpers, called disciples, and then sent them out to do His work and show His love to people. He wanted them to understand that serving Him wouldn't always be an easy job.

Although Jesus was filled with only love, goodness, and kindness, He still had enemies. His friends would share in the troubles and hardships that Jesus Himself had to face. To learn more about Jesus' disciples, read Matthew 15. Jesus even told His disciples that He was sending them out like sheep among wolves (Matthew 10:16). Ask your child what he thinks Jesus meant. Did Jesus' helpers deserve that kind of treatment? Did Jesus? Help your child develop a fortitude as a believer in Jesus so he will stand strong and determined to follow Jesus no matter the cost. What could possibly be a better gift to instill in your child's heart and life?

Here's a very lighthearted drama to reinforce a very weighty subject. Ask one family member to read the following story as the others fill in the proper sound effects. Get dramatic with this story. You might even get your gang down on all fours to play the parts.

"One sunny day a flock of sheep (baa) were munching grass (munch, munch, munch) on a quiet hillside. There were sheep (baa) of all sizes, big rams (baa), fluffy ewes (baa), and tiny baby lambs (baa). They ate the green grass (munch, munch, munch) and they drank the cool water from the stream (slurp, slurp).

Unknown to the sheep (get dramatic, this is the exciting part!), a hungry wolf (grrr!) was lurking behind the bushes, hungrily dreaming of lamb chops (lick lips and rub tummies). Suddenly, the wolf (grrr) bounded out from the bushes and found himself face-to-face with the shepherd. Seeing the determined look on the shepherd's face, and fearing the shepherd's stick, the wolf (grrr) ran off in a cloud of dust (cough like it's dusty) leaving the sheep (baa) to return to their contented munching (munch, munch, munch) and drinking (slurp, slurp). The End.

Remind your child that in the Bible Jesus is called the "Good Shepherd," and He takes good care of His sheep–us.

Four Special Kinds of Dirt
(Activities to do with seeds)

What will I need: Activity 1. A jar with a lid, a paper towel, water, and several different kinds of plant or flower seeds. Activity 2. Dirt, digging tools, birdseed, grass seed, flower or vegetable seeds, water. Activity 3. Sponges, scissors, a cookie sheet, birdseed or grass seed, water.
Where is it in the Bible? Matthew 13:1-23
How long will it take? 15-30 minutes
What age child? 3-12 years
Will it work in a group? Yes
Can it be played in the car? No

Will it work in a school classroom? Yes, preschool–6th grade

Share with your child the story of the farmer and the different kinds of dirt. Here are some highlights:
1. The seed that the farmer planted was all good. The seed represents the truth about Jesus and the life He gives us.
2. The dirt on the hard path is like the heart of someone who hears about Jesus and doesn't let it come inside his heart. So the devil, like the birds, takes the truth away.
3. The thin, rocky dirt is like the person who hears about Jesus and takes it into his heart, but the seed doesn't grow very deep roots. When trouble comes, that person doesn't live for Jesus anymore.
4. The dirt with lots of thorns and weeds is the heart of someone who hears about Jesus, but his sins and the other things that matter too much to him push God's truth out of his life, and Jesus matters less and less to him.
5. The good dirt is like the person who listens to God's message, takes Jesus into his heart, and lives a wonderful life of doing good and bringing other people to Jesus.

Try one or more of these fun activities together:
1. Get a jar with a lid. Choose 8 or 10 different kinds of seeds–flower, vegetable, beans, lentils, peas, alfalfa–and soak the seeds overnight. Cut and fold two paper towels until they are the right size to fit inside the jar. Dampen the towels slightly and line the jar with them.

Tuck each seed down between the paper towels, near the top, and put the lid on the jar. Watch the seeds every day to see how they start a little a root growing down and then a shoot growing up.

But how can the seeds grow without dirt?

They have enough food inside them to grow for awhile after they soak up water. But then they will need dirt to get enough food to keep on growing. The right kind of dirt is important for plants, and the right kind of heart for Jesus is important for you and me.

2. Find a small patch of dirt outside that your child can dig up and plant seeds in. Use toy tools and let your child dig to his heart's content. Dirt and kids go together. When there's been enough fun with dirt, it's time to plant. Provide grass seed, birdseed, flower, or vegetable seeds. Check on the garden every day, and give it whatever care it needs. Say a thank-you to God for being the One who makes all things live and grow.

3. Ask your child if he has ever eaten grass seed for breakfast. He probably has, because rice, corn, oats, and wheat are all in the grass-cereal family. God made them good for us. Give your child a few inexpensive sponges, and ask him to cut them into whatever shapes he wishes. Dip the sponge shapes into water and squeeze out any excess. Place the shapes on a paper plate, old tray, or cookie sheet. Sprinkle the damp sponges with grass seed or birdseed. Set the plate in a sunny spot and spray the sponges with water every day. See what happens in a few days.

An Itty Bitty Mustard Seed

Read to your child the very short story Jesus told about a tiny seed. You can find it in Matthew 13:31-32. Explain that our faith can begin as a very small thing, but when we place it in Jesus, the results will be amazing.

Here's a little bit of amazing seed trivia to share with your child:

1. More than 250,000 plants have seeds, and the largest seed weighs as much as 50 pounds. It comes from the double coconut tree.

2. Orchid seeds are so tiny that 800,000 seeds weigh no more than one ounce.

3. The giant redwood trees that grow in California come from seeds that are only 1/16 of an inch long.

4. Seeds wear coats like people do. Why? For the same reason, to cover and protect the seed or the person. If you soak a seed, you can peel off its coat just like you take off yours! Peanuts or sunflower seeds have coats that we call shells.

5. Seeds need only three things to grow. They need food, water, and light. For a while, a seed has enough food inside itself to grow, but before long, it needs food from the dirt, too, to keep on growing and make new plants and fruit.

6. Seeds can move, and they have to leave their parent plants to grow. Seeds travel in the wind, in water, by people who plant them, and they can even hitch a ride on animals.

7. Many seeds are great to eat just like they are, and many of our favorite foods come from seeds. Cereal, bread, pancakes, rice, corn, watermelon, apples, pickles, mustard, peanut butter, and chocolate are all from seeds.

The Greatest Rule of All
(Love activities)

What will I need? Two egg whites, 1 tsp. cream of tartar, 1/8 tsp. of salt, 1 tsp. mint flavoring, a few drops of green food coloring, sugar, 2 greased cookie sheets, a mixer, and a small plastic bag with a corner cut out.
Where is it in the Bible? Matthew 22:33-40
How long will it take? 25-45 minutes
What age child? 4-12 years

Will it work in a group? Better in a group
Can it be played in the car? No
Will it work in a school classroom? Yes, preschool–6th grade

Read in Matthew 22:33-40 the wonderful message of love. Make mint cookie kisses and give them away. Here's the recipe: Grease 2 large cookie sheets and heat the oven to 200 degrees. Combine the first three ingredients from What will I need? above. Beat with a mixer at medium speed until foamy. Turn the speed up a few notches to high and add sugar, one tablespoon at a time, until the meringue is very stiff and shiny and all the sugar is dissolved. Beat a little more as you add the mint extract and a few drops of food coloring.

Fill a plastic bag with the mixture and cut a hole in the corner of the bottom. Close the top of the bag and carefully squeeze out small amounts of the meringue as kisses on the cookie sheets. Shake some candy sprinkles on each kiss, and place them on the center rack of the oven for 2 hours. (Yes, you read right.)

Remove the kiss cookies. Let them cool on a wire rack or sheet of waxed paper.

The Happiest Day of All
(Some silly jokes and a happy story)

What will I need? Your child, a sense of humor, and a Bible
Where is it in the Bible? Matthew 28:1-11
How long will it take? 10-15 minutes
What age child? 3-12 years
Will it work in a group? Yes
Can it be played in the car? Yes
Will it work in a school classroom?
Preschoolers may not understand the jokes

Talk about happy days you and your child have enjoyed. Spend some time being happy together by telling these silly jokes:
Why do elephants wear red nail polish? So nobody can see them hiding in the strawberry patch.
What goes clomp, clomp, clomp, squish (repeat)? An elephant wearing one wet tennis shoe.
Why do elephants wear yellow baseball caps? So they can hide in the dandelions.
How can you keep an elephant from slipping down the drain? Tie a knot in his tail.

You may also do some tickling with feathers, making funny faces, walking in a silly way, using socks for hand puppets, or having a sock-ball fight. Talk about how great it is to be happy and how Jesus makes you truly happy.

Then change the mood just slightly, enough to remain happy, but not to silly. Ask your child to listen to you read about the happiest day we can imagine for all of Jesus' friends, and for us. After Jesus suffered and died for our sins, He came back to life. Read Matthew 28:1-11 with great joy, and thank Jesus for being our Living Lord!

Parents, if you want your amazing little child to have the privilege of memorizing this whole passage, read or say it with him in its entirety every day for about a week. Don't ask him to repeat after you, or drill him on it, just read it through as it is in the Bible. Then wait until the next day to read it again.

Ask him to try to say it along with you after the first day, even if he doesn't know many words. In no time, he will know some words, then more, then all the passage. He will remember it, very likely, for most of his life. Try that with other Scriptures, too. Reward him with hugs and applause.

What Can I Learn from Matthew

Matthew told us about the people in Jesus' family who lived and died before God sent baby Jesus to earth. Matthew also told us what Jesus said and did while He was on earth. Matthew wanted all people to know Jesus is God's own Son and the Savior of the world! I believe that Jesus is the Savior and Lord that God promised to send. I can trust Him with my life forever.

Important Verses to Remember

Matthew 6:21 – "For where your treasure is, there your heart will be also."

Matthew 19:14 – "Jesus said, 'Let the little children come to me, and do not hinder them, for the kingdom of heaven belongs to such as these'."

Matthew 22:37-39 – "Love the Lord your God with all your heart and with all your soul and with all your mind. This is the first and greatest commandment. And the second is like it: 'Love your neighbor as yourself'."

Matthew 28:19-20 – "Therefore go and make disciples of all nations, baptizing them in the name of the Father and of the Son and of the Holy Spirit, and teaching them to obey everything I have commanded you. And surely I am with you always, to the very end of the age."

A Devotional Thought for Parents and Teachers

Hundreds of years passed from the time the first prophecy came from God to man regarding the Savior who would come. God knew that Satan would mercilessly make it his evil business to incessantly strike against the Savior. He would make futile attempts to defeat and destroy Jesus and thwart God's divine plan for mankind's redemption. But Jesus, Messiah and Master, would strike a deadly blow on the very head of Satan through His death and mighty resurrection victory. Because of Jesus, we're in the winner's circle with Him.

However, when Jesus came to earth, He was following 400 years of silence, with not a word uttered from God to His people. Human nature being what it is, the weary "waiters" were almost certainly feeling, "Where is He, God? You promised He'd come! By the way, where are You, God?"

Jesus' presence on earth did not occur as a temporary visit, appearing then disappearing and remaining in the distant heavens far out of sight until the end of time. He reappeared as Himself in the spirit form of the ever-present Holy Spirit never to leave us without His perpetual closeness and comfort. Jesus, with the time and place limitations of his human body laid aside, may now be present everywhere His children are, because His divine, loving nature demands it and because we need Him so much.

Jesus talks about David loving God, wanting to do right, but so entangled by his own wandering eye and the sinful justifications for his behavior. We wish it weren't so, but we identify. Jesus even points out the names in His ancestry of truly evil men and reminds us that God can use anyone to accomplish His lovely purposes. Our personal worth is enhanced, our hearts are encouraged, our focus is redirected to Him where it should always be. Jesus makes up for our every imperfection, every inadequacy, as we allow Him to cleanse us and live through us in the victory that, apart from Him, would forever and ever be out of our reach.

Matthew understood who Jesus is, and the former sinner saved by the grace of the Savior knew firsthand that grace means to erase our sins and replace our old life with a brand new one. Aren't you grateful that Jesus came and stayed?

Mark God's Book About Jesus Our Savior, a Servant and King "For even the Son of Man did not come to be served, but to serve, and to give his life as a ransom for many" (Mark 10:45).

What's the Book About

The book of Mark is about the amazing things Jesus did that show He is God's Son.

A Close Friend Remembers an Amazing Life

Mark is an exciting book that speeds from one wonderful time in the life of Jesus to the next. Mark was a friend of Jesus. He saw with his own eyes all the amazing and loving things Jesus did. Mark sounds as if he can hardly wait to tell us about Jesus.

Mark said at the beginning of his book that Jesus is the Son of God. Mark tells us over and over again about the incredible things that Jesus did to prove who He is.

Let's Meet the People of Mark

Jesus is the most important person in Mark's book. He is the Son of God, and He proves it by what He says and does.

The Twelve Disciples were the special helpers Jesus chose to teach and help Him do God's work on earth.

Pilate was the Roman governor of Jerusalem who thought that Jesus had done nothing wrong. He was too weak and too worried about what Jesus' enemies and his Roman boss, the Emperor, would think if he let Jesus go free. Because he cared more about himself than about God, Pilate decided to go ahead and let Jesus be killed.

The Jewish leaders, the Pharisees, were people who said they loved and obeyed God, but they really did not. If they had loved God, they would have shown their love for Him by believing in Jesus. Instead, these unkind people tried every way they could to stop Jesus. They finally put Jesus to death even though He had done nothing wrong.

Here Are the Places of Mark

Nazareth – the town where Jesus lived when He was a child. Jesus probably helped Joseph in his carpenter's shop while He was growing up.

Capernaum – the land of Galilee, very close to the Sea of Galilee. It was a big city where many people who did not know God lived. Jesus moved there to show them that they could put their trust in Him.

Caesarea Philippi – the city that was famous for its many false gods and idols. There were even temples there where people went to worship the idol Baal, the same idol that the people worshiped in Elijah and Elisha's day.

Jericho – a city in the desert of Judea that people liked to visit for vacations. It was not far from the Jordan River.

Bethany – the town where Jesus' good friends Mary, Martha, and Lazarus lived. He went there whenever He could.

Jerusalem – the important city in Judea, where Jesus rode into town on a donkey. He was cheered by thousands of people one day, but put on a cross to die only a few days later.

Golgotha – the hill where Jesus died on the cross. It is also called Calvary.

A Great Preacher

Jesus had just moved to Capernaum from Nazareth, where He had grown up. Jesus wanted to be where there were all kinds of people with whom He could share the good news of who He was.

On the Sabbath (the day of worship), Jesus and His disciples went to church in the synagogue. The temple in Jerusalem was too far for many people to travel to worship there, so many towns had their own synagogues. There the people heard Jesus speak. They were amazed because He spoke like no one they had ever heard before.

Once, while Jesus was speaking, a man who was controlled by an evil spirit began to shout at Him, "Why are You bothering us? Have You come to destroy us? We know who You are, the holy Son of God!" Satan and his angels know who Jesus is. So do we.

Jesus has all power, including power over Satan. He told the demon in the man to come out and to say no more. At Jesus' powerful word, the demon obeyed, but as the demon came out, he shook the man and made a lot of noise! When the man was quiet and the demon was gone, the people were even more amazed that even evil spirits obeyed Jesus. The news of what had happened that day spread quickly. Don't ever be afraid that the devil will win the battle over your life or our world. Jesus is greater than Satan, and Jesus is in charge of how things will turn out.

The Spots Nobody Wanted
(A cooking activity)

What will I need? 1. Muffin pizza – English muffins, pizza sauce, cheese, or pepperoni; Fruit pizza – bagels, cream cheese, jelly, sliced bananas, kiwi, or cherries; Fluffernutter pizza – English muffins, marshmallow cream, peanut butter, and chocolate chips. 2. Spotty-Dotty Fudge – 12 oz. package chocolate chips, one can chocolate frosting, two cups miniature marshmallows, a pan, stove, and waxed paper
Where is it in the Bible? Mark 1:40-45
How long will it take? 30-45 minutes
What age child? 3-12 years
Will it work in a group? Yes
Can it be played in the car? No
Will it work in a school classroom? Yes, preschool–6th grade

Enjoy making something very tasty that has spots:
1. Toast an English muffin and top it with pizza sauce, cheese, and spots of pepperoni. Add any other topping you like. If you prefer, make a fruit pizza on a bagel by spreading on cream cheese (add a thin layer of jelly, if you want) and topping it with spots of sliced bananas, kiwi, or cherries. Another variation is the fluffernutter pizza made by toasting an English muffin and topping it with marshmallow cream or peanut butter, and some chocolate chip spots.
2. Spotty-Dotty Fudge – In a large pan over low heat, melt a 12 oz. package of semi-sweet chocolate chips. Stir constantly until the chips are smooth and melted. Remove the

mixture from the heat and add one can of ready-made chocolate frosting and two cups of miniature marshmallows. Let stand until the mixture is cool enough to handle. Divide the fudge mixture in half and roll each part into a log-shaped roll on separate sheets of waxed paper. Cover the fudge rolls and let them cool for several hours. Then cut them into spotty-dotty fudge slices.

Tell your child the spotted goodies you made are great, but not all spots are so good. Ask your child when and what spots are bad. (When they stain the carpet, when they mean you have chicken pox or a rash, or, in Bible days, when someone had a sickness called leprosy.)

Explain that leprosy started with just one little spot, but then it became much worse. It was a sickness that nobody wanted. In fact, people that had leprosy had to go away from everybody else, even their families, and live by themselves so nobody would catch their sickness. Few people ever talked to people with leprosy except to say, "Go away!" They certainly never touched someone with leprosy because they might get the disease themselves! But read Mark 1:40-45 to see what Jesus did when a man with leprosy came and knelt down in front of him. It's a wonderful story of God's love for a man who was quite unlovable to everybody else!

Jesus Stops the Storm

(Create a storm)

What will I need? You, your child, and a group of friends
Where is it in the Bible? Mark 4:35-41
How long will it take? 20-30 minutes
What age child? 3-12 years

Will it work in a group? Yes
Can it be played in the car? No
Will it work in a school classroom? Yes, preschool–6th grade

What an awesome God we serve. One who can even turn fierce storms into sunshiny days. Read the story about the day Jesus told the stormy winds to quiet down and they did. His disciples were even amazed at what Jesus was able to do.

Explain that the Sea of Galilee is in a very low valley, with hills all around it. The wind starts to blow very quickly around the sea and rushes down the hills toward the water, where it grows even stronger, and blows from all directions. The storm in the story must have been a big one, because even brave fishermen like the disciples, were scared nearly to death. They forgot that Jesus has everything under His control.

After the story do this storm activity with your child. Stand facing your child, or stand in a circle if you are in a group. Start to rub your hands, the person to your right should join in with you in rubbing her hands together, then the next player, the next, until everyone is making the rubbing sound that is much like a gentle rain. Then begin snapping your fingers and pretend the rain is beginning to fall harder and harder. Your child now imitates this sound. etc. When the new sound has gone all around the circle slap your thighs, pretending the storm is getting worse. To make the bad storm begin to let up, completely reverse your actions.

The storm Mark tells us about didn't slow down gradually. When Jesus spoke to the wind it stopped blowing, the rain stopped falling, and the water became smooth again immediately.

Herod the Horrible
(Two science experiments)

What will I need? Dancing Raisins: a jar full of water, 2 Tbsp. baking soda, five raisins, and 2 Tbsp. vinegar; Dancing Popcorn: a glass of water, 10 unpopped popcorn kernels, and two seltzer tablets
Where is it in the Bible? Mark 6:14-29
How long will it take? 15-20 minutes
What age child? 3-12 years
Will it work in a group? Yes
Can it be played in the car? No
Will it work in a school classroom? Yes, preschool–6th grade

Try one of these dancing experiments with your child.
Dancing Raisins:
1. First, fill a jar half full of water. Stir in two tablespoons of baking soda
2. Drop in five raisins.
3. Add two tablespoons of vinegar and watch what happens. The raisins will dance.

When vinegar and baking soda combine, they produce carbon dioxide in the form of bubbles. The bubbles gather on the raisins and take them along for a ride up to the surface of the water.

Dancing Popcorn:
1. Fill a glass with water and add ten unpopped popcorn kernels.
2. Drop in two seltzer tablets and watch what happens.
The bubbles lift the popcorn to the top of the water, like floats. When the bubbles reach the top of the water, they pop. The popcorn is too heavy to float by itself and it sinks down to the bottom of the glass.

Explain that there was a time in the book of Mark that dancing was not a happy event. In fact, something very unhappy took place after a girl danced for the mean King Herod. Because of her dance, and an evil request, John the Baptist had to die. You can read the whole story in Mark 6:17-29.

Pay special attention to the fact that Herod really didn't want to have John the Baptist killed, but he felt pressured by what others thought and said. Remind your child to always do the right thing, no matter which of his friends may try to get him to do wrong.

A Lot of Hungry People

Pack a picnic lunch and head out to enjoy it on a blanket somewhere. Along with any other foods that you like, include a piece or two of bread and fish-shaped crackers. Bread and fish were the typical lunch menu in Jesus' day.

As you are enjoying lunch together, tell the two stories in Mark 6:30-44 and 8:1-9, about the times Jesus fed two large crowds. They were hungry and Jesus cared about what the people needed. He made very sure that everyone there got fed. Talk about the things in each story that are alike and different. The same loving, caring Jesus was the most important person in each story.

Pay special attention to the little boy in the story who gave his own lunch so that other people could eat. Be ready to always give Jesus anything He asks.

A Picture on a Coin

(Coin rubbings)

What will I need? Different kinds of coins, white paper, and a pencil or dark crayon
Where is it in the Bible? Mark 12:17
How long will it take? 10-15 minutes
What age child? 2-11 years
Will it work in a group? Yes
Can it be played in the car? No
Will it work in a school classroom? Yes, preschool–5th grade

Collect several different kinds of coins and spread them out on a table, heads up. Cover one coin at a time with a sheet of paper and rub over it with a pencil or crayon to make its imprint. Copy the fronts of the coins first and then turn them over and rub over the backs of the coins on the paper. See if your child can match the coin-rubbings with the real coins. Name what they are and what they're worth. Be sure your child sees the very important words on each coin– *In God We Trust*. Explain how important it is that our great country really does trust in God to lead us and protect us. Take time to pray for our wonderful land and our leaders.

Read the verse about a coin that Jesus' enemies tried to use to trick Him and make Him say something that would get Him in trouble. They did not understand that Jesus is God, that He knew what they were thinking and planning, and that He will always do what is right. Ask your child if she thinks Jesus wants us to obey our country's leaders and laws, and to pay taxes. Talk about the privileges and responsibilities we enjoy because we live in a free and beautiful land. Explain to her that our tax money provides roads, parks, hospitals, libraries, schools, and many other things we need. Be sure to thank the Lord for being so kind to us to let us live in the country we love.

What Can I Learn from Mark

1. Jesus told the people He was the Son of God, and then He showed them it was true by what He did. I can tell other people that I love Jesus and I can show them by the things I do that Jesus is my Savior and my friend.

2. While Jesus was busy doing so many good things, the devil was trying to do bad things, but Jesus is much more powerful than the devil. When I do what's right, the devil doesn't like it and may try to get me to do wrong. When that happens, I need to trust Jesus to help me, because He's stronger than the devil.

Important Verses to Remember

Mark 4:39 – "He got up, rebuked the wind and said to the waves, 'Quiet! Be still!' Then the wind died down and it was completely calm."

Mark 9:35 – "Sitting down, Jesus called the Twelve and said, 'If anyone wants to be first, he must be the very last, and the servant of all.'"

Mark 9:37 – "Whoever welcomes one of these little children in my name welcomes me; and whoever welcomes me does not welcome me, but the one who sent me."

Mark 11:24-25 – "Therefore I tell you, whatever you ask for in prayer, believe that you have received it, and it will be yours. And when you stand praying, if you hold anything against anyone, forgive him, so that your Father in heaven may forgive you your sins."

Mark 12:30 – "Love the Lord your God with all your heart and with all your soul and with all your mind and with all your strength."

A Devotional Thought for Parents and Teachers

Jesus cut to the heart of things. He stepped on toes. He let the chips fall where they may. He told the truth. He wanted His followers to be the real thing, not just look like the real thing. Jesus talked about practical things like diet, fashion, pollution, finances, and communication. But when Jesus spoke, His words stirred the embers and fanned the flames within hearts, igniting the smoldering embers inside His enemies into fiery outbursts of opposition, or kindling the tiny sparks of faith within open-hearted listeners into a blazing inferno of passion to follow the Savior. Jesus' words were always explosive.

Jesus questioned why we worry so much more about our physical things than those things that nourish and strengthen our hearts, minds, and spirits. Jesus shattered the hopes and misconceptions of those whose money owned them. Jesus told us pointedly that He must be our Master, and money our servant, used wisely and given selflessly to His eternal kingdom.

The Savior even probes into our personal prayer life. Jesus wants us to pray with unselfish motives.

Jesus' words keep tugging at our hearts and calling to us by name. He says to us, "It's time to get real. I don't want you to struggle to perform any more. Just rest in My grace. You are unconditionally loved and accepted. Those corrections and adjustments that need to take place in your heart – I can fix those for you. I'm the expert at repairing and polishing up lives until they shine like gold."

Mark had been with Jesus. He had seen everything up close, and knew that everything about Jesus was real. Can the people who know us best, and the Savior who loves us most, say the same about us?

Luke God's Book About Jesus, the Perfect Man, and Our Wonderful Savior
"Praise be to the Lord, the God of Israel, because he has come and has redeemed his people." (Luke 1:68).

What's the Book About

The book of Luke tells us about the birth, life, death, and ressurection of Jesus.

Luke the Doctor Tells About a Greater Physician

Luke was a doctor who gave check-ups and medicine. He loved Jesus and watched all the incredible things that only God could do. But Luke also noticed all the things Jesus did as a man. Jesus was the only perfect man who ever lived. Luke wrote what he saw and heard so we could know and love Jesus–God who became a man.

Luke's book is very important, because he tells us things about Jesus that we wouldn't know otherwise. He tells us about Jesus' amazing birth, the shepherds, and angels who were there for that wonderful occasion. Luke tells us about Jesus when He was a boy, particularly about a trip Jesus made to Jerusalem when He was 12 years old.

Luke makes sure that we know everything Jesus did as a person was perfect. Jesus gives us a model of how we should live and love. Because Jesus is God, He has the power to help us be the way He wants us to be.

Many important details about Jesus' death, burial, and resurrection are found in Luke. The book doesn't end there, because the story of Jesus isn't finished yet. Luke makes our hearts jump for joy as he tells about the times Jesus appears to His disciples after His resurrection. He includes Jesus' wonderful promise that He will send His Holy Spirit to help and comfort us when we need Him to.

Let's Meet the People of Luke

Jesus is God's Son and the Savior of the world. He is the One the prophets of the Old Testament promised would come. Mary was His mother, and God was His Father.

Mary was the mother of Jesus, and Joseph was Mary's husband.

Elizabeth was Mary's aunt and the mother of John the Baptist, the preacher God sent to announce that Jesus, the Messiah, was coming soon.

Zechariah was the father of John the Baptist. In Zechariah's old age, an angel appeared to him and announced that he would have a son. Before long John was born.

John the Baptist was the second cousin of Jesus. He was the special preacher the prophets in the Old Testament had said would come to announce the coming of a Savior.

The disciples were the twelve men Jesus chose to be with Him. They helped Him do God's work, to spread the Good News that Jesus is Lord.

Herod the Great worked for Rome as the king of Jewish people in Jerusalem in the land of Judea. When King Herod heard that a new King of the Jews had been born he became upset. He ordered that all baby boys two years and younger should be killed. Herod thought if he destroyed all the boy babies that Jesus would be killed, too. God saved Jesus from Herod's men, because He had a plan for Jesus on earth.

Pilate was the governor of Judea. He worked for Rome. Pilate didn't like the Jewish people very much, but he was afraid he might lose his job if he didn't keep them happy. When the Jewish leaders wanted to kill Jesus, Pilate went along with them even though he could find nothing that Jesus had done wrong.

Here Are the Places of Luke

Bethlehem – the small town where Jesus was born—right where God said He would be!

Jerusalem – the city in Israel where the beautiful temple of God was and where many important things happened in Jesus' life.

Galilee – the land near the Sea of Galilee where the cities of Capernaum and Nazareth were. Jesus said and did many wonderful things in those two cities in Galilee, as He showed the people God's great love.

Judea – the land near the Dead Sea where Jesus' friends, Mary, Martha, and Lazarus lived in the town of Bethany. Jesus spent the last week before He died in Judea.

Two Very Special Families

Tell your child that Luke's story is written almost like a letter you would get in the mail. It is addressed to Theophilus. Explain that Theophilus means "my friend who loves God." The book of Luke was written to you.

The first chapter of Luke tells about two very special families, the family of John the Baptist and the family of Jesus. The family of John is mentioned first, because John was born a few months before Jesus came to earth. John was also the person God chose to announce to the world that Jesus was coming soon.

John's father and mother, Zechariah and Elizabeth, were both very old. They had no children. They loved God very much and wanted to please Him.

Zechariah was a Jewish priest. One day as he was working in the temple, something amazing happened. Read about it in Luke 1:11-25.

One month later, an angel appeared to Mary, and told her the news that she would give birth to Jesus, the Savior. See how Mary felt when the angel talked to her in Luke 1:29-38. Find out what the angel said to comfort Mary and to help her understand what was happening (Luke 1:30-33). Was Mary willing to do whatever God wanted her to (Luke 1:38)?

Read about the time the two mothers-to-be had when Mary went to visit her aunt, Elizabeth, in Luke 1:39-45. Mary sang a beautiful song of praise for God's gift of Jesus (Luke 1:46-55). Finish telling the story of Zechariah, Elizabeth, and their baby John from Luke 1:57-80.

Think of a special family for your family to visit. It can be a family that has special needs or a family of friends or relatives that you enjoy being with. If you live in a community where you can get to know families from other cultures, adopt one of those very special families. Your lives and theirs will all be enriched in the process.

Jesus Is Born

(Telling a story with presents)

What will I need? Four small boxes with lids, wrapping paper, and tape
Where is it in the Bible? Luke 2
How long will it take? 15-20 minutes for five days
What age child? 2-12 years
Will it work in a group? Yes
Can it be played in the car? Yes
Will it it work in a school classroom? Yes, preschool-6th grade

The story of Jesus' birth is a favorite of children and adults.

Here's a tradition you may want to start for your child to emphasize the story of Jesus' birth during the Christmas season. This activity will take some advance preparation, but it will be worth the result in your child's life.

Inside each box put an item or picture of something that reminds you of the Christmas story from Luke 2. Close each box and wrap in attractive wrapping paper. Ask your child to open them on different days during the Christmas season. Read and talk about the verses from the Bible that go with that object.

Here are some suggested items to put in the boxes:

1. A small, rolled-up piece of paper with words written in calligraphy. Tie with a ribbon. This paper represents the decree of Caesar Augustus in Luke 2:1-5.

2. A picture of a baby or a tiny, inexpensive doll. Read Luke 2:6-7 and talk about the fact that there was no room in the inn for God's Son that night.

3. Cut out a picture of a sheep and glue some cotton on it for the third box. Many inexpensive toddler's and children's books have pictures of sheep in them that you could use. Read about the shepherds from Luke 2:8-20.

4. Make a star from lightweight cardboard and cover it with foil or shiny paper. Luke does not include the story of the wise men in his book, but read Matthew 2:1-12.

5. After you have opened all the boxes and talked about Jesus' birth, have a special birthday party for Him. Sing Christmas songs or praise choruses while your child decorates the birthday cake.

Rich Man, Poor Man, Beggar Man

(Solving Bible mysteries)

What will I need? An object that belongs to you and other players who are helping to solve the Bible mysteries

Where is it in the Bible? Luke 9:25; 16:19-31

How long will it take? 5-10 minutes

What age child? 3-12 years

Will it work in a group? Yes

Can it be played in the car? Yes

Will it work in a school classroom? Yes, preschool–6th grade

Play a game with your child and family called "Forfeit." Explain to your child that forfeit means to "give up" something. Ask everybody in the family to put some item that belongs to them in a pile in the middle of a room. It can be a shoe, a toy, a sock, a piece of jewelry, or something else. Sit in a circle around the items.

In order to get his belonging back, each player must solve a mysterious clue about somebody in the Bible. Here are some clues:

1. "It's a good thing that I had four good friends who were willing to carry me to see Jesus, or I never would have made it! They even opened up the roof for me!" (the paralyzed man)

2. "Wow! Did I ever have some narrow escapes! I had to kill a bear and a lion to keep them from hurting my father's sheep. Sometimes I even played my harp for King Saul, to calm him down when he was upset, and then God made me the king of His people." (David)

3. "You won't believe what happened one night while we were all taking care of our sheep. There was a very bright light and lots of beautiful voices, and then we all went to see an incredible baby." (the shepherds)

4. "You've never slept until you've spent a whole night with a bunch of lions! It's a very good thing to know how to pray." (Daniel)

5. "We went on a long trip, clear across the desert, to see Jesus. We wouldn't have known where we were going, except there was a magnificent star in the sky." (the wise men)

Read Luke 9:25 and explain that Jesus was saying that a person who gives up (forfeits) what is worth more than all the money in the world, knowing and loving Jesus, for ordinary money, has made a very foolish trade. Jesus tells us that our soul, the part of us that the Holy Spirit of Jesus lives in when we ask Him to, is much more precious than everything else in the world.

Jesus tells the story of a rich man and a poor man who both died, and the poor man went to Heaven to be with God. The rich man went to hell to be with the devil forever. It's a sad story about a very unhappy ending for a man who had everything he wanted in life on earth. He didn't love God, and he selfishly wouldn't share his money with people who needed it. The man only loved himself.

The poor man in the story was homeless and hungry on earth, but he loved God and went to be with Him forever. You can read the story in Luke 16:19-31.

Less Than a Penny, More Than a Dollar

(A sale)

What will I need? Items you can sell
Where is it in the Bible? Luke 21:1-4
How long will it take? Probably a day
What age child? 3-12 years
Will it work in a group? Yes
Can it be played in the car? Use your car to help with your project
Will it work in a school classroom? Yes, preschool–6th grade

Read the story about the poor widow who gave all the money she had to God, which was only two small coins. She had to trust God to take care of her, because not only was she poor, but also she didn't have many ways to get more money, since her husband had died and she was all alone.

Jesus noticed that she loved God enough to give up what she needed for herself. He also noticed the other richer people who only gave money that they really didn't need for themselves at all. Jesus said that the widow's two small coins were worth more to Him than all the many dollars given by people who gave God what they didn't need, anyway.

Plan and have a garage sale with your child. Give everything you make from it to God. Let your child put the money in the offering plate himself. Or give a special offering to missionaries, a family in need, or whatever you choose. It will be a blessing that you and your child will always remember and may start a lifetime habit of selfless giving.

If you don't want a full-blown garage sale, just sell some items by taking them to a consignment store. Give the money you earn to God.

From the Garden to the Cross

Have a very special family worship time with your child to tell the story of the death of Jesus – for us. Do something to make it especially meaningful. Announce ahead of time where and when you will meet.

If your child is very young, you will need to adapt your plans to fit his short attention-span and to tell the story of Jesus simply and in your own words, as you hold his interest by cutting out the cross described below.

If you have grandparents or other family members and friends who may not know Jesus as their personal Savior and Lord, this would be a wonderful opportunity to invite them to share in the worship time with you.

Open your Bible to Luke 22:39–23:49, which tells the story of Jesus' last hours. Read parts of the narrative, and cut out a "surprise" cross-shape from paper as you tell the story. Don't tell what you are making until it is finished and you unfold it.

Here's the narrative: (You will need a piece of white paper and a pair of scissors. It would be a good idea to make a practice cross ahead of time without your child's knowing it, so you will know how to do it at your worship time.) After Jesus and His disciples finished eating their last supper together, they left the upstairs room and went to the Mount of Olives, where Jesus often went. When they got there, Jesus asked his friends to pray that God would make them strong and brave. Jesus knew He would very soon be leaving them to die on the cross.

Jesus went a short distance away from His disciples, got down on His knees, and began to pray very seriously. He prayed so hard that drops of blood appeared on his face, instead of the usual water that comes from our skin when we perspire. Jesus asked His Heavenly Father if there were any other way to take the sins of the world away but He knew there was not. Jesus was willing to suffer and die for us.

(Hold of the top left corner of the sheet of paper and fold it down until the right sides of the paper line up evenly. The top left corner will not match with the bottom right corner, because the paper is a rectangle and not a square. Firmly press the fold.)

When Jesus finished praying, He stood up and went back to his disciples, who had fallen asleep. Jesus woke them and told them again to pray that God would make them strong when trouble would come, and then trouble came.

Not very far away, a crowd of soldiers, Jewish leaders, and other people could be seen coming closer to Jesus and His disciples. The person leading the way was Jesus' very own disciple, Judas. Then Judas gave Jesus a friendly kiss, not because he loved Jesus, but because that kiss was the signal for the soldiers to capture Jesus and take Him away to be tried and crucified. Read Luke 22:48-53 to see what happened next. (Fold the right top corner of the paper across the first folded part to the left, until the left folded sides match up. The new folded part of the paper will completely cover the first part you folded, and it won't reach clear to the bottom of the paper, either. Press the new fold down firmly. The paper should now look like a house with a pointy roof, but it's not.)

Jesus was arrested and taken to the house of the High Priest, even though it was the middle of the night. The Jewish day of worship was coming soon and the Jewish leaders were in a big hurry to get their evil job of killing Jesus done before it was time to worship God. They didn't seem to understand that they were putting to death the very Lord they were planning to celebrate. (Fold the left diagonal side of the "roof" over across to match the right side, folding the whole paper in half from top to bottom and press the fold firmly.)

As the sun was just coming up in the morning, Jesus was taken to the most important Jewish court, the Sanhedrin, to find out if He really had done something wrong. Jesus did not defend himself or deny He was the Son of God. The mean leaders decided that was good enough reason to put Him on a cross. Then Jesus was sent to Pilate, the Roman governor. Then to Herod, the king, who sent Jesus back to Pilate again. Pilate really couldn't find any reason why Jesus should be crucified, and even offered to let Jesus go free. But the crowd of people, with the devil in charge, shouted for a robber named Barabbas to go free, instead. Because

Pilate was afraid to do something that the crowd wouldn't like, he gave Jesus to them to be killed on a cross. (Fold the folded paper in half once more, from left to right, making the right sides line up, even though they won't match this time.)

As the crowd of angry, yelling people led Jesus toward the hill where He would die, a man named Simon was told to carry Jesus' cross to the hill which was called Calvary. When Jesus and the crowd reached Mt. Calvary or Golgotha, He was nailed to the cross by His hands and feet. A sign was nailed above His head that said, "This is the King of the Jews." Two criminals were put on crosses, one on each side of the Savior. Read Luke 23:34-43 to hear what they said and find out what happened.

It was the middle of the day when Jesus was hung on the cross, but suddenly darkness covered the whole land for three hours. Jesus, God's own Son, was dying for all the sins of all people in all the world. It was a dark and very sad time. The light from God's sun was gone and God's great heart was broken.

Then Jesus died and the giant curtain in God's temple was torn completely in half, from the top to the bottom. Because Jesus died for us, everyone could now go into the special, holy presence of God and talk with Him for themselves. (Take your scissors and cut the folded paper straight down in half, from the top to the bottom, like the curtain was torn, or from the bottom to top, if that is too hard to do. Unfold the paper, with the small pieces first, which will just be small squares and rectangles. Then, unfold the remaining piece and discover a cross.)

When the captain of the Roman army saw Jesus die, and heard and saw all the things that happened, he said, "Surely this man is the innocent Son of God."

Say a prayer, or let every family member or friend say a prayer, thanking God for Jesus and thanking Jesus for dying for you.

The Most Amazing Thing That Ever Happened

Read the beautiful story about Jesus' coming alive again after He died on the cross for our sins! You can find it in Luke 24:1-12 If you want your child to memorize all or part of the Resurrection story, read it with him, straight from the Bible, word-for-word, once every day for about a week and he will then know it by heart.

Here is a reminder of the awesome truth that Jesus is alive: Talk with your child about one of God's most fascinating and beautiful little creatures, the butterfly. Explain that God had an amazing plan when He designed the life story of a butterfly. It is a little like what happened to Jesus when He died, was buried in a dark tomb, and a heavy stone door closed Him tightly inside until the wonderful day when Jesus walked out into the sunny garden alive again.

What Can I Learn from Luke

Luke told us some things about when Jesus was born, when He died and rose again, about the wonderful things Jesus did, and even about when Jesus was a child. Jesus was a real person like I am, with feelings like I have, but He was the only person who never, ever did anything wrong. Jesus was perfect.

Important Verses to Remember

Luke 1:30 – "But the angel said to her (Mary), 'Do not be afraid, Mary, you have found favor with God'. "

Luke 5:10b-11 – "Then Jesus said to Simon (Peter), 'Don't be afraid; from now on you will catch men.' So they pulled their boats up on shore, left everything and followed Him."

Luke 9:48 – "Then He said to them, 'Whoever welcomes this little child in my name, welcomes me; and whoever welcomes me welcomes the one who sent me. For he who is least among you all—he is the greatest."

Luke 11:9 – "Ask and it will be given to you; seek and you will find; knock and the door will be opened to you."

Luke 12:34 – "For where your treasure is, there your heart will be also."

A Devotional Thought for Parents and Teachers

Did anyone ever call you a perfect person? Me neither. We wouldn't even want them to, if they were ever so inclined, because we know it's just not true and we would feel embarrassed to be so overrated.

But when Jesus was called the perfect Man, He truly was. Jesus experienced the human experience from divine conception to death by crucifixion. He lived it in a unique way, perfect, without a single sin or blot on His flawless character. We can't say the same, for sure.

Then, there was the perfect ending to the perfect story. Our Savior's death was a wonderful commencement, not a tragic conclusion. He came alive again ushering in the awesome possibility that every imperfect man, woman, boy, and girl can join Him in everlasting life in the only perfect place there is – heaven.

God planned through Jesus the perfect exchange. Our sinful, blotched life would be handed over to Him in exchange for His forgiveness, salvation, promise of eternal life, and the presence of the Holy Spirit helping us to come closer to the ultimate goal of perfect surrender and obedience to Him. How could anyone refuse such an incredible offer?

John God's Book to Show Us that Jesus is God

"In the beginning was the Word, and the Word was with God, and the Word was God" (John 1:1).

What's the Book About

The book of John shows us who Jesus is. Jesus is the same God who made the world and everything in it. He came to earth as a tiny baby and grew up to be a man so that we can know God for ourselves and have life through Him.

God's Word Becomes Flesh to Save His People

John is a wonderful book that tells us a lot about what Jesus said and did. John makes sure that we understand Jesus has lived since before there was anything at all, because Jesus is God, too. God created the whole universe and every amazing thing in it. Jesus did incredible miracles to help and heal people. John recorded many events to show everyone that Jesus is God. John tells us who Jesus is through the names He is called. Many of those names for Jesus start with "I am." But the greatest proof John includes that tells us Jesus really is God, is that Jesus came back to life after He died for us. Jesus is the resurrection and the life.

Let's Meet the People of John

Jesus is God's Son and the Savior of the world that the Old Testament prophets promised would come.

John the Baptist was the man God sent to announce to everyone that Jesus would come very soon.

The twelve disciples were the special followers that Jesus chose to help teach about God and to do God's work on earth with Him.

Mary was Jesus' mother, whom He loved and took good care of, even when He was dying on the cross. (John 19:25-27).

Mary Magdalene was a woman who loved and followed Jesus, because He had given her a new life. The devil had been controlling Mary and making her unhappy until Jesus set her free. Mary was so thankful for what Jesus had done for her that she served Him faithfully all her life. She was one of the people who stayed near the cross when Jesus died, even though all His disciples, except

John, were hiding somewhere for fear. Mary Magdalene was also the first one to see Jesus after He come back to life again.

Mary, Martha, and **Lazarus** were sisters and a brother who were good friends and followers of Jesus. Jesus went to their home in Bethany every chance He got. When Lazarus died, Jesus brought him back to life again.

Here Are the Places of John

Jerusalem – the city in Israel where the temple was located. During the last week before He was crucified, Jesus rode into Jerusalem on a donkey. Big crowds of people shouted their praises to Him. Jesus was crucified just outside the city wall of Jerusalem.

Capernaum – a big city where many people lived who did not know God. That's why Jesus moved there to preach, teach, heal, and help people, and show them who God really is.

Galilee – the land near the Sea of Galilee where the cities of Capernaum and Nazareth were located. Jesus did many wonderful things in Galilee. He showed the people God's great love.

Judea – near the Dead Sea where Jesus' friends, Mary, Martha, and Lazarus lived in the town of Bethany. Jesus spent the last week before He died in Judea. The desert of Judea is where John the Baptist preached that Jesus was coming.

STORIES AND ACTIVITIES FROM JOHN

Jesus the Light
(A window to let the light in)

What will I need? A paper or plastic plate, scissors, cellophane, and tape
Where is it in the Bible? John 1:1-14
How long will it take? 10-15 minutes
What age child? 4-10 years
Will it work in a group? Yes
Can it be played in the car? No

Will it work in a school classroom? Yes, preschool–4th grade

There are two verses in the Bible that tell us about the world God made for us. Read those two Bible verses: Genesis 1:1 and John 1:1. Take a few minutes to help your child memorize one or both verses, and follow up for a few days with a little review.

Explain that Jesus made everything from nothing, that's what creating means. We can make things, but we have to use other things like paper, crayons, modeling dough, paint, glue, scissors, etc. Jesus is our incredible Creator God, He made you and me.

Jesus is called the Light of the World. The Bible says people who love Him walk in the light instead of the darkness. The devil is called the prince of darkness. He is just the opposite of Jesus. Many times in the Bible when God appears to people, there is a bright light shining around Him. When the prophets in the Old Testament had visions of God, He was very white and shining. When Jesus went up on the mountain with three of His disciples, they could see that Jesus was God because He became bright and shining as they watched in amazement. Because we know and love Jesus we walk in the light.

Here's a sunshine window your child can make. Cut a 2 X 4-inch rectangular window in the center of a paper or white plastic plate. Tape clear or colored cellophane paper behind the window. Your child will enjoy letting the light come in through his window and peeking out at whatever is around him through his sunlight window. He may also decorate the plate around the window in any way he chooses. Hang his creation in the window of his room.

The Amazing Changing Water

(Science experiments with water)

What will I need? A glass nearly full of water, a handkerchief, and a rubber band
Where is it in the Bible? John 2:1-12
How long will it take? 10-15 minutes
What age child? 3-11 years
Will it work in a group? Yes

Can it be played in the car? No
Will it work in a school classroom? Yes, preschool–5th grade

Tell your child that she can change cool water into boiling water with just a touch of her finger. Pour a glass nearly full of water and cover the top with a handkerchief. Hold the handkerchief firmly in place with a rubber band. Push down on the center of the handkerchief until it touches the water. Very quickly turn the glass upside down. The water will stay in the glass, because the tiny holes between the threads in the handkerchief are filled with water.

Now tell your child to rub her finger on her clothes until it becomes warm from the rubbing (that's called friction). Ask her to hold her finger under the glass, touching the handkerchief. Hold the glass and the handkerchief with one hand while you push down gently on the glass with the other. Where your child's finger is touching, bubbles will rise up from the handkerchief and float to the top of the water as though the water were boiling. The air is being forced up through the handkerchief, and it shows up as bubbles.

The amazing story of Jesus' first miracle is in John 2:1-12. Even when things happen that seem bad, Jesus uses His amazing changing power to make them good.

Different Kinds of Thirsty

(A water experiment)

What will I need? A balloon, a glass of water, baking soda, and vinegar or lemon juice
Where is it in the Bible? John 4:1-42; John 7:37-39
How long will it take? 10-15 minutes

What age child? 3-12 years
Will it work in a group? Yes
Can it be played in the car? No
Will it work in a school classroom? Yes,
preschool-6th grade

Ask your child if he is thirsty. If he is, get his choice of drink to enjoy as you talk about a time when Jesus was thirsty, too. Jesus and His disciples were going to Galilee, but to get there they had to go through Samaria. That spelled trouble because the Jewish people didn't like the Samaritan people. The Jewish people thought that any Jew who married somebody not Jewish was bad and that's what the Samaritans had done.

But Jesus loved the Samaritan people as much as He loved the Jewish people. This day His disciples had gone into a nearby town to buy food. Jesus sat by the well, tired from His long walk. A woman came to get water from the well. Not only was she a woman, but she was also a Samaritan. Jewish men were not in the habit of talking to women they did not know. Jesus asked her for a drink. Then He offered her some "living water."

She was amazed that Jesus would even talk to her. Read John 4:13-14 and talk about what Jesus meant by water that is so good that whoever drinks it will never be thirsty again. He was talking about a person who comes to Him because they want to know and love God so much that they are like a thirsty person who needs water.

Jesus later told the crowds of people in the temple about the living water, too. You can read His words in John 7:37-39.

Only God can give us living water, but you can have fun making a glass of water come alive and blow up a balloon, right before your very eyes.

Stretch the balloon to make it easier to blow up, and keep it nearby on the kitchen counter. Put about one ounce of water in a small glass, and add one teaspoon of baking soda to it. Pour the mixture into a clean soda bottle, and add the juice from one lemon or two ounces of vinegar. Quickly attach the balloon to the top of the bottle and, watch the water come alive, blowing air into the balloon.

Jesus is the Good Shepherd

(A sheep round up)

What will I need? Wadded-up pieces of white paper, or rolled-up sock balls, or cotton balls; two cardboard boxes
Where is it in the Bible? John 10:1-21
How long will it take? 15-20 minutes
What age child? 3-12 years
Will it work in a group? It would make a good relay with teams
Can it be played in the car? No
Will it work in a school classroom? Yes, preschool–6th grade

Explain that Jesus was sometimes called the Good Shepherd. Read about Jesus, our Shepherd, in John 10:11-15. Help your child understand that she is one of Jesus' precious sheep that He talks about. Jesus loves her, protects her, and even died for her. He is our Good Shepherd.

Play a "get the sheep in the sheep pen" game with your child. For the sheep use pieces of paper, socks, or cotton balls. Make two piles of seven sheep, one for each of you. Place them on the other side of a room. Across from the sheep place two boxes on their sides, big enough for all of your sheep to fit in. The boxes will be your sheep pen.

Each of you will also need a piece of cardboard to scoot his sheep into the pen without touching them. At the signal, begin pushing one sheep at a time toward its pen with the piece of cardboard. When the first sheep is safely home, hurry back to get another one before a wolf or lion gets it. If you want a winner, the first player to have his sheep in the sheep pen is it. If you want a more cooperative game, consider it a victory for everybody when all the sheep are home safely.

Jesus Prays for Us
(A prayer game)

What will I need? Several shoeboxes, a beanbag, or a small ball
Where is it in the Bible? John 17:1-26

How long will it take? 15-20 minutes
What age child? 3-12 years
Will it work in a group? Yes
Can it be played in the car? Not the games
Will it work in a school classroom? Yes, preschool–6th grade

Make a prayer toss game with your child by writing the names of people you'd like to pray for on the bottom of several shoe boxes. Place the boxes close together, then take turns tossing a small beanbag into the boxes. Say a short prayer for the person the bean bag lands on.

Here's another good practice to instill in your child. Each time you hear a siren, say a prayer that God will help the person in need. Help your child to develop the lifestyle of praying for people or just thanking God.

Show your child a prayer Jesus prayed for us in John 17:1-26

What Can I Learn from John

John tells us that Jesus is really God. He came to our world so we could meet Him, know Him, and love Him. I believe that Jesus really is God. If I give my heart and life to Him, I will have wonderful life right now. I will keep on having everlasting life with Jesus when I die.

Important Verses to Remember

John 1:1 – "In the beginning was the Word, and the Word was with God, and the Word was God."

John 3:16 – "For God so loved the world that he gave his one and only Son, that whoever believes in him shall not perish but have eternal life."

John 10:14-15 – "I am the good shepherd; I know my sheep and my sheep know me—just as the Father knows me and I know the Father—and I lay down my life for the sheep."

John 12:46 – "I have come into the world as a light, so that no one who believes in me should stay in darkness."

John 13:34-35 – "A new command I give you: Love one another. As I have loved you, so you must love one another. By this all men will know that you are my disciples, if you love one another."

John 14:6 – "Jesus answered, 'I am the way and the truth and the life. No one comes to the Father except through me."

A Devotional Thought for Parents and Teachers

Do you have difficulty feeling confidence in a person's pious words when his or her life gives off an entirely different message? We all want truth in packaging. We want the outside of the package to match the actual product.

John wanted us to understand that the words Jesus spoke can be fully trusted because of the who He is. Jesus is God. Many pseudo-Christs have purported themselves to be God's Messiah, God in the flesh, but only Jesus really is the Christ He claims to be. He proved His deity in the things He did and by the words He spoke.

It is awesome to think that the Creator-God is our most intimate confidant in personal affairs. He's the One who accompanies us everywhere we go, never leaving our side. He's actually more interested in what's happening in our child's life than we are. He never gets tired of hearing all about the little things our child does, even when others are rolling their eyes. He knows the best choices for us to make when we face those inevitable hard decisions in life.

Jesus is the creator of all things. When He creates, He begins with nothing. But we didn't get to where we are by starting from nothing. We began with the raw material within us that God gave us. No one is a self-made person, it simply is impossible to be.

Because of God, we can feel like someone really special, because to Him we are. Without Him, we are absolutely nothing. But Jesus can take nothing and begin to mold and shape it. He painstakingly works with the invisible, non-existent building material and makes us into something useful and beautiful.

Without an acknowledgment and acceptance that Jesus is God inside us, we truly are nothing. We are totally missing the very reason we exist – to give all honor and glory to our own Creator, Provider, and Sustainer – the Savior. He's the One who makes our lives, hopes, and dreams fulfilling, productive, and accessible with absolutely nothing to work with except our willing and available heart.

Acts God's Book About How the Church Grew

and Grew! "For we cannot help speaking about what we have seen and heard" (Acts 4:20).

What's the Book About

The book of Acts relates what happened on earth after Jesus went to heaven. God sent His Holy Spirit to live in the hearts of His children. The number of people who believed in Jesus grew bigger and bigger and spread wider and farther.

Luke Writes About the Growth of God's Family

Acts starts right where the stories of Matthew, Mark, Luke, and John end. Acts tells us what happened to the people who loved and trusted in Jesus after He went to heaven. The first church of believers was in the city of Jerusalem, but it wasn't very long until the people who loved Jesus began to be persecuted there. They began to move away into other safer cities. But God used their problems for good because everywhere the followers of Jesus went, they told other people how wonderful He is. More and more people in other cities came to love Jesus, too!

God did many amazing miracles through His disciples and through a man named Paul.

Let's Meet the People of Acts

Peter is a friend and disciple of Jesus. He wasn't very brave until Jesus died and came alive again. Then God's Holy Spirit came to live in Him. Peter became a powerful preacher who was proud to tell as many people as he could that Jesus is the Son of God and the Savior of the world.

James and **John** and **James**, Jesus' own brother, were three of Jesus' special helpers who loved and served Jesus with all their hearts. These men did many wonderful things in the name and power of Jesus.

Stephen was one of the seven men whom God's people chose to be a deacon, or special servant, in the church. Stephen loved Jesus so much that he was willing to die for his faith.

Philip was a disciple of Jesus who was one of the first people to take the news about Jesus to other lands. First, he went to Samaria.

Then, God guided Philip to Africa to tell just one man how to give his heart to Jesus.

Paul was the man who at first hated Christians. He did everything he could to punish them for following Jesus. But Paul met Jesus for himself one day as he traveled to Damascus to capture and punish more Christians. Paul's heart and life were completely changed. Paul became a missionary for Jesus.

Barnabas, Timothy, John Mark, and **Silas** were all friends of Paul's who went on special missionary trips with him.

Cornelius was a Roman army captain who came to know Jesus as his Savior when Peter had a special dream from God and traveled to Cornelius' house to tell him about Jesus. Cornelius witnessed to his whole household, and they were saved.

Lydia was a business lady who sold purple cloth. She came to know Jesus as her Savior and Lord when Paul and Silas came to her hometown of Philippi.

Ananias was the man that God sent to pray with Paul, after Paul met Jesus on the road to Damascus and became blind for three days.

Felix, Festus, and **Agrippa** were all leaders in charge of the Jewish people. They did not follow Jesus. Paul talked to each one of them and told them his own story about who Jesus was to him and the amazing things He did. Paul wanted these men to know and love Jesus, too. But the choice was up to them, and they made the wrong decisions.

Luke was the doctor of medicine who wrote the Book of Luke and who went with Paul on some of his trips to tell people about Jesus. Luke wrote about the many things he heard and saw in the Book of Acts.

Here Are the Places of Acts

Jerusalem – the city where the beautiful temple was. In the first part of Acts, Jesus followers were waiting in an upstairs room for God's Holy Spirit to come. Later, some believers stayed in Jerusalem and kept telling people about Jesus, while others went to other places and did the same thing.

Samaria – the land where many people lived who did not know of God. Besides that, the people who lived in Samaria were not totally Jewish. Some of their families were from other lands, too. The Jews didn't like that, but God loved the people of Samaria. He sent Philip, then Peter and John, and others to tell the Samaritans about Jesus.

Antioch – a city in the land of Syria where the believers in Jesus were called Christians for the first time. Paul went with Barnabas to the church at Antioch. The two men worked together there to tell people about Jesus and to help them grow strong for the Lord.

Cyprus, Galatia, Macedonia, Achaia, Athens, Corinth, Philippi, and **Ephesus** – some of the places Paul traveled to tell people about Jesus and to help them grow stronger and stronger in their trust in Him.

Caesarea and **Rome** – the places Paul was taken after he was arrested in Jerusalem for telling people about Jesus.

STORIES AND ACTIVITIES FROM ACTS

Around the World for Jesus

(Making soup)

What will I need? Water, pan, chicken or beef bouillon or broth, cut-up vegetables, seasonings

Where is it in the Bible? Acts 1:8

How long will it take? 30-40 minutes

What age child? 3-12 years

Will it work in a group? Yes

Can it be played in the car? No

Will it work in a school classroom? Yes, preschool–6th grade

Read Acts 1:8. Just before Jesus went up to heaven, He told His disciples something very important. He said the Holy Spirit would be with them and in them to help them tell other people about Him. Jesus also told His disciples to tell people in Judea and Samaria and other places around the world about Him. Jesus knew that there would be many people living in other places who had not gotten to know Him. He wanted to be sure that we tell them, too. All people in God's family from all around the world are precious to Him. He made us and loves us all, no matter how we look or talk or where we live.

Make "Round the World" soup to show how all the different ingredients and flavors blend together to make something good, like God's family of people from all around the world. Start with boiling water and beef or chicken bouillon or a can of broth. Cut up and add carrots, potatoes, celery, tomatoes or tomato sauce, meat, rice, noodles, or whatever your family would enjoy. Add salt and seasonings to taste. Cook until all the vegetables are tender. Eat your "Round the World" soup together. Be ready to share God's good news every day.

God's Amazing Holy Spirit
(Fun with air)

What will I need?
Activity 1. A ruler and a folded newspaper
Activity 2. A nail, a plastic bottle with a lid, and water
Activity 3. A large bottle and a big balloon
Activity 4. An empty oatmeal container, aluminum foil, and a piece of thick elastic big enough to fit around your child's waist
Where is it in the Bible? Acts 2
How long will it take? 10-15 minutes
What age child? 3-12 years
Will it work in a group? Yes
Can it be played in the car? Activity #4 would work
Will it work in a school classroom? Yes, preschool–6th grade

Read Acts 2:1-4 to your child. Explain that Jesus had died on the cross and came to life about 50 days before, and He had been gone to heaven for 10 days. Just before Jesus had gone up into the clouds into heaven, He had told His friends to wait in Jerusalem for Him to send His Holy Spirit to be with them. They had been praying and waiting in an upstairs room in the house where they had been staying. They must have been very excited that God Himself was going to come (because the Holy Spirit is God without a body) to be with them forever!

It was a very important celebration time in Jerusalem. There were many people from all over the world there for a celebration called "Pentecost," or the "Feast of Harvests."

As the people who loved Jesus were together upstairs on that very special day, the sky above them, and then the whole room they were in, was suddenly filled with the sound of a mighty wind. Small flames of fire stood above the heads of everyone there, but they didn't burn anyone.

After the people heard the roaring sound of wind and saw the flames of fire above their heads, God's wonderful Holy Spirit came into everyone that was there and filled them with His great love and power. They began to talk in languages that they didn't even know. God gave them that power!

It wasn't long until God's people got to use their new kind of talking, because there were so many people in town who spoke all different languages. Those people needed to know about Jesus! Explain that the believers who were filled with the Holy Spirit told everyone in his own country's language about Jesus— and Peter preached to them, too.

Find out in verses 40-41 if anybody believed in Jesus after seeing and hearing all that had happened. How wonderful! Read verse 46 to find out if the brand new believers in Jesus started going to church and worshiping with the disciples and other people who loved Jesus, too.

Then do an activity to remind you of God's incredible Holy Spirit, and to help your child understand Him better. Talk about the wind that came with the Holy Spirit at Pentecost. Explain to your child that though the wind could not be seen, the people that day could hear the wind. We can feel the breath from our own lungs that gives us life, and we know that the wind is powerful! That's like the Holy Spirit—He gives us power to do the things that God wants us to do!

Try a couple of air experiments to see the power of even a little bit of air.

1. Lay a ruler on the table with about half of it extending over the edge of the table. Cover the rest of the ruler with a sheet of folded newspaper. With your fist, hit the loose end of the ruler sharply and quickly to see if you can lift the paper. (You probably won't be able to do so, even though it seems it would be easy to do! When you suddenly hit the ruler, the air pressure (air power) on top of the newspaper holds it down.)

2. Make a small hole with a nail in the side of a plastic bottle near the bottom. Hold your finger over the hole and fill the bottle to the very top with water. Screw the top on tightly. Take the bottle to the sink (just in case) and take your finger off the hole. See if it leaks. (Air power coming through the hole in the plastic bottle from the outside is stronger than the gravity that might pull the water out and down. Besides that, there is no air inside the bottle that can push down on the water—so the water stays put!)

3. Put a large balloon into a large bottle and stretch the end of the balloon over the bottle's neck. Try to blow it up. (You can't blow up the balloon when it's inside the bottle because the bottle is full of air. When you blow into the balloon, the air in the bottle becomes packed even more tightly. The air in the bottle has more power than the air you are trying to blow into the balloon.)

4. Make an oxygen (air) tank from an empty oatmeal container, and take an imaginary trip to the moon or into space! Cover the container with aluminum foil, and make two slits on opposite sides of the canister. Thread a length of thick elastic (big enough to tie around your child's waist) through the slits and tie it into a belt-sized loop. Let your child pretend to be a space man or woman on another planet by stepping into the elastic loop on the air tank and pulling it up around their waist. Remind your child that the Holy Spirit is Jesus right here with us, as close as the air around us and as our own breath!

A Big Change
(A cooking experience)

What will I need? Food coloring
Where is it in the Bible? Acts 8:1-3; 9
How long will it take? 15-20 minutes
What age child? 3-12 years
Will it work in a group? Yes
Can it be played in the car? No. Better do the "driving and honking" at home!
Will it work in a school classroom? Yes, preschool–6th grade

One of the most exciting stories in the Bible is about the amazing change God made in a man named Saul; we know him as Paul. Read Acts 8:3 and 9:1–2 to see what Paul was like before he met Jesus.

Paul was on his way to Damascus with a letter from the High Priest in Jerusalem saying that he could arrest anyone he found there who believed in Jesus. The trip was long, about 150 miles, but Paul wanted to punish Christians anywhere he could find them.

God had a big change in mind for Paul. As he and his friends got close to Damascus, a bright light from heaven shone down on him. Paul fell down to the ground and heard a voice asking him why he was being so mean to Him. Paul asked, "Who is talking to me?" And Jesus said to Paul, "I am Jesus, the One you are being so unkind to. Now, get up and go into the city and wait to find out what you should do next."

The men who were traveling with Paul were absolutely amazed at what had happened, since they had heard the sound of somebody's voice, but they had not seen anyone talking.

When Paul got up off the ground he couldn't see a thing. He was blind. His friends had to lead him into Damascus. Paul was blind for three days. Just as Jesus had told him, Paul waited there. He didn't eat or drink anything for three days.

While Paul was waiting, God spoke to a man named Ananias, who loved Jesus. God told Ananias to go find Paul, and gave him the address of the house where Paul was waiting. When God first told Ananias to see Paul, Ananias was very afraid. He had heard how badly Paul treated believers. But God told Ananias not to be worried, because Paul now believed in Jesus, too.

Read Acts 9:17-22 to see what happened when Ananias visited Paul. Notice the amazing change that took place in Paul's heart. God's love and grace can change anybody who gives their life to Jesus.

Paul's Missionary Trip
(Fun with maps and imaginary trips)

What will I need? A piece of paper and crayons or markers; *a real map of somewhere (*optional)
Where is it in the Bible? Acts 13-15:35
How long will it take? 15-20 minutes

What age child? 3-12 years
Will it work in a group? Yes
Can it be played in the car? Yes, and you could use a real map of your city or state
Will it work in a school classroom? Yes, preschool–6th grade

Make a map of your country or the whole world with your child. If he is quite young, let him design it any way he wants, and ask him to tell you the names of some of the places he has drawn. If he has trouble naming specific places, tell him the name of your country, state, or city and show him where they might be on his map. Mark his hometown with a star.

If your child would rather use a real map, mark on it the town in which you live, one place you have visited, and a place you think you would like to go someday. Use different shapes or symbols for each special place.

If your Bible has maps in the back, show your child a map of Paul's first missionary trip—the first trip he took to tell people everywhere he went about Jesus, so they could know Him, too. Read Acts 13:1-3 and notice three special things: 1. In the church in Paul's day there were all kinds of people. There were Jewish people, black people, people who were from families where relatives didn't love Jesus (like the family of evil King Herod), Samaritan people (and many of the Jewish people who weren't believers didn't like them at all), and women, and children. The church is a wonderful family of people who love Jesus, and that's what matters. 2. God had a special plan for Paul and Barnabas: so that more and more people could come to know Jesus, and 3. God's people prayed for Paul and Barnabas and sent them away on their important missionary trip. A young man named John Mark, Barnabas' nephew, went with them. It would not be their last trip. There would be many adventures along the way!

Giving Is More Fun!
(Making snacks to give away)

What will I need? Give-away snacks like dry cereal, nuts, popcorn, pretzels, miniature marshmallows, raisins, small candy, dried fruit, chocolate or other flavored chips, chow mien noodles, a big bowl, and small plastic bags to put the snacks in
Where is it in the Bible? Acts 20:35
How long will it take? 15-30 minutes
What age child? 2-11 years
Will it work in a group? Yes
Can it be played in the car? No, but you can use your car to take your give-away snacks to people
Will it work in a school classroom? Yes, preschool–6th grade

Jesus told us in Acts 20:35 it was better to give than receive. Read that important verse to your child and explain what it means. Make give-away bags to hand out to your friends or neighbors. Mix some of the snack items together in a bowl. Then, divide the mixture into smaller amounts and put some in several small plastic bags to give away. You may want to decorate the bags before filling them. Then spend some time giving them to your neighbors, classmates, friends, people at church, etc.

A Big Crash!
Acts 27

Paul often went on trips in ships, so he was used to traveling that way. He also probably had been in rain and storms many times. But in Acts 27, Paul found himself in a very big storm.

Paul was a prisoner on his way to Rome, 2,000 miles away. He was going to go on trial before the Roman court for preaching about Jesus. Ships in Paul's day didn't have compasses or computer equipment, so sailors had to look up at the stars to see which direction to go. That was a real problem when the weather was cloudy or stormy. Paul was sailing in the month of October, a very risky time to travel in the Mediterranean Sea, which was where his ship was.

Tell the story of Paul's dangerous trip and the shipwreck in Acts 27:13-44. Were the other passengers on the ship afraid of the storm? What did they do to make the ship lighter so it wouldn't sink (verses 18-19)? What did Paul tell the other travelers on the ship (verses 21-26 and 33-34)? What finally happened in verses 41-44?

You can shipwreck a straight pin or a needle in a cup of water. Carefully place a pin in a cup of water with a pair of tweezers or a fork. As the pin is floating on the top of the water, add liquid soap around the pin one drop at a time with a medicine dropper or a small spoon. As you add more water, the pin will finally be shipwrecked and sink.

Paul, the Prisoner Who Was Free!

(A game about going to jail!)

What will I need? You, your child, and a Bible

Where is it in the Bible? Acts 28:16, 23-24, and 30-31

How long will it take? 15-20 minutes

What age child? 3-12 years

Will it work in a group? Yes

Can it be played in the car? No

Will it work in a school classroom? Yes, preschool–6th grade

Explain that Paul had wanted to tell the people in Rome about Jesus, and his wish came true. Even though Paul was sent to Rome as a prisoner, God made very sure that he got there safely, through a big storm, a shipwreck, and a poisonous snake bite! God made everything bad work together for good, just like He promises He will. Do you ever wonder why some people didn't want to believe in Jesus, even after they saw Him do amazing miracles?

Decide on a location that will be a pretend jail. Banish your child or group to that "jail." Say, "You can help Paul get out of jail by answering a question correctly." If only you and your child are playing, ask him several questions, some of which will be about what jails were like in the Bible. If several children are playing, ask only one question of each prisoner, so he can be released from jail quickly.

Here are some possible questions to ask, or make up easy questions of your own.

1. Do you think you would want to be in prison in Bible days, or ever? (No)

2. Do you think prisoners in Paul's day ever had to wear chains so they couldn't get away? (Yes)

3. Do you think prisoners were ever chained to a guard or a soldier? (Yes, Paul probably was.)

4. Have you ever heard of putting people in "stocks?" (Yes or no is okay for an answer.) Explain to your child that stocks were usually made of wood with holes for a person's hands and feet. Sometimes his head fit into it, and the prisoner couldn't get out of them. Paul and Silas were locked in stocks in the jail in Philippi, when they sang songs of praise to God at midnight!

5. Do you think all jails in Bible days always had bars on the doors and windows? (No, sometimes the jails were just empty water wells, or holes, down deep in the ground. Jeremiah, in the Old Testament, was put in that kind of jail for a while.

6. Were people ever beaten up or whipped before they were put in jail? (Yes, that often happened. It was called "scourging." Jesus was scourged by Roman soldiers before he died.)

7. Did people ever get put in prison in Bible days just because they didn't have any money to pay their bills? (Yes)

8. Are you glad not to be in jail? (Yes!)

What Can I Learn from Acts

1. The Holy Spirit came to earth to give God's people power to live for Jesus and to be strong. He also gave comfort to the disciples who were sad, because Jesus was gone away from them into heaven. The Holy Spirit will come into my heart and life when I invite Jesus in, because they are the very same Person. He will never, ever leave me!

2. The people in Acts who loved Jesus kept on telling others about Him, because they wanted everyone to know how wonderful Jesus is! There are people all around me who need to know about Jesus, and I'm just the one to tell them!

Important Verses to Remember

Acts 1:8 – "But you will receive power when the Holy Spirit comes on you; and you will be my witnesses in Jerusalem, and in all Judea and Samaria, and to the ends of the earth."

Acts 4:12 – "Salvation is found in no one else, for there is no other name under heaven given to men by which we must be saved."

Acts 4:19-20 – "But Peter and John replied, "Judge for yourselves whether it is right in God's sight to obey you rather than God. For we cannot help speaking about what we have seen and heard."

Acts 9:4-5 – "He (Saul) fell to the ground and heard a voice say to him, 'Saul, Saul, why do you persecute me?' 'Who are you, Lord?' Saul asked. 'I am Jesus, whom you are persecuting,' he replied."

Acts 20:35b – "Remembering the words the Lord Jesus himself said: 'It is more blessed to give than to receive.' "

A Devotional Thought for Parents and Teachers

Our brothers and sisters in Acts are wonderful role models for us to pattern our lives by, and that's encouraging. They were real people, not super-Christians. They are very much like we are in every way, and they were able to turn their world upside down in the power of Jesus' Holy Spirit. That means we can, too.

The basics are exactly the same in their generation and ours: 1. They heard (or saw demonstrated in someone's life) the message of Jesus, believed it, and received Him into their lives. 2. They experienced the wonderful forgiveness, peace, and joy of Jesus, and wanted to share Him with someone else. 3. They lived their lives in the strength and energy that Jesus provides for us as His children. 4.

They shared the Good News that Jesus is the Savior. 5. People whom they came in contact with accidentally or intentionally came to know and love Jesus, too.

Such a simple, effective plan, it can't be improved upon! It worked perfectly then; it works perfectly today, and we are the channels through which the message spreads and spreads and spreads. Our generation has the added benefit of tremendously advanced communications, high-tech media connections, incredible visual and audio capabilities, and much more to enhance and expand our presentation of the gospel message. But nothing is nearly as effective as when "each one teaches one."

In the book of Acts we meet heroes of the faith: Peter, Paul, Stephen, Philip, and others whose lives were completely revolutionized from cowering, hiding weaklings to God's spiritual super-heroes by the power of the resurrected Christ and His indwelling Holy Spirit.

We also meet ordinary folks, business men and women, jail-keepers, church leaders, craftsmen and craftswomen, government officials, men, women, Jews, gentiles, people of mixed lineage, rich people, poor people, and there was probably even a beggar and a thief in the crowd, who gave their lives to Jesus.

The story doesn't end with the people we meet in Acts. More and more believers continue to be added to our spiritual family and grow in their personal faith-walk, from the first century until now. Those heroes of the faith, who have repeated the message again and again for generations to hear, have no name or face to us. But they are God's precious children with whom He intimately fellowships today in heaven. One great day we'll meet them and say, "Thank you!"

Those believing men, women, boys, and girls made it possible for the precious message of Jesus to now be in our hands. Who will now pass on the life-changing, world-revolutionizing message of Jesus to generations ahead? Will it be you? Will it be your child?

Romans God's Book About How I Can Know God and What He Wants Me to Do

"I am not ashamed of the gospel, because it is the power of God for the salvation of everyone who believes" (Romans 1:16a).

What's the Book About

The book of Romans tells us that the way to know God is to believe on His Son, Jesus Christ. It also tells us other very important things God wants us to know and to do.

A Great Missionary Writes to Christian Friends

Paul wrote the book of Romans. It was really a letter to the Christian people in the church in Rome that Paul had not yet gotten to meet. Remember that very special day called Pentecost, when God's Holy Spirit came into the hearts of believers? Three thousand people gave their lives to Jesus that day, and some of the new believers were probably from faraway Rome. Those new Christians told their friends about Jesus when they went back home, and many other people in Rome became believers, too

Let's Meet the People of Romans

Paul was the man who loved God. He wrote the book of Romans. Paul had been Pharisee, a Jewish leader who knew a lot about the Bible, but hated the people who believed in Jesus and wanted to hurt them. One day Paul met Jesus for himself, and the Savior changed Paul's heart forever. From then on, Paul told everyone he could about Jesus, his Lord. Paul even went on three missionary trips to tell people in other lands that Jesus is the Son of God.

Here Are the Places of Romans

Rome – a powerful city in Italy. Rome had a mighty army and a leader they called their Emperor, or Caesar. The Romans were in charge of everyone, everywhere, they thought. But many Roman people did not know Jesus or believe in Him. They did not understand that only God is all powerful. Paul wanted so much to go to Rome to preach and teach about Jesus. He wanted to help the believers grow stronger in their faith. This book is the letter Paul wrote to the Roman Christians.

God Turns Bad Into Good
(A cooking experience)

What will I need? 1 cup pancake mix, 1 Tbsp unsweetened cocoa, 1/4 cup sugar, 2/3 cup milk, 2 Tbsp. cooking oil, 1 egg
Where is it in the Bible? Romans 8:28
How long will it take? 20-30 minutes
What age child? 2-12 years
Will it work in a group? Yes
Can it be played in the car? No
Will it work in a school classroom? Yes, preschool–5th grade

There is a verse in Romans that many people love. Read the verse with the importance it deserves. Explain that God tells us that not everything that will happens to us will be good, even though we are God's children, and He loves us. But God promises to take the good and bad things that happen us and make something wonderful for our good.

Show your child that sweet and bitter things can be mixed together to make something tasty. Let it be a picture of what Jesus does for us in real life. Here's a recipe you may want to use, or choose one of your own. As you add the ingredients, let your child taste the cocoa, pancake mix, and sugar. Pour enough batter to make a pancake onto a hot skillet. Cook 1 to 1 1/2 minutes until little bubbles form and begin to break; then flip the pancakes over for one more minute. Serve them with syrup, strawberries, chocolate sauce, or whipped cream.

Ask your child if he thought the ingredients he tasted were good or bitter by themselves. Just like the bitter and sweet ingredients mixed together to make something good to eat, God uses the good and bad times of our life for His glory.

Trusting Jesus as Your Savior.

May God give you wisdom and discernment regarding your own child's ability to understand and their readiness to receive Jesus as Savior. Don't be afraid if he is young, if he truly seems ready to trust in Jesus. However, proceed carefully because you want his commitment to be real and personal, initiated by the Holy Spirit and free from premature pressure. If God's Spirit is speaking to your child, He will keep on until your child comes to a point of genuine prayer and salvation. He will use your willing heart to help prepare him/her to personally receive the Savior as his very own at just the right time. If your child is inquisitive, but not yet ready to take the next step toward Christianity, we recommend the book *When Can I?* from Broadman & Holman Publishers.

1. Everyone has sinned
Romans 3:10-12, 23; 5:12

Activity: You will need newspaper or white paper, masking tape, one piece of construction paper or poster board, crayons or markers, and scissors.

Ask your child what sin is. If he can't really define it, ask him to name some things he thinks are sins. Does he think God's heart is sad when we sin? Why? Say, "Do you think I have ever sinned?" Ask if he thinks sin has to be punished. Why? Ask if he knows who took all our sins on Himself so we wouldn't have to be punished for them?

Explain that sin is sometimes called missing the mark. When someone tries to throw a ball at a target and misses, we say he missed the mark. Have your child make a round target with a circle for the center. Tape it on a door. Then, make paper balls wrapped with a strip of masking tape to throw at your target. Or, you may use rolled-up socks for balls. Take turns trying to hit the bulls-eye. Seeing how many hits you have together and how many misses.

We've all done wrong and missed God's mark which means we're not perfect, like Jesus. Only Jesus never sinned, and only Jesus can take away our sin, when we ask Him to.

2. Sin costs a high price
Romans 6:23a

Activity: You will need some small inexpensive items and a penny for your child.

Play pretend store with your child as the customer. Lay some inexpensive items on a table as the merchandise. Place a bag nearby for your customer's purchases. The customer will need to ask you the cost of each item, because there are no price tags. When she does, quote her some outlandish price, like $1,000 for a pencil, etc. She will probably look surprised. Say, "Do you think our prices are rather high?" Ask if she thinks a toy should cost $1,000,000. Then, slash prices for today only just because you like her. Charge her one penny for everything she purchased.

The Bible also tells us about something that has a very high price. Read about it in Romans 6:23a. Explain wages are the paycheck you get for the work you do at a job. The Bible says the price we have to pay for our sins is very high. The high cost of our sin is being away from God forever in a place called hell.

3. God's Great Love
Romans 5:8

Activity: Just you and your child

Play a game called "Prove it!" Take turns choosing things to do from the list below. All the choices start with the words, "I will_____." After you or your child have decided what to do from the list, the other one says, "Prove it!" Then do whatever you have chosen from the list.

walk backwards
whistle
snap my fingers
bend over and touch my toes
say the Pledge of Allegiance
wink with each eye

Read Romans 5:8, explaining there's a big word in the verse that means proved or showed. (The word may be "commendeth" or "demonstrates.") In this verse, Paul tells us God proved His love for us by sending Jesus to die for us while we were still sinners.

4. The best present of all
Romans 6:23b; 5:17

Activity: An inexpensive gift to wrap to give to your child because you love her.

Ask your child to tell you about the best presents she has ever gotten. Have a little surprise love gift wrapped and out of sight for your child. Give it to her after you have read the Bible together to find the very best present of all. Explain that the gift you have for her may not be the very best present she has ever gotten, but it means that you love her very much. Read Romans 6:23b. Say Jesus also gave us a present because He loves us.

In Romans 6:23b, what gift did Jesus give to us? A gift is a present someone gives because they love you. There are two things you can do with a gift: Take it or refuse it. The present is not yours until you take it. That's the way it is with the free gift Jesus gives us. His wonderful present is called eternal life.

Jesus' gift to us cost Him a lot, He had to die to pay for our sins. What a wonderful offer.

5. A very important call
Romans 10: 9-10, 13

Activity: Time for a conversation with your child

Ask your child who she would call if she could call anyone she wanted. Why are telephones so important to us? Try to imagine how people talked to their families and friends before the telephone was invented. The Bible tells us about the most important call we will ever make. But this call doesn't use phones. Read Romans 10:13 to find out how we call on Jesus. We pray. We can just talk to Him anytime we want.

Without pressuring her, ask your child if she understands that Jesus is God's Son and gave His life for her. If you know your child is ready, you can have them pray a prayer like this one: "Dear Lord Jesus, I know I have sinned. I am very sorry for my sins. I ask You to please forgive me. I give You my life and You can be my Lord. Thank You for saving me. In the name of Jesus I pray, Amen."

God's Word promises us that when we call on Jesus, He saves us from our sins. He gives us a brand new life and we are born into His spiritual family. If you prayed and received Jesus today, welcome to His family. Share the great news with someone who will celebrate with you.

What Can I Learn from Romans

God gave us some very important things to know and to do in the book of Romans. I can learn from the Bible the things God wants me to know and He will help me to do those good things!

Important Verses To Remember

Romans 3:23 – "For all have sinned and fall short of the glory of God."

Romans 5:8 – "But God demonstrates his own love for us in this: While we were still sinners, Christ died for us."

Romans 6:23 – "For the wages of sin is death, but the gift of God is eternal life in Christ Jesus our Lord."

Romans 8:28 – "And we know that in all things God works for the good of those who love him, who have been called according to His purpose."

Romans 8:38 – "For I am convinced that neither death nor life, neither angels nor demons, neither the present nor the future, nor any powers, neither height nor depth, nor anything else in all creation, will be able to separate us from the love of God that is in Christ Jesus our Lord."

A Devotional Thought for Parents and Teachers

Have you ever thought about how you fit into the big picture as a believer in Jesus Christ? Isn't it mind-boggling to imagine the millions and millions of believers who have lived? Nearly all those brothers and sisters will remain nameless and faceless to us until we meet them in heaven. As far as God is concerned, each person is a treasured only child to Him. That means you, too.

When Paul wrote Romans, he had never met the people who would read his mail. Later there were brothers and sisters in the world capital of Rome, and the family of God was growing and thriving all across the world.

Those family members in Rome needed to hear the same words of God that we read in Romans. They needed to know more about God and His will and so do we. The Roman believers wanted to know how to live according to the will of God, and so should we.

Around the world there are children of God who are related to us through Christ. Let's pray for their safe keeping, for their faith to grow by leaps and bounds, for them to know more about God's plan for them, and that they will have the Holy Spirit's boldness to do what He asks. One day those great relatives will hug you and thank you, and you'll thank them, too, because somewhere, someone is praying for you.

I Corinthians God's Book About How to Solve Problems and How to Live for Jesus

"For the message of the cross is foolishness to those who are perishing, but to us who are being saved it is the power of God" (I Corinthians 1:18).

What's the Book About

The book of I Corinthians is about God's way to handle problems and questions that arise so that we can please Him and serve Him well.

From Weakness to Strength

First Corinthians is a letter Paul wrote to a church of God's people in the city of Corinth. It was a big, bad city in lots of ways, because many people there worshiped false idols instead of the true God. The Christians in Corinth were having some trouble staying true and strong for Jesus. The church also had some fussing and fighting going on. They needed answers to some questions they had and Paul wanted to help them become everything that God wanted them to be. Paul wrote his letter to the Corinthians because they were his brothers and sisters in God's family.

Let's Meet the People of I Corinthians

Paul wrote down God's words to help the Christians at Corinth be stronger in their trust in Jesus and in the way they lived for Him. He also wanted to answer the many questions that the people had.

Timothy was the young man who traveled with Paul on some of his missionary trips and helped him do God's great work.

Aquila and **Priscilla** were tentmakers who loved Jesus. Paul had met them in the city of Corinth. Many people in the church at Corinth knew and loved Aquila and Priscilla.

Here Are the Places of I Corinthians

Houses in Corinth – Where the people who believed in Jesus met together to worship, pray, learn about God, and help each other to do God's great work since there were no church buildings yet.

Be Friends
(A sticky situation)

What will I need? You and your child, or your child and a friend
Where is it in the Bible? I Corinthians 1–4:21
How long will it take? 5-10 minutes
What age child? 3-12 years
Will it work in a group? Yes
Can it be played in the car? Yes
Will it work in a school classroom? Yes, preschool–6th grade

Open your child's Bible to I Corinthians 1–4:21 and thumb through the verses as your child watches. Tell him that in many of these verses, Paul is telling the people in the church in the city of Corinth to stick together and be friendly and kind to each other. Explain that even though some of the people in that church probably believed in Jesus, they were arguing among themselves. Some of them were jealous of each other. Paul knew it was not right to act like that. He wanted to help the Christians in Corinth to start acting in ways that would please Jesus.

Paul knew there would be many different kinds of people in churches, and they would not always think, act, or feel exactly alike. That was okay. But Paul also knew that if the people who believed in Jesus would let Him be the Lord and Master in their lives and in their church, everybody could be friends again!

Here is a way to remember that friends should stick together. Pretend that you and your child or your child and his friend, are stuck together back-to-back or side-to-side with glue. Go everywhere and do everything together until you want to be separate friends again.

Remember that Christian friends have lots of great reasons to stick together. The greatest reason of all is sharing a love for Jesus!

Be Kind
(A musical activity)

What will I need? Your whole family
Where is it in the Bible? I Corinthians 8; 13; 14:1a
How long will it take? 5-10 minutes
What age child? 2-12 years
Will it work in a group? Yes
Can it be played in the car? No
Will it work in a school classroom? Yes, preschool–6th grade

Tell your child that he has two families. He may have more than two, depending on your situation. He has a family on earth and a heavenly, spiritual family. Our Heavenly Father is God. Everyone who has ever given his or her life to Jesus is in God's family. Now that's a big family!

Explain that part of God's family are the people in your own church. A church is not a club, a class, a pretty building with lots of rooms, or a great place to go, it's a family. Paul visited some of the churches that belonged to God's family when he went on his three missionary trips.

As Paul visited churches in different towns, he could see that many of the brothers and sisters in them loved each other very much and were busy doing God's work together. But in a few places, just like happens in our families on earth, the Christian brothers and sisters were forgetting to be loving and kind to each other. Paul wanted to help them get back on track where they should be.

Jesus was filled with love. He wants His family to love each other in the same way. The thing that is so wonderful about Jesus' great love is that He can fill our hearts with His love. All our selfishness and feelings of wanting our own way or wanting to be most important will be pushed out of our hearts by His love.

Have fun together, enjoying the love that God has put in your family and pretending to be people chimes. Line up side by side, like a set of church bells, and choose one person to be the director. He will gently tap in front of the person with a yardstick, one at a time, to make a "musical" note.

After warming up your chiming skills, try to chime an actual song that you all know well, making the sound of the next note in your song when the director taps in front of you. In I Corinthians 13 Paul says that love is more important than any kind of beautiful music we can ever make. Practice being loving and kind, every single day.

Be Faithful

Explain to your child that it is important to be faithful to God. That means you believe in God, and trust Him to be there with you and for you at all times. You don't ever have to worry that Jesus will be gone away somewhere when you need Him. Jesus is faithful to us. He also wants us to be faithful to Him.

Paul tells us some of the things that being faithful to God means. Jesus wants us to decide to follow Him and then to keep on doing just that every day of our lives. When we trust in Jesus as our Savior, we give Him our whole life. Being faithful to Jesus is the best life anybody can ever have.

Ask your child to do a little detective work and discover what Paul says about some of the ways we can be faithful to Jesus:
1. Read I Corinthians 10:12-13. Being faithful to Jesus means saying, "No!" when the devil tempts you to do something wrong. Jesus will be faithful to you at those times to make you strong enough to do what's right.
2. Read I Corinthians 10:14. Being faithful to Jesus means not having idols. That probably seems sort of silly, since we don't bow down and pray to any kind of statue. But there are different of kinds of idols, because an idol is anything that is more important to us than God.

What Can I Learn from I Corinthians

The book of I Corinthians tells us that God wants His children to get along with each other and to be a strong team that works together for Jesus.

Important Verses To Remember

I Corinthians 2:14 – "The man without the Spirit does not accept the things that come from the Spirit of God, for they are foolishness to him, and he cannot understand them, because they are spiritually discerned."

I Corinthians 6:19-20 – "Do you not know that your body is a temple of the Holy Spirit, who is in you, whom you have received from God? You are not your own; you were bought at a price. Therefore, honor God with your body."

I Corinthians 10:12 – "So, if you think you are standing firm, be careful that you don't fall!"

I Corinthians 10:31 – "So whether you eat or drink or whatever you do, do it all for the glory of God."

I Corinthians 13:4a – "Love is patient, love is kind."

A Devotional Thought for Parents and Teachers

Have you ever been part of a church that had problems? Have you ever heard someone say, "I used to go to church, but I don't anymore or I never will because...." Let's face it, let's not sweep the dirt under the rug, since Paul didn't. Churches can have problems, and often do. Why is that?

Think about it for a minute:

1. We're a part of our church, and we sometimes behave in less than perfect ways. We have attitudes and thoughts at times that we would be mortified to have brought to light for all to see. Multiply us 300 or 3,000 times and there you have it – our church.

2. Every church has an ominous enemy – the prince of this world himself, Satan. His well-planned and finely-orchestrated schemes are constantly being played out, either in the dark, shadowy recesses behind the scenes or right out front for everyone to watch in stunned disbelief.

Jesus knew so many more ugly details about churches and believers than we will ever know. He so loved the church filled with weak, compromising believers, that He shed His precious blood for it. How can we truly find any excuse not to be right in there contributing our talents and gifts, adding our prayer-power, promoting peace and unity at every opportunity, expressing our optimistic hope for a bright future?

How can we send our child any other message than this: being totally involved and absolutely committed to Jesus' service, through our extended church family, is an indescribable privilege. It's an honor and an obligation from which no amount of stress and strife and trouble will cause us drop-out, because we serve in our church for Jesus.

II Corinthians God's Book About True and False Teachers

"Therefore, if anyone is in Christ, he is a new creation; the old has gone, the new has come" (II Corinthians 5:17).

What's the Book About	The book of II Corinthians is about the difference in people who tell the truth about Jesus and those who don't.
A Call to Genuine Commitment	Second Corinthians was written to help the Christians in Corinth with a problem they kept having, the problem of people who really didn't believe in Jesus at all. There were false teachers who kept telling God's people things about Jesus that weren't true. These false teachers were trying to talk the people into turning away from Jesus, and Paul didn't want that to happen. God gave Paul the words to tell the believers at Corinth to be careful, to be strong, and to be busy doing God's work.
Let's Meet the People of II Corinthians	**Paul** wrote down God's words to help the Christians at Corinth to be stronger in their faith and in the way they lived for God, and to answer their questions.
	Timothy was the young man who traveled with Paul on some of his missionary trips and helped him do God's work.
	Titus was a friend of Paul's and a servant of Jesus Christ, who sometimes went with Paul on his missionary trips to tell people about Jesus.
	False teachers were people who did not really love God and tried to get God's people confused about what to believe about Jesus.

They thought this would make the Christians stop serving Him.

Here are the Places of II Corinthians	**Corinth** – the sinful city where Paul wrote God's letter of II Corinthians to help the Christians to stay away from false teachers and to become strong servants of Jesus.
	Jerusalem – the important city of Judah, where Solomon built the beautiful temple for people to come and worship God. Many churches in Paul's day gave money to help the poor Christians in Jerusalem who were being treated badly and having a hard time.

STORIES AND ACTIVITIES FROM II CORINTHIANS

Be God's "Perfume"
(Having fun with smells)

What will I need? Three different spices or perfumes, six plastic bags, whole cloves or whole allspice, warm water, a needle, and thread.

Where is it in the Bible? II Corinthians 2:14-15

How long will it take? 15-20 minutes

What age child? 30-12 years

Will it work in a group? Yes

Can it be played in the car? Yes, you can take it along with you.

Will it work in a school classroom? Yes, preschool–6th grade

Ask your child to listen for a word that means something that smells good as you read II Corinthians 2:14-15. The word, "savor" or "fragrance" is like the word "perfume." God wants us to be His perfume. What a nice job.

Ask your child if she's ever seen the ladies in stores at the mall who want us to try their perfume? They offer to spray a little perfume on us so we can see if we like it and want to buy it. If you have ever had the perfume sprayed on you, the smell goes with you everywhere you go. Other people can smell your good perfume fragrance.

Jesus wants us to be His good-smelling perfume by the way we act toward other people, and the way we talk about Him, so they will want Jesus, too.

Try one of these good-smelling experiments:

1. Put some different kinds of spices or perfumes into little plastic bags. Use two bags for each spice. Place all the bags on the table, and ask someone in your family to close his eyes and smell each bag to find the matching bags of spices.

2. Soak some whole cloves and allspice in water for a few days or until they are soft. Thread a needle with dental floss or heavy thread and run it through the spices in whatever interesting arrangement you choose to make a good-smelling necklace.

Whenever you use spices or enjoy the pleasant smell of potpourri, remember that Jesus wants us to spread His wonderful "fragrance" everywhere we go.

What Can I Learn from II Corinthians

The devil used people in Paul's day to trick God's children into not believing in Jesus anymore. He wanted to make them stop serving God. I want to watch out for the devil and to stay close to Jesus so He can make me strong and wise.

Important Verses to Remember

II Corinthians 4:6 – "For God, who said, 'Let light shine out of darkness,' made his light shine in our hearts to give us the light of the knowledge of the glory of God in the face of Christ."

II Corinthians 5:17 – "Therefore, if anyone is in Christ, he is a new creation; the old has gone, the new has come!"

II Corinthians 9:7 – "God loves a cheerful giver."

II Corinthians 12:8b – "Be he said to me, 'My grace is sufficient for you, for my power is made perfect in weakness.' "

A Devotional Thought for Parents and Teachers

Do you ever feel like you are being bombarded with more philosophies, theories, opinions, ways of looking at things, and facts than one mind can handle? Do green beans and hot dogs cause cancer? Am I asking for trouble if I spank my child? Will I warp my child if I potty train him too early? Is the city's water supply polluted? Is the country's economy doomed? Will all teenagers inevitably rebel? What information can I trust?

We know who's right, don't we? God is! He knows the answer to every one of those questions and billions more. We have the "how-to" and "what-if" fail-proof and fool-proof guidebook within our arm's length. When we're just not sure that we ought to incorporate what we're hearing into our practical lives, we can bounce each relative idea against God's absolute truth. Then, listening to the still, small voice of the Holy Spirit within us, our personal truth detector, we'll know what to believe and what to do.

Galatians God's Book About the Old Life and the New Life in Jesus

"I have been crucified with Christ and I no longer live, but Christ lives in me. The life I live in the body, I live by faith in the Son of God, who loved me and gave himself for me" (Galatians 2:20).

What's the Book About

The book of Galatians tells Jesus' followers about the wonderful new life that Jesus gives us when we trust Him as our Savior.

Paul Writes About Freedom from an Old Life

Galatians is about the old life we lived before we met Jesus. He gave us His free gift of new life. In Paul's letter to the Christian people in Galatia, he tells them what it means to be free when we trust in Jesus. Jesus makes us free from all our sins, free to be strong in doing what's right, and free to love and help other people.

Let's Meet the People of Galatians

Paul didn't love Jesus at first, but met the Lord on the road to Damascus. Paul was planning to take Christians to jail for believing in Jesus. Paul's heart and life were completely changed. God told Paul what to write in the book of Galatians to help the people in Galatia who followed Jesus.

Barnabas and **Titus** were two of Paul's special friends who went with him on some of his missionary journeys.

Peter was one of Jesus' disciples who become one of the important leaders of Jesus' church in Jerusalem.

False teachers were the people who followed the devil, did not love Jesus, and tried to teach wrong things about the Lord so that people would stop following Him.

Here Are the Places of Galatians

Galatia – was the country where Paul went on his three missionary trips, to tell the people in the cities there about Jesus.

Jerusalem – was the city of Israel where the temple of God was located. After Jesus died, arose, and went to heaven, a church grew in Jerusalem, and Peter was one of its pastors.

Old Self/New Self

(Fruit creatures)

What will I need? Apples dipped in melted caramel with faces made out of chocolate chips, marshmallows, candy pieces, canned fruits, raisins, and nuts.
Where is it in the Bible? Galatians 2:20, 5:16-25
How long will it take? 20-30 minutes
What age child? 2-12 years
Will it work in a group? Yes
Can it be played in the car? No
Will it work in a school classroom? Yes, preschool–6th grade

Paul tells us in Galatians that all people, who have given their lives to Jesus, have an old self and a new self. The new life is much better. In fact, the old self has no good in it at all.

The old self is the person we were before we gave our heart to Jesus. Paul gives us a list of bad things that the old self wants us to do in Galatians 5:19. Have you ever had bad thoughts about someone, started fighting, getting angry, been jealous, or selfish. The old self appears when this happens and is not very pretty.

Our new self, with Jesus living inside us, is much nicer. Read what those good things are in Galatians 5:22-23. Paul calls them the fruit of the Spirit, because it is Jesus who helps to do good things instead of bad things. These good things grow out of a relationship with Jesus.

Here are some fun ideas to help you remember that the fruit from the new self is very good.

1. Make fruity faces by dipping apples in melted caramel and giving them faces.

2. Make fruity animal faces from canned pears, apricots, peaches, or pineapple. Pineapple rings made a good lion's mane; a mouse or monkey can be made from an upside-down pear or peach half with apricot ears; peach slices make good ears for a rabbit. Use raisins or nuts for eyes and noses, and apple slice's become smiles for mouths.

As you enjoy your treat talk about how good the fruits are, and compare them to the good fruits in Galatians.

Forward/Backward

(A changing directions game)

What will I need? Your family or friends, and a small object
Where is it in the Bible? Galatians 3:6-9, 14-18, 24-26
How long will it take? 15-20 minutes
What age child? 3-12 years
Will it work in a group? Yes
Can it be played in the car? Just the discussion.
Will it work in a school classroom? Yes, preschool–6th grade

Ask your child to show you what the words "forward" and "backward" mean.

People who lived before Jesus was born and died, like Abraham, Moses, and David, and people like us who live after Jesus came, are all part of God's family. We all believe in Jesus. Read Galatians 3:26,28.

Abraham lived a long time before Jesus was born in Bethlehem. Abraham believed that God would send His Son, the Savior. Abraham and the other people in the Old Testament looked forward to when Jesus would come. We look backward to see what Jesus did for us when He died for our sins. We look forward to the day we will all be with our Savior forever.

Play a backward/forward game. Stand in a line facing forward. Choose which one of you will give the signals. When that player says, "backward," the leader will pass an object (an ice cube would make the game really move) over his head without looking at the person behind him. Everyone keeps passing it backward until the designated player says "forward." Then the players must pass the object back over the head of the person in front of them. Keep the object going back and forth as long as you like. If you're playing with a large group consider passing several objects one after another.

Good Seeds and Bad Seeds

Read Galatians 6:7-10, and explain the verses in your own words. Paul says that if we do the good things that God's Spirit wants us to, it's like planting good seeds. Good things will be in our lives just like the strong plants that grow from the right kinds of seeds. But, if we let the bad things that don't please God grow in our lives, we will not be happy and good.

If a farmer plants carrot seeds, he will see carrots growing, not bananas. Whatever kind of seeds we plant, that's the kind of plant that grows.

Jesus wants us to put good things into our lives, like learning about the Bible, talking to God, going to church to praise and worship Jesus, watching television shows that are good for us, and doing kind things for people.

Plant some different kinds of flower or vegetable seeds in small cups. Then, plant a rock in a cup and a nail in another for the bad seeds. Which seeds do you think will grow good plants? Give your plants a little water each day and put them in the sunlight. Check after a week or two to see if the good seeds are growing?

What Can I Learn from Galatians

I learned that Jesus has made me free.

Important Verses to Remember

Galatians 3:28 – "There is neither Jew nor Greek, slave nor free, male nor female, for you are all one in Christ Jesus."

Galatians 2:20a – "I have been crucified with Christ and I no longer live, but Christ lives in me."

Galatians 5: 22 – "But the fruit of the Spirit is love, joy, peace, patience, kindness, goodness, faithfulness, gentleness and self-control. Against such things there is no law."

Galatians 6:9-10 – "Let us not become weary in doing good, for at the proper time we will reap a harvest if we do not give up. Therefore, as we have opportunity, let us do good to all people, especially to those who belong to the family of believers."

A Devotional Thought for Parents and Teachers

See *A Devotional Thought from Galatians, Ephesians, Philippians, and Colossians* at the end of Colossians.

Ephesians God's Book About Being a Body, a Temple, a Bride, and a Soldier

"For it is by grace that you have been saved, through faith – and this not from yourselves, it is the gift of God – not by works, so that no one can boast" (Ephesians 2:8-9).

What's the Book About

The book of Ephesians is about what it means to be a part of God's wonderful family!

Paul Tells Jesus' Followers They Are One Body.

Ephesians tells us about many wonderful things that happen to those who have trust in Jesus as their Savior. We learn that we are all an important part of the big family of people who have put their faith in Jesus, too.

Paul helps us to understand in this letter that he wrote to the church in Ephesus that we must be kind to each other and not to hurt one another with our words or the things we do. Paul paints some very interesting word pictures in the book of Ephesians. He says we are part of a body and Jesus is the Head. We are building blocks, and Jesus is the Cornerstone. Believers are the bride of Jesus, and we are His soldiers.

Let's Meet the People of Ephesians

Paul met the Lord on the road to Damascus, where he was planning to take Christians to jail for believing in Jesus. Paul's heart and life were completely changed.

Here Are the Places of Ephesians

Ephesus – the city where Paul spent three years with other followers who loved Jesus. Paul felt very close to the people there.

I'm a Rock; You're a Rock
(Building projects)

What will I need? 1. A big box, paint, a brush or markers, a sharp knife 2. A small box, frosting and graham crackers or gingerbread walls

Where is it in the Bible? Ephesians 2:19-22

How long will it take? 30-45 minutes

What age child? 3-10 years

Will it work in a group? A small group or individual project

Can it be played in the car? No

Will it work in a school classroom? Yes, preschool–4th grade

Open your Bible to Ephesians 2:19-22. Paul says all people that love and trust Jesus are a part of His wonderful family.

Paul also says that all of God's people are like a big building made of lots and lots of stones for God. Each of the stones is a person who loves Jesus. The house of God keeps getting bigger and bigger as more and more people come to know and trust Jesus. Jesus is the Cornerstone, the most important rock that the whole building is built upon. He holds everything together and makes it strong.

Make your own building from one of these:

1. Find a big box (an appliance box would work well) you can paint or decorate. Cut out a door and windows and go inside it. Draw some pictures and furniture on the walls inside. Then put a rug or old piece of cloth on the floor.

2. Use a small box you can cover with frosting for mortar, then attach graham crackers or gingerbread walls to it. Decorate it with candy pieces.

Measuring God's Great Love
(Different ways to measure)

What will I need? Your child's thumb, shoe, a flashlight, a key, a pickle, etc.

Where is it in the Bible? Ephesians 3:14-21

How long will it take? 15-20 minutes

What age child? 3-10 years

Will it work in a group? Yes

Can it be played in the car? No

Will it work in a school classroom? Yes, preschool–4th grade

Pretend that your child is a measuring wonder, and he has come to your house to measure things for you. He will not use the usual measuring things. He must measure objects and furniture with his thumb, shoe, flashlight, pickle or whatever you want him to. Tell him what you need to have measured. For instance, a book may be six thumbs wide, or your computer monitor may be two cucumbers high.

Paul tells us in Ephesians that there is something that can't be measured, no matter what we use to try to figure out how high or wide it is. God's love for us can never be measured. Read Ephesians 3:17-18, emphasizing how wide, deep, and high God's love really is. Pray together, taking turns thanking God for His love that can't be measured.

Full or Empty

(Science experiments)

What will I need? An egg, empty glass, water, dirt, rocks, and sticks

Where is it in the Bible? Ephesians 5:18-20

How long will it take? 10-15 minutes

What age child? 4-11 years

Will it work in a group? Yes

Can it be played in the car? No, water is involved

Will it work in a school classroom? Yes, pre-school–5th grade

Ask your child to think about eggs with you. Look at the outside of an egg. Ask if there is anything inside it. Say, "I can't see anything in there, I just see the outside. How can we know if there really is something in there if we can't see it?"

Do what your child will probably suggest, crack open the egg into a bowl. There was something inside the egg, wasn't there? Beat the egg and add it into a recipe for pancakes, cakes, cookies, etc. When the egg is mixed with the batter, you can't see it anymore. Ask, "Is the egg still in there? How do I know the egg is in there? I can't see it anymore. Are you sure it's still there?"

Explain that when we ask Jesus to into our heart, we can't see Him inside us. Jesus doesn't actually step into our heart with the body He had when he was on earth as a man.

Read Ephesians 5:18 and emphasize the words, "be filled with the Holy Spirit." Read verses 19-20 to see some of the things that we will do when the Holy Spirit fills our life.

Pour your child a cool drink of water, but ask him not to drink it yet. See how full you can get the glass without spilling any. Pour it

slowly, and ask your child to notice the rounded top on the water. It's higher than the glass. What keeps the water from spilling over the edge is something called "surface tension" on top of the water. It acts like an invisible skin to hold the water in place. If we touch the water or bump the glass, it's easy to break the skin and make the water spill.

We are sort of like God's empty glass, and He fills us with his Holy Spirit when we ask Jesus to become our Savior. A glass that's empty may be pretty or sit nicely in a cupboard, but it is not useful until there's something inside it.

But what would happen to the glass if there were dirt, sticks, and rocks in it. If we tried to put water in it we wouldn't be able to get as much water in the glass as before. Those things take up too much of the room.

The same is true of us, if we have not asked Jesus to come into our lives and wash out the old stuff that's taking up room where Jesus belongs. Even when Jesus lives in us, we need to be careful not to let other junk fill up our hearts.

Living Together in a Family

(A puzzling activity)

What will I need? A puzzle

Where is it in the Bible? Ephesians 5:21–6:4

How long will it take? 15-20 minutes

What age child? 3-12

Will it work in a group? Yes

Can it be played in the car? If you plan ahead.

Will it work in a school classroom? Yes, preschool–6th grade

Lay the pieces of a puzzle on a table to

work with your child. Begin putting the puzzle together fitting the wrong pieces together. Put some of the pieces together with the wrong side up. Act like you are proud of the job you've done.

Ask your child if he likes the way you do puzzles. If not, find out why. Use this opportunity to explain that puzzles that don't fit together right are like families that don't get along with each other and don't try to do things God's way.

Read Ephesians 5:25 and 28. Ask your child if he is a husband? Read Ephesians 5:22 and 33. Ask, "Are you a wife?" Then Read Ephesians 6:1-3 Ask, "Are you a children? You are a child and these verses are for you."

Explain the promise that goes along with obeying parents. Take advantage of this golden opportunity to help motivate him to be an obedient child. Because it pleases God, it makes you and Him happy. Obedience has the promise of a long, good life attached to it. That would be a good incentive to get under his belt before he becomes a teenager.

Help your child understand that God's plan for families and the way they work together is the best plan possible. Tell your child the verses in Ephesians are for parents, too. You want God to help you obey Him. Pray together that God will help each person in your family to be what God wants them to be for Him and for each other.

What Can I Learn from Ephesians

I learn that I'm a part of God's big, wonderful family. I'm also a building, a soldier, and even a bride.

Important Verses to Remember

Ephesians 2:4 – "But because of his great love for us, God, who is rich in mercy, made us alive with Christ even when we were dead in transgressions – it is by grace you have been saved."

Ephesians 2:8 – "For it is by grace you have been saved, through faith."

Ephesians 4:29 – "Do not let any unwholesome talk come out of your mouths, but only what is helpful for building others up according to their needs, that it may benefit those who listen."

Ephesians 4:19 – "Be kind and compassionate to one another, forgiving each other, just as in Christ God forgave you."

A Devotional Thought for Parents and Teachers

See *A Devotional Thought from Galatians, Ephesians, Philippians, and Colossians* at the end of Colossians.

Philippians God's Book About Joy

"Rejoice in the Lord always, I will say it again: Rejoice!" (Philippians 4:4).

What's the Book About

The book of Philippians is about the wonderful joy that Jesus puts in our heart when we put our trust in Him.

How to Get Joy and Keep It

Philippians was written by Paul when he was in jail in Rome. Paul had not done anything wrong; he was in prison for doing good things for Jesus.

It might have been easy for Paul to grumble and fuss and say, "I don't deserve this." But Paul's heart was full of joy. He wrote to tell the people at Philippi the reason that he was happy is because Jesus was in his heart. No matter what trouble Paul was having, Jesus gave him joy.

Let's Meet the People of Philippians

Paul was the man who was planning to take Christians to jail for believing in Jesus. Paul's heart and life were completely changed. Paul wrote to the people who loved Jesus in the city of Ephesus.

Epaphroditus loved God and brought a gift of money to Paul from the Philippian church. Then Epaphroditus went back to Philippi with a thank-you note from Paul.

Here Are the Places of Philippians

Philippi – the city where Paul went on his second trip to tell people about Jesus.

The Conductor

(Directing a choir)

What will I need? You, your child, a Bible, and music
Where is it in the Bible? Philippians 1:27
How long will it take? 10-15 minutes
What age child? 2-10 years
Will it work in a group? Yes
Can it be played in the car? Yes, with a little flexibility.
Will it work in a school classroom? Yes, preschool–4th grade

Talk about what a conductor is. If your child likes trains, talk about how a train conductor is the man in charge of the train. It is the conductor's job to make sure that everything goes well on the trip for the people who ride the train.

The conductor of a musical orchestra helps to make beautiful music come from what would otherwise be a bunch of noisy instruments. Paul tells us in Philippians to be conductors in our own lives. He wants us to be very sure that we act and talk in such a way that we will be like beautiful music for Jesus! Read Philippians 1:27 to your child. Pray and ask God to help you be a good conductor of the life He has given you.

Then, pretend to be a famous conductor, leading your whole family and friends in a verse of "Row, Row, Row Your Boat." Ask the choir to use their fanciest voices and to follow your conducting leading carefully. Take a bow before the imaginary, applauding audience.

Unselfish Jesus

Humility is what the beautiful verses in Philippians 2:2-11 are about. Explain in your own words about what an awesome thing Jesus did when He left His spectacular King's throne in heaven and came to earth as a baby, even though He would have to die on the cross for our sins. Jesus went from being the King of all Kings to becoming a servant. He chose to do that for us.

Help your child develop a beautiful servant spirit that will please God and help your child feel good about himself as he thinks of others. One of the best ways to teach your child to be a servant is to show him how through your own life. Your wonderful example of selflessness is sure to be contagious.

What Were You Thinking

(Time to relax)

What will I need? Some comfortable items such as a pillow, blanket, soft music, and a cold/hot drink
Where is it in the Bible? Philippians 4:8
How long will it take? As long as it is fun!
What age child? 2-11 years
Will it work in a group? Yes, everyone could find a comfortable spot to relax
Can it be played in the car? Yes, as long as the driver stays alert.
Will it work in a school classroom? Yes

Help your child get relaxed by making a comfortable place for him to rest. Do whatever would be relaxing.

Tell him to just relax and think about

happy things: a sunny day, snowflakes, the smell of cookies baking, Christmas, his birthday party, etc. Ask him what he is thinking about.

Talk about the fact that what we think about really does affect how we feel – whether we're happy and peaceful or worried, troubled, discouraged, scared, and gloomy. Read Philippians 4:8 and see what God wants us to think about. God always knows what is best for us, so let's ask Him to help us think about those things every single day.

Strong Man/Strong Lady
(A test of strength)

What will I need? A paper napkin or a sheet of paper
Where is it in the Bible? Philippians 4:11-13
How long will it take? 5-10 minutes
What age child? 3-12 years
Will it work in a group? As a demonstration
Can it be played in the car? Yes
Will it work in a school classroom? Yes, preschool–6th grade

Show your child how our muscles stretch and contract by pulling and releasing a rubber band. Discuss how God has attached our muscles to our bones to that we can move, bend, jump, and run.

Ask him to feel his muscles move by bending over and placing his hands on his calf muscles (the lower back part of his legs) and tightening and releasing those muscles. Is there a change in how the muscles look and feel?

Other important things that muscles do in our bodies are to help us breathe, swallow, and keep our heart beating. God knew that muscles would be a very important part of our bodies.

We usually think of muscles as those things that make us strong. But Paul tells us in Philippians what really makes us strong. It's not our muscles or our mind or our desire to try real hard. Read Philippians 4:13 to see what makes us strong. It's Jesus. He can give us His super power. Help your child understand that no matter how many great talents and skills we have and how healthy our bodies are, God is the One we must depend on to give us the power to be strong and live right for Him. We can do all things that God asks us to, because He is our strength. Find ways to help your child memorize that verse. Say it with him every day for a week, and help him draw a picture to remind him of it.

Ask your child this question, "Are you strong enough to fold a paper napkin in half?" If he answers yes, ask him if he can fold a paper napkin or any other piece of paper in half more than seven times. Let him try.

He will learn that no one can fold any kind of paper more than seven times, because by the time it comes to the eighth fold, the paper will be too thick to budge. That trick seems easy, but it can't be done.

Sometimes we have an attitude that says, "Sure I can do that all by myself, because I don't need any help." We find out we do need some help. Or, other times, we feel like we just can't do something, so we don't even try to do it. Both attitudes need to be traded for what Jesus tells us to do in Philippians 4:13. He promises to give us the muscles to do anything that He wants us to, because it is right and good. We trust in him and not in ourselves.

What Can I Learn from Philippians

I learn that Jesus gives me joy.

Important Verses to Remember

Philippians 1:21 – "For to me, to live is Christ and to die is gain."

Philippians 3:13b-14 – ". . . But one thing I do: Forgetting what is behind and straining toward what is ahead, I press on toward the goal to win the prize for which God has called me heavenward in Christ Jesus."

Philippians 4:4 – "Rejoice in the Lord always. I will say it again: Rejoice!"

Philippians 4:6-7 – "Do not be anxious about anything, but in everything, by prayer and petition, with thanksgiving, present your requests to God. And the peace of God, which transcends all understanding, will guard your hearts and your minds in Christ Jesus."

Philippians 4:8-9 – "Finally, brothers, whatever is true, whatever is noble, whatever is right, whatever is pure, whatever is lovely, whatever is admirable – if anything is excellent or praiseworthy – think about such things."

A Devotional Thought for Parents and Teachers

See *A Devotional Thought from Galatians, Ephesians, Philippians, and Colossians* at the end of Colossians.

Colossians God's Book About What We Have

When We Have Jesus "For in Christ all the fullness of the Deity lives in bodily form, and you have been given fullness in Christ, who is the head over every power and authority" (Colossians 2:9-10).

What's the Book About

The book of Colossians is about what Jesus did to pay for our sins, what Jesus is like and how He can make us like Him.

Paul Sends a Letter of Encouragement from Prison

Colossians is a wonderful book that Paul wrote while he was in prison in Rome. The book is really a letter to the church of believers in Colosse. God used even Paul's trouble to write these words and to teach and help us.

Let's Meet the People of Colossians

Paul was the man who met the Lord on the road to Damascus, where he was planning to take Christians to jail for believing in Jesus. Paul's heart and life were completely changed.

Timothy was the young man who was Paul's special helper on some of his travels.

Onesimus was a slave who ran away from his owner, Philemon. We read more about Philemon and Onesimus in the book of Philemon.

Here Are the Places of Colossians

Colosse – the city where there was a group of people who believed in Jesus Christ.

Jesus is Lord

(Two art projects)

What will I need? Activity 1. A cardboard rectangle about 12 by 6 inches, a sheet of pretty wrapping paper, aluminum foil, and glue Activity 2. A plain piece of paper and crayons

Where is it in the Bible? Colossians 1:15-19; 2:9-10

How long will it take? 20-30 minutes

What age child? 3-12 years

Will it work in a group? Yes

Can it be played in the car? Yes, you could take Activity 2 along to do in the car.

Will it work in a school classroom? Yes, preschool–6th grade

Tell your child that the book of Colossians tells us that Jesus is God. Explain that Jesus is completely God, not just half God and half man or just a little bit God. Jesus is God. Here are two special ways to write the name "Lord" or "Jesus is Lord."

1. Make the letters by squeezing and shaping pieces of aluminum foil and gluing them on a cardboard rectangle that you have covered with a piece of pretty paper. If your child is too young to make the letters, help him shape the letters. Very young children love to glue, so remember that the process is more important than the perfection of the finished product. It will be a great teaching moment for your child just to know that you are making a pretty name for Jesus because you love Him. Every project is an opportunity to teach God's love and truth in Him.

2. Write the word, "Lord," or "Jesus is Lord" or "Jesus" in cursive writing about 1 inch high on a plain piece of paper. Outline the words in different colors, making each outline about a quarter inch away from the last one. You will be making a rainbow of lines around the beautiful name of Jesus.

Ask your child what we mean by "Jesus is Lord?" Tell him that years ago, near the time when Paul wrote Colossians, the Roman kings often treated Christians very terribly. Sometimes the Romans even had those who followed Jesus killed, because they loved Jesus enough to say that "Jesus is Lord."

Whatever You Do

(Something for Jesus)

What will I need? Plain round cookies or iced cookies, frosting; chocolate chips or candies for eyes, noses, and mouths; coconut or chow mien noodles for hair

Where is it in the Bible? Colossians 3:17

How long will it take? 30-45 minutes

What age child? 2 -12 years

Will it work in a group? Yes

Can it be played in the car? No

Will it work in a school classroom? Yes, preschool–6th grade

Ask your child to think of something people do that makes God happy? Does praying and talking to Him make Him happy? Does being kind and nice make Him happy? Can you make Jesus happy by playing? By singing? By laughing? By cooking something? Yes. Read Colossians 3:17, and explain that we can make God happy doing all kinds of things. Whatever we're doing that's good and right makes God happy.

Say, "Aren't you glad that when Jesus sees you having a great time with your friends that He is happy." Jesus is our Friend. Read Colossians 3:17 again and decide you are going to do everything you can to please and praise God.

Then make something with your hands that pleases God. Thank Him for giving you the wonderful gift of hands that work well. After you make something, it would please God if you shared what you made with somebody else. Here's something you could make that would be fun:

Begin with a package of round, plain cookies. On the cookies make smiling faces with frosting, chocolate chips, candies, orange slices, gumdrops, red shoestring licorice, or frosting gel. Is there someone you can share your cookies with and make them happy, too?

What Can I Learn from Colossians

I learn that when I have Jesus in my life, I have everything I need!

Important Verses to Remember

Colossians 1:10 – "And we pray this in order that you may live a life worthy of the Lord and may please him in every way: bearing fruit in every good work, growing in the knowledge of God."

Colossians 2:6-7 – "So then, just as you received Christ Jesus as Lord, continue to live in him, rooted and built up in him, strengthened in the faith as you were taught, and overflowing with thankfulness."

Colossians 3:13 – "Bear with each other and forgive whatever grievances you may have against one another. Forgive as the Lord forgave you."

Colossians 3:15 – "Let the peace of Christ rule in you hearts, since as members of one body you were called to peace. And be thankful."

Colossians 4:2 – "Devote yourselves to prayer, being watchful and thankful."

Paul's "love" letters to the churches of believers in these four important places are all distinctive, as were the churches themselves. They were custom-written to fit the particular needs and weaknesses of each fellowship of believers. In all of these glimpses into the heart of Paul, in each examination of the characteristics of the "body" of Jesus in various places, and in the resulting gaze into our own lives, there is an underlying thread of beautiful truth. Jesus is God. He takes up residence in our lives, when we open the door of our heart. When Jesus moves in, the previous resident moves out, and we are brand new people. Things are vastly, permanently different or have no legitimate excuse not to be.

Even after Jesus takes up occupancy in us, His effectiveness to function as our life planner and program director depends upon how much control we allow Him to have. It depends on whether we say to that old resident, still lingering around in the shadows, "Come on back in for a while. Let's reminisce about the old days."

When God's Holy Spirit is allowed the freedom He deserves, desires, and demands to be in charge of total in-house management, those appealing attributes Paul delineates in various ways are all evident. When the "new self," under new, divine management, is in control, we are free. Isn't it ironic that we find freedom under control?

When Jesus is allowed to be Lord of all our life, we experience the love, selflessness, purpose, joy, desire to give, discernment, vigilance, completeness, and fulfillment that all comprise the one message of all Paul's inspired letters: Jesus makes all things as they should be, when we allow Him the position we promised Him, in exchange for His gift of eternal life. You know, there seems to be a lot of one-sided giving going on here. The only reason Jesus wants to be our Lord is so He can give us more of Himself.

I Thessalonians God's Book About

Staying Strong Because Jesus is Coming Back
"For the Lord him self will come down from heaven, with a loud command, . . After that, we who are still alive and are left will be caught up together with them in the clouds to meet the Lord in the air. And so we will be with the Lord forever" (I Thessalonians 4:16a, 17).

What's the Book About

The book of I Thessalonians tells us to be faithful in loving and serving Jesus, because He is coming back. We want to be ready to meet Him.

An Encouraging Report and Final Instructions

The book of I Thessalonians starts with Paul thanking the Thessalonian believers for being so strong and true to Jesus, even though they were being treated badly by people who didn't love Jesus. The Christians at Thessalonica hadn't known Jesus for very long, and there were still things they didn't understand about Him, especially about the wonderful day when Jesus would come back to earth.

Paul writes his letter to answer some of their questions and to help them keep on being brave followers of Jesus, no matter how hard their troubles were. When Jesus comes back, it will be so awesome that problems won't matter one bit anymore.

Let's Meet the People of I Thessalonians

Paul did not love Jesus or the people who believed in Him until he met Jesus for himself and was completely changed. Paul became a missionary who traveled to many places to tell people about Jesus.

Timothy was Paul's friend and helper. Timothy went with Paul on some of his missionary journeys.

Silas was another of Paul's traveling helpers.

Here Are the Places of I Thessalonians

Thessalonica – the city where Paul visited on his second and third missionary trips. Even though they were treated badly because they believed it Jesus, the Thessalonians stayed strong and true in their faith in Him.

A Very Special Crown

Tell your child that Paul wrote special letters to his friends who lived in Thessalonica. His letters are our books of First and Second Thessalonians. In I Thessalonians 2:19-20, Paul calls the Christians in the church his joy and glory. Why?

Paul loved the Thessalonian people, and he was glad he had gotten to preach to them about Jesus. He knew that one day he would see Jesus in heaven, and the Thessalonian Christians would be there, too. The people Paul had told about Jesus seemed like a tremendous glory to him. They filled his heart with joy. One day when we see Jesus, Paul and the Thessalonian believers will be there, too.

Give your child some art supplies so that he can make a beautiful crown of glory to remind him to tell other people about Jesus.

Don't Burst that Bubble!

(A bubble game)

What will I need? Bubble solution or dish detergent and water, and different kinds of bubble wands

Where is it in the Bible? I Thessalonians 4:18; 5:14-15

How long will it take? 15-20 minutes

What age child? 3-10 years

Will it work in a group? Yes

Can it be played in the car? Probably not

Will it work in a school classroom? Yes, preschool–4th grade

Tell your child Jesus wants us to help other people feel happier every chance we get. He doesn't want us to do things that will make others feel sad and discouraged. Read I Thessalonians 4:18; 5:14-15. Ask him if he can remember a time when he helped to cheer someone up. Tell him about a time when he has cheered you up.

Tell your child that people sometimes say, "I don't want to burst your bubble!" That means, you don't want to make somebody feel bad or sad. Play this bubble bursting game to help you remember to make others feel better every chance you get.

Use a small amount of bubble solution, or make your own by mixing one part liquid dishwashing detergent to two parts water. If you have no bubble blowers or want to try something different, use empty spools of thread, a clean funnel, a potato masher or kitchen whisk, or a slotted spoon.

Take turns being the one who blows the bubbles and the one who bursts the bubbles. Decide never to be somebody's discouraging bubble burster when they need you to help them feel better.

Jesus Will Come Back

(A bouncing game)

What will I need? A paddle with bounce back ball attached.

Where is it in the Bible? I Thessalonians 4:13–5:11

How long will it take? 10-15 minutes

What age child? 5-11 years

Will it work in a group? Yes

Can it be played in the car? Probably not
Will it work in a school classroom? Yes, K–5th grade

Buy an inexpensive paddle that has a little rubber ball attached to an elastic string. Show your child how to hit the ball with the paddle so that it will come back to her to hit again. Explain that I Thessalonians tells us a lot about when Jesus will come back to earth again. We sometimes call that His second coming. Paul tells us in this Bible book that Jesus will come quickly. No one knows exactly when Jesus will come back, except God Himself. It will be the happiest time that has ever been for us, because He is our Savior. It will be wonderful to get to see Him and be with Him. He promised to come back, and He will.

Pray, Pray, Pray
(An on and on trick)

What will I need? A piece of paper on a table, a pen or pencil, and a balloon
Where is it in the Bible? I Thessalonians 5:17
How long will it take? 10-15 minutes
What age child? 3-12 years
Will it work in a group? Yes
Can it be played in the car? You can pray as you ride.

Will it work in a school classroom? Yes, preschool–6th grade

Tell your child you want him to try a do a trick. You want him to write his name or draw a picture on a piece of paper on the table. Sound easy? But, that's not quite all.

As your child writes or draws, he must balance on one foot and keep the other foot turning in a circle around and around without stopping. When he has finished doing that, ask him to write his name again, but this time he has to keep a balloon in the air by tapping it again and again.

The Bible also tells us what we should keep on and on doing, without stopping. Read I Thessalonians 5:7. See if he can tell what we should keep on doing. (praying) But if we are always praying, when do we get to eat, go to school, play, or sleep? The Bible has verses about eating, sleeping, working, walking, and running, too. It tells us that it's good to pray at certain times, but it's also good to be ready to pray at any minute during the day, all day long. We can talk to God whenever we want, to say thank you or to ask Him to help us with something. We should pray and pray.

| **What Can I Learn from I Thessalonians** | See *What Can I Learn from I and II Thessalonians, I and II Timothy, Titus, and Philemon* at the end of Philemon. |

| **Important Verses to Remember** | I Thessalonians 4:7 – "For God did not call us to be impure, but to live a holy life." |

I Thessalonians 5:14b-15 – "Warn those who are idle, encourage the timid, help the weak, be patient with everyone. Make sure that nobody pays back wrong for wrong, but always try to be kind to each other and to everyone else."

I Thessalonians 5:16-18 – "Be joyful always; pray continually; give thanks in all circumstances, for this is God's will for you in Christ Jesus."

| **A Devotional Thought for Parents and Teachers** | See *A Devotional Thought from I and II Thessalonians, I and II Timothy, Titus, and Philemon* at the end of Philemon. |

II Thessalonians God's Book About
Being Busy Doing God's Work Until Jesus Comes Back

"We pray this so that the name of our Lord Jesus may be glorified in you, and you in him, according to the grace of our God and the Lord Jesus Christ" (II Thessalonians 1:12).

| **What's the Book About** | The book of II Thessalonians is about being ready for Jesus to return and believing that He will, but staying busy serving Him until comes. |

| **Be Thankful and Stand Firm** | The book of II Thessalonians begins with Paul cheering up the Christians at Thessalonica. He tells them that he's proud of them. They love Jesus, and they have stayed strong and true to Him, even though they have been treated very badly by others who don't love Jesus. |

Paul helps the people to understand more about Jesus' coming back to earth, His second coming. Some of the Christians are afraid that Jesus has already come back and that they missed Him. Paul also tells the believers in Thessalonica to keep on staying strong and serving Jesus.

Let's Meet the People of II Thessalonians	**Paul** did not love Jesus until he met Him for himself and was completely changed. Paul became a missionary who traveled to many places to tell people about Jesus.
	Timothy was Paul's friend and helper. Timothy went with Paul sometimes as he traveled to tell people about Jesus.
	Silas was another of Paul's traveling helpers.
Here are the Places of II Thessalonians	**Thessalonica** – the city where Paul visited on his second and third missionary trips to tell people about Jesus. The people in Thessalonica listened to the story of Jesus and asked Him into their lives.

STORIES AND ACTIVITIES FROM II THESSALONIANS

Don't Go There

(A game about where to go)

What will I need? A paper or cardboard sign that says, "Beware!"
Where is it in the Bible? II Thessalonians 1:7-10
How long will it take? 10-15 minutes
What age child? 5-12 years
Will it work in a group? Yes
Can it be played in the car? Yes
Will it work in a school classroom? Yes, 1st–6th grade

Make a sign that says "BEWARE!" Explain that beware means to watch out, like a warning there's danger. Give the sign to your child and tell him you are going to name some places where we should go and some where we should not go. When he hears a place we should not go, he should hold up the beware sign. When you name a place that's okay, he should nod his head yes.

Here are some places to go:

-a birthday party
-inside the fence where there is a mean dog
-where people are buying and selling drugs
-to the airport to pick up Grandma
-a neighbor's house when your Mom has said not to go
-church
-to take food to a sick friend

Explain that heaven is the place where God lives and where all people who love Jesus will go when they die. Heaven's a more wonderful place than we can even imagine. Jesus will be there with us.

The Bible warns us, like a beware sign, about a place called hell,* where the devil lives. We definitely don't want to go to hell. II Thessalonians 1:7-10 tells us that the people who will go there when their life on earth is over are those who do not know and obey God. The worst part about hell is that Jesus won't be there.

*[Note to Parents: The subject of hell is, obviously, not a popular or politically correct one.

We don't want to frighten children unnecessarily with too many details, especially when they are very young. But we cannot fail to inform them about this very real place that Jesus Himself told us about. Share what is appropriate for your child's level of understanding. If you want more information about becoming a Christian, we recommend the book, *How Do I Become A Christian*, Broadman & Holman Publishers.]

The Name You Wear

(A shirt to make)

What will I need? A T-shirt in your child's size and waterproof cloth paint

Where is it in the Bible? II Thessalonians 1:12
How long will it take? 30-45 minutes
What age child? 3-12 years
Will it work in a group? Yes, with everyone bringing his own shirt and sharing paint
Can it be played in the car? Yes, it would be great if you wear your shirt to go somewhere.
Will it work in a school classroom? Yes, preschool–6th grade

Help your child write one of these phrases on a T-shirt, "I Belong to Jesus," "I Love (use a heart) Jesus," "Jesus is my Friend," or let him decorate the shirt any way he wants while you talk about how wonderful Jesus is

What Can I Learn from II Thessalonians	See *What Can I Learn from I and II Thessalonians, I and II Timothy, Titus, and Philemon* at the end of Philemon.
Important Verses to Remember	II Thessalonians 2:16-17 – "May our Lord Jesus Christ himself and God our Father, who loved us and by his grace gave us eternal encouragement and good hope, encourage your hearts and strengthen you in every good deed and word."
	II Thessalonians 3:3 – "But the Lord is faithful, and he will strengthen and protect you from the evil one."
A Devotional Thought for Parents and Teachers	See *A Devotional Thought from I and II Thessalonians, I and II Timothy, Titus, and Philemon* at the end of Philemon.

I Timothy — God's Book About Being Good

Leaders "Don't let anyone look down on you because you are young, but set an example for the believers in speech, in life, in love, in faith and in purity" (I Timothy 4:12).

What's the Book About	The book of I Timothy is about leading God's people in the way that pleases Jesus.
Paul Gives The Church Instructions and Advice	The book of I Timothy was written by Paul to his young friend Timothy. Timothy had known about Jesus since he was a little baby, because his mother and grandmother loved Jesus. Timothy came to know Jesus, too, as his own Savior and Lord. Then Timothy became a preacher who told other people about Jesus.
Let's Meet the People of I Timothy	**Paul** did not love Jesus, but then Paul met Jesus for himself and was completely changed. He became a missionary, who traveled to many places to tell people about Jesus.
	Timothy was Paul's friend and helper. Timothy went with Paul sometimes as he traveled to tell people about Jesus. I Timothy was written to him as a letter from Paul.
Here Are the Places of I Timothy	**Ephesus** – the city where Timothy was the pastor. Timothy was helping the church in the city of Ephesus when Paul wrote this letter to him.

STORIES AND ACTIVITIES FROM I TIMOTHY

Jesus Is Our Bridge

(Different kinds of bridges)

What will I need? Paper, crayons, or markers
Where is it in the Bible? I Timothy 2:4-6
How long will it take? 20-30 minutes
What age child? 3-12 years
Will it work in a group? Yes
Can it be played in the car? You could work on your picture in the car as you travel

Will it work in a school classroom? Yes, preschool–6th grade

Ask your child what a bridge does and why bridges are important. Explain that Jesus is our Bridge to get to God. Read I Timothy 2:5 and tell him that a mediator is a kind of bridge. Make a simple line drawing to help explain what the verse means. Draw a mountain on the left of the paper with you (stick figure) on top of it. On the right side make another mountain, and write the word "God" on top of it. Put rays around the word to show that He is very special.

Explain that our sins, all the wrong things we have done, are in the empty space between you and God. Our sins keep us from God. Before Jesus came, people tried all kinds of ways to get to know God. They tried idols, but that didn't work. They tried having big celebrations to get God to notice them, but that didn't work. They tried being very good, following all kinds of rules they had made up, but that didn't work. They tried everything they could think of to get to God for themselves, and it did no good.

But then Jesus came and died on the cross. Now draw a cross that connects the two mountains like a bridge between the two cliffs. Now we can get to God. Make your fingers walk across the bridge. Jesus is our bridge to God.

Kid Power
(Influence experiments)

What will I need? A bowl of water, pepper, dishwashing soap, a sugar cube, a piece of bar soap, and toothpicks
Where is it in the Bible? I Timothy 4:12
How long will it take? 15-20 minutes
What age child? 3-12 years
Will it work in a group? Yes
Can it be played in the car? No
Will it work in a school classroom? Yes, preschool–6th grade

Read I Timothy. Explain that Timothy was a young man who had learned about God from his mother and grandmother when he was just a very little boy. Now Timothy is a young man, and he helps Paul on his missionary journeys to tell others about Jesus.

But Paul doesn't want Timothy to think that being young is not good. He doesn't want Timothy to think he has to wait until he's older before he can serve Jesus well. Paul tells Timothy to do the right things in the way he talks, lives, and loves people. Paul wants Timothy to know that even young people have influence. What's influence?

Influence is similar to being an example. It means that other people watch what you do. When we are a good influence, we help others to serve God. When we are a bad influence, we lead other people away from God.

Try some of these experiments:
1. Fill a bowl with water, and sprinkle quite a bit of pepper on top. Tell your child that your finger has influence and can make the pepper move away so your finger can slide across the water. Dip your finger in dishwashing soap and make a sweep through the pepper. Your soapy finger will influence the pepper to move and sink so that your finger can swim alone.
2. Arrange six toothpicks or matches like the spokes of a wheel in a bowl of water. Place a sugar cube (you may use a teaspoon of sugar, but it will not work quite as well) in the center of the circle of toothpicks. What happens? Now remove the sugar cube, and place a little piece of soap in the center of the toothpicks, instead. Does something different happen to the toothpicks this time? Jesus wants us to be His good influence, making people want to come close to Him.

Good/Bad Money

(Money you can eat)

What will I need? Frozen cookie dough or dough from your own recipe, a cookie sheet, and oven, an ink pen that's out of ink, and a a white plastic or paper plate.

Where is it in the Bible? I Timothy 6:6-10, 17-19

How long will it take? 30-45 minutes

What age child? 2-12 years

Will it work in a group? Yes

Can it be played in the car? Only the discussion

Will it work in a school classroom? Yes, preschool–6th grade

Ask your child if she thinks money is good or bad. If she says it's good, ask her if it is ever bad (when it is used to buy drugs or to pay people to do bad things, when it is money that someone has stolen, when money gets to be too important to someone and they love it too much)? If she says money is bad, ask her if it ever is used to do good things (to help people come to know about Jesus, to buy food and clothes for people who need them, to help a family who have lost their job, to give at church to help meet needs).

Tell your child that money all by itself is just paper or metal, but the way people use it is what makes money good or bad. Read what Paul tells Timothy about money in I Timothy 6:10 and 6:17-19.

Some people think that having lots of money makes them happy. They want to be rich. Those people think, by mistake, that if they can just get more money all their problems will go away and they will be peaceful and happy. But that's just not true. Only Jesus fills our heart with happiness and peace, whether we have a little bit of money or none at all.

Paul warns Timothy, and all of us, to be careful about loving money, because when we do that, we bring all kinds of bad things into our lives. We hurt other people, too. We need to be so thankful for any money that God lets us have, because He has promised He will take care of us and meet all our needs (Philippians 4:19). He wants us to watch out so we don't get greedy and want more and more. Money doesn't make our heart happy and content, Jesus does.

Make "coin" cookies from frozen cookie dough or your own recipe to help you remember that money is God's gift to us, to be used for Him in the right ways. Slice or flatten the dough into round circles. With a toothpick carve funny faces and pretend words on your coin cookies. You might even want to carve a coin design deeply on the plate, then press your cookie dough against the design to make it transfer to the dough. Bake your coin cookies, cool them, and eat 'em all up!

Remember that money is a gift from God and we should give part of it (at least 10%) back to Him to say, "thank you."

Run Away, Chase, or Fight

Paul tells his good young friend Timothy to do three important things:

1. Run away. Read I Timothy 6:11-12 and talk about what Paul is saying. Paul tells Timothy to get out of there when there are bad things going on that would not make God happy. If it's too hard to say no to wrong things, we need to just leave the place and the

people we're with. Jesus wants us to run away from bad.

2. Pursue or chase after things that are good – Read I Timothy 6:11b to find out some of those good things that we should hold on to.

3. Sometimes he must fight. Fight what? Fight whom? Read verse 12a and explain that sometimes living for God involves a fight, because we have an enemy, the devil. He is always trying to fight against God and us in every way he can.

But some things are worth fighting for. Our faith in God is the most valuable thing we have, so we will gladly fight for Him against the devil. Jesus will make us strong enough to fight and win.

What Can I Learn from I Timothy

See *What Can I Learn from I and II Thessalonians, I and II Timothy, Titus, and Philemon* at the end of Philemon.

Important Verses to Remember

I Timothy 1:15a – "Here is a trustworthy saying that deserves full acceptance: Christ Jesus came into the world to save sinners."

I Timothy 2:5-6a – "For there is one God and one mediator between God and men, the man Christ Jesus, who gave himself as a ransom for all men."

I Timothy 4:12 – "Don't let anyone look down on you because you are young, but set an example for the believers in speech, in life, in love, in faith and in purity."

I Timothy 6:10a – "For the love of money is a root of all kinds of evil."

A Devotional Thought for Parents and Teachers

See *A Devotional Thought from I and II Thessalonians, I and II Timothy, Titus, and Philemon* at the end of Philemon.

II Timothy   God's Book About Staying Faithful

to Jesus "But as for you, continue in what you have learned and have become convinced of, because you know those from whom you learned it" (II Timothy 3:14).

What's the Book About

The book of II Timothy is about serving Jesus because we love Him and never giving up until we see Him one great day.

A Very Personal Final Greeting from Paul

The book of II Timothy begins as Timothy is leading and helping God's church in the city of Ephesus. Paul is far away from him in jail in Rome. Paul loves and misses Timothy as much as if he were his own son. Paul knows that he will soon die and go to heaven to be with Jesus. He has some special words he wants to tell Timothy.

Paul tells Timothy he is thankful to God for such a fine young man as Timothy. Paul is thankful that Timothy loves Jesus with all his heart and is serving Jesus so faithfully. Paul also tells Timothy not to be afraid of what people might think or do. Paul is writing his letter at a time when Emperor Nero is persecuting people who believe in Jesus. That's why Paul is in a jail, and that's why Paul will finally die for his faithfulness to his Savior.

Paul reminds Timothy that he needs to be a strong, brave soldier for Jesus Christ, to be like an athlete who works and exercises hard. Paul even tells Timothy to be like a farmer who works hard to grow a big crop of food. God wants Timothy to do his best work for Jesus.

Let's Meet the People of II Timothy

Paul was a changed man who became a missionary and traveled to many places to tell people about Jesus. Paul wrote the Book of II Timothy to his good friend Timothy.

Timothy was Paul's friend and helper. Timothy sometimes went with Paul as he traveled to tell people about Jesus. The book of II Timothy is really a letter that Paul wrote to Timothy. It is very important and a little sad, because it is Paul's last words to his friend.

Luke was Paul's doctor friend who wrote the book of Luke. He was with Paul in Rome when he wrote the book of II Timothy.

John Mark (Mark) was Paul's helper during some of the Paul's missionary journeys. Paul asked Timothy to bring Mark to Rome, so he could help Paul there.

Rome – the giant headquarters for the powerful Roman Empire. Rome is where Paul was put in prison two different time for preaching about Jesus. Rome is where Paul was when he wrote II Timothy.

Ephesus – the city where Timothy was a pastor.

STORIES AND ACTIVITIES FROM II TIMOTHY

Love You, Grandma
(Enjoying grandparents)

What will I need? Ingredients to bake cookies, your child, a piece of paper, and markers or crayons

Where is it in the Bible? II Timothy 1:5

How long will it take? 20-30 minutes

What age child? 3-12 years

Will it work in a group? Invite grandparents in for refreshments

Can it be played in the car? Riding with Grandma and Grandpa

Will it work in a school classroom? Yes, preschool–6th grade

Read II Timothy 1:5, and explain that Timothy had a mother named Eunice, and a grandmother named Lois. Both wonderful ladies taught him about God's great love in sending Jesus. Timothy learned also to love Jesus when he was just a little boy. His grandmother and mother probably took real good care of him, showed him lots of love, played with him, and gave him food and clothes. But nothing they did for him was as important as telling Timothy about Jesus.

These two important ladies in Timothy's home wanted to be sure that he grew up knowing Jesus.

Parents are a special gift from the Lord, and so are grandparents. Here are some grandparent ideas to show them you love them and that you thank God for them.

1. Bake cookies and decorate them to give to your grandparents.

2. Think of questions to ask your grandparents; sit down and listen to their answers:
What was your favorite toy or game when you were my age?
What was your favorite book?
Did you watch television or movies?
Did you play sports?
What did you do on your birthdays?
What did you want to be when you grew up?
Did you go to church?
What was your church like?
Who told you about Jesus?

3. Make a grandparent's card to give them. Fold a piece of paper in half and draw a picture on the cover half. Inside tell them something you appreciate about them. Ask your child to sign his name, and give it to his grandparents.

If you have grandparents who love Jesus and tell you about Him, be very thankful. If your grandparents don't know Jesus as their Savior, you can be the one who shows them Jesus' love. Always pray for them.

Study Hard for Jesus

(Doing our best)

What will I need? Your Bible and voice
Where is it in the Bible? II Timothy 2:15
How long will it take? 5-10 minutes
What age child? 3-10 years
Will it work in a group? Yes
Can it be played in the car? Yes
Will it work in a school classroom? Yes,
preschool–4th grade

Tell your child that you have a very important verse to read to her. It's II Timothy 2:15. It is about something you are doing right this minute. Read the verse and explain that it means God is happy when we study His Word, the Bible, and learn more about Him.

The verse also means that when we study and work hard, we are doing our very best for Jesus. Explain that Paul doesn't tell us what kind of work we should be doing, he lets us choose what kind of work to do. He just wants us to do our very best at whatever we do.

Here's a saying to help you remember to always do your best for Jesus:

Good. Better. Best. Never let it rest, 'til your good is better and your better is best.

Let's be the very best person we can be for our Savior, Jesus.

What Can I Learn From II Timothy	See *What Can I Learn from I and II Thessalonians, I and II Timothy, Titus, and Philemon* at the end of Philemon.
Important Verses to Remember	II Timothy 1:7 – "For God did not give us a spirit of timidity, but a spirit of power, of love and of self-discipline." II Timothy 2:1 – "You then, my son, be strong in the grace that is in Christ Jesus." II Timothy 2:3 – "Endure hardship with us like a good soldier of Christ Jesus." II Timothy 3:16-17 – "All Scripture is God-breathed and is useful for teaching, rebuking, correcting and training in righteousness, so that the man of God may be thoroughly equipped for every good work." II Timothy 4:7 – "I have fought the good fight, I have finished the race, I have kept the faith."
A Devotional Thought for Parents and Teachers	See *A Devotional Thought from I and II Thessalonians, I and II Timothy, Titus, and Philemon* at the end of Philemon.

Titus

God's Book About Serving Jesus "But when the kindness and love of God our Savior appeared, he saved us, not because of righteous things we had done, but because of his mercy" (Titus 3:4-5a).

What's the Book About	The book of Titus describes what it means to be a good leader and servant of Jesus Christ.
These are the Things That Must Be Taught	Titus tells us what a good leader should be like. A good leader is also a servant of Jesus. He or she should be careful to serve Jesus well, whether other people notice what a good job we're doing or not. The One we want to please is Jesus, because He has been so good to us.
Let's Meet the People of Titus	**Paul** did not love Jesus, but then Paul met Jesus for himself and was completely changed. Paul became a missionary who traveled to many places to tell people about Jesus.
	Titus was from Greece. He was a Gentile. Titus loved Jesus and went with Paul on some of his missionary trips. Titus was the leader of some churches on the island of Crete. Paul wrote the book of Titus to to help him be a good leader for Jesus.
Here Are the Places of Titus	**Crete** – an island near Titus' home in the country of Greece. Most of the people in Crete were Gentiles and not Jews.

STORIES AND ACTIVITIES FROM TITUS

What's an Example?
(Pictures to copy)

What will I need? Thin paper like onion skin paper to trace a picture or a sheet of carbon paper to make a duplicate of your traced picture.
Where is it in the Bible? Titus 1:7, 8 ; Titus

2:12-14
How long will it take? 20-30 minutes
What age child? 3-10 years
Will it work in a group? Yes
Can it be played in the car? No
Will it work in a school classroom? Yes, preschool–4th grade

Help your child make some duplicate copies of coloring book pictures or pictures cut out of magazines. Tape the picture to a piece of white card and use a sharpened pencil to poke holes around the edge. The picture outline will show on the cardboard below.

Read Titus 1:7 and explain that Paul is telling Titus that men who lead the church, especially the pastor, should be a good example for people to copy, like your child copied some of the pictures he made. Even though this verse and the ones around them are for pastors, God expects all the rest of us to be good examples to others, too. Have fun coloring the copies your child made.

Read Ephesians 5:1-2 and see who is the example that all of us should be like!

What Can I Learn from Titus	See *What Can I Learn from I and II Thessalonians, I and II Timothy, Titus, and Philemon* at the end of Philemon.
Important Verses to Remember	Titus 2:7 – "In everything set them an example by doing what is good."
	Titus 3:4-5a – "But when the kindness and love of God our Savior appeared, he saved us, not because of righteous things we had done, but because of his mercy."
	Titus 3:1-2 – "Remind the people to be subject to rulers and authorities, to be obedient, to be ready to do whatever is good, to slander no one, to be peaceable and considerate, and to show true humility toward all men."
A Devotional Thought for Parents and Teachers	See *A Devotional Thought from I and II Thessalonians, I and II Timothy, Titus, and Philemon* at the end of Philemon.

Philemon
God's Book About Running Away and Coming Home "Perhaps the reason he was separated from you for a little while was that you might have him back for good – no longer as a slave, but better than a slave, as a dear brother" (Philemon 15-16a).

What's the Book About

The book of Philemon is about a slave who ran away from his master and about Paul's efforts to get the two men back together again, but this time as brothers.

Everyone Is Equal in Christ

Philemon begins as a slave named Onesimus has run away from his master, Philemon. Not only had he run away, slaves in those days weren't supposed to leave, but Onesimus had also stolen some things from Philemon.

When Onesimus ran away, he went to the city of Rome. God planned that Onesimus should run into Paul there, where he was in prison for preaching about Jesus. Onesimus gave his heart to Jesus, too. Paul talked the slave into going back home and making things right with his master. Paul isn't saying it is a good idea to have a slave. That was man's idea, not God's. But Paul gives some rules for masters and their slaves so that they will treat each other with kindness, as God wants us all to do.

Paul wrote a short letter to Philemon asking him to please let Onesimus come back home, now that God has erased his sins and given him a brand new life. That makes Philemon, who is a Christian, and Onesimus, who is also a Christian, brothers, instead of a master and his slave.

Jesus changes people when we give our hearts to Him. He gives us a brand new life, just like He gave Onesimus!

Let's Meet the People of Philemon

Onesimus was the slave who ran away from his master and ran into Paul in Rome. Onesimus became a Christian when he gave his life to Jesus. He decided to go back and make things right with his master, Philemon.

Philemon was a Christian man who had a slave named Onesimus. Onesimus stole some things from his master and then ran away. Slaves weren't supposed to do either of those things!

Paul was God's man who wanted to be a peacemaker and get Philemon and Onesimus back together as brothers.

Here Are the Places of Philemon

Colosse – the town where Philemon lived and went to church.

Rome – the city where Paul was in prison, when he wrote his letter to Philemon.

STORIES AND ACTIVITIES FROM PHILEMON

Share Your Faith
(A day of sharing)

What will I need? Different ideas for sharing
Where is it in the Bible? Philemon 6
How long will it take? All day long
What age child? 2-12 years
Will it work in a group? Yes, a group would be great.
Can it be played in the car? Sure
Will it work in a school classroom? Yes, preschool–6th grade

Ask your child to join you in a day of sharing. On this special day think of ways you can share something with someone. Share hugs, handshakes, and smiles. Think of creative ways to share, like baking cookies for your neighbors, sharing Jesus with someone, inviting them to church, or giving them a Bible. Sharing Jesus is the very best thing you will ever share.

The book of Philemon is about a slave who ran away. Read Philemon 10-12. Paul is writing a letter to Philemon, who is a Christian. In fact, Philemon had become a Christian on one of Paul's earlier visits to Colosse. The church in Colosse met in Philemon's home, because they didn't have a church building.

Philemon had a slave, who worked in his home and helped with things that needed to be done. Many people in those days had slaves. Some people were nice to them, and others were not. Having slaves was not God's idea, but He did lay out some rules in the Bible so people would be kind to their slaves. It was the law in that day that if a slave ran away, the master could actually kill him. Philemon's slave was Onesimus, and he had run away from Philemon. Onesimus ended up in Rome. Because of the law, he was afraid Philemon might kill him.

God made sure that Onesimus found Paul in Rome. Paul introduced Onesimus to Jesus. Now Onesimus was a new person, he was a child of God. God always wants His children to do the right thing, so Paul told Onesimus he needed to go back to Philemon's house and finish the work he was supposed to be doing for the family.

Philemon was written to ask Philemon to let Onesimus come back home without punishing him. In Philemon 16, Paul is asking Philemon to let Onesimus come back home as a brother in the family of Jesus, since both of them are God's children. Read Philemon 21 to see if Paul thinks Philemon will say yes, or no, to what he asks of him. What do you think? What does the book of Philemon teach us (that everyone is important in God's family and no one is better than somebody else)?

What Can I Learn from I and II Thessalonians, I and II Timothy, Titus, and Philemon

These books teach me many things about being a good leader and a good follower. I will probably get to be both of them in my life. They also remind me to keep on loving and obeying Jesus, because one day He will come back to earth. Then I will see Him, and I'll be so glad He is my Savior. Because Jesus wants me to be a good leader, follower, and worker for Him, I will be.

Important Verses to Remember

Philemon 4 – "I always thank my God as I remember you in my prayers, because I hear about your faith in the Lord Jesus and your love for all the saints."

Philemon 6 – "I pray that you may be active in sharing your faith, so that you will have a full understanding of every good thing we have in Christ."

A Devotional Thought for Parents and Teachers from I and II Thessalonians, I and II Timothy, Titus, and Philemon

Are you a leader? A follower? Both? Right. Very few people in life fail to experience both important roles at some time. Paul directed some of his intimate writings to people whose position as leader or follower may be very different from yours, but the principles remain the same.

Be busy staying faithful to Jesus; keep on fulfilling your unique calling in your own distinctive, gifted way. Do everything in your power to live an exemplary life of commitment to Jesus and service to others. Never let Jesus slip from the top of your priority list from this very minute until He comes back again and says directly to you, "Well done, good and faithful servant!" (Matthew 25:21a)

Hebrews
God's Book About Why Jesus is God's Very Best

"In the past God spoke to our forefathers through the prophets at many times and in various ways, but in these last days he has spoken to us by his Son, whom he appointed heir of all things, and through whom he made the universe" (Hebrews 1:1-2).

What's the Book About

The book of Hebrews is about how much better Jesus is than anyone, anything, and everything else.

We Should Persevere and Learn from Faithful Saints

Hebrews is a wonderful book that shows us many reasons that Jesus is better than anything or anyone else. Jesus is God. Some of the new Christians were getting mixed-up about what to believe about Jesus. They needed to be told again how wonderful and powerful Jesus is.

In Hebrews we also find out about some men and women who had great faith in God, even though they had experienced hardships in their life. God tells us to keep on trusting Him like those heroes of faith. God will give us His strength just as He did for those faithful followers.

Let's Meet the People of Hebrews

Jesus, God's Son, is totally perfect. He is God.

Heroes of Faith are the Old Testament men and women who had great faith in God.

STORIES AND ACTIVITIES FROM HEBREWS

God Speaks through Jesus
(Different ways of talking)

Sometimes in the Bible God spoke out loud to people, like Abraham, Moses, or Paul. Sometimes God spoke to people in dreams, like He did to Philip, Peter, Mary, and Joseph. Once God spoke from a burning bush, and once His voice came from a donkey. Several times God's voice came from the clouds.

God spoke through His prophets and teachers in the Bible. He still speaks through His preachers and teachers today. Many times God speaks to someone's heart in a voice that can't be heard. Over and over again God has spoken and speaks today through His Word, the Bible.

But the book of Hebrews tells us about one of the most amazing ways God has ever spoken. Read how God spoke in Hebrews 1:1-2. What did God say to us through Jesus? Don't forget that God wants us to speak to

Him by talking to Him in prayer. This would be a great time to speak to God.

Jesus is Better

(An important S.O.S.)

What will I need? A piece of paper and pencil or a chalkboard and chalk
Where is it in the Bible? Hebrews 3:1-6
How long will it take? 10-15 minutes
What age child? 3-12 years
Will it work in a group? Yes
Can it be played in the car? Yes
Will it it work in a school classroom? Yes, preschool–6th grade

Ask your child what S.O.S. means? (It means "save our ship," but it also means that someone is in trouble and needs help.) Tell her that you have a different kind of S.O.S. to show her. Write the letters down on a piece of paper or a chalkboard.

Explain that the book of Hebrews tells us that Jesus is the best, because Jesus is God. But Hebrews tells us someone else that Jesus is better than. Ask your child to listen as you read Hebrews 3:3-6 to see who that person is. (Moses)

Explain that Moses was very important to God's special people, the Jews, in Old Testament days. He had been the leader that took them from being slaves and had led them across the desert to the new land God had given them. Moses would have been something like our President of the United States. But Jesus was much more important than Moses, because of S.O.S. What's that, you say? The answer is in those verses you read. Moses was a servant of God, but Jesus is God's Son. So the difference between Moses and Jesus is the difference in servant or Son – S.O.S.

Hard Heart, Soft Heart

(Things to feel)

What will I need? A box with a hole cut in it or a sack, and hard and soft objects
Where is it in the Bible? Hebrews 3:7-15
How long will it take? 20-30 minutes
What age child? 3-10 years
Will it work in a group? Yes
Can it be played in the car? Yes
Will it work in a school classroom? Yes, preschool–4th grade

Make a "feel-it" box for your child to reach into. It can be a very simple shoebox with a hole cut in it big enough for your child to slip his hand in, or use a brown paper sack like a grab bag. Inside the box place items that are either hard or soft. Consider using a rock, a golf ball, a block, a cotton ball, a tissue, a rolled-up sock, etc. Ask your child to reach through the hole into the box and to tell you if he feels something hard or soft. He should try to guess what the object is.

Talk about things that are good to be soft (a pillow or tissue) or hard (bricks for building or ice for skating). Explain that the Bible talks about something God never wants to be hard. He tells us what that is in Hebrews 3:7-8,15. Read those verses. They say that God never wants our hearts to be hard against God and what He says to us in His Word.

Jesus Prays for Us

Tell your child there's a big word you want to help him learn. Ready? The word is INTERCESSOR. Ask him if he has ever been an intercessor? Tell him that he has! An intercessor is someone who prays for somebody else, and your child has definitely done that. When your child prays for somebody, he is being like Jesus, because Jesus is our Intercessor. Jesus prays for us. Read Hebrews 7:25 to your child.

Explain to your child that everyday Jesus is our faithful Intercessor. He prays for us all the time.

To help you remember who Jesus is to you, close your hand, fingers together, and trace around it. Then draw another line about a quarter in away around just the thumb and fingers of your drawing. The second line will make your drawing appear to be three-dimensional, like two hands folded together in prayer.

Cut out your praying hands, and punch a hole in the top. Write the word "intercessor" on them. Color the hands, if you wish. Loop a ribbon or piece of yarn through the hole, and hang the praying hands in a window.

Run the Race
(A family relay)

What will I need? A pan, an empty egg carton, a spatula, cotton balls, homemade medals and trophies.

Where is it in the Bible? Hebrews 12
How long will it take? 30-45 minutes
What age child? 4-11 years
Will it work in a group? Yes
Can it be played in the car? Not the race
Will it work in a school classroom? Yes, preschool–5th grade

Your family will be an Olympic cotton ball balancing team trying to win a gold medal by taking turns picking up one cotton ball on the spatula and running with it to the opposite end of the room, placing it in a section of the egg carton. If you lose the cotton ball, you must begin again. Your team wins when it has put twelve cotton balls into the egg carton.

Have fun congratulating each other on the great race you all ran. Make gold or silver medals for all your super athletes from circles cut from plastic plates. Spray paint and decorate your medal. Punch a hole in the top of each, and tie a string through it for pinning or hanging on your super athletes. You can make a family trophy by working together gluing some plastic bottles, cups, or bowls together as a trophy. Paint your trophy with gold or silver spray paint.

The Bible says that the Christian life is a race. That's great, because a race is full of excitement, challenge, energy, and fun. It's great to run the race of life on Jesus' team. If we run on Jesus' team, we know that we will win the race.

What Can I Learn from Hebrews

I learned there are lots of great people who have loved God and have had faith in Him. The best person who has ever been or ever will be is Jesus. Because Jesus is the best there is, I will put all my trust in Him.

Important Verses to Remember

Hebrews 4:12 "For the word of God is living and active. Sharper than any double edged sword, it penetrates even to dividing soul and spirit, joints and marrow; it judges the thoughts and attitudes of the heart."

Hebrews 12:2 – "Let us fix our eyes on Jesus, the author and perfecter of our faith, who for the joy set before Him endured the cross, scorning its shame, and sat down at the right hand of the throne of God.".

Hebrews 13:1-2 – "Keep on loving each other as brothers. Do not forget to entertain strangers, for by so doing some people have entertained angels without knowing it."

Hebrews 13:8 – "Jesus Christ is the same yesterday and today and forever."

A Devotional Thought for Parents and Teachers

Faith. Do you ever struggle with that little five letter concept? Does the faith struggle manifest itself in a rapid heartbeat, sweaty palms, and a very dry mouth in the undeniable manifestation of fear – fear because of real or imagined danger, fear to expose yourself to disapproval, disappointment, or failure; fear of the unknown or the known. You're not the first, the last, or the only person to experience faith struggles.

The book of Hebrews has much to say about faith. Why we can trust the One who says He is God? Because He is. We need not fear our own journey of faith, because there are many footprints already visible along that road. We can hear those triumphant heroes and heroines shouting excitedly to us from eternal grandstands, "You'll make it. Jesus is real. Your faith has a solid basis. You won't fall. He was with us, and He is with you!"

James God's Book About Wind and Waves, Forest Fires, Horses, Big Ships, and a Mirror
"Do not merely listen to the word, and so deceive yourselves. Do what it says" (James 1:22).

What's the Book About

The book of James is about hearing what God says to us and then doing it.

Instructions for Listening Carefully and Speaking Slowly

James is an interesting Bible book, because it uses so many different ways to teach us important things. James tells us that we are like ocean waves that rock back and forth when we don't trust in Jesus. He tells us that shadows change their shapes and sizes, but God never changes. James also tells us to be careful how we use our tongues, because our words can be powerful.

James uses interesting word pictures to teach us to watch what we say. One of the most important things that God tells us in James is about a mirror. He says for us not to look into God's Word like we would look into a mirror. Don't walk away from it and forget what we saw. Jesus wants us to hear His Words, and then to do what He says.

Let's Meet the People of James

All the faithful prophets, preachers, and those who loved God from the Old Testament.

Here Are the Places of James

Everywhere that Christians lived then and now.

I'm Getting Seasick!

(Making an ocean in a bottle)

What will I need? A picture of ocean waves, an empty soda bottle or jar with a lid, water, green and blue food coloring, cooking oil, and glue

Where is it in the Bible? James 1:5-7; 3:13-18

How long will it take? 20-30 minutes

What age child? 4-12 years

Will it work in a group? Yes

Can it be played in the car? Yes, take your "ocean wave bottle" along with you.

Will it work in a school classroom? Yes, preschool–6th grade

God wants to help us do right, wise things, but we need to trust Him to help us. Read James 1:6-8 and see what we are like when we don't really believe God will help us when we ask Him. (We are like an ocean wave that is blown back and forth by the wind.) Then do one of these "ocean wave" activities to show you what we are like when we ask God to help us, and then don't really believe that He will.

1. Play "Waves of the Sea." Show a picture of an ocean wave, or just talk about how the waves and the tides come and go, back and forth, from the seashore. Tell your child that God made the world and the oceans so that the moon has a lot to do with how the ocean waves come and go. One of the reasons for the back and forth motion of the ocean waves is so that they can clean up the beach and wash whatever is messing it up back into the ocean away from the sand. God has amazing ways of seeing that all His awesome world work well together!

Pretend that you and your child are going to be the ocean waves rolling on the floor over and over again. When you get to the point where you need to go the other direction say, "Shall I stay here? Shall I go back? Shall I stay here? Shall I go back?" Just like the ocean waves, you can't make up your mind.

James says not to be like ocean waves when we ask God for something, especially when we ask for His help in doing the right thing. We shouldn't be like the waves and say, "Can I trust God? Can I not trust God? Can I trust God? Can I not trust God?" The answer is "Of course, I can trust God to help me. He already promised He would, and He will."

2. Make an "Ocean in a Bottle." Fill an empty jar or two liter soda bottle partly full of water. Add a few drops of blue and green food coloring and some cooking oil on top. Put a little white glue inside the lid and tighten it on the bottle. Let your child watch as the "ocean waves" move back and forth and back and forth. Let's not be like those waves in our trust in Jesus.

Watch Those Words

(Two activities about our tongue)

What will I need? A tube of toothpaste and a plate; several colors of gelatin powder, some cups or bowls

Where is it in the Bible? James 1:19-20, 26; James 3:1-12

How long will it take? 1 5-20 minutes

What age child? 3-12 years

Will it work in a group? Yes

Can it be played in the car? No, better done at home
Will it work in a school classroom? Yes, preschool–6th grade

Read James 1:19-20 and James 3:2-4 to your child. Ask him if he knows what James is talking about. (our tongue) Is he telling us to be careful what we taste with our tongue? No, Jesus wants us to be careful what we say with our tongue. James says our tongue is a very small part of our whole body, but small things can be powerful, and our tongue is.

James says that a very small piece of metal called a "bit" goes into a horse's mouth and pushes down on his tongue. The horse will go wherever he's supposed to go. That small bit is powerful. James says that our tongue is very small, but very powerful. What does James say our tongue can be like in James 3:5-8? (A fire and a wild animal.) Does that mean that our tongues are very, very bad? No, our tongue can be bad or good, depending on how we use it. Read what James says about how we should use our tongue in verse 9-10. We should let our tongues be used for good to tell others about God. We also need to use our tongue to say kind, encouraging things to other people and not hurtful words, either to them or about them.

Here are two activities to try that involve our tongue and what we say:

1. Ask your child if he thinks he can squeeze some toothpaste on a plate. Let him do it. Then, ask him if he can put the toothpaste back into the tube. He may make a little progress, but that's much harder to do. What we say is like the toothpaste. Once our words are out of our mouth, we can't put them back in. We need to be extra careful that what we say the first time is kind and good and pleases God!

2. This game's just for fun and to remind you that when the Bible talks about our tongue in James, it's not talking about tasting. Pour small amounts of various colors of gelatin into cups or bowls. Let your child and some friends get some of only one color on a spoon and pour it on their tongue or lick it until their tongue turns that color. Ask everyone to get different colors, unless you have a large group playing, and duplicate colors will be okay then.

Call out a color and ask the player whose tongue is that color to do what you have asked them to.

All the options must involve speech:
Say a Bible verse.
Tell somebody something nice about them.
Sing a short praise song.
Say, "I love you," or "I like you" to someone.
Tell something you like about your family.
Tell something you like about your church.
Tell something wonderful about Jesus.

What Can I Learn from James

James tells me lots of important things to remember, like believing in God, watching what I say, not being more kind to some people than I am to others, staying strong when I have problems, and not forgetting to pray. One of the most important things I learn from James is to listen to what God has to say in His Word and then to do it! I will keep on learning from the Bible, and God will help me to do what it says.

James 1:5 – "If any of you lacks wisdom, he should ask God, who gives generously to all without finding fault, and it will be given to him."

James 1:17 – "Every good and perfect gift is from above, coming down from the Father of the heavenly lights, who does not change like shifting shadows."

James 1:19b-20 – "Everyone should be quick to listen, slow to speak and slow to become angry, for man's anger does not bring about the righteous life that God desires."

James 3:17 –"But the wisdom that comes from heaven is first of all pure; then peaceloving, considerate, submissive, full of mercy and good fruit, impartial and sincere."

James 4:17 – "Anyone, then, who knows the good he ought to do and doesn't do it, sins."

A Devotional Thought for Parents and Teachers

James was a pragmatist! His book is full of practical glimpses, illustrations, and bits of valuable, every-day advice. It's current. It's relevant. We can tell at a glance that what James tells us would work, if applied to daily life. If we just followed his very sensible, people-friendly suggestions, our lives and the lives of everyone around us would be tremendously enhanced.

Did you ever think why James is a pragmatist? Is it because some of us are just naturally practical thinkers, and others of us are head-in-the-clouds dreamers? No, it's because his writings aren't really his own; like all the Bible, they are God-breathed and Holy Spirit illuminated and God is a pragmatist. His Word works. Jesus was a pragmatist. He spoke of seeds and birds, flowers and wind, farming and dirt. People knew about those things.

As God speaks to us through His written Word and His internal, subjective "Holy Spirit" Word, it doesn't matter in the least if the sound is coming from the top of smoking Mt. Sinai, from behind the curtain in the Holy of Holies, beside the Hollywood Freeway, or Time's Square. God's Word to us is ageless and timeless. His message, for all practical purposes, fits our lifestyle and meets our needs.

The key to unlocking the practicality of God's Word is "Do it!"

I Peter

God's Book About How to Live When Times are Hard. "These have come so that your faith – of greater worth than gold, which perishes even though refined by fire – may be proved genuine and may result in praise, glory and honor when Jesus Christ is revealed" (I Peter 1:7).

What's the Book About

The book of I Peter is about the help and hope that Jesus gives us when we are going through hard times.

Respect Authority and Be Willing to Suffer for God

I Peter is a letter from Peter to people around the world who love Jesus. Things were getting difficult for believers, so Peter wrote this letter to remind Christians that God was always with them. God will use even the bad things that come our way to make us more useful for Him. Peter reminds us to stay faithful to Jesus, whether it's easy or hard.

Let's Meet the People of I Peter

Peter was the disciple of Jesus who had seen Him do amazing miracles. When Jesus was about to be crucified, Peter became very afraid and turned his back on the Savior. After Jesus was crucified and resurrected Peter became a great preacher for Jesus. In the book of I Peter, he tells other Christians how to stay strong and true for the Lord.

Silvanus was the man who delivered Peter's letter to Christians to read.

Here Are the Places of I Peter

Jerusalem – the city of Israel where the temple of God was. Jesus rode into Jerusalem on a donkey at the beginning of the last week before He was crucified. Big crowds of people shouted their praises to Him as he rode through Jerusalem. After Jesus died many of His followers in Jerusalem met together to worship and pray. Many of them moved to other places when they were mistreated because they loved Jesus. When the Christians moved to other areas they helped to spread the great news about Jesus farther and farther away.

Rome – the powerful city where Emperor Nero lived and where Peter was when he wrote I Peter.

Faith is Golden

(Making beautiful golden things)

What will I need? Gold wrapping paper, scissors, tape or glue; or a small picture frame, seashells, pasta shapes or buttons and gold spray paint.
Where is it in the Bible? I Peter 1:3-7, 18-19
How long will it take? 30-45 minutes
What age child? 3-12 years
Will it work in a group? Yes
Can it be played in the car? No
Will it work in a school classroom? Yes, preschool–6th grade

Make something golden with your child. Here are a few ideas to try:
1. Make a golden chain from short strips (about one inch wide and five inches long) of shiny, gold wrapping paper. Make a circle out of one strip and glue the ends together. Then add one link of gold paper at a time, looping it through the link before it and gluing it closed. Make your chain as long as you would like. Hang your chain somewhere in the house for everyone to enjoy.
2. Cover a plain picture frame with small sea shells, pasta shapes, buttons, or other interesting tiny objects you have around the house. Glue them on the picture frame. When the glue is dry, spray paint your creation gold. You may want to put a picture of Jesus in the frame, and set it somewhere in your house.

Why did you make golden things? Read I Peter 1:7 to see what Peter says is also golden (our faith and trust in Jesus). Did you know that gold gets more shiny and beautiful when it is put in fire? The Christians in Peter's day were having lots of trouble. The devil was being very mean to them (like gold being put in a hot fire) but their faith in Jesus just got stronger and stronger. Read I Peter 1:18-19 and find out something that is much more valuable than gold. Just remember when you have a problem or something doesn't go well for you, that you are God's golden child and you're getting polished up to shine for Jesus. God is always good, even when the devil and every thing he tries to do are bad.

Ask Me a Question

(Questions and answers)

What will I need? Time with your child
Where is it in the Bible? I Peter 3:15
How long will it take? 10-15 minutes
What age child? 3-10 years
Will it work in a group? Yes
Can it be played in the car? Yes
Will it work in a school classroom? Yes, preschool–4th grade. Upgrade the difficulty of the questions for older children.

Play a question and answer game with your child. Here are some possible questions:
1. Can you make a sound like a siren?
2. Can you make a sound like an alarm clock?
3. How are birds and airplanes alike and different?
4. Do you think you could draw a picture in the dark?
5. Do you have a heart? How can you be sure? Have you ever seen it?
6. What's your name? Can you spell it?
7. Could you cut a raw egg in half?

8. Can you name one of Jesus' disciples?

9. Who is Jesus?

10. What did Jesus do for us? Why?

Read I Peter 3:15 to your child and explain that the Bible says we should always be ready to answer any questions people may ask us about our faith in Jesus and our love for Him. When a person asks us about Jesus we should answer in love and kindness. If we treat others with kindness and respect they may want to come to know Jesus, too!

There's a Lion Out There

(Making lions)

What will I need? An empty, square tissue box, construction paper, scissors and glue; or a paper plate, construction paper, scissors, a stick or ruler.

Where is it in the Bible? I Peter 5:8-9

How long will it take? 20-30 minutes

What age child? 3-12 years

Will it work in a group? Yes

Can it be played in the car? Yes, you could wear your lion mask in the car.

Will it work in a school classroom? Yes, preschool–6th grade

Tell your child that you are going to read him a Bible verse about a lion. Read I Peter 5:8-9 and talk about lions. If you want, do a little research about the king of beasts from the library or internet. Be sure to talk about verse 8 that says a lion prowls around and is very quiet and sneaky.

Talk about the fact that the lion in these verses is the devil, and he loves to cause us trouble. The devil wants to get us to do things that will hurt God's heart, because Satan hates God.

Ask your child what he would do if he saw a lion coming toward him? Read I Peter 5:9 and see what we should do when the devil wants us to do wrong and disobey God. The Bible says we should stand firm and say, "No!" to Satan. We don't need to be afraid of the devil, because Jesus is our courage and strength. He is stronger than Satan.

To help you remember to be on guard against the devil make a lion from one of the following ways:

1. Make a lion from an empty facial tissue box (the smaller, square kind). Cover the box with tan or brown construction paper. Use markers to draw a face, then cut out narrow strips of yellow or tan paper. Glue them on the sides and top of the lion's face for his mane. Curl the ends of each strip slightly. Glue on pointy ears and two round paws. Use your lion box to hold whatever you want it to, even tissues.

2. You can make a lion mask from a paper plate by coloring the nose and mouth, and cutting out eye-holes. Color around the edges of the plate with yellow or brown. Then cut little slits around the edge like fringe for the lion's mane. Tape the mask to a stick or ruler to use as a mask.

What Can I Learn From I Peter

See *What Can I Learn from I and II Peter, I, II, and III John, Jude, and Revelation* at end of Revelation.

Important Verses to Remember

I Peter 1:15 – "But just as he who called you is holy, so be holy in all you do; for it is written: 'Be holy, because I am holy'."

I Peter 1:18 – "For you know that it was not with perishable things such as silver or gold that you were redeemed from the empty way of life handed down to you from your forefathers, but with the precious blood of Christ, a lamb without blemish or defect."

I Peter 3:8 – "Finally, all of you, live in harmony with one another; be sympathetic, love as brothers, be compassionate and humble."

I Peter 5:8-9a – "Be self-controlled and alert. Your enemy the devil prowls around like a roaring lion looking for someone to devour. Resist him, standing firm in the faith."

A Devotional Thought for Parents and Teachers

See *A Devotional Thought from I and II Peter, I, II, and III John, Jude, and Revelation* at end of Revelation

II Peter God's Book About True and False Faith

"We did not follow cleverly invented stories when we told you about the power and coming of our Lord Jesus Christ, but we were eyewitnesses of His majesty" (II Peter 1:16).

What's the Book About

The book of II Peter is a warning for believers to watch out for people who don't love Jesus and who want to make them stop trusting Jesus. II Peter is also about growing stronger in our faith.

Guard Your Faith and Beware of False Teachers

The book of II Peter starts with a challenge from Peter to believers. He tells them they should make every effort to show they love Jesus by doing good things for Him, knowing Him better, not giving in to self, staying strong, not giving up, and showing love.

Peter also tells believers to watch out for danger from false teachers who will try lead them away from Jesus.

Let's Meet the People of II Peter	Peter – the disciple of Jesus who had seen Him do amazing miracles, but turned his back on the Savior when he was sentenced to be crucified. Peter later repented and became a very important preacher for Jesus.
Here Are the Places of II Peter	Rome – the very powerful city where Emperor Nero lived. Peter was in Rome when he wrote this letter.

STORIES AND ACTIVITIES FROM II PETER

Add These Up

(A calculator activity)

What will I need? A calculator
Where is it in the Bible? II Peter 1:5-10
How long will it take? 15-20 minutes
What age child? 3-12 years
Will it work in a group? Yes
Can it be played in the car? Yes
Will it work in a school classroom? Yes, preschool–6th grade

Tell your child you need someone to help you add up something. Open your Bible to II Peter 1:3-11 and look for the seven things God wants us to add to our lives. They already belong to us. We just need to add them to our faith. Here they are:

+ Goodness (being and doing good)

+ Knowledge (knowing God better and finding out what He wants us to do)

+ Self-control (not always doing what you want and getting your own way)

+ Perseverance (being patient, waiting for God to work, and not giving up)

+ Godliness (letting God have His way with you, being like God)

+ Brotherly kindness (being nice to other people and enjoying them)

+ Love (the deepest kind of liking)

= A strong and useful boy or girl for Jesus

God's Awesome Day

Will Jesus ever come back to earth? Read Matthew 24:30 to see what Jesus said about coming back.

Discuss these three questions about Jesus' second coming.

1. When will Jesus come back? (No one knows exactly when it will be.)

2. Why hasn't Jesus come back yet? Why is He waiting this long to come? (II Peter 3:8-9, 15. Jesus wants to give people an the time to give their hearts to Him before He comes. He will come at His right time.)

3. What shall we do until Jesus comes back? (II Peter 3:14. We should try to live like Jesus wants us to. We should tell others about Him.)

It will be a great day when Jesus comes back.

What Can I Learn From II Peter	See *What Can I Learn from I and II Peter, I, II, and III John, Jude, and Revelation* at end of Revelation.
Important Verses to Remember	II Peter 1:5-7 – "For this very reason make every effort to add to your faith goodness; and to goodness, knowledge; and to knowledge, self-control; and to self-control, perseverance; and to perseverance, godliness, and to godliness, brotherly kindness; and to brotherly kindness, love."

II Peter 1:19 – "And we have the word of the prophets made more certain, and you will do well to pay attention to it, as to a light shining in a dark place, until the day dawns the morning star rises in your hearts." |
| **A Devotional Thought for Parents and Teachers** | See *A Devotional Thought from I and II Peter, I, II, and III John, Jude, and Revelation* at end of Revelation. |

I John   God's Book About Jesus, our Light, our Love, and our Life
"And this is the testimony: God has given us eternal life, and this life is in his Son. He who has the Son has life; he who does not have the Son of God does not have life" (I John 5:11-12).

What's the Book About	The book of I John is about who Jesus is and about what He gives us – light, love, and life.
Children of God, Love One Another	The book of I John begins with John telling us how awesome and wonderful Jesus is. John tells us to be very careful not to believe people who teach false things about Jesus, because Jesus is Truth. We can trust every word He says to us.

Then John tells us that when we invite Jesus to be our Lord and Savior, He gives to our lives His light, His perfect love, and He gives us life. John says that when we have Jesus we have everything we need.

We never need to look for anything or anyone else to believe in. John says that Jesus is the only true God. He is eternal life. |

Let's Meet the People of I John	**Jesus** is God's Son, the Savior of the world.
	John was one of Jesus' closest disciples and best friends on earth.
Here Are the Places of I John	**Everywhere** – that there are people who love and believe in Jesus.

STORIES AND ACTIVITIES FROM I JOHN

God's Three Big L's:

The Book of I John tells us about three important things about Jesus that start with the letter "L."
1. Jesus give us Light.
2. Jesus gives us Love.
3. Jesus gives us Life.

John tells us at in the first part of his book that he saw Jesus with his very own eyes and even touched Him. John knows that Jesus is the Son of God and he is happy because of what Jesus has done for people who believe in Him.

Jesus Gives Us Light
(Making a light-catcher)

What will I need? Some old crayons, waxed paper, an iron, newspaper, scissors, and yarn or dental floss to hang your light-catcher.
Where is it in the Bible? I John 1:5–2:11
How long will it take? 20-30 minutes
What age child? 3-12 years
Will it work in a group? Yes, be careful with the iron.
Can it be played in the car? No
Will it work in a school classroom? Yes, preschool–6th grade

Ask your child why light is important. What's his favorite kind of light? Sunlight? A flashlight? A laser beam? A Christmas tree light?

Emphasize the word light each time you read it in I John 1:5–2:11. Ask him if he remembers other Bible stories about God or Jesus and light. Jesus is called, "the Light of the World" (John 8:12). Light is good because it is white and bright, and it shines so we can see where we are going. Jesus lights our way.

Make a light-catcher as a reminder to let the light of Jesus shine through us. Cover your work area with newspaper and let your child shave pieces off of old crayons with a potato peeler. Use lots of different colors. Sprinkle the crayon shavings onto a piece of waxed paper. Cover them with another piece of waxed paper.

Top the whole thing with another layer of newspaper and iron gently with a warm, not hot, iron, until the shavings have melted into pretty designs. When your stained glass window has cooled, cut it into any shape you want. Put a frame around it, if you want. Punch a hole in the top and hang it with yarn, thread, or dental floss.

What Can I Learn from I John	See *What Can I Learn from I and II Peter, I, II, and III John, Jude, and Revelation* at end of Revelation.
Important Verses to Remember	I John1:7 – "But if we walk in the light, as he is in the light, we have fellowship with one another, and the blood of Jesus, His Son, purifies us from all sin." I John 3:1a – "How great is the love the Father has lavished on us, that we should be called children of God!" I John 3:18 – "Dear children, let us not love with words or tongue but with actions and in truth." I John 4:9b – "He sent his one and only Son into the world that we might live through him."
A Devotional Thought for Parents and Teachers	See *A Devotional Thought from I and II Peter, I, II, and III John, Jude, and Revelation* at end of Revelation.

II John   God's Book About Truth and Love

"Grace, mercy and peace from God the Father and from Jesus Christ, the Father's Son, will be with us in truth and love" (II John 3).

What's the Book About	The book of II John is about believing that Jesus is Truth, then acting in the same way that He would.
Powerful Words from a Beloved Friend	The book of II John is short, but very important, because it is God's Word to us. John had seen Jesus with his own eyes and touched Him with his own hands. John knew that Jesus is the only truth we will ever need. John had also seen God's great love in action though Jesus.
Let's Meet the People of II John	**Jesus** is God's Son, the Savior of the world. **John** was one of Jesus' closest disciples and best friends on earth.

| **Everywhere** – that there are people who love and believe in Jesus.

STORIES AND ACTIVITIES FROM II JOHN

Walk Like This
(Different ways of walking)

What will I need? Your child and a few things from around the house

Where is it in the Bible? II John 4-6

How long will it take? 10-15 minutes

What age child? 3-10 years

Will it work in a group? Yes

Can it be played in the car? No, it's hard to walk inside the car

Will it work in a school classroom? Yes, preschool–4th grade

Have fun walking in different ways through your house or yard. You can take turns trying these ways of walking, or you can do them together at the same time.

1. Walk with something on top of your head, like a book or pillow.

2. Walk with your hands clasped behind your back.

3. Walk with your hands on your knees.

4. Walk with your right hand patting the top of your head and your left hand rubbing your stomach.

5. Walk while reading a book.

6. Walk like you are in a big hurry.

7. Walk like you have a hurt foot.

   Think up your own ideas for different ways of walking.

   Explain that II John talks to us about the way we should walk with Jesus. Read II John 4-6 and explain there are three ways Jesus wants us to walk. When the Bible says "walk" it means the way we act and the things we do. Here are the three ways Jesus wants us to walk:

1. He wants us to believe the truth about God.

2. He wants us to obey God.

3. He wants us to love Him and other people.

What Can I Learn from II John | See *What Can I Learn from I and II Peter, I, II, and III John, Jude, and Revelation* at end of Revelation.

An Important Verse to Remember | II John 6 – "And this is love: that we walk in obedience to his commands. As you have heard from the beginning, his command is that you walk in love."

A Devotional Thought for Parents and Teachers | See *A Devotional Thought from I and II Peter, I, II, and III John, Jude, and Revelation* at end of Revelation.

III John — God's Book About Walking in the Truth

"I have no greater joy than to hear that my children are walking in the truth" (III John 4).

What's the Book About

The book of III John is about three men. Two of them followed Jesus and showed kindness to others, like Jesus would. The third man loved himself more than he cared about other people. He wanted to be in charge more than he wanted to be a servant.

Be Faithful, Have Joy, and Love Others

The book of III John is a letter to Gaius, who loved Jesus and loved to open his home to other believers. Gaius was not the only person John wrote about who loved Jesus and served Him faithfully. John also has kind words for Demetrius.

John also talks about Diotrephes. John says that this man was way too proud of himself. He didn't want to serve and help anyone. He wanted them to serve him by doing whatever he said.

Not only was Diotrephes bossy, he didn't want anyone to be kind to the missionaries and preachers who came through their town. Can you even imagine such a selfish, unkind person? He certainly did not have Jesus living in his heart and life, because Jesus is love.

Let's Meet the People of III John

Gaius was a very kind man who loved Jesus and opened his home so that people traveling through could stay and visit there.

Diotrephes was nothing like Gaius. He was a selfish man who wanted to be the boss.

Demetrius was another man who loved Jesus and served Him faithfully.

Here Are the Places of III John

The home of Gaius – the place where Christians and missionaries who were traveling could come and stay.

Don't Copy That!

(Copying each other)

What will I need? Two sheets of paper and pencils or crayons

Where is it in the Bible? III John 11

How long will it take? 15-20 minutes

What age child? 3-10 years

Will it work in a group? Yes

Can it be played in the car? Yes

Will it work in a school classroom? Yes, preschool–4th grade

Have fun copying things with your child. First, copy (imitate) what each other says.

Then, take turns making gestures that each other can copy.

Finally, sit down together at the table and take turns copying designs you make on a piece of paper.

When you've finished copying each other's drawings, have fun making silly pictures on your own.

Open your Bible to III John 11 and read what God says about copying. Explain that the word imitate means to copy. What does God want us to copy? What should we not copy? Where does good come from? How about evil?

Jesus is the very best One for us to copy.

What Can I Learn from III John	See *What Can I Learn from I and II Peter, I, II, and III John, Jude, and Revelation* at end of Revelation.
Important Verses to Remember	III John 3-4 – "It gave me great joy to have some brothers come and tell about your faithfulness to the truth and how you continue to walk in the truth. I have no greater joy than to hear that my children are walking in the truth."
A Devotional Thought for Parents and Teachers	See *A Devotional Thought from I and II Peter, I, II, and III John, Jude, and Revelation* at end of Revelation.

Jude God's Book About Guarding the Truth

"Dear friends, although I was very eager to write to you about the salvation we share, I felt I had to write and urge you to contend for the faith that was once for all entrusted to the saints" (Jude 3).

What's the Book About

The book of Jude is about standing firm in what we know is true, God's truth.

God Is Love, but He Punishes Those who Turn from Him

Jude was written to remind the followers who love Jesus that He is the Truth. Jude also wants us to understand how precious it is to know Jesus as our Savior and to have His promise of everlasting life. Jude wants us to always be on guard to protect God's wonderful truth from being changed by false teachers who don't know and love Jesus.

Jesus also wants us to help other people who do not believe the right way to live and act. The Lord wants us to always be ready to help our brothers and sisters in God's great family who need our help to become strong in their faith. He warns us to be on guard so that we don't fall prey to the beliefs and actions of those who don't love Jesus.

Let's Meet the People of Jude

Jesus is God's Son, the Savior of the world.

Jude was Jesus' half-brother. Mary was the mother of both Jude and Jesus, but Jude's father was Joseph. Jesus' Father was God. James was Jude's other brother, Jesus' half-brother, who wrote the book of James.

Here Are the Places of Jude

Everywhere – that there are people who believe in Jesus and love Him.

Don't Be a Grumbler-Mumbler

(Funny ways to talk)

What will I need? Your child and a silly mood

Where is it in the Bible? Jude 16, 17-23

How long will it take? 10-15 minutes

What age child? 3-12 years

Will it work in a group? Yes

Can it be played in the car? Yes

Will it work in a school classroom? Yes, preschool–6th grade

Pretend that you and your child are from another land called "GrumbleMumbleopolis."

It's not a very pleasant place to live, because the people there grumble, gripe, and complain all the time. Show each other how grumbling and mumbling people might talk and what facial expressions they might make.

Read Jude 16 to see what some real grumblers in Jude's day were like. These unpleasant people were false teachers who were doing bad things and even laughing at God's people for their faith in Jesus. Jude is telling God's people to watch out for them and to not be like them at all.

Read Jude 20-21 to see how God's people can keep from being like the people who complain all the time.

What Can I Learn from Jude	See *What Can I Learn from I and II Peter, I, II, and III John, Jude, and Revelation* at end of Revelation.
Important Verses to Remember	Jude 20-21 – "But you, dear friends, build yourselves up in your most holy faith and pray in the Holy Spirit. Keep yourselves in God's love as you wait for the mercy of our Lord Jesus Christ to bring you into eternal life."
	Jude 24 – "To him who is able to keep you from falling and to present you before his glorious presence without fault and with great joy – to the only God our Savior be glory, majesty, power and authority, through Jesus Christ our Lord, before all ages, now and forevermore! Amen."
A Devotional Thought for Parents and Teachers	See *A Devotional Thought from I and II Peter, I, II, and III John, Jude, and Revelation* at end of Revelation.

Revelation God's Book About Jesus, Our King and Lord.

"On his robe and on his thigh he has this name written: KING OF KINGS and LORD OF LORDS" (Revelation 19:16).

What's the Book About

The book of Revelation is about Jesus, the Savior of the world and our all-powerful God. Revelation is also about when and how our Lord will come back, and be victorious over the devil forever.

John Gives Us a Glimpse of Heaven

Revelation is an incredible vision that God gave to John in a dream while he was all alone on the island of Patmos, in the Mediterranean Sea. John was a special friend of Jesus. He had spent a lot of time with the Jesus while He lived on earth. John had watched Jesus do amazing miracles. When John had his dream from God and wrote it down, he was an old man. He knew he would soon be going to heaven to be forever with the Lord he loved.

Jesus came to John in a wonderful dream and told him to write down everything that he would see and hear, so that all the people who loved Jesus could understand He would come back in great power as the King of all Kings.

The people who loved Jesus were being mistreated when John wrote Revelation. God's words gave them great comfort and hope.

Let's Meet the People of Revelation

Jesus is God's Son, the Savior of the world.

John was one of Jesus' closest disciples and best friends on earth.

Here Are the Places of Revelation

The Island of Patmos – the rocky island where God gave John a very special vision about Jesus. John wrote down everything he saw and heard in the book of Revelation.

Heaven – the New Jerusalem is the beautiful home where God lives. One day everyone who knows Jesus as their Savior and Lord will go there to live with Him forever.

Washed Clean

(Making a washing machine)

What will I need? A plastic container with a lid, water, laundry or dish detergent, a small block or plastic toy, and socks to wash
Where it is in the Bible? Revelation 1:5-6
How long will it take? 10-15 minutes
What age child? 4-12 years
Will it work in a group? Yes
Can it be played in the car? No
Will it work in a school classroom? Yes, 1st–6th grade

Tell your child that you and he are going to make a washing machine. Does he look surprised? Find a plastic container with a lid that fits tightly. Put a block or a small plastic toy in it. Put in something small, like a pair of your child's socks, to be washed. Finally, add a small amount of laundry or dishwashing detergent. Fill the container about 3/4 full of warm water and tighten the lid.

Take turns shaking your tiny washing machine for a minute or two. You and your child are the motor that make it work. The block or toy is the part called the agitator because it stirs the water to loosen the dirt from whatever is being washed.

There are two verses in Revelation 1:5-6 about a kind of washer that works better than any other washer. Talk about who has washed away our sins. Thank Him for the awesome way He did it – on the cross.

Think with your child about this important question, "Is everybody automatically washed clean by Jesus?" We know that Jesus loves everyone and wants to wash everyone's sins away, but that would mean that everyone who has ever lived, even the worst of bad guys would be in heaven. There would be no hell but Jesus said there is such a terrible place for some people to go. Jesus gives everyone a choice whether they want their sins washed clean. Also read Acts 10:43, John 3:16, and I Corinthians 6:9-11.

God's Beautiful Heaven

(A drawing about heaven)

What will I need? Sidewalk chalk in different colors, hot water, a bowl or pan, sugar, a piece of paper to draw on, and a plastic bag
Where is it in the Bible? Revelation 21– 22
How long will it take? 20-30 minutes
What age child? 2-12 years
Will it work in a group? Yes
Can it be played in the car? Probably not
Will it work in a school classroom? Yes, preschool–6th grade

The Bible tells us some wonderful things about heaven in the book of Revelation. It is a beautiful place that words cannot describe. The most awesome part of heaven, besides all the people we will get to be with forever, is that Jesus will be there with us.

Read some of words about heaven in Revelation 21:1-2 that Jesus told John to write. Read your child Revelation 21:10-11; 21:18-20, and 21:23-27 about heaven. See who says to "come" to be with Him in heaven (Revelation 22:16-17).

Nothing you could make or do with your child will really adequately represent heaven and eternity with Jesus, but let him make something pretty as a reminder. Add one part sugar, as heaven will be a sweet place to be, to four parts very hot water and drop sticks of colored sidewalk chalk into the mixture. Leave the chalk in the hot water for about five minutes, until all the fizzing stops. Take the chalk out of the sugar water and start to draw with it right away on a piece of paper. Draw a picture of what you think heaven might be like. When your picture is finished and dry, drizzle a little glue on it and sprinkle on glitter.

To keep and reuse your sugar chalk, let it dry completely in the air and put it in a plastic bag. When you want to draw with it again, dunk it first in plain water. Do not use the chalk on chalkboards, however, only use it on paper.

What Can I Learn from I and II Peter, I and II and III John, Jude, and Revelation

I learned from these important books that Jesus is light, love, and life. These books tell me that I can trust Jesus to help me when times are good or bad. Jesus will help me stay strong when other people don't love God and try to get me to stop believing His Word. I can trust Jesus all the time.

Because Jesus is wonderful and His Word is absolutely true, I will follow Him.

Important Verses to Remember

Revelation 3:20 – "Here I am! I stand at the door and knock. If anyone hears my voice and opens the door, I will go in and eat with him, and he with Me."

Revelation 4:11 – "You are worthy, our Lord and God, to receive glory and honor and power, for you created all things, and by your will they were created and have their being."

Revelation 22:17 – "The Spirit and the bride say, 'Come!' And let him who hears say, 'Come!' whoever is thirsty, let him come; and whoever wishes, let him take the free gift of the water of life. "

A Devotional Thought for Parents and Teachers from I and II Peter, I and II and III John, Jude, and Revelation

In the New Testament we are introduced to many different people that God used to write down His Word for others to hear. Those inspired scribes may deliver God's message from various perspectives, but the words they write are not their own – not a single one.

Two unmistakable facts prevail in all the different writings:
1. The Words are all God's from His heart and from His infinite, omniscient mind, challenged through the Person of the Holy Spirit.
2. The human instruments through which God spoke were pas-

sionately convinced of the truth they received and communicated. They were also uncompromisingly committed to the One who told it to them.

Nothing better could ever be said of us when our life is over than that we were passionately convinced of the truth of God's Word and that we were uncompromisingly committed to the Lord of Truth. One day, when we will face our Savior, what will Jesus say? That's what matters, isn't it?